Praise for *The Field Gui*

"*The Field Guide to the 6Ds* is the most pragmatic guide book I have ever seen. It provides learning professionals with specific tools, concrete cases, and how-to guides. We are greatly impressed by the authors' practical and business-oriented approach to enhancing the value of learning and development."

—Tao Zhou, P.hD., president, Shanghai TopLearning
Management Consulting Company, China

"This book is an amazing treasure chest to those looking for ideas and evidence of learning value in the organization. Real cases illustrating field applications of the 6Ds are especially valuable to help you come up with your own solutions suitable to your organization. It doesn't matter which industry you work for or what country you live in."

—Mijeong Kim, Ph.D., director, Learning &
Performance Institute, Credu, Korea

"The sharing of the successful implementation by many organizations and the 'how-to' guides on implementation of the 6 Disciplines make this a complete field guide and a tremendous resource for all heads of training who are serious about delivering training for business results."

—Jim Kee, associate director, Group
Education & Development, AIA Group, Singapore

"By incorporating the principles found in *The Field Guide to the 6Ds,* we were able to better implement our programs, and measure the actual learning transferred. This was evident in both the new skills and attitudes learned, and performance in the field as well."

—Randy Eppard, Ph.D., executive director,
International Department of Education and
Training, United Brotherhood of Carpenters

"*The Field Guide to the 6Ds* is the perfect follow-up to *The Six Discipines.* It takes the concepts of the 6Ds and provides a framework for immediate implementation. Anyone who is leading the learning function will benefit from the case studies and tools to help take their organization's learning to the next level."

—Meg Pletcher, national director of
learning & development, Emeritus Senior Living

"Pollock, Jefferson, and Wick have developed an immensely resourceful guide for anyone in the training and human development field. With the focus on business outcomes, efficient delivery, conducive environment for learning transfer, and results documentation, the 6Ds is ultimately about going the extra mile to ensure that training attains its best possible value to the learners, trainers, and the organization."

—Zairi Chew Long Po, product & technical
faculty, Prudential BSN Takaful Berhad, Malaysia

The Field Guide to the 6Ds

*How to Use the Six Disciplines
to Transform Learning into Business Results*

TIPS, TOOLS, CASE STUDIES, AND PRACTICAL ADVICE

Roy Pollock
Andrew Jefferson
Calhoun Wick

WILEY

Cover design by Wiley
Cover photograph © Creativeye99 | Getty
Authors' photographs by Terence Roberts

Illustrations in Part I: The 6Ds © 2014 The 6Ds Company unless otherwise noted.
6Ds Illustrations by Ris Fleming-Allen

For additional copies or bulk purchases of this book or to learn more about Wiley's Workplace Learning offerings, please contact us toll free at 1-866-888-5159 or by email at workplacelearning@wiley.com .

Wiley also publishes its books in a variety of electronic formats and by print-on-demand. Some material included with standard print versions of this book may not be included in e-books or in print-on-demand. If the version of this book that you purchased references media such as a CD or DVD that was not included in your purchase, you may download this material at http://booksupport.wiley.com. For more information about Wiley products, visit www.wiley.com.

Library of Congress Cataloging-in-Publication Data

Pollock, Roy V. H.
    The field guide to the 6Ds: how to use the six disciplines to transform learning into business results: tips, tools, case studies, and practical advice / Roy Pollock, Andrew Jefferson, Calhoun Wick.
       pages   cm
    Includes index.
    ISBN 978-1-118-64813-1 (paper/website); ISBN 978-1-118-67738-4 (ebk)—ISBN 978-1-118-67714-8 (ebk)
       1. Organizational learning.   2. Employees—Training of.   3. Performance.   4. Organizational effectiveness.
I. Jefferson, Andrew McK.   II. Wick, Calhoun W.   III. Title.
HD58.82.P65   2014
658.3'124—dc23

                                                                                2013047961

Printed in the United States of America
PB Printing   10 9 8 7 6 5 4 3 2 1

Contents

About This Book

Since the first publication of *The Six Disciplines of Breakthrough Learning* in 2006, companies around the world have realized greater value from training and development by applying its principles. We included case studies and recommendations for implementation in both the first and second editions, and we continue to provide advanced training in the 6Ds® through online and live workshops. Even so, readers have asked us for additional examples, tools, and recommendations. *The Field Guide to the 6Ds* is designed to fill that need.

The Field Guide is intended to be used as you would a guidebook to Yellowstone Park or the Pantanal in Brazil, that is, to help you go where you want to go and know what to do when you get there. Especially valuable in such guides are first-hand accounts of travelers who have gone before you. That is why we are particularly pleased that this guide includes forty-three accounts ("how-we" case histories) submitted by innovators across five continents who agreed to share their stories and advice. Without them, this book would not have been possible.

The Field Guide is organized by the Six Disciplines (the 6Ds). It contains numerous cross-references and diagnostic tools to help you find what you are looking for. Part I includes an overview of each discipline for those who have not yet read *The Six Disciplines,* accompanied by quick checks with recommendations for action. Part II contains tools, checklists, and flow charts to help you implement the 6Ds in your organization. Part III includes forty-three examples of putting 6Ds princi-ples into action across a wide range of programs, companies, industries, and countries. Part IV contains specific "how-to" guides on twenty-five topics.

Additional information, materials, and tools are available at the 6Ds website: www.the6Ds.com and through 6Ds Workshops.

Acknowledgments

This book would not have been possible without the help of the hundreds of learning professionals around the world who have used the 6Ds and shared with us their insights, challenges, and triumphs. We are especially indebted to those who took the time to prepare case studies and obtain the necessary permissions to publish them.

Special thanks also to our colleagues at the Fort Hill Company with whom we began this journey, to the exceptional professionals at Wiley who have partnered with us to bring the 6Ds to market, to the 6Ds Company staff, and, of course, to our families, who continue to encourage and support our efforts to make a difference.

Contributors

Steve Akram, Director, North American Sales Force Development, Oracle

Sujaya Banerjee, Ph.D., Chief Talent Officer and Senior Vice President, HR, The Essar Group

Colonel Bernard B. Banks, Ph.D., Professor and Department Head, Department of Behavioral Sciences and Leadership, United States Military Academy at West Point

Ishita Bardhan, Assistant General Manager, Learning and Development, Management Development Centre of Excellence, Tata Motors Academy

Rob Bartlett, Corporate Trainer, DirectWest

Paul Beech, Manager, Emirates Global Contact Center

Karen Bell-Wright, Vice President, Emirates Retail and Contact Centers

Melanie Brunet Relyea, Training and Development Manager, Oneida Nation Enterprises, LLC

ChiChung Chan, Lean Sigma Master Black Belt, Underwriters Laboratories PLC

Anand Justin Cherian, Manager, Learning and OD, The Essar Group

Michelle Cooper, Training Supervisor, Oneida Nation Enterprises, LLC

Terrence Donahue, Corporate Director, Training, Emerson, Inc.

Joyce Donohoe, Manager, Strategic Commercial and Service Initiatives, Emirates Group Learning and Development College

Joshua Ebert, Lean Sigma Master Black Belt, Underwriters Laboratories PLC

Russell Evans, Managing Director, Primeast Ltd.

Mike Girone, Director, Global Learning and Leadership Development, Agilent Technologies, Inc.

Christopher Goh Soon Keat, Director, Global Learning and Leadership Development, Agilent Technologies, Inc.

Patricia Gregory, Senior Director, North American Sales Force Development, Oracle

Maria Grigorova, Marketing College Director, Mars University

Lauren Grigsby, Learning Coordinator, Plastipak Packaging, Inc.

Charlie Hackett, Corporate Improvement Team Leader, Hypertherm Inc.

Eric Haddon, Lean Sigma Master Black Belt, Underwriters Laboratories PLC

Wanda J. Hayes, Ph.D., Director, Learning and Organizational Development, Emory University

Diane Hinton, Director of Corporate Learning, Plastipak Packaging, Inc.

Glenn Hughes, Director of Global Learning, KLA-Tencor

Jon Hurtado, Senior Learning Consultant, Coventry Workers' Comp Services

Royce Isacowitz, Performance Consultant, Sydney, Australia

Kaliym A. Islam, M.Ed., Vice President, Depository Trust & Clearing Corporation

Alex Jaccaci, Corporate Improvement Training Facilitator, Hypertherm Inc.

Cecil W. Johnson, III, Director, Management Development, Janssen Pharmaceuticals

Ted Joyce, Esq., LL.M., Adjunct Professor, Rouen Business School, and Visiting Professor, Université Paris 1, La Sorbonne, France

Justin Keeton, Manager of Organizational Effectiveness, Development and Training, Methodist Le Bonheur Healthcare

Sonal Khanna, Senior eLearning Instructional Designer, Kaiser Permanente

James Kirkpatrick, Senior Consultant, Kirkpatrick Partners

Wendy Kirkpatrick, Founder and President, Kirkpatrick Partners

Marc Lalande, M.Sc., CTDP, CRP, President, Learning Andrago, Inc.

Duncan Lennox, CEO, Qstream

Jonathan Low, Managing Partner, PowerUpSuccess Group

Richard Low, Senior Specialist, Learning and Development, Merck & Co., Inc.

Alberto Massacesi, Lean Sigma Master Black Belt, Underwriters Laboratories PLC

Susan McDermott, Lean Sigma Master Black Belt, Underwriters Laboratories PLC

Sumita Menon, Divisional Manager, Learning and Development, Tata Motors, Ltd.

Debra Modra, Lean Sigma Master Black Belt, Underwriters Laboratories PLC

Robert Moffett, Customized Learning Director, Mars University

Praise Mok, Principal Consultant, ROHEI Corporation Pte. Ltd.

Sylvain Newton, Senior Leader for Business and Regions, GE

Rebecca Nigel, Manager, Marketing Communications, BST

Cheryl Ong, Director and Principal Consultant, Global Trainers, Inc.

Peggy Parskey, Strategic Measurement Consultant, KnowlegeAdvisors

Raymond Phoon, Managing Partner, PowerUpSuccess Group

Anjali Raghuvanshi, Program Manager, Tata Motors, Ltd.

Hemalakshmi Raju, Assistant General Manager, Learning and Development, Tata Motors, Ltd.

John Resing, Lean Sigma Master Black Belt, Underwriters Laboratories PLC

Geoff Rip, Research Director, Institute for Learning Practitioners

Steve Rosenbaum, President, Learning Paths International

Conrado Schlochauer, Ph.D., Partner, AfferoLab

Mike Schwartz, Learning Program Manager, Cox Media Group

Kanika Sharma, Senior Manager, Learning and Development, Management Development Centre of Excellence, Tata Motors Academy

Mary Singos, Learning Professional, Plastipak Packaging, Inc.

Tom Stango, Learning Consultant, Coventry Workers' Comp Services

Tahseen Wahdat, Senior Manager, Learning and OD, The Essar Group

Emma Weber, Founder and Director, Lever Learning

Clive Wilson, Deputy Chairman, Primeast Ltd.

Introduction

Shortly after the turn of the millennium, we became interested in the challenge of creating even greater value from training and development. We knew that learning speed and effectiveness would become even more important in an increasingly competitive, global, and knowledge-based business climate. We were convinced that well-executed training would be an important source of competitive advantage, but we were certain that training could—and should—yield a greater return on investment than it does today.

We recognized that training creates value only to the extent that it is transferred and applied to work in a way that improves performance (Figure I.1). We focused our efforts on improving learning transfer, since there was overwhelming evidence that transfer is the weakest link in the value chain for learning (see, for example, review by Grossman and Salas, 2011).

More often than not, training accomplishes its learning objectives—that is, the instruction successfully imparts new skills and

Figure I.1. Transfer Is an Essential Step in the Process by Which Training Creates Business Value

knowledge—but then the process falters. Trainees fail to transfer their new skills and knowledge to their work environment or apply them well enough to improve performance. We coined the term "learning scrap" to describe the wasted time, effort, and opportunity represented by training that was delivered, but never used (Wick, Pollock, Jefferson, & Flanagan, 2006, p. 101). The analogy, of course, is to the cost of manu-facturing scrap—the materials, labor, capital, and opportunity cost wasted producing products that fail to meet customers' expectations. Both manufacturing scrap and learning scrap are expensive; both adversely impact a company's competitiveness.

Initially, we focused on the post-training period, as that was where the bulk of the slippage seemed to occur. Historically, the process by which training is converted into business results had received inade-quate attention (Figure I.2). Together with our colleagues at the Fort Hill

"I think you should be more explicit here in step two."

Figure I.2. A Typical Approach to the Post-Training Period
© Sidney Harris /www.cartoonbank.com. Used with permission.

Company, we developed a software system (*ResultsEngine®*) specifically designed to support learning transfer. We were able to show that it measurably increased transfer and results . . . but only in some programs and not others. That perplexed us. Given that the software and approach were constant, there had to be additional factors that influenced why some organizations achieved much better results than others. We set out to understand why.

Origin of the 6Ds

By studying the results of our clients, reading the literature, talking to learning leaders, and observing programs across a range of companies, disciplines, and industries, we came to realize that many factors—before, during, and after training—influence whether learning is transferred to produce business benefit or scrapped. Surprisingly—although we really should have known it—these factors extended far beyond the traditional responsibilities of the training department. For example, we discovered that unless the *business purpose* of the training was clearly and explicitly defined at the onset, it was perceived to be of little value. Likewise, training—no matter how brilliantly conceived and delivered—foundered unless it had buy-in and active support from the trainees' supervisors.

Moment of Truth

We came to realize that the value of all the effort that went into analysis, design, development, implementation, and evaluation of training was determined at what we came to call "the moment of truth" (Pollock & Jefferson, 2012). The "moment of truth" is that instant, back on the job, when employees decide (consciously or

Figure I.3. The "Moment of Truth" That Determines Whether Training Adds Value or Is Scrap

unconsciously) how they will accomplish a task. They have two choices: perform the new way they have just been taught or perform the old way they have always done it—which might include doing nothing! (See Figure I.3.)

Which path the employee chooses depends on the answer to two questions:

- Can I?
- Will I?

Both must be answered in the affirmative in order for the employee to use the new approach, which we have drawn as uphill because it requires additional effort to change behaviors. The whole learning experience—from the invitation, to the instruction, to the post-training work environment—needs to be designed to ensure that at the moment of action, employees respond, "Yes, I can!" and "Yes, I will!" Unless employees answer yes to both questions, they will slide down the easy path back to old habits and the training will fail to create value (Figure I.4). We will refer to these two questions throughout the discussion.

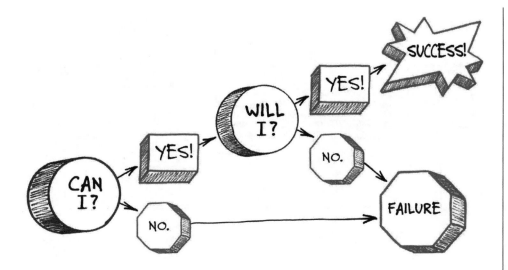

Figure I.4. Both Critical Questions Must Be Answered "Yes!" for Training to Create Value

The Six Disciplines

We distilled our insights into the six disciplines practiced by the most effective training organizations, which we named the 6Ds® to make them easier to remember (Figure I.5). We called them *disciplines* because they had all been described before; one could almost say they are common sense. But they were not—and still are not—common practice. What differentiates more effective training organizations from less effective ones is not their *knowledge* of these principles, but the thoroughness, consistency, and *discipline* with which they execute them.

Relationship to Instructional Design

It is important to note that the 6Ds are not a *replacement* for the science and art of instructional design. Rather, they are an *extension* and *complement* to instructional design models, such as ADDIE, which are mainly concerned with the instruction itself. In contrast, the 6Ds are a holistic

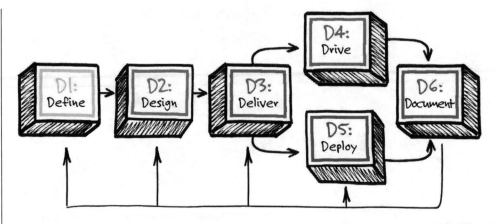

Figure I.5. The 6Ds®: The Six Disciplines That Turn Learning into Business Results

process approach that strengthens the business linkage on the front end and that drives and measures learning transfer on the back end (Figure I.6).

The core concept of the Six Disciplines is that in corporations, training is a *business* function. It is a means to an end—improved performance—and not an end in itself. The more that training departments shift their focus to *performance*, rather than learning *per se*, the more they will be valued by their business partners. Applying the 6Ds has helped training organizations go "on beyond ADDIE" to create greater

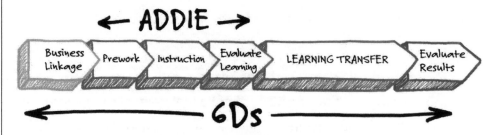

Figure I.6. The 6Ds Extend and Complement Instructional Design Models Such as ADDIE

business value and greater appreciation for the contribution of the training function. We trust that you will enjoy similar success.

Evidence of Effectiveness

In the years since we first began teaching and writing about the 6Ds, more and more training organizations have adopted them as operating principles. Proof of their value is illustrated by the forty-three case histories ("How We") from around the world included in this *Field Guide.*

The 6Ds apply to both internal training departments as well as external consultants and training providers. In Case I.1, Sonal Khanna, senior e-learning instructional designer at Kaiser Permanente, describes how the 6Ds helped her Front Office Operations Improvement Department take an end-to-end approach focused on performance. In Case I.2, Cheryl Ong, principal consultant for Global Trainers in Singapore, explains how she uses the 6Ds to do a better job of meeting customers' needs and to create a competitive advantage for her training and consulting practice. In Case I.3, Royce Isacowitz, an independent performance consultant in Sydney, Australia, explains how he created a 6Ds outline to help him explain and deliver his value proposition to clients, and in Case I.4, Alberto Massacesi and a team of Black Belts from Underwriters Laboratories describe how they used the 6Ds process to continuously improve a worldwide training program on continuous improvement.

The 6Ds have proven useful not only in designing and executing individual programs, but also in thinking holistically about an entire curriculum spanning a number of courses or complete career path. In Case I.5, Cecil Johnson III, director, management development, for Janssen Pharmaceuticals, describes how he and his team used the 6Ds framework to help them successfully redesign their entire sales leader-ship curriculum.

Getting Started

Our goal for this book has been to create a guide to the 6Ds that is both readable and action-oriented. You can start at D1 and read through to D6, if you like, but a field guide should help you get to where you want to go without having to read from beginning to end. So you can also go straight to a topic of interest or just browse. Each chapter and each case are intended to stand on their own.

If you aren't certain where to start, use the 6Ds Application Scorecard (Tool I.1, page 143) to help identify your greatest opportuni-ties for improvement. Then use the 6Ds Pathfinder (Tool I.2, page 147) to locate relevant sections, case studies, tools, and how-to guides.

An alternative approach is to use the 6Ds Flow Chart (Tool I.3, page 151) to help identify the best trail to follow.

If you prefer, you can go straight to the compilation of the recom-mendations from the field (Tool I.4, page 159) and start with the ones that are most relevant to you.

Whichever route you choose, you will find ideas that—when put into practice—will increase the value of training and development and firmly establish you as a strategic partner in the success of your business.

Introducing the 6Ds

The 6Ds are best practiced as a "team sport," that is, when all of the learning professionals in your organization share a common under-standing of the 6Ds' concepts and terms and when the six disciplines are built into your design and implementation processes. In Case I.6, Ted

Joyce explains the creative way in which he introduced the 6Ds to his learning team at Deloitte.

You could, as Ted did, start by having everyone read *The Six Disciplines* and then discuss and debate the ideas and their application. Alternatively, the 6Ds Company and its certified providers can deliver customized, in-house 6Ds Workshops for learning teams and their business partners. There are also public workshops offered by Wiley, ASTD, and other organizations. These interactive, live, and online workshops provide an opportunity to explore the 6Ds in depth and to practice applying them to your own programs. Dates and locations can be found at the 6Ds website: www.the6Ds.com.

PART I

The Six Disciplines

D1 Define Business Outcomes

In her book, *Strategic Learning Alignment,* Rita Smith (2010) succinctly summarized the core concept of D1: "The *only* reason that learning organizations exist is to drive business outcomes" (p. 10). In other words, organizations invest in training and development with the goal of improving performance in areas critical to their strategy and objectives. Thus, training is valued to the extent to which it visibly and convincingly contributes to improved performance. When training consumes resources (time and money), but fails to demonstrably improve performance, it is seen as wasteful and expendable.

Therefore, the first and most critical discipline is to truly understand what the business needs to accomplish. As Patricia Gregory, senior director, and Steve Akram, director, North American Sales Force Development at Oracle explain in Case D1.1, focusing on business outcomes repositions training and development professionals from mere order takers to strategic business partners.

Conversely, failing to clearly define the business outcomes dramatically increases the risk of pouring time, effort, and money into a training program that won't actually scratch the itch. In Case D1.2, Sujaya Banerjee, chief talent officer and senior vice president, and her colleagues of the Essar Group, explain how investing the time to truly understand the business needs helped their Corporate Training Group avoid creating another "feel good" training program. By focusing on business outcomes, she and her colleagues were able to make a significant contribution to business transformation and produce results that the CEO recognized and applauded.

Key steps in the practice of D1 include:

- Understanding the business you support
- Talking to your stakeholders
- Deciding whether training is appropriate

- Completing the performance-gap analysis
- Differentiating learning objectives from business objectives
- Using business outcomes to explain the benefits

Understand the Business You Support

A core principle of the 6Ds is that training is a business function. It follows that the better that training professionals understand the organization they serve—its goals, vision, mission, and operations—the better they are able to contribute, and the greater the respect they command. Training departments that are viewed by business leaders as truly aligned with their businesses enjoy much greater support than those that are seen as "doing their own thing" (Bersin, 2008, p. 82).

Use Quick Check D1.1 to evaluate your alignment with the business and to identify actions to take that will improve this important skill set.

QUICK CHECK D1.1:
BUSINESS ALIGNMENT

1. Can you succinctly explain how your organization makes money (or for nonprofits, fulfills its mission) and the key challenges it faces in doing so?

Yes	No
Congratulations. Understanding the business you are part of is essential for you to become a trusted advisor rather than simply an order-taker.	You will increase your contribution and your value to your organization by deepening your knowledge of the business. Greater business savvy will allow you to design more relevant and more effective programs. Suggested actions include: ❏ Find a mentor in the business who can help by explaining key terms and concepts. ❏ Review the business plans for the units you support. ❏ Ask to sit in on business reviews and planning sessions; ask your mentor about any aspect you don't understand.

2. How would the business leaders rate the alignment of your training department with their business needs?

Good to Excellent	Fair to Poor	I Don't Know
Terrific. Training departments that are seen as aligned to the business's needs receive greater support and, interestingly, less scrutiny.	This is a problem. If Training is not seen as fully aligned with the business, then it will have to produce more data to justify its value and it is more likely to have its budget cut. Suggested actions include: ❏ Interview business managers to find out where they feel there is misalignment. ❏ Require a clear understanding of business needs before beginning any design work. ❏ Interview business leaders using the Planning Wheel (page 173) to identify the real business needs and criteria for success.	You need to address this gap in your knowledge, as it could prove fatal for your department. If Training is not seen as aligned with the business, then it is likely to be viewed as expendable. Suggested actions include: ❏ Survey or interview training's business clients to assess their perceptions of training's alignment with their needs. ❏ Take appropriate action to rectify the situation based on the results.

Talk to Your Stakeholders

The business is training's customer. Directly or indirectly, the business pays for the cost of providing training and, in the end, decides whether or not the resulting value justified the expense. What the business "buys" from training is the expectation of improved performance; courses and programs are only a means to this end. Whether the training department stays in business depends on whether its customers feel they "got their money's worth" and are therefore willing to continue to invest.

Customer satisfaction requires listening to the "voice of the customer" and understanding their goals, needs, and definitions of success. In this regard, keep in mind that in corporate training, the participants are *not* the ultimate customer; they don't usually make the purchasing decision. So while we need participants to be engaged, to learn, and to apply what they learned, it is the *business leaders* who need to be satisfied with the results. Thus, there is no substitute for talking directly to these stakeholders; they are the ones who should decide which training needs are the highest priority—not the training department.

A good starting place is the 6Ds Outcomes Planning Wheel™ (Figure D1.1). Although the wheel's four questions seem deceptively simple, they have helped both large and small organizations create much greater—and shared—clarity about the real business issues behind a request for training.

The "how-to" guide H2 D1.1 provides a brief introduction to using the Planning Wheel (Tool D1.1). Additional details can be found in Wick, Pollock, and Jefferson (2010, pp. 41–45).

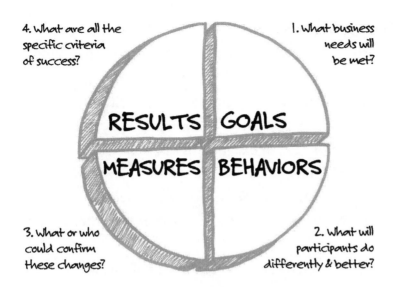

4. What are all the specific criteria of success?

1. What business needs will be met?

RESULTS | GOALS
MEASURES | BEHAVIORS

3. What or who could confirm these changes?

2. What will participants do differently & better?

Figure D1.1. The 6Ds Outcomes Planning Wheel™

In Case D1.3 Hemalakshmi Raju, assistant general manager, and Anjali Raghuvanshi, program manager, at Tata Motors describe how they used the Planning Wheel to clarify the business outcomes for internal facilitators training. Russell Evans, managing director, and Clive Wilson, deputy chairman, of Primeast Ltd. describe in Case D1.4 how they used a comprehensive framework called PrimeFocus™ to ensure that they deliver the right intervention and achieve the business objectives. In Case D1.5, Richard Low, senior specialist, Learning and Development, Merck & Co., Inc., describes how adding the Planning Wheel to the Learning Services Tool Box has helped the Merck Polytechnic Institute better meet the needs of its clients in research and development.

Finally, in Case D6.1, Peggy Parskey, strategic measurement consultant with KnowlegeAdvisors, describes the use of logic modeling to help business leaders answer two critical questions:

- Why are you doing this?
- What do you expect to happen as a result of the training?

Logic modeling helps to ensure that there is a well-defined and logical "chain of influences" between the training and the expected business benefit.

When there is more than one key stakeholder, it is critical to speak to all of them, as they may have very different expectations. One of our clients found himself in exactly this dilemma. He used the Outcomes Planning Wheel to interview the four co-owners of a major training initiative. He discovered that they held widely divergent views on both the business objectives as well as the criteria for success.

Clearly, under these circumstances, nothing that the training department designed or delivered would have satisfied them all. So he circulated the results of his interviews to all four stakeholders and then convened a meeting to discuss them. What emerged—after some lively debate—was a clear consensus on the purpose of the program, the desired results, and the criteria for success. The point is that had he not used a structured approach to interview all four stakeholders, he would never have realized how divergent their points of view were and the program would have failed to deliver on expectations for some or all.

Use Quick Check D1.2 to evaluate the extent to which you really understand the business drivers and to identify potential actions you can take to strengthen your alignment with the business.

QUICK CHECK D1.2:
BUSINESS OUTCOMES

1. Can you succinctly state the business need(s) the training is designed to address? (Remember that "training" is not a business need. Business needs are ultimately related to increasing revenue, improving productivity, lowering costs, etc.)

Yes	No
Congratulations. You are in possession of a key requirement for designing and executing effective learning interventions.	Don't proceed until you have clarity on this point. The only reason to invest in training is to (directly or indirectly) drive business outcomes. Suggested actions include: ❏ Interview the business leader(s) using the Planning Wheel or related tool to gain clarity on the underlying business drivers.

2. Can you identify the key changes in on-the-job behavior that will result if the training and reinforcement activities are successful? (What will participants do better and differently?)

Yes	No
Excellent. This is essential knowledge; only actions produce results. To improve performance, people have to behave in new and more effective ways. Or, as Einstein supposedly put it: "One definition of insanity is to keep doing the same thing and expect a different result."	Don't proceed until you can get clarity on this point. You need to be able to describe *actions* and *behaviors* (how the new skills and knowledge will be applied on the job) to deliver truly effective interventions. Suggested actions include: ❏ Interview the business leader(s) using the Planning Wheel or related tool to get clarity on the desired change in behavior. ❏ Compare the actions of more effective to less effective employees. ❏ Keep asking questions until you get beyond "knowledge" to observable actions.

3. Have you discussed what would change or who would notice when the new behaviors are practiced?

Yes	No
Carry on. This is important to know. It identifies the data source(s) for deciding whether or not the training is achieving its objectives.	Stop and revisit this issue. While you can, technically, deliver successful training without considering who or what will confirm the changes, the problem is that you will never know one way or the other.
❏ Begin thinking about which metrics you might use to assess training's impact and how you would get and analyze the data.	Suggested actions include: ❏ Think logically about the business goals and desired behaviors. Who or what will they impact? ❏ Suggest and confirm potential sources of data (customers, company records, etc.) with the sponsor. Get a reaction to the relative merit of various sources.

4. Are you clear about how the program sponsor defines success?

Yes	No

Is it realistic?
 	
❏ Yes
 	
    Proceed to design the training. Include in your plans how you will gather the data to satisfy the sponsor's "conditions of satisfaction." Stress management's role in achieving the results.
 	
❏ No
 	
    You need to have a "crucial conversation" with the sponsor in which you help him or her understand why the training is unlikely to produce the desired results given the available time, resources, management support, and so forth.
	Stop! If you do not know how the manager will decide whether the training is a success, then you are very likely to fail, since you may be operating on an erroneous set of assumptions.
	    Suggested actions include:
	
	❏ Ask the business sponsor directly: "What will it take for you to conclude that the training was a success?"
	
	❏ Try to gain clarity on "how much, by when?"

Decide Whether Training Is Appropriate

"To a young boy with a new hammer, everything is a nail." Unfortunately, for many business managers, training is a hammer and every sort of performance challenge is a nail (Pollock, 2013). For training professionals to be more than "order takers," we must learn how to explain to business leaders when training is, and is not, an appropriate part of the solution (see H2 D1.2: "How to Decide Whether Training Is Necessary").

You can ask your doctor for any medicine you like, but it's malpractice for him or her to prescribe it without a diagnosis. Similarly, learning professionals should never deliver training just because some manager asks for it, without first being sure it is the right prescription.

When a lack of skill or knowledge is holding back performance, training is an essential part of the solution. But there are many other causes of suboptimal performance that training cannot resolve—and indeed, that training may make worse (Figure D1.2). Among them:

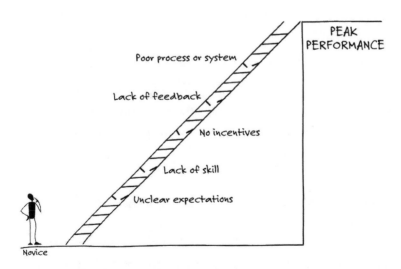

Figure D1.2. Lack of Knowledge or Skills Is Only One of Many Potential Causes of Suboptimal Performance, But It Is the Only One That Training Can Remedy

- Unclear expectations or performance criteria
- Inadequate feedback on performance
- "Bad attitude"
- Lack of motivation
- Insufficient information, tools, or time for the task
- Lack of incentives or consequences

Why raise the issue here? Doesn't every learning professional already do this? Apparently not. The inappropriate use of training appears to be much more widespread than generally appreciated. Participants in our 6Ds Workshops estimate that from 10 percent to as high as 50 percent of all the training they do is directed toward issues that training won't help resolve. That is a terrible waste of time, money, and talent. It frustrates both trainers and learners.

What can we do about it?

- Build the process for approving training so that it requires a clear business case and needs analysis.
- Use the flow chart in Tool D1.2 to ensure that training really is the right solution and that other possible causes and solutions have been explored and eliminated.
- Keep in mind that, even when training is an appropriate *part* of the solution, it is never the *whole solution*. For training to be effective, it has to be directed toward the right problems *and* it has to be supported by active managerial engagement before and afterward (see D2: Design the Complete Experience).

Complete the Performance-Gap Analysis

Once you have a clear view of the business objectives of the training, and you are convinced that training is an essential part of the solution, you need to figure out specifically what people need to learn. The

Planning Wheel asks the stakeholder (usually a senior business leader) "What do people need to do better and differently?" That is a good starting point, but senior leaders rarely have detailed insight into specific knowledge and skill gaps.

Designing an effective learning intervention requires a performance-gap analysis based on observations, interviews, surveys, and task analyses with those who actually do the work or who directly supervise it. We prefer "performance-gap analysis" to "training-needs analysis" because the latter pre-supposes that the solution is training, which, as we just discussed, is not necessarily so.

To truly understand what people need to learn, you have to get close to the action; senior managers and human resource professionals may have important insights, but they are often too far removed from the day-to-day interactions to know key details. Refer to one of the numerous texts on the subject—such as the Robinsons' *Performance Consulting* (2008), Mager and Pipe's *Analyzing Performance Problems* (1997), or Barbazette's *Training Needs Analysis* (2006)—for detailed guidance.

Quick Check D1.3 will help you decide whether you have adequate insight into the issues to move to the design phase and, if not, some actions to take.

QUICK CHECK D1.3:
PERFORMANCE
GAP ANALYSIS

1. Are you convinced that knowledge and skill deficiencies contribute to the performance gap?

Yes	No	Not Sure
Great. That means training will be an important part of the solution. Remember, however, that training is never the whole solution and there may be multiple contributing causes. Be sure to design a complete experience, which includes managing the transfer climate.	**Stop!** If you are not convinced that knowledge or skill deficiencies are significant contributors to the problem, then training is unlikely to help. As Bob Mager put it: "If a genuine lack of skill is not the problem, then you can forget training as a potential solution" (Mager & Pipe, 1997, p. 93). ❏ Use Tool D1.2 to try to get to the root causes and help devise remedies for the real issues.	**Stop!** If you are not sure whether a lack of knowledge or skill is a significant contributor, don't agree to provide training until you are convinced it is. Ask "If their lives depended on it, could they still not perform?" If the answer is that they could not, then training is probably part of the solution. If they know how to perform, but aren't, then something other than training is needed. ❏ Use Tool D1.2 to try to elucidate and fix the real cause of suboptimal performance.

2. If you are convinced that lack of knowledge or skill is a significant contributor, can you identify where the specific gaps are?

Yes	No
Terrific. Convert your knowledge into learning objectives and design—or work with an instructional designer or vendor—to create learning experiences to address them.	Spend the time to identify where, specifically, the gaps are. If you don't, then you run the risk of creating a lot of content that people don't really need while missing key things that they do. ❑ Consult a text or expert on needs analysis and do enough to be sure you pinpoint the critical skill deficiencies.

Differentiate the Business Objectives of Training from Learning Objectives

In the practice of D1, it is important to differentiate between the business objectives of training and the learning objectives.

Learning objectives explain *what* the participants will learn—the capabilities that they will have acquired by the end of the instruction ("At the completion of this module, the participant will be able to . . ."). Business objectives for training, in contrast, describe the *on-the-job* results that application of the training will produce. The business objectives explain *how* the training will help the organization and the participants perform better. The differences are highlighted in Table D1.1. Examples are shown in Table D1.2.

Training initiatives, of course, are only one of many initiatives that a business undertakes to meet its targets and ambitions. There are business objectives for each unit or function which, taken together, add up to the overall success of the organization (Figure D1.3).

The business objectives for training explain how it fits into the overall picture and contributes to the organization's success. They are, therefore, of interest to both senior management and to the leaders of departments. Learning objectives are a lower level of detail. They exist only to support achievement of the business objectives. Numerous learning objectives (as well as other kinds of support) are usually needed to support one business goal. As explained below, learning

Table D1.1. Comparison of Learning Objectives to Business Objectives of Training

	Learning Objectives of Training	Business Objectives of Training
Time Frame	End of instruction	On the job
Focus	Knowledge or capability	Actions and results

Table D1.2. Examples of Business and Learning Objectives for Training

Business Objective of Training	Learning Objective of Training
Improve employee engagement by 10 percent within one year	At the completion of this workshop the participant will be able to demonstrate the proper use of the SBR method for giving feedback in a simulated conversation with a direct report.
Keep number of customers who switch to competitor's product to less that 5 percent by year's end	At the completion of this e-learning module, the learner will be able to identify all three key advantages of our product versus the competitor's product.
Increase the "net promoter score" on customer surveys by 10 percent within six months	At the completion of this self-paced learning, the customer service representative will be able to correctly score at least eight of ten recorded calls as "acceptable" or "unacceptable" according to the principles taught in this course.

Figure D1.3. The Learning Objectives of Training Exist to Support Business Unit Objectives, Which Together Create Business Success

objectives, by themselves, don't adequately explain training's value; their use should be restricted to internal communications among training professionals (see H2 D1.3: "How to Use (and Not Use) Learning Objectives").

Use Business Objectives to Explain Benefits to Participants and Managers

One of the first things a new salesperson must learn is to differentiate between a product's features and its benefits. *Features* are characteristics of the product itself, like the amount of RAM memory, a car's horsepower, or an armchair's fabric. *Benefits* explain the value of those features to the customer; they answer the WIIFM ("What's in it for me?") question for the potential buyer or user.

In our view, learning objectives are like features: "Here is what you will learn." They leave it up to the participant or the participant's manager to figure out the benefits. Any time anyone is asked to attend a corporate training program (or when a manager is asked to send his or her staff), the key questions that spring to mind are

- Will this be worth my time?
- Will it help me?

Learning objectives don't answer that question directly; they are too particularistic and too formulaic. In her short and readable *Design for How People Learn* (2012), Julie Dirksen advises, "… just say no to learning-objective slides at the beginning of the course" (p. 73). Why? Because it means that "learners are subjected to horrible instructional design jargon" (p. 72). Moreover, while learning objectives list *what* trainees will learn, they don't really answer the question on every adult learner's mind: "*Why* should I learn this?"

Don't misunderstand our point. Learning objectives are essential to define what needs to be taught and the criteria for demonstrating mastery. Our concern is that they do not adequately communicate the benefits of the training to either the participants who must attend or the business managers who pay the bills. Use learning objectives to communicate internally within the training department, but use the business objectives (rationale) to communicate with attendees and their managers. You will enjoy greater buy-in and participation when you make the business benefits explicit.

Use Quick Check D1.4 to evaluate your current practices and the actions you could take to strengthen this aspect of D1.

QUICK CHECK D1.4:
BUSINESS OBJECTIVES

1. Can you concisely and convincingly state the business objective of the training and how it relates to the overall business goals?

Yes	No
Congratulations, you have passed an important milestone on the path to creating training that delivers business results. ❑ Be certain to stress the business objectives and business benefits of the training in any communications to the rest of the organization.	You will greatly improve the probability of success of your training if you stop to clarify the business rationale. ❑ If you are unsure of the business objectives, you need to talk to the business sponsors. They own the business objectives, although they may need your help in clarifying them (Planning Wheel, etc.). ❑ If you think you understand the business objectives, but are struggling to express them, give it your best shot and then ask a business leader to react to it.

2. Are you using learning objectives in your course descriptions and course introductions?

Yes	No
Don't do it! Learning objectives inadequately convey the program's benefits and are usually boring.	Good, so long as you are using business objectives and benefits statements. One of the principles of adult learning is that adults want to know why they should learn something before they will willingly do so.
❏ Take Julie Dirksen's advice: "There are a multitude of ways that *aren't* bullet points on a slide to accomplish the goals of focusing the learners' attention, and letting them know where they are headed" (2012, p. 73).	❏ Explain the business rationale for the training to learners and their managers—what this will help them do and how it fits into the overall strategy. ❏ If you aren't sure, ask.

SUMMING UP

The most effective learning organizations build D1 into their standard operating procedures. Before they embark on the design and implementation of a training program, they make sure that:

- A clear and agreed-on business need has been defined by the business leadership.
- Training is an appropriate part of the solution.
- Other essential elements of the solution also have been identified.
- It is clear what participants are supposed to do better and differently as a result of the training.
- How success will be measured and judged has been discussed with the business sponsor.
- The benefits to the business and individuals are succinctly stated.
- The business outcomes, rather than the learning objectives, are used in communications with managers and participants.

A checklist of the most important elements of D1 is provided as Tool D1.3. The checklist should be completed before a training initiative moves into the design and implementation phases.

D2 Design the Complete Experience

The core concepts of D2: Design the Complete Experience are (1) that turning training into improved performance is a process, not an event and (2) that what happens before and after training is as important as the instruction itself. As the cases in this section illustrate, the most effective training organizations consider the learner's *complete* experience by incorporating everything from pre-course communications to post-training support into their plans. Such a holistic approach to training requires additional efforts and new skills from learning professionals, efforts that are amply rewarded by improved learning transfer and business impact.

Key aspects of the practice of D2 include:

- Treating learning as a process
- Managing expectations
- Creating intentionality
- Emphasizing benefits rather than features
- Initiating learning before class
- Redefining the finish line
- Providing a sense of accomplishment

Treat Learning as a Process, Not an Event

Process thinking contributed significantly to the dramatic increase in manufacturing productivity in the 20th century. We now enjoy higher-quality, lower-cost goods in greater abundance than ever before. Championed by Deming, Juran, and others, and later expanded into the Six Sigma Way by Motorola, a process approach to continuous improvement recognizes that everything in a business is a process and that every process can be "continuously and forever improved." A process approach defines quality as the consistency with which the output meets the customer's needs. "Each time that a process or product does not meet stakeholders' expectations, it is counted as a defect" (Islam, 2006, p. 16).

In the case of training, management's expectation is that the investment will produce improved performance (Figure D2.1). If performance fails to improve after training—even if people demonstrably gained new knowledge and skills—then from a management perspective, the training was defective. This may help explain why in a survey by the Corporate Executive Board, 56 percent of managers responded that employee performance *would not change or would be improved* if learning and development were completely eliminated (Corporate Executive Board, 2009).

While it is true that the process fails more often in the transfer of training step than in the instruction itself, the result is still customer

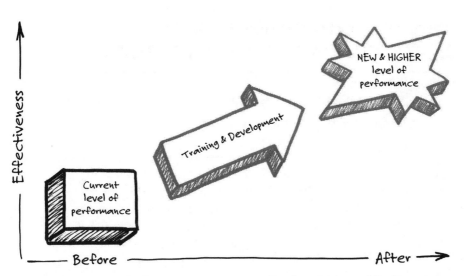

Figure D2.1. Management Expects Training to Produce Improved Performance

dissatisfaction and a reluctance to support training in the future. When learning professionals practice D2, their role changes from event planners to process owners. A process approach challenges us to think through and manage *all* of the factors that contribute to the output and to identify, fix, measure, and continuously improve the weak links.

The power of process thinking and process reengineering is described in Case D2.1, in which Kaliym Islam, vice president, Depository Trust & Clearing Corporation, describes how he used a process reengineering approach to dramatically improve the productivity and output of the DTCC Learning Group. For a general discussion of process improvement see Langley, Nolan, Nolan, Norman, and Provost (2009), *The Improvement Guide.* For detailed information on applying process thinking to training, see Islam's *Developing and Measuring Training the Six Sigma Way* (2006) and *Running Training Like a Business* by Van Adelsberg and Trolley (1999).

Quick Check D2.1 provides a quick assessment of the extent to which you treat learning as a process and suggests some actions you can take to strengthen this aspect of your practice.

QUICK CHECK D2.1:
TRAINING AS A PROCESS

1. Are you able to apply the basic techniques of process improvement (Six Sigma, Total Quality Management, Lean, etc.)?

Yes	No
Excellent. These are valuable tools that can be applied to any business process.	Knowing the basic approaches to process improvement can help you in a wide range of endeavors in addition to making training more effective and efficient.
❑ If you have not done so already, map the process from the learner's point of view and look for probable points of failure.	❑ Consider reading a book or taking a short course on the methodology used by your organization.
	❑ Alternatively, "learn by doing" by joining a process-improvement team in your organization. Most companies have experts and ongoing projects in manufacturing and other fields.

2. Does your instructional design process include developing plans for both the pre-training and post-training period?

Yes	No
Good. You are ahead of most training organizations that are still stuck in the "event paradigm."	If you are focusing all your attention on the "event," then much of your training is probably going to waste. The evidence suggests that what happens before and after training can make or break its success.
❏ Use the D2 Checklist to look for opportunities to further improve your process.	❏ Use the D2 Checklist to identify opportunities.
	❏ Start small, such as concentrating on improving pre-course communications.

Manage Expectations

Expectations matter. Indeed, expectations shape people's experience of reality. The classic example is a study done many years ago at MIT in which students were given two slightly different descriptions of the guest lecturer prior to class (Kelley, 1950). Although all the students participated in the *same* discussion, led by the *same* professor, their post-class reaction ratings differed substantially depending on whether the guest lecturer had been described to them beforehand as "warm and friendly" or "cold and aloof."

In a brilliant series of experiments, which contributed to their sharing the Nobel Prize, Kahneman and Tzversky showed that even seemingly irrelevant input, such as the spin of a roulette wheel or the throw of dice, affects people's subsequent judgments (Kahneman, 2011). In a more humorous study, Ariely (2010a) showed that which beer students preferred depended on whether they were told in advance the identity of the "secret ingredient" added to one of the two samples. It was the foreknowledge that affected their preference, not the knowledge. If they tasted the beer first and then were told that the secret ingredient was balsamic vinegar, it did not change their opinions. It was only knowing that the "secret ingredient" was balsamic vinegar *in advance of tasting* that put them off.

The relevance of these observations to training and development is that the pre-conceptions that participants form about an upcoming training program influence both their expectations and their actual experience. Expectations tend to be self-fulfilling prophesies. In other words, if someone arrives at training convinced that it will be a waste of her time, then it is very likely to be so. Once she has made up her mind that the training is not going to have any value, then she is less open to new ideas and less likely to engage in the experience in a way that will lead to new insights.

Conversely, when participants arrive at training with the expectation that it will be relevant and useful (two key criteria for adult learners), then there is a much greater probability that they will indeed find it to be so. They will be more willing to engage and more open to new ideas. As a result, they have a more positive learning experience.

Taken together, these observations suggest that investing effort to positively shape learners' attitudes about upcoming training will pay dividends in greater training effectiveness. In Case D2.2, Wanda Hayes of Emory University describes the creative steps she has taken to ensure that potential participants in Emory's Excellence Through Leadership Program have a clear understanding of the level of commitment required and the outcomes they can achieve. The "how-to" guide H2 D2.1 provides additional guidance on using pre-training communications to create a positive incoming attitude.

Create Intentionality

Training is more effective when participants arrive expecting to learn something of value. It is also important that they arrive *intending* to learn. Brinkerhoff and Apking (2001) originated the concept of "learning intentionality"—coming to training with specific, personal learning goals in mind. Brinkerhoff and Montesino (1995) demonstrated that a pre-training discussion between the trainee and his or her manager had a positive effect on learning intentionality and, ultimately, learning transfer and results. Tool D2.1 is a guide for pre-training discussions for managers. Tool D2.2 provides a sample learning contract.

Peter Block goes further. At the beginning of a training session, he challenges the audience to answer questions like the following and to share their answers with two people seated next to them:

1. How valuable an experience do you plan to have?
2. How engaged and active a participant do you plan to be?
3. How much risk are you willing to take during the session?
4. How much do you care about the quality of the experience of the others in this session?

He reports that having people share their answers to these questions changes the culture in the room to a more participative one (Block & Markowitz, 2001, p. 372). Asking such questions makes the point that creating a great learning experience depends on the participants' active engagement; it is as much their responsibility as the instructor's.

What the trainees learn in class is only the first step in the process of converting training into business value. They must also transfer and apply what they learn to their work. So we should really aim to have learners come to training with not only learning intentionality, but *results intentionality*—the expressed intent to go back and apply what they learned to improve their performance (See H2 D2.2: "How to Create Results Intentionality."). In Case D2.3, Mike Girone, director, Global Learning and Leadership Development, Agilent Technologies, Inc., explains the rigorous approach that Agilent uses to design a complete experience and create results intentionality throughout their high-potential leadership program.

Emphasize Benefits, Not Features

How your programs are described contributes to the expectations and results intentionality trainees bring to class. Unfortunately, most course descriptions focus primarily on the *features* of the training (length, locale, method, learning objectives) and fail to adequately articulate the *benefits*—that is, how the training will help the participant and his or her business unit.

Read the description of your training—or better yet, have someone who is not familiar with the program read it.

- Does it unambiguously answer the WIIFM ("What's in it for me?") question for the learner?
- Does it make clear the value that a manager can expect by sending his or her direct reports to the training?
- If not, rewrite the descriptions and/or invitations so that they clearly convey the business benefits, not just the activities that will take place.

The results of doing so may surprise you. One of the participants in a workshop we taught in China took our advice and rewrote the descriptions of all her courses so that they emphasized the business linkage and the business outcomes that could be expected. None of the courses or content was altered, only the way in which they were described.

Nevertheless, shortly after she rewrote the descriptions, she started to receive calls from employees and managers who were so excited about what they perceived as the new and greatly improved course offerings because they met their needs and goals so much better than the old ones!

Use Quick Check D2.2 for ideas to improve your practice in this regard.

QUICK CHECK D2.2:
FEATURES VERSUS BENEFITS

1. Can you confidently explain the difference between features and benefits and correctly identify them in descriptions?

Yes	No
Congratulations. Be sure that you are putting this skill to work in the way in which you describe training programs.	This is a skill worth learning, since it will help you do a better job of marketing the value of training to both participants and managers.
❏ Review your course descriptions and invitations. Circle the benefits statements and rewrite feature statements into statements of value.	❏ Talk to one of the marketers in your organization. Have him or her describe the differences and help you rewrite your descriptions to focus more on benefits.
	❏ Alternatively, talk to one of your colleagues who teaches sales training, or review sections in the sales training materials on features versus benefits.

2. Do your course descriptions clearly state the *benefits* of participating in the training? Are these clear to the participants and their managers?

Yes	No	Not sure
Great. This will help generate positive attitudes and learning intentionality among participants and encourage managers to send their direct reports to training.	Fix this. It will help generate more support for training and make facilitation easier and more effective. ❏ Rewrite your course descriptions and invitations to emphasize the personal and business benefits of attending. ❏ Test them with some participants and managers to be sure the message is clear. ❏ Have a colleague in marketing review them and offer suggestions for improvement.	You need to do some market research to answer this question, since it impacts training's effectiveness. ❏ Test your descriptions by showing them to some potential participants and managers. Can they readily identify the benefits? It not, rewrite the descriptions. ❏ Have a colleague in marketing review your descriptions and offer suggestions for improvement.

Initiate Learning Before Class

Time is a non-renewable resource and an increasingly precious commodity. At the pace of business today, training organizations are being pressured to make learning more efficient and reduce the time people spend in learning activities away from their day-to-day work. As the time for instruction continues to be compressed, independent Phase I learning (commonly called pre-work[1]) takes on even greater importance.

For Phase I learning to be effective, five conditions must be met:

1. There must be a sound learning rationale for it.
2. Its purpose should be clearly and convincingly communicated to participants.
3. The amount must be reasonable for the time available.
4. It must be engaging and thought-provoking.
5. Subsequent instruction should depend on and build on, but not repeat, Phase I learning.

See H2 D2.3: "How to Start Learning Before Class and Improve Efficiency" for additional details. Tool D2.3 is a flow chart to help select appropriate Phase I learning. Tool D2.4 provides examples.

Quick Check D2.3 is an opportunity to assess your current use of Phase I learning. It includes suggestions for actions you can take to make this important aspect of the complete experience more effective.

 Redefine the Finish Line

Cal Wick added an important insight to designing the complete experience: the need to redefine the finish line (Wick, Pollock, & Jefferson, 2009).

---

[1]We have waged an (as-yet-unsuccessful) attempt to strike the word "pre-work" from the learning lexicon because we feel that calling something "pre-work" implies it isn't the real work—that comes later. Calling assignments "pre-work" may be part of why they don't get done.

QUICK CHECK D2.3:
PHASE I LEARNING

1. Does your instructional design process require consideration of Phase I learning?

Yes	No
Excellent. Phase I learning should be considered for every program. For certain programs, you might decide not to have learners do some independent learning prior to the training, but this should be an active and considered choice, not merely oversight.	It should, even if you decide ultimately not to require preparatory work for some programs. ❏ Revise the standard operating procedure and sign-off process for instructional design to ensure that the merits of Phase I learning are always considered and that the plan includes a rationale for what type of preparation is required and why. ❏ Use the D2 Checklist to help ensure that Phase I learning is always considered as part of the plan.

2. If Phase I learning is assigned, is it required to continue in the training program?

Yes	No
Excellent. Your organization is among the few who do. Doing so sends a strong signal that preparation is important and expected.	You are like most organizations. Not requiring learners to earn the right to continue by completing assignments signals that they are optional and that you don't consider them very important. ❏ Modify the course requirements so that completing the Phase I learning assignments is a requirement to continue. ❏ For prestigious or mission-critical courses, work with HR and management to establish a policy of sending people home who have not completed the assignments.

3. Does the instruction depend on and build on the Phase I learning assignments rather than simply repeat them?

Yes	No	Not Sure
Excellent. Your training is, sadly, in the minority. ❑ Be sure to monitor and continue this policy.	If the training doesn't depend on the preparatory work, why was it assigned? 　　If the facilitators cover everything that was in the pre-work in class anyway, you are wasting time. ❑ Revise the instructional design so that it fully utilizes and builds on the Phase I learning. ❑ Revise the pre-training assignments if necessary to make them more meaningful.	This is worth investigating. If facilitators are going over all the pre-work again in class, they are wasting valuable time. ❑ Interview some recent attendees or sit in on a class to find out what is really going on.

In the great majority of corporate training programs today, attendees receive credit or certificates of completion as soon as the instruction (Phase II) ends. In our view, that sends entirely the wrong message. It implies, "You're done." In fact, the real work begins when the class ends. The real work is the effort required to transfer and apply the new knowledge and skills in ways that improve performance.

The most effective training programs "move the finish line" to a point in time weeks or even months after training and make evidence of improved performance the requirement for satisfactory completion (Figure D2.2).

In Case D2.4, Justin Keeton, manager of organizational effectiveness for Methodist Le Bonheur Healthcare, describes how he and his team redefined the finish line for their Coaching Clinic. In Case D2.5, Christopher Goh Soon Keat, director, Global Learning and Leadership Development for Agilent Technologies, describes how Agilent redefined a core leadership program for first-level managers as a three-month process instead of a one-time event.

See H2 D2.4: "How to Move the Finish Line for Learning" for specific guidance, and Wick, Pollock, and Jefferson (2010, p. 188–189) for additional examples. Tool D2.5 provides a guide to help managers hold a quick but effective post-training discussion.

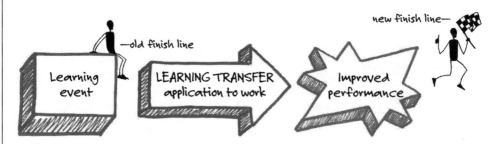

Figure D2.2. The Finish Line for Training Should Be Redefined as Improved Performance at Work

Provide a Sense of Accomplishment

In *Drive: The Surprising Truth About What Motivates Us* (2009), Daniel Pink summarized the evidence on the power of intrinsic motivation, concluding that, for most people, the drive to do a good job and be recognized is more important than money and position. In an exhaustive study of the daily work logs of knowledge workers, Amabile and Kramer (2011) found that a sense of progress in meaningful work was associated with greater productivity, creativity, and commitment to the work. Unfortunately, they also discovered that "Far too many managers are unaware of the importance of progress and therefore neither worry about it nor act to support it" (p. 158).

The devastating effect of having your efforts ignored was demonstrated by Ariely (2010b). People were given a straightforward task of identifying all the places in which the double-letter "ss" occurred on a printed page, for which they were paid a nominal amount. Each time they completed a page, they could turn it in for another or they could stop at any time. The pay decreased with each round until it eventually became zero after the eleventh sheet.

When workers turned in their sheets, one of three things happened. For the first group, the experimenter looked it over, nodded in a positive way, and placed it on a pile of completed sheets. In the second group, the participants were ignored; no eye contact was made, and their completed sheet was added to a stack without so much as a glance at the work. In the third group, when the participants turned in a completed worksheet, it was immediately placed in a paper shredder right in front of their eyes.

Not surprisingly, the group that received acknowledgement completed the most sheets before voluntarily stopping and the shredded group completed the fewest. The key lesson for training professionals is the surprising result that the group whose work was ignored was much closer in performance to the shredded group. In other words, having your work ignored destroys intrinsic motivation almost as much as having it shredded. Historically, training departments have not done enough to harness intrinsic motivation by ensuring that trainees receive recognition when they make the effort to apply what they learned back on the job.

So, in conjunction with "moving the finish line," we need to make certain that there is some acknowledgement of the effort exerted and some recognition for achievements as a critical and fourth phase of the learning-to-results process (Figure D2.3). That may be simply awarding credit or providing a certificate of completion, or more powerfully, it can include recognition by the participant's manager as described in Case D4.6: "How We Engage Managers to Acknowledge the Achievements of Leadership Program Participants."

See Quick Check D2.4 for ideas on how to improve this aspect of your programs.

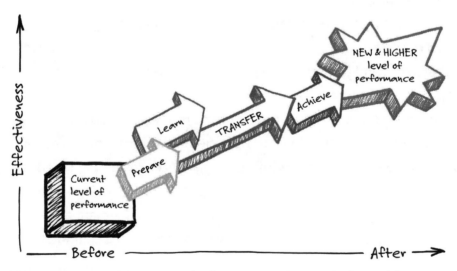

Figure D2.3. Providing a Sense of Achievement Is the Fourth Phase of the Learning Process

QUICK CHECK D2.4: PROGRESS AND ACCOMPLISHMENT

1. Do you award certificates or credit as soon as the instruction (class or e-learning module) ends?

Yes	No
If so, then you are sending the wrong message. Attending the training does not itself create value; only application does. ❏ Redefine the finish line. Make credit or certificates of completion dependent on some evidence of application. Choose a time and mechanism appropriate to the subject and the strategic importance of the outcomes.	Good for you. You are ahead of the pack if you extend the learning back to the workplace.

2. Do you provide participants with a way to gauge their progress in applying what they learned?

Yes	No
Well done. A sense of making progress in meaningful work is a strong motivator for continuing effort.	You have an opportunity to increase the business impact of your training by giving people a sense of progress after training. This can be as simple as a self-evaluation. ❏ Read *The Progress Principle* (Amabile & Kramer, 2011) on the importance of progress. ❏ Consider using a learning transfer support system, like Qstream, to foster spaced learning and a sense of progress.

3. Is there a mechanism to recognize and reward accomplishments resulting from the use of the training?

Yes	No
Excellent. Too many training programs just fizzle out. With no reinforcement or recognition for accomplishment, it isn't surprising that a significant amount of training is never used.	You are missing an important opportunity. Remember that having your work ignored is almost as demotivating as seeing it destroyed (Ariely, 2010b). ❑ Put a stake in the ground—a point in time and a mechanism by which achievement will be assessed and recognized. It can be a follow-up session, capstone call, self-evaluation, or more formal evaluation. For maximal impact, have the recognition come from the trainee's manager.

Putting It All Together

For training to deliver results, the learner's *whole* experience from beginning to end needs to "hang together." That is, each of the components must make sense in relation to the others and must reinforce key themes and concepts. Training should be organized in ways that make it the easiest to learn, not necessarily the easiest to teach. The design must be comprehensive and consider the full range of formal instruction and on-the-job experience, as well as the coaching and mentoring necessary to achieve proficiency. That is the core concept behind Steve Rosenbaum's and Jim Williams's Learning Path Methodology (2004). As Steve explains in Case D2.6, taking a holistic approach to the design and management of the learning path for new employees dramatically shortens the time it takes them to get up to speed while, simultaneously, improving retention.

Two additional examples illustrate the power of designing the complete experience. In Case D2.7, Ishita Bardhan, assistant general manager, and Kanika Sharma, senior manager, Tata Motors Academy, describe the benefits of the complete learning experience for new employees in a manufacturing facility. Last, in Case D2.8, Raymond Phoon and Jonathan Low, managing partners, PowerUpSuccess Group, explain how by marrying an in-depth analysis of the business needs with a comprehensive approach to learning and performance support, their group was able to help a spin-off software provider achieve significant business results.

SUMMING UP

What happens before and after training is as important in determining the final results as the instruction itself. The second of the 6Ds is to design the complete experience, not just a learning event. Tool D2.6 is a checklist to help ensure disciplined execution of D2.

D3 Deliver for Application

The central tenet of the 6Ds is that training produces business value only when it is transferred and applied to the work of the individual and enterprise. The third discipline, Deliver for Application, is about ensuring that the delivery of the training itself—in terms of method, medium, sequence, timing, participation, and so forth—facilitates its subsequent application on the job. It requires discipline to deliver training in ways that are the easiest to learn and apply, as opposed to the easiest to design and teach.

The effective practice of D3 involves:

- Addressing the "Can I?" and "Will I?" questions
- Teaching for how people learn
- Avoiding cognitive overload
- Ensuring adequate practice
- Connecting the dots
- Monitoring perceived relevance and utility

Address the "Can I?" and "Will I?" Questions

In the Introduction, we proposed that whether training was used or was added to the scrap heap depended on how participants answered two questions at the "moment of truth," when they were about to take an action:

- Can I actually do this the way I was just taught?
- Will I make the effort?

How the training is designed and delivered has a profound effect on the answers to these two critical questions.

For employees to answer "Yes" to the "Can I?" question, three conditions have to be satisfied:

- They feel confident in their ability.
- They have the opportunity.
- They can get help if they need it.

Confidence is born of experience. New trainees are more likely to be confident in their ability if the instruction emphasized "*how*" more than just *"why"* and if they had sufficient opportunities to practice the new approach in a safe environment (see Ensure Adequate Practice, below). Job aids and the availability of help from more experienced practitioners also boost confidence and help ensure an affirmative answer to "Can I?" (see D5: Deploy Performance Support).

For employees to answer "Yes" to the "Will I?" question, three things must be true:

- They perceive what they learned to be relevant and useful.
- They are convinced that the new approach is better than whatever they were doing before.
- They believe that their efforts will be noticed and rewarded in some way that they value.

How the training is delivered (D3) significantly impacts the first two. A fundamental principle of andragogy (adult learning) is that "Adults are motivated to learn to the extent that they perceive that learning will help them perform tasks or deal with the problems that they confront in their life situations" (Knowles, Holton, & Swanson, 2005, p. 67). For employees to make the effort to learn the material in the first place, and then to apply it, they need to be persuaded that it will "help them perform tasks or deal with the problems they confront." In other words, the training needs to be delivered in a way that "sells" them on its value (see "Connect the Dots" below).

A useful criterion for evaluating training designs is to ask: "Will this design result in affirmative answers to the 'Can I?' and 'Will I?' questions?" If not, fix it. Use Quick Check D3.1 to assess your current practice and identify opportunities for improvement.

QUICK CHECK D3.1:
THE TWO QUESTIONS

1. Do your end-of-instruction reaction forms ask participants whether they feel prepared to use the training on the job?

Yes	No
Very good. This is an important piece of information; it tells you how participants will answer the "Can I?" question. While a positive response doesn't guarantee transfer and application, if participants don't feel prepared to apply what they learned, they won't. ❏ Identify and resolve the root causes of any courses that score low in this regard.	You are missing out on some vital insights. ❏ Add one or two questions to the end-of-instruction survey to gauge participants' perception of their ability to actually use what they learned. ❏ Identify and resolve the root causes of any courses that score low in this regard.

2. Do you measure the transfer rate (how many learners actually apply the training to their work) for key programs?

Yes	No
Excellent. You are ahead of the game; not many learning organization know the actual transfer rate. ❏ Practice continuous improvement. Look for ways to increase the number of "Yes" answers to "Can I?" and "Will I?" even in courses that score well.	If you do not measure (in some way) how many people actually use what they learn, then you don't really know how effective the training is. ❏ At a minimum, ask participants (after a suitable period) whether they have been able to apply the training to their jobs and achieve positive results. ❏ Ideally, confirm application through independent observers or metrics.

Teach for How People Learn

Recent years have witnessed tremendous progress in our understanding of how people learn and remember. See, for example, *How the Brain Learns* by David Sousa (2011), *Brain Rules* by John Medina (2008), *Evidence-Based Teaching* by Geoff Petty (2009), or *The Brilliant Report* by Annie Murphy Paul (2013). The research shows that much of what we do in corporate education is actually counter-productive.

For example, we now know that paying attention is a first and vital step in learning. The brain continuously receives far more input than it can process (see Figure D3.1). We can only consciously attend to a single stream or channel at a time; everything else is discarded without being processed. A familiar example is how, if you are genuinely interested in the person you are speaking with at a party, you "tune out" other conversations. Even though you can hear other voices, you aren't really conscious of what is being said unless something hijacks your attention, like overhearing your name being mentioned or a voice raised in anger.

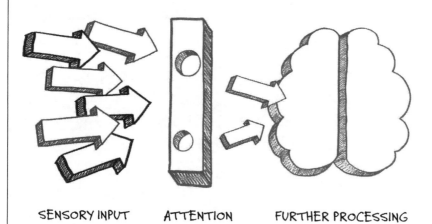

SENSORY INPUT   ATTENTION   FURTHER PROCESSING

Figure D3.1. The Brain Receives More Input Than It Can Process. Attention Is Strictly Limited; Most Input Is Filtered Out and Ignored

All the evidence suggests that multi-tasking is a myth (Paul, 2013). People can switch between tasks rapidly, but can only attend to one at a time. So attention is a very narrow funnel through which all learning must pass. People can't learn what they don't attend to and "we don't pay attention to boring things" (Medina, 2008). Unfortunately, a great deal of corporate training is pretty boring stuff, aided and abetted by slide after bullet-point slide. See H2 D3.1: "How to Use (and Not Abuse) PowerPoint."

Paying attention is hard work. Jonathan Haidt, in his thought-provoking *The Happiness Hypothesis* (2006), borrowed an analogy from the Buddha and characterized the conscious brain as the rider on an elephant:

> The rider . . . is conscious, controlled thought. The elephant, in contrast, is everything else. The elephant includes the gut feelings, visceral reactions, emotions, and intuitions that comprise much of the automatic emotional brain.

Julie Dirksen, in *Design for How People Learn* (2012), expanded Haidt's analogy and applied it to training and development. The rider can control the elephant, but only up to a point, and it is hard work. The elephant is bigger and stronger; it has a mind of its own and is easily distracted. We have to deliver training in a way that respects both and helps them work together. Even the most dedicated rider cannot force the elephant to pay attention indefinitely (Figure D3.2).

How long can adults pay attention without some kind of change of pace? Not as long as most people think: about ten minutes for most of us. The practical implication, according to Medina (2008), is that instruction needs to be broken into a series of ten-minute segments. Every ten minutes or so you need to change things up in a way that re-engages the audience, using something he calls "hooks"—emotionally competent stimuli. These can be any number of things: case histories, business

"I think I'd like to start seeing other elephant trainers, Rolf."

Figure D3.2. The Elephant and the Rider Must Work Together for Training to Succeed
Michael Crawford/The New Yorker Collection/www.cartoonbank.com. Used with permission.

anecdotes, humorous stories, thought-provoking questions, and so forth, provided they are relevant to the topic and arouse some sort of emotion like happiness, curiosity, nostalgia, or the like.

We find audience-response technology, such as that available from Turning Technologies or Poll Everywhere, to be very effective for re-engaging learners and simultaneously checking for understanding. For additional ideas and methods, see H2 D3.2: "How to Gain and Hold Learners' Attention."

People need breaks to satisfy both mental and physiological needs, but getting their heads "back in the game" can be challenging. In H2 D3.3, Terrence Donahue, corporate director of training for Emerson, describes using quick puzzles to re-engage learners, a technique we learned from him and have used with great success.

Experiential learning can be particularly powerful because it holds attention and engages emotions, which are both strong catalysts for memory. In Case D3.1, Praise Mok, principal consultant for the ROHEI Corporation in Singapore, explains how they use experiential learning to engage learners' hearts as well as their minds.

Bottom line: You have to teach in the ways that people learn best. The first and critical step is to get and hold their attention. That requires awareness, planning, and creativity by designers and trainers.

Avoid Cognitive Overload

Processing speed and capacity are another bottleneck in learning. Information that is attended to is passed to working (short-term) memory (Figure D3.3). It must be further processed (encoded) if it is to be retained in long-term memory and later retrieved for application. The more elaborate the encoding—that is, the more neural connections that are formed between the new and existing knowledge—the longer the information will be stored and the easier it will be to recall and apply. The problem is that such processing takes time and effort.

When too much content is delivered too quickly, it overwhelms the brain's capacity to adequately process and make sense of it, a condition known as cognitive overload. At some point, everyone has felt like the young man in Gary Larson's *Far Side* cartoon who asks to be excused because his "brain is full." That's cognitive overload: so much information coming in so fast that your brain is overwhelmed and can no longer process it.

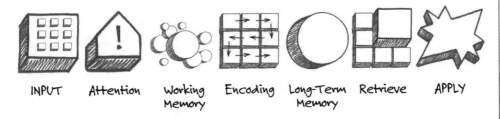

INPUT   Attention   Working Memory   Encoding   Long-Term Memory   Retrieve   APPLY

Figure D3.3. Schematic of Key Steps in Learning, Storage, Retrieval, and Application

The problem with cognitive overload isn't just that the overage is not retained: "When overload gets large enough, the learning system shuts down altogether" (Clark, Nguyen, & Sweller, 2006, p. 29). In other words, trying to stuff in too much extra information adversely impacts learning even the basics.

Cognitive overload occurs in e-learning and multi-media programs when:

- Too many different channels are used to present information simultaneously—for example, concurrent text plus narration plus animation.
- Too many extraneous details are included in drawings, diagrams, and videos; simple line drawings of only the salient features usually result in better comprehension.
- More importance is given to dazzling visuals than to learning principles.

Cognitive overload occurs in instructor-led training when:

- Subject-matter experts include far more detail than is needed or can be grasped by non-experts.
- Slides are text-dense, which creates conflict between listening to the presenter and reading the slide.
- Visuals contain non-essential and distracting "noise."

In Case D3.2, Glenn Hughes, director of Global Learning for KLA-Tencor, describes a program that transformed the presentation culture in his company and produced more efficient meetings, clearer communication, and better decisions. A key element of that program was teaching people to improve the "signal-to-noise" ratio in their slides. Tool D3.1 is the "Glance Test" for slides that can be used to assess their signal-to-noise ratio.

Programs that stuff too much content into too little time lock the instructor and participants into a forced march ("We just have to get through this"). When this happens, inadequate time is available for practice, reflection, reinforcement, or clarification. As a result, some learners are left behind. Those who did not understand a foundational concept are completely lost when the instruction moves to more advanced topics.

Delivery for application requires allowing enough time and active practice for participants to comprehend the material, link it to existing knowledge, and encode it in a way that facilitates its later retrieval and use. The process can be enhanced by returning to a key theme repeatedly. "Spaced learning"—revisiting the same topic at intervals—is one of the best-studied phenomena in cognitive science (see review by Thalheimer, 2006). Spacing out learning over time reduces cognitive load, encourages elaborative encoding, and produces learning that is both more durable and richer than when a topic is presented only once, *even if the total amount of time spent is identical.*

■ Ensure Adequate Practice

In a review of two hundred articles on the science of training and development, Salas and colleagues (2012) concluded: "We know from the body of research that learning occurs through the practice and feedback components" (p. 86). Sufficient practice with feedback is essential for learners to have the confidence to answer "Yes, I can" when it comes time to apply the training to their work.

Although it is impossible to make a hard-and-fast rule that applies to all training, the consensus among learning professionals in our workshops is that to deliver training that participants can apply, at least half to as much as 90 percent of the class time should be spent on practice, as opposed to content delivery. And yet, when we ask these same professionals what the ratio is in the training they deliver today, they frequently admit that it is the complete opposite of what they recommend! This contradiction between theory and practice is an indication of how deeply the "cult of content" is embedded in the design and delivery of training. Most corporate training programs would be improved by reducing the amount of content (thus avoiding cognitive overload) and increasing the amount of practice.

What counts as practice? Anything that requires the learners to *apply* what they have learned. This can include problem solving, case discussions, simulations, games that require application, role play, and many others. Practice is most effective when it takes place under conditions similar to the work environment in which the knowledge will be used and when it includes several different scenarios. That's because the goal in business is usually "far-transfer"—the application of knowledge to novel situations. Far-transfer ability is enhanced when participants have practiced on several different and increasingly challenging problems.

Interestingly, practice should be designed such that students are likely to make mistakes. A number of studies have shown that such "error training" produces superior post-training application compared with the more common approach of trying to minimize errors (Keith & Frese, 2008). Making mistakes in a safe environment seems to encourage greater effort to learn and a deeper understanding of tasks, as well as the development of tactics for handling on-the-job errors.

Quoting Salas and colleagues (2012) again: "We recommend the incorporation of errors, particularly when training complex cognitive tasks. Training tasks can be designed so that trainees are more likely to commit errors, and trainees can be encouraged to try new responses even if it leads to errors" (p. 87).

Bottom line: An important aspect of "delivering for application" is ensuring that the training provides enough practice, in enough different scenarios—including those in which the participants are likely to err— that they are sufficiently confident to try to apply the learning when they return to work.

Use Quick Check D3.2 to evaluate current practices in this regard and to identify opportunities for action.

QUICK CHECK D3.2: PRACTICE VERSUS CONTENT

1. Do you compare the amount of time spent on passive information transfer to active practice working with the content in your programs?

Yes	No
Well done. Ensuring sufficient time for trainees to actively work with the material is vital to its subsequent application on the job.	You should. It does not take long and you may be surprised at the percent of class (or e-learning) time trainees spend sitting passively.
❏ Continue to look for ways to minimize the amount of training time spent on information transfer to free up more time for practice.	❏ Go through the program agenda and add up the time spent in simple content delivery (lecture, demonstration, etc.) versus the amount of time spent solving problems, in simulations, role plays, etc.
	❏ If more than half the time is spent delivering content, look for ways to reduce it in favor of more active learning.

2. Do you push back on subject-matter experts and designers when you feel the amount of material is excessive for the time available or the level of performance required?

Yes	No
Good for you. A true learning professional uses his or her expertise in the science of learning to appropriately challenge flawed designs and assumptions.	You have an untapped opportunity to contribute. ❑ Ask the experts how they themselves became good at what they do; it was by working through problems, not being spoon fed. ❑ Share with them the research on learning that overwhelmingly supports the need for more practice.

Connect the Dots

Learning is the product of sense-making and meaningfulness. In other words, people *can* only learn things that make sense to them and *will* only learn things that are meaningful to them personally (Sousa, 2011, p. 52). In other words, if I don't speak Urdu, then I can't make any sense out of a class conducted in Urdu and I cannot learn anything from it. By analogy, if I attend a training program that uses terms and concepts that make no sense to me, then it will be a waste of my time and the company's resources.

Alternatively, the concepts and terms could make perfect sense to me. But if I don't see how the topic relates to me (it isn't meaningful to me personally), then I won't make the effort and won't learn anything either.

Thus, there are two aspects to "connecting the dots" that are relevant to D3:

- Helping learners connect new information to what they already know so it makes sense
- Making the training meaningful by answering the WIIFM question

All learning is a process of connecting new information to things you already know. That is why Gagné included "stimulating recall of prior learning" as the third of his "Nine Events of Instruction" (right after gaining attention and stating the objectives). Helping learners relate what is being taught to what they already know is essential to help them make sense of it. Introduce new material at a rate that learners can assimilate and provide a framework for understanding, especially if the concepts build on one another. See H2 D3.4: "How to Build Scaffolding."

Training not only needs to make sense, it must also be meaningful to the learner. For adult learners, that means it must be perceived as relevant and useful (Knowles, Holton, & Swanson, 2005). In other words, the training must, early on, provide a convincing answer to "Why should I learn this stuff?" otherwise known as the WIIFM or "What's in it for me?" question.

Providing a convincing answer to that question requires that the trainers themselves clearly understand the links between the training and the business needs and outcomes. A useful tool for mapping these relationships is the Value Chain (Figure D3.4).

Tool D3.2 is a job aid for applying the Value Chain concept. It challenges instructional designers to map out how each topic and exercise supports a skill that is needed to achieve a business outcome. H2 D3.5: "How to Build a Value Chain for Learning" explains how to construct a value chain and the benefits of doing so.

The connections between instructional events and business outcomes should be explained during the training to reinforce the relevance and importance of each topic and exercise. In fact, Margolis and Bell (1986) argued that every exercise should be introduced by first

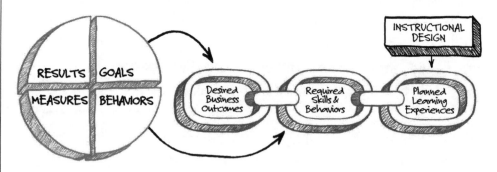

Figure D3.4. A Value Chain for Learning Shows the Links Between the Training and the Ultimate Business Outcomes

explaining its performance rationale in order to answer the WIIFM question. See H2 D3.6: "How to Introduce Exercises."

In Case D3.3, Diane Hinton, director of corporate learning, and her colleagues at Plastipak Packaging, Inc., explain how they developed a learning experience to address a serious business problem and how they ensured that the program participants understood its immediate relevance and applicability.

Delivering for application also means re-orienting participants to focus on the opportunities they have to put their learning into action as part of their daily work. Several contributors emphasize the power of this approach. In Case D3.4, Melanie Brunet Relyea and Michelle Cooper of Oneida Nation Enterprises explain how they ensured application in a key leadership program by having participants set—and then report on—a behavior change goal each week. In Case D3.5, Rebecca Nigel of the safety consulting firm BST describes their approach to teaching supervisors to spot and seize critical "moments of truth" at work that they can use to shape their safety culture and simultaneously build leadership best practices. And in Case D3.6, Colonel Bernard Banks of the U.S. Military Academy describes the impact of changing the course objective from "can apply" to "will apply."

Sharing achievement stories of prior participants before, during, and after training also helps trainees see the relevance and applicability to their own work. In "Feasting on Achievement," Cal Wick and Michael Papay (2013) describe a variety of ways in which companies are using achievement stories to help communicate training's relevance (see also Case D2.2). An automated web-based system (*Waggl*) is available to facilitate the collection and assessment of post-training achievements.

Other ways to help participants see the relevance and utility of the training include:

- Using company-specific, rather than generic, examples
- Employing company leaders as teachers
- Emphasizing the business objectives instead of the learning objectives
- Starting each exercise with how it relates to on-the-job performance
- Designing exercises to be as close to the actual work experience as possible
- Using real data, systems, equipment, or tools during the training

Finally, if you use tests to gauge achievement or certify completion, make sure that they align with the learning objectives and accurately reflect the job performance required. See H2 D3.7: "How to Improve the Predictive Value of Assessments."

Use Quick Check D3.3 to help evaluate your practices and provide ideas for action.

QUICK CHECK D3.3:
CONNECTING THE DOTS

1. As part of the instructional design, do you create a value chain, impact map, or similar device to connect the training to the business outcomes?

Yes	No
Excellent. This is a good discipline that helps ensure learners will answer the "Will I?" question in the affirmative. Having a clear picture of the rela- tionships makes it easier to explain the value to business leaders and participants.	Consider doing so. Because adult learners place so much importance on relevance and practicality, it is impor- tant to be able to clearly illustrate the linkage to business performance. ❏ Use the 6Ds Value Chain or Brinkerhoff's Impact Map to link the training to business needs and the skills and behaviors required to achieve them. ❏ Communicate the linkages before, during, and after the training.

2. Do the trainers frequently reiterate the relevance of the training to the business needs and performance expectations of the participants?

Yes	No
This is a best practice. ❏ Look for continuous improvement opportunities by using current business challenges as examples or citing the on-the-job achievement stories from recent trainees.	They should. Adults are more willing to learn and to participate in exercises when they understand "What's in it for me?" ❏ If the business connections are not emphasized in the facilitator's manual, add them and train the trainers to underscore them.

Monitor Perceived Relevance and Utility

It is one thing for the learning organization to be convinced of the training's relevance and utility. It is another to be sure "the message got through" to the trainees. That's essential, because if participants leave a training session without being convinced that what they learned was relevant, useful, and likely to help them succeed, then they will answer "No" to the "Will I?" question and they won't even attempt to apply what they learned.

To assess the *perceived* relevance and utility of the training, ask participants to rate statements like those below immediately following instruction (Level 1 evaluation):

1. What I learned is directly relevant to my job.
   ○ Strongly disagree   ○ Disagree   ○ Agree   ○ Strongly agree
2. Using what I learned will improve my performance.
   ○ Strongly disagree   ○ Disagree   ○ Agree   ○ Strongly agree
3. I feel I am well prepared to use what I learned.
   ○ Strongly disagree   ○ Disagree   ○ Agree   ○ Strongly agree
4. I am motivated to put my learning to work.
   ○ Strongly disagree   ○ Disagree   ○ Agree   ○ Strongly agree

Track and monitor the responses to these questions for all programs. Analyze those that score low on relevance or utility to understand the root causes and take action to correct the situation. Otherwise, the training will be scrap. Table D3.1 lists the most common causes of low relevance/utility ratings.

Use Quick Check D3.4 to assess your current practice in this regard and review suggestions for improvement.

Table D3.1. Causes of Low Perceived Relevance or Utility Scores

Wrong audience	The training really was not relevant to the learners' job responsibilities; they should not have been there in the first place.
Wrong timing	The training was not relevant to the learners' current job responsibilities and the design did not adequately create a "need to know" regarding future responsibilities.
Wrong examples	The audience was unable to relate to the examples used in the training and the instructors were not able to build credible bridges.
No sale	There was not enough evidence that using the techniques taught would truly benefit the employees or the evidence was not presented in a convincing manner.
Too much material or too theoretical	The message was lost in an onslaught of too much material or too much theory without enough practical application.
Wrong instructional methods	The instructional methods did not allow opportunities for learners to experience the relevance and utility for themselves.

QUICK CHECK D3.4:
MONITORING RELEVANCE

1. Do you track participants' end-of-training perceptions of its relevance and utility?

Yes	No
Good. Understanding whether participants perceived the training to be relevant and useful in their work is much more important than knowing whether they liked the food or facility.	You should. Because if trainees don't *perceive* the value, they won't even try to use it. Sometimes the message gets lost, and if you don't ask, you'll never know. ❑ Include questions about perceived relevance and utility on Level 1 evaluations.

2. Do you have a process to routinely review relevance ratings and take action?

Yes	No
This is a best practice. Regularly reviewing participants' reactions will help you identify courses or instructors that, for whatever reason, failed to persuade learners that the training was relevant and useful.	It is not enough to collect data; you have to do something with it.
❏ Look for recurring patterns that will allow you to make changes that benefit several programs simultaneously.	❏ If you don't now track relevance and utility ratings, add them to your Level 1 evaluations.
	❏ Establish a schedule to review the ratings, understand the cause of low ratings, and fix them.

SUMMING UP

D3: Deliver for Application emphasizes the following points:

- How the training is structured and delivered affects the ease or difficulty of applying it on the job.
- Most corporate training programs will benefit by reducing the amount of content delivered in order to increase the amount of time devoted to guided practice and feedback.
- People learn only when they can make sense of what is being taught and when they are convinced it is meaningful to them.
- Finally, it is important to monitor whether or not participants perceived the training to be relevant and useful and to take corrective action if for some reason they do not.

Tool D3.3 is a checklist to help you execute D3.

D4 Drive
Learning Transfer

The importance of the fourth discipline—Drive Learning Transfer—is underscored by the evidence that learning transfer is currently the weakest link in most corporate training programs. Learning professionals themselves estimate that only one learner in five applies what he learns in training long enough and well enough to improve his performance. In other words, as much as 80 percent of the potential value of training goes unrealized because transfer fails (Figure D4.1).

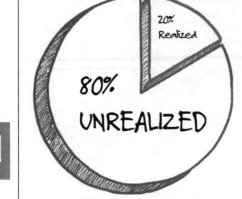

Figure D4.1. Learning Leaders Estimate that 80 Percent or More of Training's Value Is Never Realized for Lack of Transfer

Insufficient transfer of training back to the workplace is the leading cause of customer dissatisfaction with learning and development programs. Business leaders do not differentiate between training and training transfer. When they invest in learning initiatives, but fail to see the expected improvement in performance, they conclude that "the training failed," even though the actual point of failure is most often in the post-training work environment (transfer climate). Regardless, the net effect undermines confidence in training. Indeed, in a survey conducted by McKinsey & Company, only 25 percent of respondents said their training programs measurably improved business performance (DeSmet, McGurk, & Schwartz, 2010).

An important reason why learning transfer is suboptimal is that no one "owns" it; until recently it has fallen into the no-man's land between management and training, with neither side taking the responsibility to plan for and manage the process. As Winston Churchill aptly said, "Failing to plan is planning to fail." In other words, training designs that fail to include plans to drive transfer are plans to fail. Driving transfer has not traditionally been part of instructional design, so it is easy for even well-informed learning professionals to overlook it. In Case D4.1,

- Engaging managers
- Ensuring accountability for both learners and their managers

Apply Process Thinking

As we discussed in the Introduction, turning training into business results is a *process* in which learning transfer is a vital step (Figure I.1). Like every other business process, transfer can be improved by a never-ending cycle of planning, implementing, analyzing the results, and acting accordingly—an approach known as the PDCA or the Deming Cycle (Figure D4.3) in honor of one of the founders of the quality revolution, W. Edwards Deming.

Most learning organizations today use ADDIE or some other instructional-systems design (ISD) process to create training programs. That's good practice, but it doesn't go far enough in applying process thinking. The problem is that these approaches focus "entirely on instructional analysis, audience analysis, instructional strategies, and the evaluation of those strategies" (Islam, 2006, p. 13). They were developed for general education rather than corporate training and, as a result,

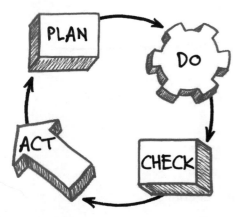

Figure D4.3. The PDCA or Deming Cycle for Continuous Improvement

Cal Wick, the founder of The Fort Hill Company, describes just such a case and presents an "Immediate Transfer Checklist" to circumvent the problem.

Recall that for training to create business value, trainees must answer "Yes" to both the "Can I?" and "Will I?" questions when they are back at work and confronted with a job to do (Figure D4.2). The practice of D4 principally affects the answer to the "Will I?" question. That is, whether or not participants are sufficiently motivated to make the effort to apply what they learned. It doesn't matter what they learned, or how well they mastered new skills; unless they are willing to make the effort to transfer and apply them, the learning is scrap. Some learners are naturally more motivated than others, but all employees are influenced by their environment—the transfer climate (see below)—in particular, the attitude and actions of their managers. Learning professionals should play a pivotal role in positively influencing the environment in which transfer will occur.

Figure D4.2. The Answers to Two Critical Questions Determine Which Path Learners Take

The effective practice of D4 includes:

- Applying process thinking to the transfer challenge
- Assessing and improving the transfer climate
- Maintaining share of mind for learning after training

- Engaging managers
- Ensuring accountability for both learners and their managers

◼ Apply Process Thinking

As we discussed in the Introduction, turning training into business results is a *process* in which learning transfer is a vital step (Figure I.1). Like every other business process, transfer can be improved by a never-ending cycle of planning, implementing, analyzing the results, and acting accordingly—an approach known as the PDCA or the Deming Cycle (Figure D4.3) in honor of one of the founders of the quality revolution, W. Edwards Deming.

Most learning organizations today use ADDIE or some other instructional-systems design (ISD) process to create training programs. That's good practice, but it doesn't go far enough in applying process thinking. The problem is that these approaches focus "entirely on instructional analysis, audience analysis, instructional strategies, and the evaluation of those strategies" (Islam, 2006, p. 13). They were developed for general education rather than corporate training and, as a result,

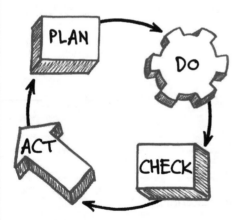

Figure D4.3. The PDCA or Deming Cycle for Continuous Improvement

provide little guidance on satisfying the business requirements of corporate training. Traditional instructional design processes concentrate on ensuring and assessing achievement of *learning* objectives, but stop there. They don't include plans to support training transfer to work or to evaluate whether the initiative achieved its *business* objectives.

Ensuring that training is applied on the job requires a process approach that encompasses all four phases of learning (Figure D2.3) and all six disciplines. In Case D4.2, Alex Jaccaci and Charlie Hackett of Hypertherm, Inc., describe the process they implemented to ensure application of Lean Manufacturing principles.

A central tenet of Total Quality Management, Six Sigma, Kaizen, Zero Defects, Lean, and other process-improvement methods is that quality is defined as how consistently the output meets the expectations of *the customer*, not just some internal standard. The true measure of the quality of training, therefore, is how consistently it produces the improved performance that management wants and expects.

Applying process thinking to corporate training, then, means designing and monitoring every step in the process to ensure that it consistently delivers what the customers want—improved performance—whether or not those steps are within the traditionally perceived boundaries of training and development. When the focus is shifted from achieving learning objectives to producing the on-the-job results, it is apparent immediately that the work environment (transfer climate) to which an employee returns will have a profound impact on whether the training is transferred or not. Numerous studies have confirmed that this is so (see, for example, the review by Grossman & Salas, 2011). Therefore, an essential element of D4 is to assess and improve the post-training transfer climate.

Use Quick Check D4.1 to assess your current practices and identify opportunities for improvement.

QUICK CHECK D4.1:
PROCESS THINKING

1. Does your instructional planning process require consideration of all four phases of the learning-to-results process?

Yes	No
You are ahead of the game. Most learning organizations are still stuck in the "event" paradigm.	When you leave one or more of the phases of learning to chance, you increase the risk of failure.
❏ Learn and apply the techniques of process improvement to continue to strengthen your programs.	❏ Build a check step into the design creation and approval process that requires consideration of what must happen before and after training to produce business impact.

2. When you make a change to a program, do you think through how you will know whether or not it was an improvement?

Yes	No
Congratulations. You have grasped a fundamental concept of process improvement: you must assess the results of a change to know whether you have made things better or worse.	If you implement changes, but don't check the results, then you could actually be making things worse or having no impact one way or the other. ❏ Whenever you propose a significant change (such as switching to virtual or autonomous delivery) ask "How will we know if this worked?" ❏ Use the PDCA cycle (Figure D4.3) and, in particular, be sure to complete the check step to inform future actions.

Assess and Improve the Transfer Climate

Rouiller and Goldstein (1993) defined the learning transfer climate as all of the practices and procedures in an organization that signal to people what is and what is not important. In other words, at the "moment of truth" after training (Figure I.3) when employees decide "Will I make the effort to try to use what I was taught?" they weigh whether it is important enough to make it worth their while. What factors affect their assessment? At a minimum:

- Their perception of their supervisor's interest and support
- What their peers think about the new approach
- Their personal perceptions of its usefulness and potential payoff
- The cultural norms about "making a good try" versus getting it perfect

Holton and his colleagues at Louisiana State University developed a model for assessing the transfer climate, which they called the Learning Transfer Systems Inventory (Holton, Bates, & Ruona, 2000). The complete inventory comprises fifty-one questions grouped into sixteen factors. These can be aggregated into three larger categories:

- Ability to use
- Motivation to use
- Environmental catalysts or impediments

All of the elements of the transfer climate interact to reinforce or undermine each other, as shown in Figure D4.4.

A simplified version of the Transfer Climate Scorecard is given in Tool D4.1. Use it to assess which elements in your current climate are conducive to learning transfer and which are impediments that contribute to learning scrap. Then refer to the Transfer Climate Improvement Planner, Tool D4.2, to identify potential courses of action.

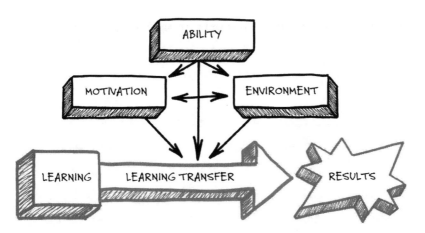

Figure D4.4. Main Components of the Transfer Climate

Maintain Share of Mind by Reminding Learners

Most learners leave training with the intent to use what they learned. However, their good intentions are frequently overwhelmed by day-to-day tasks and hundreds of messages and other priorities that compete for their attention. Absent active reminders about the training and the need to apply it, even well-intentioned action plans lose "share-of-mind," slip from consciousness, and are forgotten.

Advertisers face the same issues. That is why even the best-known brands, like Coca-Cola, Apple, and McDonald's continue to invest millions of dollars each year in advertising. They know that a message must continue to be repeated over and over to get through the welter of competing ideas (Ries & Trout, 2001).

Similarly, communication from the training organization must not stop at the end of the instruction. Participants need to be reminded periodically to sustain their attention and prompt them to action. The most basic reminders are simply emails. Surprisingly, despite the email overload that everyone complains about, email reminders work. In a study involving two thousand employees, Plotnikoff and colleagues (2005) showed that employees who received weekly email reminders for twelve weeks made greater progress in changing health habits than those who did not. A study at Kaiser Permanente showed similar differences between those who received reminder messages and those who did not (Pallarito, 2009).

The advantage of email reminders is that they are simple and economical to implement. In Case D4.3, Rob Bartlett describes how he successfully implemented a low-cost, low-effort reminder system at DirectWest; those were essential attributes, since he constituted the entire training staff at the time! See H2 D4.1: "How to Remind Learners to Apply Their Training" for additional guidance and ideas.

Although passive reminders, tips, and content can enhance transfer, methods that require active engagement and processing are more effective. In Case D4.4, Duncan Lennox, the CEO of Qstream, describes a system that takes advantage of spaced learning and gamification to engage learners post-training. The approach, originally developed at the Harvard Medical School, has been proven effective in a series of controlled trials (see, for example, Kerfoot & Baker, 2012).

Use Quick Check D4.2 to assess your current practices for reminding participants and identify opportunities for improvement.

QUICK CHECK D4.2:
REMINDING PARTICIPANTS

1. Do you remind participants about the training after the period of instruction ends?

Yes	No
Good. You are helping to maintain "share of mind", which increases the probability of transfer. ❏ Look for continuous improvement opportunities to make the communications more interactive and more valuable.	Sending reminders is a low-cost, simple way to increase learning transfer. ❏ Prepare several communications to be sent at intervals following the training. ❏ Make them interesting by including tips, examples, achievement stories, or questions to answer. ❏ Explore the use of transfer support systems like Qstream®, ResultsEngine®, Cameo®, and others that help automate the process.

Engage Managers

Managers have a profound impact on whether or not training is transferred and used; they are a key factor that determines whether the transfer climate is supportive or inimical to the application of training. Managers' reactions to training fall along a continuum (Figure D4.5). The most destructive response is to actively prevent its use: "That may be what they taught you in training, but that's not the way we do things around here." Tragically, this happens more often than generally acknowledged.

Figure D4.5. The Spectrum of Managers' Actions Related to Training

On the other end of spectrum is the ideal and most supportive response: when the manager insists that new work be performed in a way that is consistent with what was taught in training. Although "neutral" is in the center of the continuum, it is not benign. Recall Ariely's study of what happens when your work is ignored that we discussed in D2 (page 43). When a manager says nothing one way or the other about the training, an employee is likely to conclude that it cannot be very important and therefore that it is not a priority. It may be that the manager said nothing simply because she was distracted or overwhelmed by other tasks, not necessarily that she did not value the training. It doesn't matter. The effect is the same: learning scrap.

A study at American Express (2007) concluded that:

> The key criteria for a high transfer climate includes having a manager
> who clearly communicates endorsement and support for the training

and sets goals and expectations before the employee initiates the learning event; who follows up with the participant after the event to discuss what was learned; and who recognizes and rewards improved leadership behavior (p. 9).

Rob Brinkerhoff summed it up this way: "When managers support training and learners, it works. When they do not, it does not" (2006, p. xii).

The bottom line is that training departments need to figure out how to more effectively engage managers in support of transfer and application. Keys to effective managerial engagement include:

- Engaging business leaders in defining and prioritizing the business's training needs.
- Clearly defining the expected business benefits (D1).
- Making sure that participants' managers understand the business rational for the program and the potential benefits for their departments.
    - When managers understand "what's in it for them," they are more likely to invest time and effort in coaching.
- Providing a short synopsis of the course content.
    - Managers are more likely to coach if they feel they know something about the topic and program.
    - Keep it short and to the point—preferably no more than one page. Provide hyperlinks to more detailed information for those who want it.
- Being sure that managers feel comfortable coaching in general.
    - Coaching is usually one of the least-developed skills among managers; they may benefit from training in how to coach and give feedback.
    - Case D3.5 provides an example of how to help business managers build coaching skills while simultaneously learning new content.

- Providing specific guidance on coaching for each program.
  - Give managers specific, practical steps they can take to be sure that their direct reports extract the greatest possible value from training (see H2 D5.1: "How to Provide Performance Support for Managers and Coaches").
  - Managers do more coaching when you provide specific guidance than when you simply exhort them to do so.
- Increasing accountability for managerial support.
  - Clearly, the training department can't hold managers accountable; that is the job of senior management.
  - But you can raise senior management's awareness by asking trainees whether their managers actively helped them apply what they learned. Report the results to senior management so they can decide whether they are satisfied with the current level of support or want to take action.

In Case D4.5, Geoff Rip, research director, Institute for Learning Practitioners, Australia, describes a program to ensure that managers were prepared to coach and to make sure they understood the importance of doing so. In Case D4.6, Mike Schwartz, learning program manager, Cox Media Group, explains how Cox has engaged managers to help provide a sense of accomplishment in Phase IV learning and the beneficial effect this has had on both the managers and the participants.

Use Quick Check D4.3 to assess your current practices for engaging managers and to identify opportunities for improvement.

QUICK CHECK D4.3:
ENGAGING MANAGERS

1. Before their direct reports attend training, do you provide managers with a brief synopsis of the course, its business objectives, and what they can do to increase the value to their department?

Yes	No
This is a best practice. When managers discuss training with their direct reports in advance, it positively influences both learning and learning transfer. ❏ Look for continuous improvement opportunities. Ask managers whether the materials are useful and how they could be improved.	You can improve the effectiveness of your training initiatives by engaging managers in advance. ❏ Prepare and send managers a brief synopsis of the program, including its business rationale (not the learning objectives). ❏ Provide specific, short, practical actions they can take—such as having a brief discussion prior to training—that will boost its value.

2. If participants set goals for application, do you copy and send these to their managers?

Yes	No
Well done. This eliminates a common cause of slippage and increases the accountability participants feel for using the learning (even if the manager fails to follow up). ❏ Explore ways to automate or streamline the process.	Although you probably encourage participants to discuss their goals with their managers, many won't for a variety of reasons. ❏ If you are serious about having people apply what they learn, send their goals for application to their managers. ❏ Explore the use of online learning transfer support systems to streamline the process.

3. Do you communicate with managers after training and provide them with steps they can take to enhance the application and value of the investment?

Yes	No
Excellent. Managers have a big impact on the transfer climate. Providing practical advice will pay dividends in greater manager engagement, improved learning transfer, and better business results.	You can improve the transfer climate and return on investment in training by making it easy for managers to get involved. ❑ Prepare and send the managers of participants very short, very practical, and specific things they can do to ensure the training pays dividends (see H2 D5.1).

Ensure Accountability for Training Transfer

Peter Gilson, former chairman of Swiss Army Brands, Inc., described his experience with training this way: "As a young corporate executive, I attended dozens of development programs, but no one ever once followed up with me to see what I had done with what I learned. The most information ever collected was how I rated the instructor" (quoted in Wick, Pollock, & Jefferson, 2010, p. 70). Sadly, that is still common. Employees are held accountable for many things—hitting revenue targets, meeting production schedules, filing timely reports—but rarely for applying what they learned in training. Absent any accountability for training transfer, it isn't a priority and employees don't spend time on it (Figure D4.6).

To get the most out of training, companies need to hold employees accountable for applying what they learn. That begins by setting the expectation for application up-front (see H2 D2.2: "How to Create Results Intentionality"). The description of the training should stress the expectation that it will be used on the job. This message has to be reinforced during training by having the participants create goals for application and an action plan. In Case D4.7, Marc Lalande, president of Learning Andrago, describes a method for having participants create a "commitment to apply contract," which is then used as the basis

Figure D4.6. For Most Learners, Applying What They Learned in Training Is a Low Priority

for follow-up. See also H2 D4.2: "How to Engage Learners in Action Planning," which describes an effective and engaging group activity to encourage participants to review their learning and develop plans for application.

Action planning is a good start, but unless participants are held accountable for executing their plans, the effect is likely to be limited. Many programs have participants write goals for application, but the process stops there. The goals are put in the course binder, which is put on the shelf . . . and promptly forgotten. After several such experiences—in which no one followed up or cared about execution—participants learn not to take goal-setting seriously. An example that illustrates the extent to which this is true occurred some years ago in a class at one of our clients. Our research had shown that most managers had no clue what their direct reports' goals were for applying training. So we had persuaded the training department that participants' goals should be collected, copied, and shared with their managers.

The facilitator of the program, however, forgot to tell the partici-pants that their managers would be receiving copies of their goals until *after* they had already written them. When she did so, the room was suddenly filled with the sound of papers being torn up and people asking for new goal forms! The participants' previous experience with training had taught them that no one was even going to look at their goals, much less follow up. They did not take the exercise seriously until they learned their goals would be shared with their managers. If we want employees to respond "Yes, I will" when it comes to the "moment of truth," they need to be held accountable for doing so.

Several online systems are now available to support learning trans-fer, such as *ResultsEngine*® and *TransferLogix*™. These systems increase accountability by engaging the participants' managers, peers, and oth-ers during the learning transfer phase. They have the advantage of auto-mating many aspects of the process.

A different, but highly effective, approach is described by Emma Weber of Lever-Learning, Australia, in Case D4.8. In the Turning Learning into Action® process she describes, participants create and sign action plans and schedule three follow-up ACTION conversations with an external specialist. The focus of these conversations is on *action*—the changes that the participants are going to make in the interval between follow-up calls to make progress on their stated objectives. The results are compiled into a dashboard. Participants are informed that the dashboard will be shared with the program sponsor (typically senior management) to underscore accountability.

SUMMING UP

The practice of the fourth discipline—Drive Learning Transfer—includes:

- Recognizing that turning training into results is a process that does not stop when instruction ends.
- Making the business case for investing time and resources to enhance learning transfer (see H2 D4.3).
- Building active transfer support into training plans.
- Holding both the participants *and* their managers accountable for transfer.
- Creating a positive transfer climate and engaging the participants' managers in the process.

Tool D4.3 is a checklist of the key elements of D4.

6Ds

D5 Deploy Performance Support

The goal of the fifth discipline—Deploy Performance Support—is to facilitate learning transfer by increasing the probability that learners will be successful when they try to apply new skills to their work. Extraordinary advances in technology—especially smart-phone technology—have afforded training departments with unprecedented opportunities to provide high-quality support when and where it is needed.

Human memory is extraordinary. But most people are much better at remembering the gist of things than the specifics. They have trouble remembering all the details of new information, processes, or procedures. Even well-trained individuals are likely to forget a key step when they are pressured by time constraints or complexity. As Atul Gawande observed in *The Checklist Manifesto* (2009), "Checklists seem able to defend anyone, even the experienced, against failure in many more tasks than we realized" (p. 48). The right performance support reduces dependence on fallible human memory to ensure that everyone does everything right every time.

Performance support is especially valuable after training, when people are trying to master a new skill, because it reduces cognitive load. Instead of having to simultaneously remember both the sequence of steps and how to perform them, well-designed performance support (job aids, checklists, etc.) allows novices to concentrate their short-term working memory on the performance of the task.

> Designers should encourage their learners to use working memory to *process* information, *not* to store it. For example, as learners first practice a new procedure, give them access to clear written summary steps for reference so all working memory can be directed toward executing the procedure. The use of job aids . . . can be especially powerful for this purpose. With enough repetition of the task, it will become automatic and bypass working memory. Then the job aid will become unnecessary.
>
> Clark, 1986, p. 19

Performance support enhances learning transfer by giving trainees more confidence to answer the "Can I?" question (see page 52) positively. It also contributes to an affirmative answer to "Will I?" by

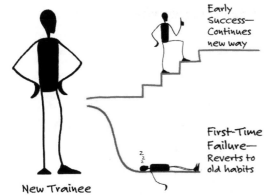

Early Success— Continues new way

First-Time Failure— Reverts to old habits

New Trainee

Figure D5.1. Learners Who Experience Early Success Are Motivated to Continue; Those Who Experience Early Failure Are Likely to Abandon the Effort

increasing the probability of "early wins"—success in the first few tries. Early success is essential to maintain motivation and effort; if people fail the first time they try something new, they are more likely to revert to old habits (Figure D5.1).

Last, moving content that was previously taught, memorized, and tested into performance support frees up time for more active learning and practice. The result is training that is both more effective and more efficient. Indeed, for some tasks, well-designed performance support can completely obviate the need for training. For example, you do not need a training program on how to change the toner in the copier: the instructions are both on the box and built into the machine.

The effective practice of D5 includes:

- Making performance support part of the design
- Identifying when and where support will be most valuable
- Designing, testing, improving, deploying, and improving again
- Ensuring job aids are used

Tool D5.1 is a job aid to help you think through the process of selecting, designing, and delivering performance support.

Make Performance Support Part of the Design

The 6Ds are called disciplines to emphasize that they must be executed in a disciplined manner—thoroughly, consistently, and well—in order to produce optimal results. With respect to D5, that means building performance support into the planning process for every program. That is not to say that every training program must have performance support—although almost all will benefit from it—but that whether or not support will help achieve the business outcomes is *considered* as part of every program design. If performance support is not part of the ultimate plan, it should be the result of an active decision not to provide it, rather than simply an oversight.

The best practice is to make performance support one of the required items on the training design approval checklist. A number of our clients have done so; one even offers an award annually to the instructional design team that developed the most effective solution.

In Case D5.1, Conrado Schlochauer, partner at AfferoLab, the largest training provider in Brazil, describes how they deployed performance support through a customized mentoring program. Consistent with both D2 and D5, the mentoring support was fully integrated into a larger cultural change initiative.

Use Quick Check D5.1 to assess the extent to which you incorporate performance support as part of the design.

QUICK CHECK D5.1:
PART OF DESIGN

1. Is performance support a required part of your instructional design process?

Yes	No
Good; it is an important element of designing a complete (and effective) training experience.	Almost every training program can be made more effective by providing an appropriate kind and level of performance support. ❏ Make thoughtful discussion of performance support a required component of every instructional design. ❏ Ensure that any decision not to provide support is a considered judgment, not just an oversight.

Identify When and Where Support Will Be Most Valuable

Rossett and Schafer (2007) identified eight situations in which performance support is especially valuable:

- Infrequently performed tasks and procedures
- Tasks that are complex and involve many steps or attributes
- When the consequences of error are very serious or costly
- When performance depends on a large body of information
- If the procedures, approaches, or information change frequently
- When self-assessment against a standard will help improve performance
- If employee turnover is high and the tasks are straightforward (for example, fast-food restaurants)
- When there are few resources or not enough time for training

Performance support is especially valuable immediately after training, since the new procedures have been "infrequently performed" at that point. Even if the training included several opportunities to practice, new trainees will not yet be proficient in their execution. Job aids and other forms of performance support will help them succeed initially, so they are motivated to continue to move up the experience curve (Figure D5.1). With practice, they will become more proficient and less dependent on the support. Nevertheless, in situations in which the consequences of failure are intolerable (such as flying an airplane or performing surgery), routine use of the job aid—such as a preflight checklist—should be mandatory.

To identify when and where performance support will be most valuable:

- Talk to people who perform the tasks being taught. Ask them to think back to when they were first trying to perform them. Where did they struggle? What did they have trouble remembering? What would have helped them get up to speed more quickly?

- If the course has been previously offered, interview recent trainees. What did they find most difficult to apply and why? What would have made the application of new learning easier?

- Ask employees whether they have developed their own job aids, such as sticky notes, spreadsheets, reminders, etc. Employees often develop simple but effective tools that they are willing to share.

- Interview managers of employees who perform the work that is the subject of the training. In their experience, where are employees new to the task most likely to have difficulty? Are there any critical points of failure that could be very costly to the company, the employee's career, or customer confidence? Target these for support.

- Tap the expertise of learning professionals. From the designers' experience and knowledge of human performance, where do they anticipate that people are likely to have trouble remembering "what to do" and "how to do" simultaneously? Check with trainers: Where do learners struggle the most in class during role plays and other forms of practice?

- Do not forget that managers also need performance support. Just because someone has been promoted to manager doesn't mean he or she knows how to give effective feedback (Figure D5.2) or to coach for maximal performance against the specific topic of the training. In your interviews with managers, ask them where they struggle to support employees upon their return from training. Likewise, ask employees where their managers could have been of even greater assistance. Develop performance support for managers based on your findings (see H2 D5.1: "How to Provide Performance Support for Managers and Coaches").

"Keep up the good work, whatever it is, whoever you are."

Figure D5.2. Managers Also Need Performance Support
© James Stevenson/The New Yorker Collection/www.cartoonbank.com. Used with permission

Use People, Technology, and Materials Creatively to Provide Support

Traditional paper-based job aids, reminder cards, and the like are entirely satisfactory and cost-effective performance support for many tasks. But you should also tap into the expertise of your instructional designers and IT professionals to explore creative and potentially more effective ways to deliver support. For example, one of our clients was struggling to meet sales objectives for a new medical product targeted at a particularly complicated region of anatomy. They discovered that their representatives were hesitant to open the discussion with physicians because they were not confident of their knowledge and, in particular, their ability to correctly pronounce the many multi-syllabic structures in the area. The representatives were afraid they would embarrass themselves or look foolish.

So the training and marketing departments collaborated on an interactive job aid for the representatives' iPads that not only showed them the name of any structure they touched, but pronounced it using the system's audio capabilities. The representatives could quickly review the material immediately before making a call. Confidence went up, detailing increased, and sales began to exceed targets.

Never be afraid to use a good idea just because you did not think of it first. Look around to see how other organizations, especially consumer product companies, have solved a customer support problem. Then adapt the ideas to your own needs. Consider IKEA, an international leader in assemble-it-yourself furniture. The vast majority of IKEA's customers are able to successfully assemble even complex pieces of furniture following the instruction manuals, even though they do not contain a single word—only pictures. Could we follow their example and use more pictures and fewer words? Pictures take advantage of right-brain image-processing capabilities and are often more readily and more quickly understood than text.

Training organizations can also be much more creative in the use of people for performance support. There are many instances in which the requisite knowledge or nuance cannot be reduced to a simple job aid. Employees may need the kind of feedback on their real-time performance that can only be provided by a more experienced worker or trained coach. An under-utilized resource in this regard is peers—either co-workers in the same training cohort or those who have successfully completed the program previously (see H2 D5.2: "How to Utilize Peer Coaching").

In Case D5.2, Geoff Rip, research director, Institute for Learning Practitioners, Australia, describes a process called Proficiency Coaching that uses "Proficiency Development Workouts" (typically with peers) and a "Proficiency Story" to ensure that learning doesn't stop or get dropped at the classroom door. In Case D5.3, Ishita Bardhan, assistant general manager, and Kanika Sharma, senior manager, Management Development Centre of Excellence, Tata Motors Academy, describe how they helped trainees enhance their coaching capability by ensuring support from the work environment.

When rolling out a new software system, many companies designate "black belts"—highly trained and experienced users—to help with complex questions or problems that aren't covered in the basic job aids. One company went further and hosted a weekly call-in webcast modeled after the radio show *Car Talk*. Users called in their questions to two experts who addressed them on the air in an authoritative but light-hearted manner. The "show" became enormously popular. Many people who didn't even have a question would log in because they usually picked up a tip or learned about a feature they did not know existed.

Our key point here is that we should challenge ourselves and our design teams to think creatively about how to provide effective, efficient, and useful support, whenever and wherever it is needed.

Use Quick Check D5.2 to assess your practices regarding creative performance support.

QUICK CHECK D5.2:
CREATIVE APPLICATIONS

1. Have you created performance support for a recent course that employed an approach other than paper forms or cards?

Yes	No
Good for you. There are lots of creative opportunities for support made possible by new technologies.	Paper forms and reminder cards are adequate solutions in many cases. But if that is all you are using, then you are not capitalizing on technology to make support even more valuable.
❏ Keep on the lookout for creative approaches used by other training departments or by consumer brand companies.	❏ Challenge your team to think "outside the box" by coming up with technology-enhanced support based on what they have found valuable outside of work.
❏ Adapt these to your own needs.	❏ Apply the principles to your training programs.

2. Do you acknowledge and celebrate team members who develop creative and effective performance support?

Yes	No
Good for you! One of the best ways to foster creativity and innovation is to recognize and celebrate it. Intrinsic motivation is a powerful catalyst of creativity.	You should. The intrinsic drive to excel is a very powerful motivator. If people know that their efforts will be noticed and recognized, they are more creative, more productive, and more committed to their work (Amabile & Kramer, 2011). Plus, it costs nothing. ❑ Put in place a system that specifically seeks out especially creative or effective performance support and be sure to recognize its creators. ❑ Consider creating an award for the best performance support solution in any given year.

Design, Test, Improve, Deploy, and Improve Again

Once you have identified where performance support can add the most value, you need to create it. The key decisions are the nature of the support and the delivery vehicle(s).

Support can take many forms, from printed checklists to expert systems, smart-phone applications, or access to human experts. Tool D5.2 provides examples of the variety of different kinds of support possible. It may make sense to provide the support in more than one form, and to provide second-tier, advanced support for unusually difficult issues.

The key attributes of great performance support are that it is

- Readily available
- Specific
- Practical
- Concise
- Clear
- Effective
- Economical

See H2 D5.3: "How to Develop Great Performance Support" for details.

To ensure that your solution fulfills these criteria, you need to test it with typical users under conditions of actual (or closely simulated) work, gather feedback, and improve the support before deploying it. Even after deployment, continue to monitor use and solicit suggestions for further improvement. In *The Checklist Manifesto* (2009), Atul Gawande describes the rigorous process by which the airlines develop, test, and continually improve checklists and performance support for pilots. He also describes the dramatic impact that a simple checklist had on the care of surgical patients, affirming that checklists and other job aids are not just for novices; they also benefit even the most highly trained and experienced professionals in the world. It is recommended reading.

In Case D5.4, Hemalakshmi Raju, assistant general manager, Learning and Development, and Sumita Menon, divisional manager, Learning and Development, for Tata Motors, explain how they contributed to impressive gains in manufacturing quality by identifying the need for performance support in a quality initiative, designing and deploying it, and measuring the results.

Ensure That Job Aids Are Used

Job aids and other forms of post-training performance support—like training itself—are only of value if they are actually used. To ensure that job aids are put to use:

- Use them during the training itself.
- Ensure that managers reinforce their use.

Introduce Job Aids in (or Even Before) the Training

Don't hand out job aids or other forms of performance support after the training is over and then expect people to use them. If you want to accelerate speed to proficiency, introduce the support aids during the training itself. Have participants practice using them in the exercises so they become familiar and comfortable with their use. They will then be much more likely to use them on the job.

Terrence Donahue, corporate director of training for Emerson, goes further. He believes that for many kinds of training, you should create the job aid *first*, then design the training to ensure that people know when and how to use it effectively. One of our clients distributes a computer-based job aid prior to class and lets students explore it on their own before using it during the in-class exercises.

Have Managers Reinforce the Use of the Job Aids

As we have noted before, managers have a profound influence on whether or not learning is transferred and applied on the job. That includes the use of job aids and other forms of performance support. Ideally, managers should *require* their direct reports to use the job aids and tools from the training. At the very least, they should encourage their use.

Be sure managers know of the existence of the job aids, their purpose, and their use. Provide them copies and offer a briefing or mini-training program about the tool. Try to have performance appraisal or feedback forms modified so that they mirror the steps and techniques covered by the performance support tool. Ideally, the use of appropriate job aids should be a checklist item on performance evaluations.

Use Quick Check D5.3 to assess your current practices and identify opportunities to improve the use of job aids.

QUICK CHECK D5.3:
ENSURING USE

1. Do you wait until the end of class to distribute job aids?

Yes	No	No Job Aids
You are missing an opportunity to increase their use and the likelihood of learning transfer. ❏ Distribute job aids during instruction and design the exercises to include their use in class. ❏ Better yet, create the job aid first and then design the training to teach people how to use it.	Assuming "no" means that you pass them out during instruction, great. It is important for employees to get used to using job aids as part of the training to make it clear that using them on the job is not only OK, but expected.	If you are not providing job aids or other forms of post-training performance support, then you are missing an opportunity to enhance training's effectiveness. ❏ Ask prior trainees where they had trouble applying what they learned and design job aids that will help.

2. Do you provide managers of employees with copies of the job aids and instructions for their use?

Yes	No
Well done. This practice helps to engage the manager and reinforce the message that job aids are meant to be used on the job. ❑ Practice continuous improvement by soliciting managers' ideas to make the job aids more effective.	Another opportunity. It is important that the manager reinforce the use of the job aid in day-to-day work. ❑ Send the managers of participants copies of the job aid with a very concise explanation of its intended use. ❑ Ideally, build the use of the job aid into checklists or rating forms that managers use to assess performance on the job.

SUMMING UP

In this section we emphasized the following about D5: Deploy Performance Support:

- Post-training performance support should be part of every instructional design.
- Effective performance support facilitates learning transfer and application by helping participants affirmatively answer both the "Can I?" and "Will I?" questions.
- Performance support reduces the load on working memory as employees try new approaches and improves the probability of "early wins" that motivate continued effort.
- Support can be supplied in many ways; the best choice depends on the kind of task and work environment.
- Effective aids are specific, clear, concise, and practical.
- Managers should be informed about the kinds of support being provided and the benefits of encouraging their use.

Tool D5.3 is a checklist of the most important elements of the practice of D5.

D6 Document Results

Businesses expect a return on their investment in training and development as a result of improved performance, greater productivity, enhanced employee retention, and so forth. The sixth discipline—Document Results—is essential to justify ongoing investment and to continuously improve subsequent offerings. It also provides clear and unambiguous evidence of how your participants answered the "Can I?" and "Will I?" questions.

Not all results are created equal, however. There is a tendency in training and development to measure activity and participant satisfaction and report them as if they were business outcomes; they are not. The key decisions in the practice of D6 are *what* to measure, *when* to measure, and *how* to measure.

Given the enormous range of businesses, industries, goals, and job functions that training supports, it is obvious that no one approach to evaluation will work for all. It is, however, possible to define four universally applicable principles to guide the evaluation of any program (Wick, Pollock, & Jefferson, 2010, p. 267).

An effective evaluation is

- Relevant to the business purpose for which the training was created
- Credible to the stakeholders
- Compelling to decision-makers
- Efficient in its use of resources

Creating program evaluations that satisfy these criteria begins in D1 (see "Start with the End in Mind" below). Although results can only be evaluated some time after the training has taken place, evaluation plans should be developed and approved by the program sponsors *in advance* of the training, not afterward.

The successful practice of D6 involves:

- Starting with the end in mind
- Distinguishing between activity and productivity
- Deciding *what* to measure before worrying about *how*
- Selecting the most relevant measures
- Ensuring that the results are credible to the intended audience
- Presenting a compelling argument for a course of action

- Using resources efficiently
- Improving, as well as proving, training's value
- Building a strong learning brand

Start with the End in Mind

Steven Covey's famous adage, "Start with the end in mind" applies to the evaluation of training in two ways. The first is to start with the business results in mind that you expect from the training. As Peggy Parskey, strategic measurement consultant with KnowlegeAdvisors, explains in Case D6.1, the more clearly the business goals of the program can be described at the outset, the easier it is to design an effective evaluation, and the higher the probability of success.

In other words, the effectiveness of D6 depends on the quality of execution of D1 (Figure D6.1). It is impossible to meaningfully evaluate a program without a clear understanding of the business outcomes it was intended to achieve.

It is worth making the distinction here between measurement and evaluation. To measure is to quantify: for example, to say that a piece of rope is 10 meters long, or that profits this year were $112 million.

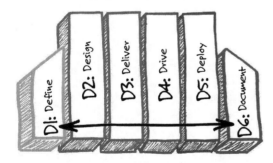

Figure D6.1. Clear Definition of the Business Objectives (D1) Is Prerequisite to Meaningful Evaluation (D6); They Are Bookends

To *evaluate* is to assign value or worth, which to a great extent depends on the need or expectation. The measure of a 10-meter-long rope is constant; its value is quite different depending on whether you have to rappel 8 meters or 15. Likewise, $112 million in profit is the same amount of money, but it is valued very differently depending on whether the company projected profits of $100 million or $125 million. Training programs can only be meaningfully evaluated relative to their purpose and expected results; getting D1 right is critical.

The second application of Covey's principle to evaluation is having the end (purpose) of the *evaluation itself* in mind before commencing. That means knowing the answers to questions like:

- For whom is the evaluation intended?
- What are we trying to prove or learn?
- How will the results be used? (What decision are we trying to inform?)
- How will the findings be communicated?

Use Quick Check D6.1 to help you assess your current practice in this regard and identify actions to take to improve this aspect of D6.

QUICK CHECK D6.1: BEGINNING WITH THE END IN MIND

1. Do you have a clear definition of the business outcomes the training was designed to produce and an agreed-on definition of success?

Yes	No
Congratulations, you have the information you need to start designing a relevant, credible, and compelling evaluation. ❏ Turn your attention to how to collect the needed data reliably and efficiently. ❏ Seek expert help if you are not specifically trained in evaluation.	This is a serious problem that needs to be addressed before you can design an effective evaluation. ❏ Revisit the planning documents. If the business rationale and outcomes are not clearly stated there, meet with the sponsor to understand his or her definition of success.

2. Are you clear about the intended audience and their preferences regarding data and presentations?

Yes	No
Very good; you will need this information in deciding how to communicate the results most effectively.	Audience analysis is as important in planning how to report training results as it is in planning training itself. ❑ Ask for advice from those who communicate frequently with the target audience or simply ask the business sponsors directly what kind of information they want to see and how they want it presented. Forewarned is forearmed.

Don't Confuse Activity with Productivity

Einstein famously remarked that "not everything that can be counted, counts." That principle applies as much to documenting the results of training programs as it does to science. Many aspects of training can be quantified: the number of classes, how many people were trained, how many e-learning programs were developed or completed, costs per training hour, reactions ratings, and so forth. Such operational metrics are important for the management of the training department, but although they can be counted, they don't count in terms of documenting results. They are measures of means (inputs and activities), not measures of ends (outputs and results) (Figure D6.2).

So when we say "Document Results" in D6, we mean to document "*outcomes* that are *of interest to the business* and *to which training contributed* in a demonstrable way" (Wick, Pollock, & Jefferson, 2010, p. 263). But what results are "of interest to the business"? Business leaders are most interested in the measures for which they themselves are held responsible—key performance indicators like sales and

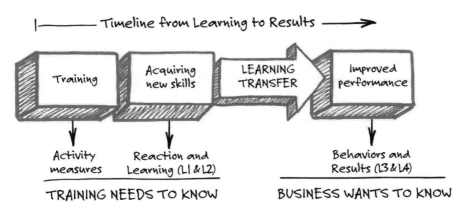

Figure D6.2. Measures of Training Activity Are Not What the Business Really Wants to Know

profits, as well as measures that are strongly correlated with financial performance, such as customer satisfaction, product or service quality, employee engagement, and so forth. Business leaders are also interested in documented changes in relevant behaviors and on-the-job actions that are "leading indicators" of future business-relevant outcomes.

Case D6.2 is a good example. In it, Joyce Donohoe, Paul Beech, and Karen Bell-Wright of the Emirates Group, together with Jim and Wendy Kirkpatrick, explain how they used the Kirkpatrick Foundational Principles to design a customer service training initiative and then measured improvements in both the behavioral and customer satisfaction objectives. As is often the case, the evaluation uncovered an issue unrelated to training that nevertheless adversely affected performance. Had the evaluation not been done, or had it focused only on the learning objectives, rather than performance, neither this issue nor the insight management needed to address it would have been discovered.

Use Quick Check D6.2 to assess the extent to which you are reporting activity rather than results and to identify opportunities for improvement.

QUICK CHECK D6.2:
MEANS VERSUS ENDS

1. Do you routinely report number of courses, trainees, e-learning modules completed, and so forth to management?

Yes	No
That's OK, as long as you also have evidence of on-the-job impact such as behavioral changes (Kirkpatrick Level 3) or results (Level 4) to put them in perspective. If you are only reporting activity or reaction scores, then you risk being perceived as only a net consumer of resources.	You probably do need to report this kind of information to management occasionally, for example, as part of the budget planning cycle. But be sure these are not the *only* metrics you report, as they are just measures of activity, not productivity.
❑ Select a high-priority or high-profile program, measure on-the-job results, and report them.	❑ Always start with an example of the on-the-job impact of one or more programs before reporting activity measures.

2. If a business manager said to you: "I see the training department has been very busy. But what I want to know is, 'How has all this activity helped us achieve our business objectives?'" would you be able to give a good answer?

Yes	No
Congratulations, you are focusing on the right things and measuring what the business wants to know, which is "What value are we getting for all this effort and expense?"	If you cannot, off the top of your head, rattle off several good examples of business impact, you have work to do. Being unable to convincingly articulate training's value puts the function at risk. ❏ Interview the key business managers and find out what they consider acceptable evidence of contribution. Then go find the data. ❏ If the department has evidence of results, but you aren't sure about it, make it a point to learn and be able to explain two or three strong examples.

Decide What to Measure Before Worrying About How

The most common error we encounter in efforts to evaluate training is "putting the cart before the horse," that is, worrying about *how* to measure the results without first clarifying *what* results have to be measured. By analogy, imagine the absurdity of choosing whether to use a measuring tape, balance, or graduated flask without first knowing whether you were going to be asked to measure length, mass, or volume.

Whether one eponymous evaluation approach is better than another depends entirely on the situation: what the training was supposed to produce and what the customer considers relevant, credible, and compelling evidence (see below). Remember that it is the customers (typically the business leaders) who define what constitutes an acceptable evaluation, not the training department or self-professed gurus.

The most important decision in designing an evaluation is choosing *what* to measure. If you measure the wrong thing, it does not matter how elegantly or efficiently you do so, it still amounts to garbage-in, garbage-out.

So what should you measure? Whatever will provide the most relevant and believable evidence that the training contributed to the desired outcomes and, at the same time, will provide insights to make the initiative even more effective in the future (see below).

Measure the Relevant Outcomes

An effective evaluation answers the question: "Did the training (and related performance support) produce the desired outcomes for the business?" To answer that question convincingly, the measures must be directly related to the desired outcomes; they must have what is known as face or construct validity. That is, just on the face of what you see, would you say that the proposed parameter is really a legitimate gauge of what it purports to measure?

So, for example, measuring how much people *liked* a training program is not a valid measure of whether they learned what they needed to know, or more importantly, are performing better as a result. If the goal was to improve performance in a specific area, for example, presentation skills, then you have to first define what you mean by improved performance and then (and only then) figure out how to measure it. You wouldn't choose your surgeon based on how highly she rated her medical school experience; you would want to know how many of this particular operation she has done and how those turned out. Table D6.1 provides examples of relevant measures for various training objectives. See also H2 D6.1: "How to Ensure Your Measures Are Relevant" for additional recommendations.

Table D6.1. Examples of Relevant Measures for Business Objectives for Training

Business Objectives for Training	Relevant Measures Include
Improved leadership effectiveness	Repeat 360 assessments focused on areas covered in training Surveys or interviews of direct reports before and after the training or post-training assessments that ask them to compare the leader's effectiveness now versus previously
Reduced time to productivity for new hires	Average time to consistently achieve a specified level of performance (proficiency)

Table D6.1. *Continued*

Business Objectives for Training	Relevant Measures Include
Greater customer satisfaction	Customer surveys or interviews Mystery shoppers (evaluators who pose as customers and use a checklist or rubric to rate service)
Less machine downtime on production line	Average changeover time before/after training Average time to troubleshoot and repair problems before/after training Total uptime before/after training
Better coaching of sales representatives	Surveys or interviews of representatives before and after training—or post-training surveys asking them to compare effectiveness now to previously Observations of coaching interactions by field-based trainers (or other trained observers) using a rubric or checklist
More effective handling of pricing objections	Interviews or surveys of customers before and after training Observations of sales interactions by managers or field-based trainers using a rubric or checklist
Improved safety/fewer accidents	Number of accidents or "near misses" before and at a suitable time after training
Improved (more effective and efficient) presentations	Observation and rating of presentations using a rubric (such as the "Glance Test" described in Case D3.2)
More rapid software development	Average times pre- and post-training for comparable projects and levels of customer satisfaction

Ensure Credibility

The second criterion for an effective evaluation is that the results are credible—that is, believable—to the target audience. It doesn't matter how fantastic the results appear to you, if the business sponsors don't believe them—for whatever reason—then the evaluation will be a failure; it will not persuade them to accept training's contribution or your recommendations.

Many factors affect the credibility of your results. Among them:

- How much data you have (more is generally better)
- From whom it was collected and how
- The expertise of the person who did the evaluation
- Real or perceived bias

See also H2 D6.2: "How to Improve the Credibility of Evaluations."

The credibility of the findings is also affected by the timing of the evaluation. Asking people immediately after training to estimate the impact it will have and then treating that as if it were a result is not very credible. You have to wait long enough that the results of the training will be evident in the real work of the trainees. That might be just days after technical skills training or several months if the training is intended to change opinions, such as of leadership effectiveness or employee engagement.

Credibility is also affected by the extent to which you control for, or at least acknowledge, the impact of other factors. In a corporate setting, training is almost never the only variable. As a practical matter, for example, it is extremely difficult to isolate the impact of training on sales versus the impact of competitors' actions, marketing programs, a new product, advertising effectiveness, and the like in the interval between training and measuring results. That's why we prefer to focus on a change in observable behaviors, since behavioral change is more closely tied to the training and performance support and because behaviors are "leading indicators" of results to come. If the training and transfer climate fail to change behavior, then they can't claim credit for any subsequent change in results.

Credibility is also influenced by the magnitude of the results. If the results are "too good to be true"—as they sometimes are in ROI studies—then they are likely to be dismissed out of hand. Remember that the more unexpectedly positive your results, the greater the skepticism will be, and the heavier the burden of proof required. Finally, credibility suffers if the training department tries to take too much credit. Recall that positive managerial engagement is a critical element of any training success; be sure to acknowledge the contribution of trainees' managers.

Use Tool D6.1: "Checklist for Evaluation Credibility" to help ensure your evaluations will be believed and therefore be persuasive.

Make a Compelling Case

The only reason to evaluate is to inform action (Bersin, 2008). Given that, the third criterion for an effective evaluation is that it must be compelling—that is, persuade the target audience to accept the analysis and follow your recommendations with respect to questions like these:

- Should the training be continued as is or revised?
- Should future offerings be expanded, held constant, or cancelled?

For your evaluation to be compelling, it must first be relevant and believable. Beyond that, it must also:

- Start with a complete yet concise executive summary
- Include specific recommendations based on the data and analysis
- Include examples and stories to make it memorable
- Use clear language and business terms
- Eschew learning- and HR-jargon

See H2 D6.3: "How to Make Your Evaluations More Compelling" for additional details.

Use Resources Efficiently

The final criterion for an effective evaluation is that it is efficient. That is, it uses the minimum resources necessary to collect data commensurate with the importance of the initiative. The cardinal rule is to never invest more in an evaluation than the value of the information it generates (Phillips, Phillips, & Aaron, 2013, p. 16). The more mission-critical or expensive the program is, the more important the decisions are regarding it, and therefore, the more rigorous the evaluation must be.

Surveys are an inexpensive, quick, and commonly used method for collecting data. However, they are *efficient* only if the data collected are relevant and reliable. Gathering bad information quickly and cheaply is not efficient; it leads to erroneous and potentially costly decisions. See H2 D6.5: "How to Write Better Surveys" for an overview of the topic and the references cited for more detailed discussions.

Don't collect data you are not going to use to inform decisions. Most training organizations are awash in data that no one reviews, much less uses to make hard decisions about training. It is a waste of everyone's time and the company's money to gather data that is never used.

Use Quick Check D6.3 to help you assess your current application of the guiding principles for effective evaluations and to identify actions to improve this aspect of D6.

QUICK CHECK D6.3:
GUIDING PRINCIPLES

1. Do your proposed measures have *prima facie* validity? That is, would a reasonable person—without a lot of explanation from you—conclude that they are legitimate measures of the desired business outcomes?

Yes	No
Good. What you are measuring reflects what the training was designed to accomplish *for the business*. Mere reactions (Level 1) and even amount learned (Level 2) fail this test.	You have work to do. Unless there is a clear and obvious link between the measures and the claim, there is no point in collecting the data. ❑ Go back to basics and ask yourself: What evidence is required for a reasonable person to conclude that training achieved its goal?

2. Are the stakeholders likely to accept your results without raising a lot of objections about the accuracy?

Yes	No
Good. You have fulfilled the second requirement of credibility. ❑ Be sure you do not undermine your credibility by presenting results you cannot explain or by failing to share the credit with other departments or contributing factors.	You have a problem. Hopefully, you have discovered this *before* you conducted the evaluation. If your audience doesn't believe your numbers, they won't believe your conclusions. ❑ Go back to the drawing board, propose different measures or means of collecting them, and check whether the stakeholders will find them credible or not.

3. Do you have an unambiguous recommendation for action that is supported by the data and analysis?

Yes	No
Great. You have completed your responsibility as a staff member.	Having done the evaluation, you should summarize, suggesting the right course of action based on the results: to expand the program, revise it, keep it the same, or kill it altogether. ❏ If your report does not have clear recommendations, go back and add them. ❏ Be sure you justify them by reference to the analysis of the data.

Prove and Improve

Proving that the training did, or did not, deliver the business outcomes for which it was intended is necessary, but not sufficient. Evaluations should serve to both *prove* and to *improve*—that is, to also provide insights to support continuous improvement. The most effective learning organizations set targets for improvement, experiment, and assess the results as part of a never-ending Plan-Do-Check-Act cycle of improvement (Figure D4.3, page 80).

The only way to know whether changes you have made to a program are actually producing improvement is to measure the results and compare them to the target. In Case D6.3, Sylvain Newton, senior leader for Business and Regions, GE Crotonville, explains how he and his team set a bold target to improve an already highly rated program using the NPS (net promoter scores) from the managers of the participants.

Effective evaluations actively seek to understand the causes of learning and transfer *failures*, as well as their successes. The Success Case Method developed by Rob Brinkerhoff (Figure D6.3) is especially useful in this regard. It seeks out both success stories to illustrate training's

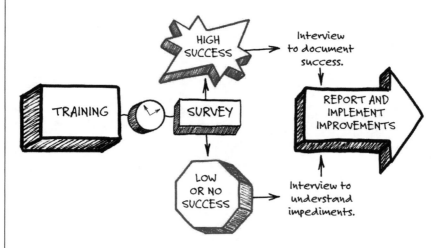

Figure D6.3. Brinkerhoff's Success Case Method

impact as well as impediments to progress that can be addressed in subsequent initiatives. See H2 D6.4: "How to Conduct a Success Case Evaluation."

Success stories can be a relevant, credible, and compelling way to communicate training's value. In Case D6.4, Steve Akram, director, and Patricia Gregory, senior director, North American Sales Force Development, Oracle, explain how they use success stories to make the value of sales training tangible to sales leadership and how this has increased management's interest and involvement in training.

Build a Strong Learning Brand

The reputation of your training department (your learning brand) affects management's willingness to invest in training and learners' willingness to engage. "Your learning organization has a brand, whether you choose to manage it or not" (Todd, 2009). Therefore, it is in your best interest to define and actively manage how you want training to be viewed in your company.

Key elements of building a strong brand include:

- Defining what you want to be known for (your brand promise)
- Gaining buy-in from everyone in the training department
- Making sure every customer experience reinforces the brand promise
- Marketing the brand: reinforcing the key brand elements at every opportunity

In Case D6.5, Maria Grigorova and Robert Moffett of Mars University, explain "How We Created a High Impact Mars University Brand." See also Dresner and Lehman (2009), "The Astounding Value of Learning Brand."

SUMMING UP

The sixth and critical discipline is to document the results, that is, to demonstrate that the investment in training and development did, in fact, help the company achieve the results for which the training was created in the first place. The most important aspects of D6 can be summarized as follows:

- Training organizations can improve both their effectiveness and the regard in which they are held by doing a better job of documenting on-the-job results, rather than just training activity.
- Effective evaluation begins with doing a thorough job in D1. It is impossible to adequately evaluate a program unless the goals are clear.
- Effective evaluations are built into the program design, not tacked on after the fact.
- The reported measures must be relevant to the expected outcomes; that is, they must have strong and obvious connection to the promised results.
- The measures, and the methods used to obtain them, must be perceived as trustworthy by the target audience.
- The evaluation should include a clear and compelling case for a recommended course of action.

Use the Evaluation Planner (Tool D6.2) to help you think through the design of the evaluation. Tool D6.3 is a checklist to help you ensure that all the key components of D6 have been considered.

Coda: Getting Your Money's Worth

Getting your money's worth from this book requires transferring and applying these ideas to your work—just as it does with training.

Get Started Now

"A journey of a thousand miles begins with a single step" (Lao-tzu, 6th century BCE). The most important thing to do is to start. This guide contains myriad things you *could* do. It would be easy to become overwhelmed and paralyzed by choice.

The antidote is to pick one thing and get started. You can start pretty much anywhere. Completing the 6Ds Personal Action Planner (Tool C.1) may help you focus. Regardless of which aspect of the 6Ds you select, start with something you feel confident you can accomplish; some early wins will help sustain you and encourage others to adopt the 6Ds as well.

In Case C.1, Tom Stango, learning consultant, and Jon Hurtado, senior learning consultant, at Coventry Workers' Comp Services, explain how they are implementing the 6Ds in their organization, one step at a time, and the impact it has had already.

Our bias is to begin by emphasizing business outcomes in your discussions with both business leaders and other training professionals. Many of our clients have found that this produces positive reactions almost immediately. However, if another of the ideas in this *Field Guide* appeals to you more, start there. Just get started.

Share your goal with others; you will be more likely to accomplish it if you do.

Build the 6Ds into the Process

The 6Ds are most effective when they are built into the processes by which your department defines, designs, delivers, supports, and evaluates training initiatives. For example, you might make a statement of business purpose a prerequisite before any design work can begin, or you could include all four phases of learning on a checklist for approving a training proposal.

Embed 6Ds concepts into your language and standard operating procedures so that new members joining your team pick up and adopt them as a matter of course. Use 6Ds concepts in your discussions, for example:

- What's your plan to drive learning transfer?
- Is this really the best way to deliver for application?
- Will this process ensure that participants say "Yes" to both the "Can I?" and "Will I?" questions?
- What is your plan for performance support?
- How will we document the results?

There is tremendous synergy to be gained when everyone in the department shares a common language and has the discipline to focus on business outcomes.

Continue to Learn and Grow

Clearly, there is a great deal more to say about creating business value through learning than we could include in even this fairly lengthy guide. Be a role model for lifelong learning. Read widely, starting with *The Six Disciplines of Breakthrough Learning* if you have not already done so. Attend high-quality workshops and meetings. Talk to other learning professionals within your organization and from outside it. Challenge your own assumptions and be skeptical of purveyors who promise quick fixes and overly simplistic solutions.

If you want to learn more about the 6Ds in particular, we and our certified partners around the world offer in-company training for learning teams. Public workshops are available through our publisher, Wiley, and also in cooperation with ASTD and other professional organizations.

Finally, consider joining the 6Ds group on LinkedIn and letting us know of your achievements and challenges. We want to continue to learn ourselves and to share best practices with others.

PART II

Tools: Maps, Planners, Scorecards, and Checklists

This section contains a variety of tools—maps, planners, scorecards, and checklists—that have proven useful in implementing the 6Ds. Printable copies are available on the 6Ds website: www.the6Ds.com.

Tool I.1

6Ds Application Scorecard

Use this tool to evaluate the readiness of a program to deliver results and identify strengths on which to build as well as opportunities for improvement. For each item, check the box that best describes the program using the following key:

  0 = Not at all
  1 = To a small extent
  2 = Somewhat
  3 = To a large extent
  4 = To a very great extent

Identify the lowest-scoring disciplines and then use the 6Ds Pathfinder (Tool I.2) to help you locate relevant topics, case studies ("How-We's"), tools and How-To guides.

		0	1	2	3	4
Define	1. The business needs are well understood. Anticipated on-the-job results of the training are clearly defined and measurable.	❏	❏	❏	❏	❏
	2. Course objectives are communicated to participants and managers in terms of expected business impact.	❏	❏	❏	❏	❏
Design	3. The pre-instruction preparation phase is an integral part of the design. Meetings with managers are facilitated. Pre-work is fully utilized during exercises and instruction.	❏	❏	❏	❏	❏
	4. The training is considered complete only when there is evidence of successful transfer and application on the job.	❏	❏	❏	❏	❏
Deliver	5. The cognitive load of the program is manageable; there is sufficient time for practice with feedback to ensure that participants develop basic proficiency.	❏	❏	❏	❏	❏
	6. Each topic and exercise has a clear "line of sight" to required behaviors and business results. Participants' perceptions of the program's utility and relevance are monitored and acted upon.	❏	❏	❏	❏	❏

		0	1	2	3	4
Drive	7. After the program, participants are periodically reminded of their learning in ways that encourage reflection, retention, and application.	❏	❏	❏	❏	❏
	8. Participants' managers are actively engaged during the post-training period. They monitor and actively support application on the job.	❏	❏	❏	❏	❏
Deploy	9. Post-training performance support is an integral part of the design. Participants are provided job aids, expert help, coaching, and other support as needed to facilitate transfer.	❏	❏	❏	❏	❏
	10. Participants continue to learn from each other after the program. Peer coaching and sharing of best practices are facilitated.	❏	❏	❏	❏	❏
Document	11. On-the-job actions and results are evaluated based on the business outcomes agreed to by the sponsor prior to the program.	❏	❏	❏	❏	❏
	12. Information to support continuous improvement of the preparation, program, and learning transfer is actively solicited, analyzed, and acted upon.	❏	❏	❏	❏	❏

Tool I.2

6Ds Pathfinder

Once you have identified the areas of greatest interest or opportunity, use the pathfinder below to identify relevant sections of the text, tools, how-tos, and how-we case examples.

Discipline	Topic	Text	Tools	How-Tos	Cases
Two Key Questions	Can I?	xxii 52–54 98	Tool D3.3 Tool D5.1 Tool D5.2 Tool D5.3	H2 D3.4 H2 D3.7 H2 D5.3	Case D2.6 Case D3.2 Case D3.3 Case D3.4 Case D4.8 Case D5.2 Case D5.4
	Will I?	xxii 52–54 79 98-99	Tool D2.1 Tool D2.5 Tool D3.2 Tool D4.1 Tool D4.2 Tool D4.3	H2 D2.1 H2 D2.2 H2 D2.4 H2 D3.5 H2 D3.6 H2 D5.3	Case D2.2 Case D2.3 Case D2.4 Case D2.8 Case D3.1 Case D3.3 Case D3.5 Case D3.6 Case D4.1 Case D4.4 Case D4.5 Case D4.8 Case D6.5

Discipline	Topic	Text	Tools	How-Tos	Cases
Introducing the 6Ds		xxi xxvi	Tool I.1 Tool I.2 Tool I.3 Tool C.1	H2 D4.3	Case I.1 Case I.3 Case I.4 Case I.5 Case I.6 Case C.1
D1: Define Business Outcomes	What is the business need?	3–5 8–10	Tool D1.1 Tool D1.3	H2 D1.1	Case I.1 Case D1.1 Case D1.2 Case D1.3 Case D1.4 Case D1.5 Case D6.1
	Is training required?	15–16	Tool D1.2	H2 D1.2	
	What behaviors are needed?	8–10 16–17	Tool D1.1	H2 D1.1	Case D1.2 Case D1.4 Case D1.5 Case D2.6 Case D6.1
	Criteria for success	20–21	Tool D1.1 Tool D6.2	H2 D1.1	Case D1.1 Case D1.2 Case D6.1 Case D6.2
D2: Design the Complete Experience	Phase I: Prepare	32–33 38	Tool D2.1 Tool D2.2 Tool D2.3 Tool D2.4	H2 D2.1 H2 D2.2 H2 D2.3 H2 D5.1	Case D2.2 Case D2.3 Case D4.2
	Phase II Instruction	56–62	Tool D3.1 Tool D3.2 Tool D3.3	H2 D3.1 H2 D3.2 H2 D3.3 H2 D3.4 H2 D3.5 H2 D3.6	Case D2.1 Case D2.8 Case I.4

Discipline	Topic	Text	Tools	How-Tos	Cases
D2: Design the Complete Experience, cont'd	Phase III: Transfer	38–42 77–86	Tool D2.5 Tool D2.6	H2 D2.4 H2 D4.1 H2 D4.2 H2 D4.3	Case D2.3 Case D2.4 Case D3.5 Case D4.1 Case D4.2 Case D4.3 Case D4.4 Case D4.5 Case D4.7 Case D4.8
	Phase IV: Achieve	43–47	Tool D4.3	H2 D2.4	Case D2.4 Case D2.5 Case D4.2 Case D4.6
D3: Deliver for Application	Maximize learning and retention	52–64	Tool D3.1 Tool D3.2 Tool D3.3	H2 D3.1 H2 D3.2 H2 D3.4 H2 D4.1	Case D2.6 Case D2.8 Case D3.1 Case D3.3 Case D4.4
	Ensure relevance and utility	65–74	Tool D1.1 Tool D3.2 Tool D3.3	H2 D2.1 H2 D2.2 H2 D2.4 H2 D3.5 H2 D3.6 H2 D3.7	Case D1.4 Case D2.6 Case D2.7 Case D3.3 Case D3.4 Case D3.5
D4: Drive Learning Transfer	Set goals	94–96		H2 D4.2	Case D4.7 Case D4.8
	Maintain share of mind	85–87		H2 D4.1	Case D4.3 Case D4.4 Case D4.7 Case D4.8

Discipline	Topic	Text	Tools	How-Tos	Cases
D4: Drive Learning Transfer, cont'd	Create positive transfer climate	84–85 88–96	Tool D2.1 Tool D2.2 Tool D2.5 Tool D4.1 Tool D4.2 Tool 4.3	H2 D4.3 H2 D5.1 H2 D5.3	Case I.4 Case D2.5 Case D3.5 Case D3.6 Case D4.1 Case D4.4 Case D4.5 Case D4.6 Case D4.8 Case D5.1
D5: Deploy Active Support	Create job aids	97–110	Tool D5.1 Tool D5.2	H2 D5.2	Case D5.4
	Engage managers and coaches	88–90 102–106	Tool D2.1 Tool D2.2 Tool D2.5 Tool D5.3	H2 D5.1 H2 D5.2 H2 D5.3	Case D4.6 Case D5.2 Case D6.3
D6: Document Results	Relevant	117–127	Tool D1.1 Tool D6.2	H2 D1.1 H2 D6.1 H2 D6.4	Case I.1 Case I.3 Case D6.1 Case D6.2
	Credible	128–129	Tool D6.1	H2 D6.2 H2 D6.5	Case D6.1 Case D6.3 Case D6.4
	Compelling	129–130 135	Tool D6.3	H2 D6.3	Case D6.4 Case D6.5
	Support Continuous Improvement	134–135	Tool D6.3	H2 D6.4	Case D6.3 Case C.1
Sustaining the 6Ds		137–139	Tool I.1 Tool I.4 Tool C.1		Case I.2 Case I.3 Case I.5 Case C.1

Tool 1.3

6Ds Flow Chart

This flow chart will help you to design and execute training that will yield results and to identify relevant resources in the *6Ds Field Guide.*

1. We clearly understand what the business is trying to accomplish as a result of the training.

   Yes. Go to 2

   ✗ **No** or not exactly. **STOP!** Go back and clarify the business needs.

   To be considered successful, training must help achieve business outcomes. Use the 6Ds Outcomes Planning Wheel (Tool D1.1) or a similarly structured process to develop an agreement between the business and the training providers.

2. We have explored non-training solutions and concluded that training is necessary to achieve the business objectives.

   Yes. Go to 3

   ✗ No. **STOP!** Go back and explore non-training solutions.

   Given the time and expense of training, you should always consider whether the issue truly requires training or whether it can be addressed more effectively or efficiently by some other intervention. See the flow chart for ensuring that training should be part of the solution (Tool D1.2).

3. We have a thorough understanding of the skills and behaviors employees must perform to achieve the desired results, as well as their current level of proficiency.

Yes. Go to 4.

  ✗ No. **STOP!** Go back and do a performance needs analysis.

You cannot design effective training and support unless you understand the on-the-job skills and behaviors needed to achieve the desired business outcomes. Use the Planning Wheel (Tool D1.1) to obtain business leaders' perspective. Then complete a task or performance analysis to gather additional detail and insight.

4. We have a robust set of learning objectives to inform the instructional design.

Yes. Proceed to 5.

  ✗ No. **STOP!** Go back and define the learning objectives.

"If you don't know where you are going, you won't know when you get there." Well-crafted instructional objectives are essential to inform the training design and appropriate assessment of learning outcomes.

5. We have discussed the business sponsor's criteria for success and have explored the kind of data the sponsor would consider relevant, credible, and compelling.

Yes. Proceed to 6.

  ✗ No. **STOP!** Go back and discuss sponsor's definition of success.

Evaluation should be built into the process from the very beginning, not tacked on at the end. It is essential to establish how the sponsor defines success and what kinds of evidence he or she considers relevant and believable.

6. We have included meaningful preparation, preferably experiential, which will be used as an integral part of the training.

▪ **Yes**. Proceed to 7.

✗ No. **STOP!** Go back and plan Phase I learning.

Meaningful preparatory work (Phase I learning/pre-work) should be part of the design to maximize the value and efficiency of the time available for guided instruction. See H2 D2.3: "How to Start Learning Before Class to Improve Efficiency."

7. The course description and invitation emphasize the business purpose and clearly explain the WIIFM (What's in it for me?) to the participants and their managers.

▪ **Yes**. Proceed to 8.

✗ No. **STOP!** Go back and rewrite the descriptions.

Coming-in attitudes have a significant impact on how much people learn in training and how much they eventually transfer. Rewrite course descriptions and invitations to emphasize the benefits of the training, not just its features. See H2 D2.1: "How to Communicate to Motivate."

8. The plan includes steps to ensure a pre-training discussion between the attendee and his/her manager.

▪ **Yes**. Proceed to 9.

✗ No. **STOP!** Go back and plan to facilitate pre-training discussions.

Even a brief, pre-training discussion between the attendee and his or her manager helps create "learning intentionality" and improves the results of training. See Tool D2.5 for a pre-training discussion guide you can adapt and provide to managers and H2 D2.2: "How to Create Results Intentionality."

9. The instructional design is robust; at least 50 percent of the total instructional time is devoted to participants' active engagement with the material (practice with feedback).

Yes. Proceed to 10.

✗ No. **STOP!** Go back and adjust plan to devote more time for practice.

Learning occurs most effectively when participants actively practice working with the material and receive feedback on their efforts. Excessive content leads to cognitive overload and reduced mastery. Eliminate content, if necessary, to free up time for practice.

10. We have structured the instruction and exercises to underscore their relevance and utility for the participants.

Yes. Proceed to 11.

✗ No. **STOP!** Go back and revise to emphasize relevance and utility.

Adults want to know why they should learn something before they will do so willingly. Construct a value chain (See H2 D3.5: "How to Build a Value Chain for Learning" and Tool D3.2) to illustrate the links between the training, on-the-job application, and business results. Introduce exercises with the rationale (see H2 D3.6: "How to Introduce Exercises").

11. If we plan to collect immediate post-instruction (Level 1) reaction data, then the evaluation form includes questions regarding the participants' perception of the training's relevance and utility and there is a plan in place to monitor and act on the results.

Yes. Proceed to 12.

✗ No. **STOP!** Go back and plan to track and monitor perceived utility.

Add questions regarding reliance and utility to the end of instruction assessments and monitor them regularly (see "Monitor Perceived Relevance and Utility" in D3, page 71). It's important, because if participants leave the training without being convinced that it will help them in their work, they will not even attempt to apply it.

12. If we plan to assess whether the learning objectives have been met or give a certification test at the completion of training, then we have made sure that there is congruity between the learning objectives and the manner of assessment and that we are assessing their ability to *perform*, not merely recall facts.

Yes. Proceed to 13.

✗   No. **STOP!** Revise assessments to reflect on-the-job requirements.

The all-too-common multiple-guess tests of factual recall do not predict performance. They lead to the common complaint: "How come they can pass the test, but can't do the job?" Assessments should match the job conditions and performance requirements as closely as possible.

13. There is a plan in place to remind learners periodically after the program about what they learned and the need to apply it.

Yes. Proceed to 14.

✗   No. **STOP!** Go back and develop a plan to remind participants.

Reminders are important in today's fast-paced world to be sure that learning stays top of mind and is used. Reminders can take many forms. What is important is that some form of reminders is built into the program design. See H2 D4.1: "How to Remind Learners to Apply Their Training."

14. We have defined and clearly communicated a "finish line" for the training other than end of instruction.

Yes. Proceed to 15.

  ✘ No. **STOP!** Go back and redefine the finish line.

    Awarding credit or certificates of completion as soon as instruction ends sends the wrong message. It implies that the learner's work is done, when, in fact, the real work is applying what they learned on the job. Defining a new finish line for completion—even if it is just a self-assessment—harnesses people's intrinsic drive and fosters learning transfer (see H2 D2.4: "How to Move the Finish Line for Learning").

15. We have a plan in place to engage managers and support their efforts.

Yes. Proceed to 16.

  ✘ No. **STOP!** Go back and develop a plan to engage managers.

    Managers are one of the most significant elements of the transfer climate. Their support is critical to ensure that training is applied on the job (see pages 88 and 89). You can help managers fulfill their role by providing short, specific, practical guides for getting their money's worth from training and development (see Tool D2.5 for a manager's guide to post-training discussions that you can adapt and distribute).

16. We have developed specific job aids or other forms of performance support to assist learners in utilizing their training once they return to work and we have incorporated them into the training itself.

Yes. Proceed to 17.

  ✘ No. **STOP!** Go back and plan performance support as part of the complete learning experience.

Job aids and performance support help learners answer the "Can I?" question. They are especially valuable the first few times that someone is trying to utilize a new skill or approach. They should be created as an integral part of the program and used during instruction. See H2 D5.3: "How to Develop Great Performance Support."

17. We have a plan to ensure that coaching will be available to participants from peers, experts, managers, or others.
   Yes. Proceed to 18.
   ✗ No. **STOP!** Go back and develop a coaching plan.

   The availability of coaches is an important transfer support element. It should be considered and built into most programs—especially soft skills programs—as an integral part of the design. There are many different ways to ensure the availability of coaching (see Cases D4.5 and D5.2 for examples).

18. We have a plan in place to evaluate on-the-job results commensurate with the cost and strategic importance of the training. The evaluation approach and criteria have been discussed with and agreed to by the business sponsors.
   Yes. Proceed to 19.
   ✗ No. **STOP!** Go back and develop an evaluation plan.

   Training and development organizations must document the results of their programs in order to prove that value was created and to improve future offerings. See D6 "Document Results" and H2 D6.1, H2 D6.2, and H2 D6.3)

19. The evaluation plan specifically seeks out information that will help us improve the effectiveness of subsequent programs.
   Yes. Proceed to 20.
   ✗ No. **STOP!**

Today's competitive climate demands continuous improvement of every business function, including training and development. An evaluation that only measures impact, without identifying opportunities through the entire process, is incomplete. See "Prove and Improve," page 134 and Tool D6.1: "Checklist for Evaluation Credibility."

20. We have a plan in place to effectively communicate the results of the evaluation, good, bad, or indifferent.

    Yes. Proceed to design and implement the training.

    ✗ No. **STOP!** Go back and develop a communications plan.

    The only reason to conduct an evaluation is to inform subsequent action. An important part of planning an evaluation is considering how and to whom you will communicate the results. See Tool D6.2: "Evaluation Planner" and Case D6.5: "How We Created a High Impact Mars University Brand."

Tool I.4

Wisdom from the Field

We asked each case study contributor to provide a few key pieces of advice for learning professionals based on their "lessons learned" from the field. This table summarizes the collective wisdom and provides an index to cases, organized by theme. For the details behind a recommendation, refer to the specific case.

Regarding	Advice	Case
Becoming a trusted advisor	Avoid making assumptions on issues. Solicit feedback at ground level and mid-levels of performers, influencers, and under-performing staff to corroborate management views.	D2.8
	Develop interpersonal relationships and a good reputation through working history. Become a trusted resource for your company that leaders reach to when they first begin to experience a performance problem.	D3.3
	Develop a long-term strategy that aligns with your organizational goals and culture.	I.1
	Learn, expand, and evolve. The more widespread the use of the logic modeling process, the more impact it will have on "changing the conversation" with the business.	D6.1
	Recognize that shifting the focus to business outcomes for an L & D function can be a cultural change for the function and the business leaders in the organization.	I.5

Regarding	Advice	Case
Becoming a trusted advisor, cont'd	When building a program to support accelerated talent development, alignment to strategic business need is critical.	**D2.3**
	Understand the context and your client's strategic needs.	**D5.1**
	Ensure that your team has business savvy as well as technical and instructional design skills; expertise in both business and instruction are needed to deliver business impact from training.	**D6.4**
	Establishing a partnership with stakeholders is paramount. Without the support of the stakeholders, it is not possible to ensure that behavioral changes will occur as a result of training.	**C.1**
	Following a structured approach enhances the credibility of the learning function.	**D1.3**
	Always start any discussion of training needs with a discussion of the business's strategic and tactical objectives and the skills that will be required to achieve them.	**D1.1**
Implementing the 6Ds	Have some fun with the task—such as our photo contest—learning should be enjoyable!	**I.6**
	Stick with it; the change won't happen overnight. It has taken us several years to move from order-taker to strategic business partner.	**D1.1**
	Use the *Six Disciplines for Breakthrough Learning* as an effective roadmap to achieve learning transfer and improvement results for your company.	**D4.2**
	Creating a strong learning brand requires creativity initially, then discipline to stay the course.	**D6.5**
	Never underestimate how others will use 6Ds tools once they have been presented. 6Ds tools and concepts can serve business purposes outside of just training.	**D1.5**
	Be patient with these and other changes. Changing leaders' attitudes about new finish lines for learning won't happen overnight. Explain the "why" and the benefits of feedback.	**D2.4**
	Have a methodology that you follow to secure results.	**D4.8**
	Identify where you can embed this process into your end-to-end solution design process. Pilot it in specific areas, for example, leadership development or sales skill programs.	**D6.1**

Regarding	Advice	Case
	Identify early adopters who can execute this process and have the skills and confidence to engage the sponsors in business-oriented discussions.	D6.1
	Keep in mind that making changes to a business takes time! Develop a long-term strategy that aligns with your organizational goals and culture. Then continue to chip away at it.	I.1
	Visit every step of the 6Ds, stay on track, close the loop.	I.2
	Teach your teams the 6Ds and use them as a framework for evaluating both individual courses and whole curricula.	I.5
	Train the whole team on the 6Ds; there is synergy in a common understanding and vocabulary.	I.6
	Don't try to tackle the whole 6Ds book at once; work your way through the chapters, with time for discussion after each section.	I.6
	We found it helpful to also attend a 6Ds workshop as a group to gain additional insights and have time practicing application to our specific programs.	I.6
Defining business outcomes	Be prepared if your stakeholders are reluctant to answer the Outcomes Planning Wheel questions, especially if they are not accustomed to them. You may need to help them understand *why* you're asking the questions.	C.1
	Use of the Planning Wheel can be the first step toward ensuring business impact; it ensures partnering of learning with business and their involvement.	D1.3
	Thoroughly defining business outcomes (D1) is the foundation for success. DO NOT NEGLECT THIS STEP IN ANY WAY!	D1.4
	Utilize the 6Ds D1. Define concepts to validate or re-validate what the expected business needs are. This should be applied for both new and ongoing projects.	D1.5
	Clear business and workshop outcomes ensure that instructors, managers, and participants all understand what the course is designed to achieve. Alignment is critical.	D3.2
	Always start the design of a developmental experience with the end in mind and ensure the appropriate linkages are present.	D3.6

Regarding	Advice	Case
Defining business outcomes, cont'd	In practicing the first discipline (D1), discuss or agree on the transfer terms before the project starts. People are too busy with other pressing priorities after the training.	**D4.7**
	Establish the success criteria from the start.	**D5.1**
	Practice the process with one key program, even if it's after the fact.	**D6.1**
	Prior to any mission-critical training initiative, meet with and draft a "memorandum of understanding" among all parties, spelling out critical roles and steps along the way.	**D6.2**
	Always start with the end in mind—the goals of the business. Remember that training is only a means to an end; it is not an end in itself.	**I.2**
	Baseline current performance versus future goals to determine relevant gaps.	**D2.8**
	Clarify how the sponsor defines success—which is almost always application on the job that achieves some business purpose—and then gather evidence that this is happening.	**D1.1**
	Use the overarching direction as defined by the principal sponsor as the pole star for all decisions.	**D1.2**
Involving leaders	Involve leaders as teachers to capitalize on their tacit knowledge, experience, and expertise.	**D1.3**
	Share the 6Ds Outcomes Planning Wheel with your business clients and encourage them to use the tool in their internal decision process for evaluating training needs prior to contacting training.	**D1.5**
	Engage the senior executive team in reviewing and tracking the emerging leadership participants before, during, and after the program.	**D2.3**
	Sponsorship is key; be sure you secure it before embarking on the branding journey.	**D6.5**
	While the support of the direct manager is essential, a broader support structure, or "board of directors," helps ensure visibility and sponsorship for future opportunities and continued coaching and development.	**D2.3**
	Involve a team of stakeholders to provide critical information and to build ownership.	**D2.6**

Regarding	Advice	Case
	Teaching executives the basic concepts of your workshop can turn them into a legion of auditor/advocates.	D3.2
	Establish leadership alignment (through all levels) to establish priority and focus for the learning and improvement activity.	D4.2
	Involving business leaders in the entire learning journey will ensure their ownership and support.	D5.4
	Have the leaders who sponsor these programs help drive them.	D6.4
	Always engage business partners in the discussion regarding business objectives and expected benefits to the business of any training proposal.	I.5
	Pursue the *real* sponsor of the program to invest in clearly articulating what the real business challenges are and how the program will impact desired business outcomes.	D1.2
Creating results intentionality	Clearly communicate how the program will benefit the learner, the department, and the business.	D3.4
	Add video testimonials to your orientation sessions.	D2.2
	Share videos of achievement and results, such as project presentations.	D2.2
	We ensured that each participant had a pre-training meeting with a leader. The result was that participants showed up to the first learning event motivated to learn and viewed this training initiative as a priority.	D3.3
	Provide your participants with a clear destination of improved performance.	D4.1
Learning as process	Learning cannot be looked at as a one-time event. It has to be built as a journey with specific milestones. This also gives a better structure and focus to the process.	D1.3
	The preparatory phase ensures better preparation and the post-program phase is essential to ensure transfer of learning.	D1.3
	In the same way that 6Ds provides clarity and a common language for driving high-impact learning, it is important to use an organizational framework (such as PrimeFocus™) to drive performance improvement.	D1.4

Regarding	Advice	Case
Learning as process, cont'd	Design your training program as a continuous learning process rather than a single learning event.	**D2.5**
	Stretch your participants' learning experience by building in pre-, actual training, and post-event activities as part of your program design.	**D2.5**
	Ensure that there is a plan for all the essential learning activities (such as observing more experienced workers); leave nothing to chance.	**D2.6**
	Provide a platform for application of learning at the workplace beyond the training class.	**D2.8**
	Design the entire learning experience up-front based on desired business outcomes.	**D3.4**
	Learning must move from the classroom to the workplace; training can't stop at the classroom door.	**D3.5**
	Treat training as a process rather than an event.	**D5.2**
	Plan the complete experience; isolated training events rarely produce meaningful performance improvement.	**I.2**
	Make sure to stay close to the process and wording, as per the 6Ds book.	**I.3**
	Using the Define stage effectively leads to driving an intervention as opposed to just putting on a program.	**D1.2**
Designing instruction	Much can be learned from the design and content structure of the 6Ds Workshop manual with its supporting documents. It provides an example of conveying information in a manner that invites repeated use and reference.	**D1.5**
	Ensure that the learning organization is structured in a way that best supports an Agile approach. Functional silos can make an Agile implementation difficult or impossible.	**D2.1**
	Be aware of the demands that agile development creates. From a workload perspective, agile program development is a buzz saw.	**D3.3**
	The learning team must know that they are empowered to make decisions and that they ultimately have ownership for the results.	**D2.1**

Regarding	Advice	Case
	Moving part of the content before or after the class is very effective. Nothing is more true than the concept that "less is more" while teaching.	I.4
	The second key to success was that we were agile in the development of the program. We continuously asked for feedback from both the leaders and program participants and implemented thoughtful changes to the materials and activities as we went.	D3.3
	Where possible and appropriate, incorporate various learning approaches to enhance your participants' learning experience and to accommodate the different learning styles of your participants.	D2.5
	When training an intact team where tensions run high, it is crucial to employ a variety of methods that increase engagement and influence the participants' motivation to learn.	D3.3
	Move away from topic-by-topic design and focus on finding an organizing principle that integrates how the job is really done and incorporate accelerated learning principles.	D2.6
	Select an appropriate instructional strategy first, followed by method of delivery.	D2.7
	Use a variety of instructional methods to facilitate on-the-job application.	D2.7
	Use Bloom's Taxonomy to identify the instructional goal and method. An ideal method should maximize application.	D2.7
	Set learning goals that support specific business goals (not just overall big picture).	D2.8
	Develop specific learning solutions that are relevant to roles and staff proficiencies.	D2.8
	Ensure that objectives of each learning module are clear and associated training actions connect with good fit.	D2.8
	When designing the experience, ask more and tell less, both for the clients as well as for the participants.	D3.1
	Leverage off the power of reflection that adult learners possess and work on building strong debriefs.	D3.1

Regarding	Advice	Case
Designing instruction, cont'd	When creating an experience, identifying and compressing the key elements helps to heighten the experience (for example, doing X task in Y timeline).	**D3.1**
	The foundation of all design should be to encourage the participants and to engage them in a way that preserves/highlights their value as individuals.	**D3.1**
	Don't rely solely on packaged content from a vendor. Pull in resources and examples from a variety of sources to enhance the content and ensure that participants will be able to connect with the concepts.	**D3.3**
	Begin with the end in mind—identify the business and improvement outcomes desired by team leaders, and design the program to achieve these outcomes.	**D4.2**
Accelerating on-boarding	Start with a proficiency definition and then build the training to move to proficiency as fast as possible.	**D2.6**
	Eliminate the "nice to know" and even the "need to know"; teach people to do what they need to do.	**D2.6**
	Use neuroscience while designing programs. Instructional methods should give the learners intellectual stimulation as well as opportunities to use as many as possible of their five senses.	**D2.7**
Focusing on performance	Optimize for impact as perceived by the customer (managers of participants), rather than just the consumers (the participants themselves).	**D6.3**
	We need to provide participants with "connection adapters" to help them make connections between learning and practice.	**D4.1**
	"Learning can make a business impact" is an important experience for creating development-savvy leaders.	**D1.2**
	Knowing and doing are two very different things. The most valuable learning happens when you focus on doing.	**D2.6**
	Instructional methods, media, and exercises should be designed with the "end in mind," as defined in the first two segments of the Planning Wheel.	**D2.7**
	Avoid generic learning topics and focus on key outcomes that support business goals.	**D2.8**
	To change attitudes and behaviors, you have to engage the heart as well as the head, which means people need visceral, not just cerebral experiences.	**D3.1**

Regarding	Advice	Case
	Don't allow the "day to day" to get in the way of delivering the entire experience.	D3.4
	The best leaders are both task-oriented and relationship-oriented; developing quality leaders means cultivating both of these areas.	D3.5
	Make sure that the learning you will deliver is well connected with the workplace situations your participants face.	D4.1
	Design the classroom learning to be as practice- and application-oriented as possible to assist the participants to gain experience putting their learning to work.	D4.2
	Remember it is the participants who will make the change. Having them engaged, committed, and held accountable is even more important than engaging the manager.	D4.8
	Offer a learning and performance package approach to any major business need, as opposed to just a training initiative.	D6.2
	Remember, it is not just about the content. The best content in the world is worthless unless it is transferred and used on the job.	I.2
Moving the finish line	Stop sending people the wrong message ("you're done") by awarding credits and certificates at the end of class.	D2.4
	Ensure that the purpose emphasizes application (will use) as opposed to just learning (can use).	D3.6
	Define learning transfer as a goal of the program and communicate the rationale and approach to leaders and participants.	D4.2
	Rethink the finish line for your key strategic programs.	D2.4
	Make submitting a proficiency story the criterion for completing the training.	D5.2
	If you want training to stick, commit to do it right or stay away from it. We should not compromise on where the finish line should be.	D4.7
	If intersession assignments are part of the program, make completing them a requirement for continuing the course.	D5.3
	Move the finish line; be sure that you include post-training follow-up as part of designing the complete experience.	I.2
	Be patient with these and other changes. Changing leaders' attitudes about new finish lines for learning won't happen overnight.	D2.4

Regarding	Advice	Case
Engaging managers	Engage participants' managers and support them in encouraging new skills back on the job.	**D2.4**
	Create a parallel leadership development track in the program that trains and supports leaders.	**D4.2**
	Be proactive in harnessing management involvement and influence on transfer.	**D4.5**
	Provide training so that managers understand their crucial role and have the know-how to leverage results from learning.	**D4.5**
	Keep it practical and straightforward. If influencing transfer looks too hard or time-consuming, managers will just give it lip service.	**D4.5**
	Give the manager notice at the beginning of the program that you will seek an acknowledgment of the participant's progress and provide samples of previous acknowledgments.	**D4.6**
	Secure permission to pursue the transfer plan ahead of time with the various stakeholders and participants.	**D4.7**
	Provide simple "how-to" documents enabling managers to engage easily and effectively in the learning process.	**D6.3**
	It is rare to find a supervisor willing to act as a coach. This needs to be factored in so that a specific action can be deployed at least to mitigate those effects.	**I.4**
Ensuring learning transfer	Define learning transfer as a goal of the program and communicate the rationale and approach to achieve learning transfer to leaders and participants.	**D4.2**
	Prepare new participants to take action and expect to achieve results.	**D2.2**
	Leverage available social learning technology to foster knowledge sharing and collaborative learning.	**D2.5**
	Help supervisors become better leaders by honing leadership skills while engaging in core activities.	**D3.5**
	Ensure you are incorporating learning transfer. Hope is not a method.	**D3.6**
	Don't launch a training program without completing an Immediate Application Checklist.	**D4.1**

Regarding	Advice	Case
	Check that your participants have the opportunity to immediately apply what they learn to their work.	**D4.1**
	Design the classroom learning to be as practice- and application-oriented as possible.	**D4.2**
	Define action learning projects or assignments that extend participant learning into a period of learning transfer.	**D4.2**
	Do something after training to cause recall of the information. It doesn't have to be perfect; you just need to help participants to recall what they learned and how they were going to use it.	**D4.3**
	Have the reminders come from the sponsor rather than from the trainer. Strong sponsorship from the leader is critical to success.	**D4.3**
	Planning for pull-through is critical. The ideal time to roll out a reinforcement solution is after your initial knowledge transfer programs are completed.	**D4.4**
	Users, particularly on-the-go sales representatives, enjoy the learning experience more when given simple tools with game elements.	**D4.4**
	If you are creating a reinforcement program for the first time, start by asking yourself what information you want rolling off the tongues of your sales team.	**D4.4**
	Encourage clients to keep the learning alive; provide a list of suggested steps, and they end up doing more.	**D4.7**
	The transfer plan is like the exercising sequence you get when you enroll in a gym. It makes the routine a lot easier to follow and stick to.	**D4.7**
	Bite the bullet with learning transfer. Do a small pilot, learn from it, and keep trying.	**D4.8**
	Utilize the telephone as a powerful secret weapon.	**D4.8**
	Use different sources of influence (social motivation, social ability, and personal ability) to create a positive transfer climate.	**D5.3**
	Support transfer by reinforcement and measurement.	**D5.3**
	The real challenge is the existing behaviors of the trainee, and especially of the supervisor. To have the trainee apply the learning, we need to work hard to create a safe environment where he or she can actually apply it.	**I.4**

Regarding	Advice	Case
Providing performance support	Deploy performance support (D5) by ensuring that there are suitable ongoing flexible learning opportunities for managers to further leverage their personal strengths in support of identified business objectives.	**D1.4**
	Ensure there is sufficient one-on-one coaching (D5) for managers to fully deliver on their commitments when faced with ongoing challenges of "business as usual."	**D1.4**
	Establish one-on-one engagement opportunities, for example, coaching, mentoring, buddy system, etc.	**D2.8**
	Be sure to prepare both the coaches and the managers of participants for their roles.	**D5.2**
	Post-program performance support is the key to success for any training intervention.	**D5.4**
	Use peer proficiency coaching to extend learning back into the workplace and ensure the practice necessary to achieve proficiency rather than merely familiarity or capability.	**D5.2**
	Provide support to strengthen learning to assure participants manifest the desired new competencies and produce business value.	**D5.3**
	Matching the mentors and mentees is a crucial success factor.	**D5.1**
Providing a sense of achievement	Recognition at the end of the learning journey adds to the sense of completion and also acts as a trigger to move forward.	**D1.3**
	Give recognition for even small, incremental change and suggestions for overcoming their challenges.	**D3.4**
	Ask the managers of participants to submit acknowledgments in which they highlight observable performance improvements.	**D4.6**
	Give the manager plenty of advance time to prepare the acknowledgment and set a deadline well in advance of the "graduation."	**D4.6**
	Have the manager's acknowledgment of achievement by the trainee read at graduation by another participant in the program.	**D4.6**

Regarding	Advice	Case
Documenting results	Be rigorous about the measurement of business results and personal successes (D6). This provides the business case to embed this type of intervention as an ongoing strategic alignment process.	**D1.4**
	If you don't have the training or experience to do valid measurements, involve others in your organization who are trained in measurement and statistics. You can usually find them in the quality department.	**D2.6**
	Check transference of learning by regular assessment (empirically as well as anecdotally).	**D2.8**
	Check back against impact to business bottom line on a quarterly basis.	**D2.8**
	Define and include measure(s) of learning transfer and share the results with participants and stakeholders.	**D4.2**
	Measuring business outcomes rather than learning outcomes is essential for buy-in from the senior leadership.	**D5.4**
	Reviews need to be built into the process.	**D5.4**
	Practice the logic modeling process with one key program, even if it's after the fact.	**D6.1**
	Monitor critical behaviors and other important metrics during the execution stage. Make adjustments along the way based on the data.	**D6.2**
	Don't stop with end-of-class evaluations; gather data after employees have had the opportunity to apply the training in the course of their work.	**D6.4**
	While you can use logic modeling for any program, it is most useful for strategic, costly, or highly visible programs.	**D6.1**
Communicating value	Align the corporate communications plan for the business to celebrate the gains made by managers as a means to leverage cultural development (D6).	**D1.4**
	Capture stories of success and achievement from past program participants.	**D2.2**
	Measure results and share them with leaders.	**D2.2**
	Having a successful, credible pilot group that is willing to advocate for the program is like strapping a rocket booster to your initiative.	**D3.2**
	Celebrate your successes in a meaningful and visible way, crediting learners, business partners, and anyone else who contributed to the success of the experience.	**D3.4**

Regarding	Advice	Case
Communicating value, cont'd	Report back to the team the results that they have achieved.	D4.2
	Use the results to demonstrate training's effectiveness and provide insights into the capabilities, trends, and knowledge gaps of your teams.	D4.4
	Share the results with the key stakeholders to demonstrate the value you have delivered.	D4.8
	Communicate successes achieved by using a new approach. Build support for logic modeling across L & D.	D6.1
	Success stories can provide credible and compelling evidence that the program is helping achieve business outcomes.	D6.4
Improving continuously	Learning is a process rather than a one-time event. Once you map out a learning process, you can apply process improvement tools to reduce time, waste, and variability.	D2.6
	Benchmark with other companies for best practices. Before designing this program, we benchmarked with another company who shared tips and tools that they use for spaced learning programs.	D3.3
	Measure your results and adjust the approach when multiple measures indicate a failure to achieve your stated aims.	D3.6
	Experiment! Even small changes to your approach can dramatically improve engagement and retention.	D4.4
	Define a stretch goal with a measurable target. Make it so challenging that it forces you to think "out of the box."	D6.3
	Bring in ideas from the outside; don't feel you have to invent everything yourselves. Ask a lot of questions; read widely. Adopt good ideas from other companies and industries—including your competitors!	D6.3
	Don't expect everything to work the first time. Indeed, if you aren't having some failures, you aren't stretching enough.	D6.3
	There is no end point to the improvement of our teaching process.	I.4
	Consider engaging an independent 6Ds consultant for strategic projects; they can add external perspective and best practices from other firms to the discussion.	I.5

Tool D1.1

6Ds Outcomes Planning Wheel™

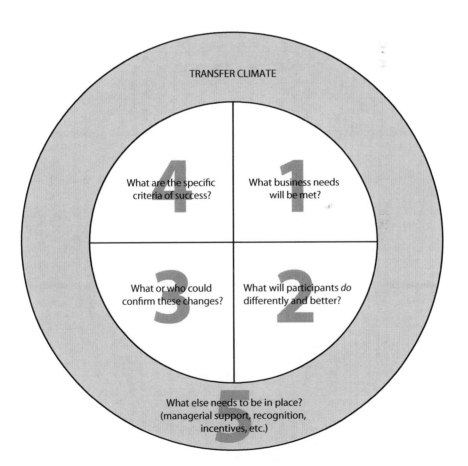

TRANSFER CLIMATE

4 What are the specific criteria of success?

1 What business needs will be met?

3 What or who could confirm these changes?

2 What will participants *do* differently and better?

5 What else needs to be in place? (managerial support, recognition, incentives, etc.)

Tool D1.2

Flow Chart: Is Training Necessary?

Some business leaders look to training to solve all manner of performance problems. As flattering as that may be, it is a mistake for a training and development group to agree to provide training when the root cause of the suboptimal performance is something other than a lack of knowledge or skill. Conducting training under such circumstances is guaranteed to produce learning scrap and to undermine the credibility and support for the function as a whole.

Use the flow chart on the next two pages to determine whether training should be a component of the solution—it is never the whole solution—and, if not, what the real issues are and how to address them.

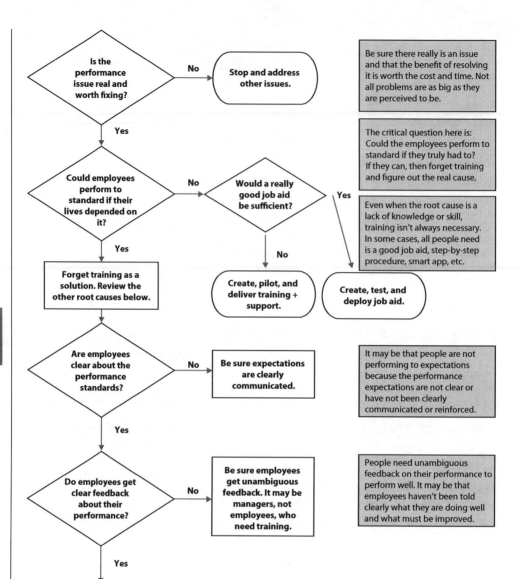

Is the performance issue real and worth fixing?

No → Stop and address other issues.

Be sure there really is an issue and that the benefit of resolving it is worth the cost and time. Not all problems are as big as they are perceived to be.

↓ **Yes**

Could employees perform to standard if their lives depended on it?

No → Would a really good job aid be sufficient?

The critical question here is: Could the employees perform to standard if they truly had to? If they can, then forget training and figure out the real cause.

Yes → Create, test, and deploy job aid.

Even when the root cause is a lack of knowledge or skill, training isn't always necessary. In some cases, all people need is a good job aid, step-by-step procedure, smart app, etc.

↓ **No**

Create, pilot, and deliver training + support.

↓ **Yes**

Forget training as a solution. Review the other root causes below.

↓

Are employees clear about the performance standards?

No → Be sure expectations are clearly communicated.

It may be that people are not performing to expectations because the performance expectations are not clear or have not been clearly communicated or reinforced.

↓ **Yes**

Do employees get clear feedback about their performance?

No → Be sure employees get unambiguous feedback. It may be managers, not employees, who need training.

People need unambiguous feedback on their performance to perform well. It may be that employees haven't been told clearly what they are doing well and what must be improved.

↓ **Yes**

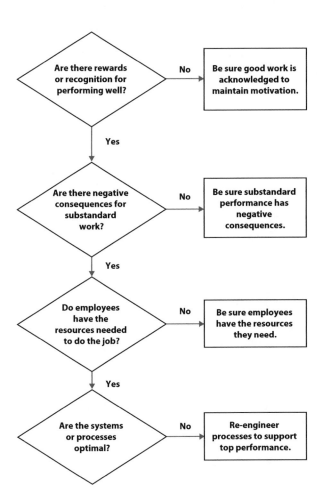

Are there rewards or recognition for performing well?

No → **Be sure good work is acknowledged to maintain motivation.**

There need to be incentives for performing well. These need not be monetary; simple recognition of a job well done is motivating for most people.

Yes ↓

Are there negative consequences for substandard work?

No → **Be sure substandard performance has negative consequences.**

If poor quality or incomplete work is tolerated, it will soon become the norm. If employees are not held accountable for using training, they probably won't.

Yes ↓

Do employees have the resources needed to do the job?

No → **Be sure employees have the resources they need.**

It may be that people lack a critical resource (time, tools, or information) to perform to standards.

Yes ↓

Are the systems or processes optimal?

No → **Re-engineer processes to support top performance.**

The real problem may be the process or system. As Geary Rummler famously remarked, "Pit a good employee against a bad system, and the system will win every time."

Tool D1.3

Checklist for D1

❏ The proposed training addresses a performance issue related to lack of knowledge or skill.

❏ A gap analysis has identified the specific knowledge and skills that must be mastered to improve performance.

❏ Non-training solutions have been explored or tried and rejected.

❏ The training is clearly linked to high-priority, high-value business needs.

❏ Objectives for the training state the actual performance that will be achieved (as opposed to knowledge, ability, or capability) and use business terms and concepts.

❏ Objectives clearly indicate how success could be measured and specify the performance standard to be met (how much, by when).

❏ The business benefits (objectives) are made explicit in course descriptions and other communications.

❏ The sponsor's criteria for success (how much change in which parameters by when) have been discussed, agreed to, and shared with the relevant training and business managers.

❏ Environmental factors that will affect successful intervention (such as incentives, consequences, coaching, etc.) have been discussed.

❏ Management accepts its responsibility for the transfer climate.

Tool D2.1

Manager's Guide to a Pre-Training Discussion

Having a pre-training discussion is one of the single-most important things you can do as a manager to be sure that both you and your direct report get your money's worth from training.

Meet with your direct report—ideally in person, but at least by phone—before the training session. It needn't be a long meeting—even ten to fifteen minutes will be beneficial. Talking to your direct report before the training creates learning intentionality. It helps him or her focus and makes it clear that you place value on the investment. A pre-training discussion also sets expectations for application and results, establishes a timeline for follow-through, and spells out the definition for success.

Agenda

1. Prior to the meeting, think about the areas in which your direct report could improve his or her performance. Even if someone is a top performer already, there is always opportunity for improvement.
2. Look at the topics covered by the training and decide which will be most valuable for your report.

3. In the meeting, ask your report what he or she thinks are the greatest opportunities for improvement and the most important course topics.
4. Compare to your answers; discuss points of agreement and differences.
5. Agree on the most important learning opportunities.
6. Commemorate the agreement in a learning contract or brief memorandum.

More specific guidance is given below.

Detailed Coaching Guide

1. "What do you see as your three best opportunities to further improve your performance?" [Write them down as your direct report describes them.]
    - Why those three in particular? [Listen to rationale.]
    - Share the three you came up with.
        - If you are in agreement: "We picked very much the same things. Let's see how you can use this course to further your career."
        - If you are not in agreement, then use this as a coaching opportunity to talk about the differences in your points of view. The choices include:
        "I did not put this one on my list because I feel that it is already a strength for you."
        "I agree that this one you listed would also be good to improve, but I think this other one is more important because. . . ."
        "You know, I agree that this item on your list is more important than this one on mine, so let's focus on that."
2. "Let's talk about how to get the most of out the upcoming training. What do you see as the most important or valuable aspects of this learning opportunity for you personally?"

- Listen your direct report's answers.
- Compare them with yours.
- Start by pointing out the areas in which there is substantial agreement.
- If your direct report's answers are quite different from yours, coach by asking, "Help me understand why you chose. . . ." Then listen actively to the answer.
- Be willing to accept a different answer than your own if it is justifiable or perhaps better than yours.

3. Given the above, agree on one to three (no more) of the most important things for your direct report to take away from the course.

4. Ask your direct report to complete a learning contract (such as the one shown in Tool D2.2) or to send you a brief email summarizing the discussion.

5. Schedule a short meeting or call with your direct report as soon as possible after the training to hear a report on the program and his or her goals and plans for implementation.

Adapted from Jefferson, A., Pollock, R., & Wick, C. (2009). *Getting your money's worth from training and development*. San Francisco: Pfeiffer. Used with permission.

Tool D2.2

Sample Learning Contract

Participant's Responsibilities

In order to maximize the business results of attending the upcoming Parts Department Management Program, I agree to (check all that apply and complete the phrases below):

- ❏ Identify opportunities in advance of attending to use the new learning to create business results
- ❏ Complete all required pre-work assignments
- ❏ Attend and be actively engaged in all sessions
- ❏ Develop goals for applying what I learned to my work
- ❏ Execute a follow-through plan that improves my performance
- ❏ Report the results
- ❏ Share highlights and insights with my co-workers
- ❏ Specifically, I will focus on inventory management during the program in order to improve my ability to maximize profitability and efficiency of repair process afterward.

Signed: Arthur Doyle
Date: August 8, 2014

Manager's Agreement

As the manager of the employee above, I agree to:

❏ Understand the relationship between the training and on-the-job business results.

❏ Attend and participate in any advance briefing sessions for supervisors;

❏ Meet with my direct report before the program to discuss the business outcomes that should occur as a result of attending

❏ Release my direct report from sufficient work assignments that he/she has time to complete the preparation for the training and attend all the sessions;

❏ Minimize interruptions during the training.

❏ Meet again after the program to discuss the highlights of the session and explore opportunities for application.

    ❏ Our post course follow-up meeting is scheduled for: <u>Friday, September 19th</u>

❏ Provide encouragement, support, and reinforcement for efforts to apply the training.

❏ Provide specific opportunities for my direct report to practice the new behaviors and skills on the job.

❏ Provide suggestions for continued development.

Signed: <u>Melinda Rogers</u>
Date: <u>August 12, 2014</u>

Adapted from Jefferson, A., Pollock, R., & Wick, C. (2009). *Getting your money's worth from training and development.* San Francisco: Pfeiffer. Used with permission.

Tool D2.3

Flow Chart for Phase I Learning (Pre-Work)

1. Does everyone have a common understanding of the basic terms and concepts that will be used in class?
   - ❑ Yes. Go to 2.
   - ❑ If not, then assign reading, e-learning, prerequisite courses, required experience, or other assignments to get people up to speed (see Tool D2.4: "Purposes and Examples of Phase I Learning").

2. Do at least some of the learners overestimate their knowledge and understanding of the subject ("know it alls")?
   - ❑ If yes, consider providing a relevant self-test to help them gain a more realistic assessment and create a "need to know."
   - ❑ If no, go to 3.

3. Will learners be naturally interested in the topic and want to learn more?
   - ❑ If yes, you are truly blessed; go to number 4.
   - ❑ If no, then consider how you could stimulate interest or impress the learners with the relevance and utility of the training. Examples include:
     - Horror stories about what can go wrong
     - A provocative video or question

- Success stories from prior participants. See Case D2.2.
- Experiential learning on the shop floor or as a customer, line worker, customer support representative, and so forth

4. Will learners arrive with "learning intentionality"—that is, knowing what, specifically, they want to take away from the program?
   - ❏ If yes, that is wonderful. Carry on with the training.
   - ❏ If not, then consider actions to help generate intentionality, such as facilitating pre-training discussions between the manager and participant, requiring a learning contract, having them self-rate and prioritize opportunities for improvement, and so forth (see H2 D2.2: "How to Create Results Intentionality").

Tool D2.4

Purposes and Examples of Phase I Learning (Pre-Work)

Purpose	Examples
Establish foundation knowledge; be sure all learners are "on the same page"	Reading short, targeted selections
	Completing an introductory e-learning program
	Having prerequisites, such as successful completion of a foundation course or specific work experiences
	Passing a relevant test
Stimulate interest in the topic	Experiential learning, such as interviewing a customer, patient, or senior leader; visiting a plant or office; listening to customer calls; and so forth
	Reading a provocative article or watching a provocative YouTube or other video
	Writing a short description of their own best/worst experience with something of relevance to the program
	Video testimonials from prior participants about the value of what they learned
	Completing a simulation that illustrates the importance of the topic

Purpose	Examples
Create learning intentionality	A guided pre-training discussion between the manager and participant about what is most important
	Requiring a "learning contract" signed by both manager and participant
	Holding a pre-training teleconference that both managers and participants attend
	Giving a pre-training assessment to highlight knowledge gaps and make participants aware of how much they still have to learn
Provide input to be used in the training	Having each participant bring a real and current issue to work on during the instruction
	Collecting 360-degree (or other) feedback on current performance
	Having each participant find and bring relevant examples from their work
	Having each participant interview customers, co-workers, or other stakeholders
	Having participants bring pictures or videos that illustrate the issues or opportunities to be discussed

Tool D2.5

Manager's Guide to a Post-Training Discussion

A quick follow-up discussion as soon as possible after your direct report returns from training will help you underscore its importance and ensure that you get your money's worth for the time and resources invested.

Overview

1. Schedule a post-training follow-up discussion (in person or by phone) as soon as practical after the training program.
2. *Having* the conversation is more important than its length; even five to ten minutes will underscore your interest and improve learning transfer.
3. Spend most of your time listening and asking questions. Your direct report should do most of the talking.

Ask four key questions:

*   What was the most valuable thing you learned?
*   What are your plans to apply the training?
*   How will applying what you learned benefit the department and your career?
*   What support do you need?

The objectives of the conversation are to underscore your interest, encourage your direct report to reflect on the experience (thereby reinforcing it), and secure his or her commitment to practice new behaviors to achieve a valuable outcome.

Detailed Coaching Guide

1. Meet and greet. Thank the person for taking the time to meet with you. Express your interest in hearing about the program and how he or she plans to apply it.

2. Ask: "What was most valuable to you?"
   - Listen carefully to the answer.
   - Play back what you heard to be sure you understood: "So, for you, the most valuable part of attending was. . . ."
   - Ask for further clarification or amplification to help your direct report cement his or her understanding and practice critical thinking. "Tell me a little more about that . . ." or "Do you think that other people found different parts to be the most valuable, and, if so, why?"

3. Your direct report should have one to three (no more) strong goals for applying the program's content.
   - Review the goals (if you have not already).
   - Do they focus on the right things?
   - If you agree with the goals, move on to the benefit question.
   - If not, provide guidance: "I'd like to see you be clearer about the outcomes" or "I'd like you to focus more on . . . because that is where I see the greatest opportunity for you to improve your performance," etc.

4. Ask: "How will achieving these goals benefit the department and your career?"
   - Help your direct report focus on benefits to be sure he or she has internalized their value and to increase commitment to achieving them.
5. Ask: "What support/opportunities do you need?"
   - Show your support by giving your direct report the opportunity to ask for resources, time, or projects to help achieve his or her goals.
   - If these are reasonable, provide them.
   - If the request is more than it is possible for you to grant, then explain the limitations and, if necessary, revise the goal to be achievable with the resources and time at your disposal.

6. Finally, set a specific time for follow-up. "I'd like to see a progress report on [date]." It is important to do so to underscore that you are serious about application. As the saying goes, "people respect what you inspect."

Adapted from: Jefferson, A., Pollock, R., & Wick, C. (2009). *Getting your money's worth from training and development*. San Francisco: Pfeiffer. Used with permission.

Tool D2.6

Checklist for D2

- ❏ The invitation/course description is clear and compelling. It focuses on the benefits rather than just the features.
- ❏ There is meaningful Phase I learning (preparatory work)—reading, exercises, simulations, performance feedback, etc.—that will help maximize the time spent during instruction.
- ❏ A pre-program meeting with the participants' manager is strongly encouraged (ideally, required). Guidelines and worksheets for that meeting are provided.
- ❏ The instruction itself is designed to maximize application (see also Checklist for D3).
- ❏ Structure, support, and accountability for learning transfer are included in the program design (see also Checklist for D4).
- ❏ Post-instructional performance support is an integral part of the program design (see also Checklist for D5).
- ❏ The "finish line" for the program is defined as improved on-the-job performance weeks or months after the instruction.
- ❏ There is a plan in place to assess achievement and participants know what it is.
- ❏ There is a mechanism to ensure that participants receive recognition for their efforts and what they achieve as a result of applying the training.

Tool D3.1

Glance Test for Slides

Glance Test

	signal	NA	noise
Did it pass the glance test?	○		○
One Message (one point vs. many)	○	○	○
Audience Relevance (resonant content vs. inapplicable)	○	○	○
Visual Elements			
Background (supporting vs. distracting)	○	○	○
Text (scannable vs. document)	○	○	○
Color (system vs. random)	○	○	○
Photo (simple vs. involved)	○	○	○
Data (emphasis vs. non-emphasis)	○	○	○
Diagram (shapes clarify relationships vs. confuse them)	○	○	○
Arrangement			
Contrast (clear prioritization vs. indistinct)	○	○	○
Whitespace (open space vs. cluttered)	○	○	○
Hierarchy (identifiable parent|child vs. no relationship)	○	○	○
Unity (structured grid or look vs. unstructured)	○	○	○
Flow (clear path for eye vs. meander)	○	○	○
Proximity (intentional placement vs. random)	○	○	○
Animation (intentional meaning vs meaningless distraction)	○	○	○

◯ vs ◯

Tool D3.2

Value Chain Planner

The Value Chain Planner illustrates the links between the business outcomes and the behaviors required to achieve them, as well as the relationship between the learning activities and the requisite behaviors.

Use the drawing tools in Word, PowerPoint, or similar software to illustrate the hierarchical relationships in a chart like the one on the next page. Be sure that the learning activities include plans for all four phases of the learning process—from preparation to the recognition of achievement.

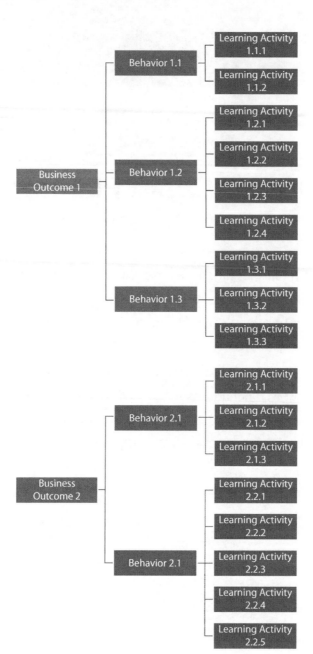

Tool D3.3

Checklist for D3

❑ An Impact Map, Value Chain, or similar process is used to make the linkage between training elements and the business goals clear.

❑ Program descriptions, materials, and instruction answer the "What's in it for me?" (WIIFM) question for participants and their managers.

❑ The links between the program content, current business needs, and job responsibilities are clearly stated and reiterated for each major exercise or topic.

❑ Relevant examples, stories, simulations, discussions, and so forth are included to help learners see how the material applies to their jobs.

❑ Success stories from prior graduates of the program are used to underscore its utility.

❑ Any Phase I learning (preparatory work) is utilized in the program—so much so that those who did not complete it are at a disadvantage (or, ideally, are not allowed to attend).

❑ The instructional design includes conscious efforts to gain and hold learners' attention.

❑ The agenda provides adequate time for learners to practice the desired skills or behaviors and receive feedback so that they can answer the "Can I?" question in the affirmative.

❑ The instructional strategy takes advantage of the power of spaced learning.

❏ The amount of content, visuals, and pace of instruction is designed to avoid cognitive overload.

❏ Job aids are introduced during the instruction and used in exercises.

❏ The materials, equipment, situations, and settings are as close to the actual work environment as possible.

❏ Participants' perceptions of the program's relevance and utility are solicited, tracked, analyzed, and acted upon.

❏ Assessments gauge the learners' ability to apply the skills and concepts, not just recall them.

Tool D4.1

Learning Transfer Climate Scorecard

Instructions:

1. Rate each of the climatic factors below using the scale at right.
2. Use the descriptors below each item to help you.
3. Investigate those you are unable to rate.
4. Target low-scoring areas as opportunities for improvement.

Climatic Factor	0. Very Weak	1. Weak	2. Fairly Strong	3. Very Strong	? Don't Know
Learner Readiness Learners understand what the training is about and how it relates to their development and job performance Learners have the necessary background knowledge and skills to benefit from the training					

Climatic Factor	0. Very Weak	1. Weak	2. Fairly Strong	3. Very Strong	? Don't Know
Opportunity to Use Employees have opportunities to apply their new knowledge and skills on the job soon after training Employees have the resources (information, equipment, materials, and supplies) necessary to use the training					
Personal Capacity Employees have the time and energy to try new methods; their workloads are not too overwhelming Employees are able to cope with the amount and pace of change in the organization					
Perceived Relevance and Utility Employees feel that the skills and knowledge taught are relevant and useful to their work The instructional methods, aids, materials, and equipment used in training are similar to those used on the job.					
Motivation Employees are motivated to use what they learned because they: Are convinced it will help them perform better Expect better performance to be rewarded in a way that they value					
Organizational Culture Performance expectations are clear Individuals are recognized for good performance People take pride in performing well					

Climatic Factor	0. Very Weak	1. Weak	2. Fairly Strong	3. Very Strong	? Don't Know
Managerial Alignment Managers speak positively about the techniques taught Managers model the same approaches, behaviors, and skills as those taught in training Managers set clear expectations for the application of training					
Managerial Encouragement Managers encourage the use of new skills Managers recognize individuals who make the effort to apply their learning					
Managerial Feedback and Coaching Employees receive constructive input and assistance from their managers when they try to apply what they learned Managers assist individuals when they encounter problems as they try to apply new learning					
Peer Group Impact The employees' co-workers support the use of new techniques; they don't try to force conformity to current practice Peers help each other identify opportunities and implement new methods					

Climatic Factor	0. Very Weak	1. Weak	2. Fairly Strong	3. Very Strong	? Don't Know
Personal Experience Employees experience positive benefits from using what they have learned, such as increased productivity, recognition, additional opportunities, or the like					
Employees experience negative consequences for *not using* what they learned such as criticism or reprimands					
There are *no negative consequences* when they try to apply their learning to their work					

From Pollock, Jefferson, and Wick (2013). *The 6Ds Workshop: Participant Workbook.* San Francisco, CA: John Wiley & Sons. Used with permission.

Tool D4.2

Transfer Climate Improvement Planner

Actions to Consider to Improve Transfer Climate

Learner Readiness	Rewrite the course descriptions and invitations to explain the benefits and expectations of the training. Establish criteria or prerequisites for attendance to make sure the right people are in the room.
Opportunity to Use	As part of the analysis, make sure that employees will have the necessary resources to perform as taught. Insofar as possible, provide "just-in-time" training, so that trainees have the opportunity to use it soon afterward. Secure managerial alignment, in advance, about the use of the methods being taught so that employees do not experience conflicting messages.
Personal Capacity	Pay attention to how much change is being expected of employees; a new training initiative launched in the midst of a major reorganization is unlikely to succeed.
Perceived Relevance and Utility	Monitor the perceived relevance and utility of courses and address low scores promptly. Make the relevance of the training as a whole, and the individual exercises, clear. Use equipment, materials, and circumstances that are as close to actual job performance as possible.

Motivation	Provide examples of how prior participants have benefited.
	Ensure that rewards and recognition are in alignment with what is being taught.
Organizational Culture	Evaluate the extent to which the current culture supports or impedes new behaviors.
	Share your insights with senior management; changing culture is a long-term and difficult project that they must lead.
Managerial Alignment	Ensure managerial buy-in by seeking their input into the selection and prioritization of training programs.
	Provide managers with job aids to help them set expectations in advance of training.
Managerial Encouragement	Provide managers with short, specific, and practical things they can do to support learning transfer—including scripts if appropriate.
	Provide training on coaching to managers if necessary.
Managerial Feedback and Coaching	Answer the WIIFM question for managers by showing them the evidence on how much additional value their coaching can create for their departments.
	Provide short, specific, and practical guides for coaching for maximum performance.
Peer Group Impact	Train intact teams so that the whole work group is exposed to the new methods simultaneously.
	Offer incentives for team as well as individual performance.
Personal Experience	Ensure that the performance appraisal and incentives systems are in line with what is taught in training rather than working against them.
	Gain agreement with managers beforehand on the importance of both positive consequences for using the training as well as negative consequences for allowing it to go to waste.

From Pollock, Jefferson, and Wick (2013). *The 6Ds Workshop: Participant Workbook.* San Francisco, CA: John Wiley & Sons. Used with permission.

Tool D4.3
Checklist for D4

❏ The quality of the transfer climate for the training initiative has been assessed.

❏ There is a plan in place to address any negative elements in the work environment to which trainees will return.

❏ Processes are in place to periodically remind participants of their obligation to apply their learning.

❏ There is a mechanism to hold participants accountable for using what they learned, and to recognize superior efforts and accomplishments.

❏ Participants and managers meet following the course.

❏ Managers are provided concise, specific, and practical coaching guidelines.

❏ Managers actively support the use of new skills and knowledge, help identify opportunities to apply new skills, set relevant goals, provide feedback, and help work through difficulties.

❏ Managers are informed of their direct reports' personal goals for application, if appropriate.

❏ Job aids and specific guidance are provided to coaches and managers to help them fulfill their roles in facilitating learning transfer.

❏ There is a process to assess the extent to which managers are supporting their direct reports' application of training and to report the results to senior management.

❏ Senior management underscores the importance of managerial support by recognizing and rewarding managers who do a superior job of developing their direct reports.

❏ Appropriate recognition is given to trainees who make great progress and/or complete their objectives.

Tool D5.1

Performance Support
Planner

Name of Program: _____

_____

What are people likely to have trouble remembering or performing back
on the job?

What kind of support will be most helpful?

☐ Checklist   ☐ "How-to" video or diagram
☐ Step-by-step procedure   ☐ Script
☐ Worksheet   ☐ Searchable database
☐ Flow chart / If-then diagram   ☐ Help Desk / Access to Experts
☐ Other: _____

Where will trainees be at the time?

Given the above, what delivery system(s) make the most sense?

☐ Paper-based job aid   ☐ Online help or database
☐ Smart phone app   ☐ Posted instructions
☐ Phone support   ☐ Other: _____

Taken together, describe the kind of performance support necessary to ensure that everyone is able to perform satisfactorily:

Tool D5.2

Kinds of Performance Support and Their Application

Performance support can take many forms; common examples and their uses are listed below.

Type	Especially Good For
Checklist	Making sure all the key items in a procedure are included or completed. Especially important when many actions are required involved or when omission could lead to serious adverse consequences.
Step-by-Step Procedure	Making sure that a procedure is followed in the correct sequence. Especially valuable for complicated or rarely performed procedures or when someone is learning a new procedure.
Worksheet	Completing procedures that require calculations at various steps. A tax form is a good (albeit unpopular) example.
Flow Chart/If-Then Diagram	Guiding decision making or troubleshooting for well-defined problems that can be broken down into a series of defined choices. Helps ensure logical, stepwise approach to problems. Online and app versions can be made "smart" so that the choices presented take into account prior answers.

Type	Especially Good For
Photo or Diagram	Showing where to locate a particular part or item. See Case D5.4, for example. Online and app versions can be made interactive, for example, allowing zoom, rotation, or turning labels off and on. Using pictures can be especially valuable when literacy or language is an issue.
"How-to" Video	Demonstrating exactly how to perform a specific procedure or sequence. Many examples on the Internet; www.ehow.com, for example.
Script	Ensuring consistency. For example, use a script to ensure that all customers receive the same marketing message or when conducting telephone surveys. Scripts can be especially helpful for new employees learning company procedures.
Searchable Database	Providing rapid access to a large body of information. Online databases of products, models, and parts are good examples.
Smart Phone App	Many of the above formats can be programmed as smart phone apps, which have the advantage of being available virtually any time and anywhere. Apps also have unique capabilities, such as "touch here for additional explanation or pronunciation," that cannot be duplicated on paper.
Peer or Expert Coach	Providing tips of the trade, qualitative assessment of performance, coaching guidance, or encouragement.
Help Desk/Access to Experts	Providing assistance with complex problems that simpler job aids failed to solve.

Tool D5.3

Checklist for D5

❏ Performance support is an integral part of the training design.

❏ The difficulties or memory lapses that trainees might encounter have been anticipated and addressed.

❏ Former participants have been polled to discover what additional support would have helped them.

❏ Job aids that participants have developed for themselves have been solicited and, if appropriate, incorporated.

❏ Learners are provided with job aids, online materials, apps, help desks, and so forth to help ensure they are successful when trying new skills and behaviors.

❏ Job aids and other forms of support are fully integrated into the training exercises.

❏ The design team has been encouraged to explore new technologies and creative approaches to providing performance support.

❏ Continued learning and peer-to-peer sharing is encouraged and facilitated.

❏ Learners are provided easy and efficient ways to engage their managers, subject-matter experts, instructors, or other advisors during the transfer and application process.

❏ Job aids and other forms of performance support are tested and continuously improved based on feedback.

❏ Managers are provided copies of job aids and provided guidance on how to maximize their value.

Tool D6.1

Checklist for Evaluation Credibility

❏ The evaluation plan has been reviewed by someone "skilled in the art" for validity and reliability prior to its implementation.

❏ The data include all participants in a small program or a large sample of participants (fifty or more) for large programs.

❏ If a sample has been used, is was randomly (as opposed to haphazardly) selected to avoid bias.

❏ More than one source of data has been used.

❏ Persons asked to provide input or collect the data have no vested interest in the outcome, or any potential bias is discussed in the analysis.

❏ Those who are asked to provide input have had meaningful opportunity to observe and have the expertise or guidance necessary to make an informed judgment.

❑ Standardized scoring forms or rubrics are used to increase inter-rater reliability.

❑ Any surveys that will be used to collect data have been reviewed for conformance to best practices and, ideally, pilot-tested to ensure clarity and reliability.

❑ The comparisons that support claims of "better," "improved," and so forth, are legitimate.

❑ The limitations of the study and conclusions are honestly assessed and communicated, including non-training factors that may have influenced the results.

❑ Assistance from the finance department has been secured if the sponsor has defined return on investment as a criterion for success.

❑ The contribution of managers to the success of the training has been acknowledged.

Tool D6.2
Evaluation Planner

Name of Program: _____

Concise statement of program's promise (expected performance improvement):

Leading indicators (observable behaviors that are prerequisites to producing the desired results):

Relevant outcomes that need to be measured to support the program's claim:

Mechanism(s) for collecting data (check all that apply):

❏   Direct observations by:
    ❏ manager   ❏ mystery shopper   ❏ trained evaluator
    ❏ other _____

- ❑ Surveys of:
  - ❑ trainees   ❑ managers   ❑ customers
  - ❑ other _____

- ❑ Interviews of:
  - ❑ trainees   ❑ managers   ❑ customers
  - ❑ other _____

- ❑ Evaluation of work product(s)
- ❑ Review of company records
- ❑ Focus groups
- ❑ Other: _____

Timing (How long between the training and the evaluation?)

Comparators (to what will you compare the "after training" results)

How will you minimize or control for the impact of non-training factors?

How will you identify opportunities for improvement?

Tool D6.3

Checklist for D6

❏ The ways in which the program will be evaluated have been discussed with and agreed to by the program's sponsor(s) in advance.

❏ The proposed evaluation meets the guiding principles of efficiently generating relevant, credible, and compelling results.

❏ The earliest (leading) indicators that the program is working have been identified.

❏ A plan is in place to use leading indicators as in-process checks to drive improvement during the rollout.

❏ The sources of the data that will be used in the evaluation have been identified and their availability has been confirmed.

❏ A plan is in place to gather needed data that are not already collected routinely.

❏ Consideration has been given to what the post-training results will be compared with to support claims of "better," "improved," and so forth.

❏ Assistance from the finance department has been secured if the sponsor has defined financial return on investment as a criterion for success.

❏ The evaluation plan actively seeks out information to identify opportunities for improvement of subsequent programs.

❏ The evaluation plan has been reviewed by someone "skilled in the art" for validity and reliability.

❏ How the data will be reported and presented has been considered.

❏ The key audiences for the results have been identified and there is a communications plan for each.

Tool C.1

6Ds Personal Action Planner

Directions

1. Reflect on what you consider the most important insights, reminders, or ideas you gained from reading *The 6Ds Field Guide*.
2. Write them down in the first space below.
3. Reflect on how you current practices compare to the six disciplines of the most effective training initiatives.
4. Write down which aspect of your current practice—if improved—would yield the greatest benefit to your organization.
5. Now write down what you want to accomplish in the next two to three months with respect to implementing the 6Ds. Don't try to change the world in two months. Pick an area in which you can make progress and reach a milestone. See Exhibit C.1.1 below for examples.
6. Figure out how you will know you are making progress and the benefit of accomplishing what you propose.
7. Anticipate what kinds of challenges you may face and what help will be needed to achieve your goal.
8. Share your goal with your manager and/or co-workers.
9. Now go achieve it.

My three most important "takeaways" from the 6Ds are

1.

2.

3.

The aspect of our current work that will provide the greatest benefit if improved is

My goal in the next three months is to:

Evidence of my progress will be

The benefit of accomplishing this will be

Challenges I am likely to face or help I am likely to need

EXHIBIT C.1.1. EXAMPLES OF GOALS FOR APPLYING THE 6DS

D1: Define Business Outcomes

In the next eight weeks, I will interview key stakeholders using the 6Ds Planning Wheel to make sure I understand the business drivers and required behaviors following the XYZ Program. I will summarize the results of those discussions and check for understanding so that I am certain I know what is expected from the program and that it is focused on the most important business needs. Evidence of my progress will include completed interviews, my Planning Wheel, and a written agreement with the sponsors.

D2: Design the Complete Experience

In the next eight weeks, I will revise and implement an improved process for inviting people to participate in the ABC Program so that they are more motivated to attend and so that the expectations are clear. Indicators of my progress will include these things:

- ❏ Defining a new process and having it approved
- ❏ Having the senior vice president sign the invitation
- ❏ Making sure the invitation states clear expectations for application on the job
- ❏ Including examples of success by prior participants
- ❏ Having former participants agree the new invitation is a much clearer and more motivating message than they had received

D3: Deliver for Application

In the next eight weeks, I will review and revise the end-of-course assessment to ensure that it tests participants' ability to *apply* the course material and not merely play it back.

Indicators of my progress will include:

- ❏ Scoring the cognitive level of all our current test questions according to Bloom's taxonomy
- ❏ Replacing or rewriting 75 percent of the questions that test only recall
- ❏ Having the new questions reviewed for cognitive level by a learning professional with expertise in test design

D4: Drive Learning Transfer

In the next eight weeks, I will pilot the use of an online learning transfer support system so that I can test its value in our programs to increase post-instruction transfer and application.

Indicators of my progress will include selection of the system and a completed plan for integrating learning transfer, including assessing its impact after the first pilot group.

D5: Deploy Performance Support

In the next eight weeks, I will create and implement a comprehensive plan to increase the engagement of participants' managers. It will include tips, forms, and timelines, as well as a letter of expectation from the relevant senior leader, so that managers of participants know that they are expected to coach their direct reports and are supported in doing so.

Indicators of my progress will include seeing a higher level of coaching reported by participants and feedback from managers about the coaching support's value.

D6: Document Results

In the next eight weeks, I will create an evaluation plan for the JKL Program that will produce relevant, credible, and compelling evidence of its business impact so that we can convincingly prove its value and also gather insight to improve it further.

Indicators of my progress will include developing the design and gaining buy-in from management that these are the right measures of success.

Source: Pollock, Jefferson, & Wick (2013). *The 6Ds workshop: Participant workbook.* San Francisco, CA: John Wiley & Sons, used with permission.

PART III

Case Histories ("How We")

This section contains forty-three cases, submitted by learning leaders around the world, that illustrate the application of 6Ds concepts and principles in action. They span a broad range of industries and training programs. Each is accompanied by the authors' advice to their fellow learning professionals.

Use the tables below to help you find specific case studies. Three indices are provided: by primary discipline (although most studies touch on more than one); by industry; and by type of training.

By Discipline

By Industry

By Type of Training

Case I.1

How We Transitioned Our Focus to Results

Sonal Khanna

Senior eLearning Instructional Designer, on behalf of the Front Office Operations Improvement Department, The Permanente Medical Group, Inc., Kaiser Permanente Northern California

Background

Kaiser Permanente is a health plan, hospital system, and medical group, all working together to serve over 8.8 million members in nine states and the District of Columbia. Our mission is to provide high-quality, affordable health care services and to improve the health of our members and the communities we serve.

The Front Office Operations Improvement (FOOI) Department is a group of professionals with a single focus: serving our clients. Primarily, we work in five key areas: consulting, communications, training, reporting, and evaluating. Our vision is to drive an exceptional patient experience by:

- Preparing and supporting front office staff to excel in their roles,
- Ensuring products and benefits integrity from concept to implementation, and
- Delivering accurate and actionable tools to achieve operational excellence and innovation

In 2011, we were introduced to the 6Ds framework and realized that it supports our vision to prepare and support front-office staff to excel in their roles. We started making changes within our department to move to a more business results and job performance orientation. In doing so, we reorganized job responsibilities, defined processes, developed templates, and made sure that we continued to work with our clients even after deployment to ensure job support and learning transfer.

What We Did

The actions we took are summarized below and in Figure I.1.1.

D1: Define Business Outcomes: We have templates in place so that projects start with either a full-scale analysis document or for smaller initiatives, a one page "memorandum of understanding" document in which the high-level business requirements are set out in detail, reviewed, and signed off by all stakeholders.

D2: Design the Complete Experience: Since we are defining measurable business outcomes and objectives upfront, our solutions are driven with the end in mind. While designing the solution we also

Figure I.1.1. Summary of Actions We Took to Transition to a Results Focus

consider strategies for risk management, implementation, learning transfer, and job support.

D3: Deliver for Application: We have made sure that a communications strategy is woven into the solution design/project so that implementation is not a surprise to stakeholders and our end-users. The stakeholders have buy-in and are partners in the implementation.

D4 and D5: Drive Learning Transfer and Performance Support: We now have learning consultants in place who drive our solutions through to the end. They are in the field, promoting our deliverables, supporting the end-users, and serving as our "ears on the ground" to ensure a flow of feedback back to our design team. They are also the single point of contact who can provide additional support when required.

D6: Document Results: This final piece is made possible by detailed performance data via reports, evaluations, 360-degree reviews, and lessons-learned forums. This is one of the areas that we are currently working to strengthen as we try to further refine and improve.

Results

By implementing the 6Ds framework, we see a more defined end-to-end process in place within the team. Having such a framework has helped us as a department have a better handle on resourcing needs and planning ahead for projects.

We also have seen an improvement in our relationships with our clients. With learning consultants in the field, we have a better understanding of our clients' needs and are thus better able to meet them. Our clients also tell us that having a single point of contact in the field helps them to reach out easily when they need help.

Finally, our reports provide data that keep a pulse on actual performance and help in identifying areas for future performance improvement initiatives.

Advice to Colleagues

- Keep in mind that making changes to a business takes time! It has taken us two years to make small changes at a time, and we continue to refine our implementation.
- Develop a long-term strategy that aligns with your organizational goals and culture.
- Then continue to chip away at it.
- Knowing that your strategy supports your vision helps you gain leadership support and dissolve any resistance.

Case I.2

How We Use the 6Ds to Differentiate Our Services

Cheryl Ong

Director and Principal Consultant, Global Trainers, Inc.

Background

Global Trainers is a world-class provider of customized solutions for people development and learning needs throughout the Asia-Pacific region. Headquartered in Singapore, Global Trainers has special expertise in the financial and insurance sectors.

We believe that people are an organization's greatest assets and, ultimately, drive its bottom-line results. Our aim is to maximize the strengths of all individuals and unleash their full potential. To that end, we place our customers' preferences, aspirations, and business needs first. We "begin with the end in mind," utilizing a structured, 6Ds approach to understand our clients' business needs. We then tailor solutions to meet those needs, providing end-to-end performance improvement solutions, rather than isolated training events.

What We Did

I first became acquainted with the 6Ds when a fellow training professional recommended that I read *The Six Disciplines of Breakthrough Learning*. The first edition had just been published. I read it and realized that the approach would help my team and me deliver even greater value from our training and development efforts. I was, at the time, vice president-agency training for American International Assurance (AIA). I was responsible for sales training throughout the Asia-Pacific Region, with special focus on enhancing the training skills of the regional agency trainers and business development executives. As we shifted our emphasis from providing training to driving improved performance, we enjoyed greater and greater support from the business. We were viewed as true business partners helping to drive results, rather than as just a cost center.

When I later became senior vice president, regional training, for the Life and Health Business for Allianz SE Insurance Management Asia Pacific, I introduced the 6Ds with positive effects to our operations in Thailand, China, Taiwan, Malaysia, Singapore, and Indonesia and into the Allianz Achievers Academy (Asia). I came to appreciate the 6Ds as industry best practice and I was anxious to introduce them more broadly throughout Asia. Based on more than five years' experience working with the 6Ds, I knew I could use them to make a significant difference on the business impact of training.

When I decided to create my own company in 2012, I made the 6Ds a centerpiece of our strategy because it would allow us to differentiate ourselves; we would use the 6Ds to focus on business needs and offer complete solutions, rather than just learning "events."

In particular, defining the business outcomes (D1) is a critical part of our process. Too often, training departments "fill the order" for training, without first truly understanding what the business managers need to accomplish. We recommend training *only* when we fully understand the business challenges and are convinced that training is an appropriate part of the solution. Then we look at the whole change process—not just program delivery—to ensure that we optimize conditions for lasting change and performance improvement.

Results

In my leadership roles at both AIA and Allianz, I experienced first-hand the value of the 6Ds approach. In particular, focusing on business outcomes and performance improvement allowed us to forge a much stronger working relationship with the business.

As an independent provider in a crowded market, we have found that the 6Ds provide Global Trainers with a competitive advantage and differentiation. Our focus on business linkage and results is—unfortunately—still rare among training providers. Business leaders appreciate our focus on *their needs* rather than *our solutions*. They also appreciate our emphasis on how to define success and capture evidence that training is being translated into performance. The result is that we gain access to business leaders at much higher levels in the organization than typical training providers. We also are consulted on more interesting and challenging assignments.

In short, the 6Ds have allowed us to move from a training provider to a strategic business partner and trusted advisor.

Advice to Colleagues
- Always start with the end in mind—the goals of the business.
- Remember that training is only a means to an end; it is not an end in itself.
- Plan the complete experience; isolated training events rarely produce meaningful performance improvement.
- Remember, it is not just about the content. The best content in the world is worthless unless it is transferred and used on the job.
- Move the finish line; be sure that you include post-training follow-up as part of designing the complete experience.
- Visit every step of the 6Ds, stay on track, close the loop.

Case I.3

How We Prepare a Proposal and Design a Process Using the 6Ds Outline

Royce Isacowitz
Performance Consultant, Sydney, Australia

Background

Based in Sydney, Australia, I was in the process of a career transition. Whilst researching theories in instructional design, I was referred to the *Six Disciplines of Breakthrough Learning*.

I was immediately convinced of the validity of the concept and the value behind the process. Being more design/architect-oriented than development or implementation, I set out to establish myself as a groundbreaking performance consultant for this part of the globe.

At the start, I encountered two problems:

1. How to approach potential clients given the amount of detail required
2. How to tackle a project incorporating all the required steps of the process in order to achieve a successful outcome

Exhibit I.3.1. Portion of the Spreadsheet Flow Chart for the 6Ds

		On the job behaviors and business results	Define SMART Goals	
D1: Define Business Outcomes (verifiable outcomes of relevance to the business of the organization)	**Begin with the end in mind**	Traditional: end of course and (cap) abilities		
	Express outcomes in business terms	Programs that help participants improve their performance will pay dividends in job satisfaction, motivation, discretionary effort and motivation	…wide range of metrics in addition to financial; e.g., increased customer satisfaction, greater employee commitment, enhanced leadership effectiveness, more productive sales approaches, improved work quality.	
	Pick the right problems	Know the business – see exhibit D1.1, p. 32	Desired business outcomes > required changes in actions / behaviors > experiences needed to produce them. Which path and which behaviors are most critical depends on the business model, climate, and state of development.	Two sources of info: - Explicit knowledge: business plans and report → See: Business Unit Plan - Tacit knowledge: leaders, managers and employees. → Exhibit D1.2, p. 38
	Translate needs into deliverables	Outcomes Planning Wheel 1. What business need(s) will be met? 2. What will participants do differently and better? 3. What or who could confirm these changes? 4. What are the specific criteria of success?	Gain clarity of the real business issue or opportunity behind the request for training. (p. 41) Participants must put their new knowledge and skills to work in ways that are different, better and more effective than previously. How is success defined by the client? (p. 43). See Table D1.3, p. 44. Goals is to come to agreement with business leaders on the key outcomes and acceptable approaches to document results.	Enforce priorities, p. 47.

			Create co-ownership: Besides training, what else needs to be in place?
	Training as a cure-all. See Exhibit D1.3, p. 50.		
Avoid training traps		Having a program to have a program	What are the expected results beyond having a program? How will having a program benefit the business? What outcomes are we trying to achieve?
		Confusion between means and ends	Efficiency (cost containment) vs. efficacy (cost benefit); activity (program) vs. results (increased sales, greater efficiency, better leadership, more effective marketing, higher service, etc.
		Laudable intent	Politically correct courses should receive the same scrutiny as others.
		Inadequate input from sources such as line leaders. Recommended: at least two sources such as employees, managers, customers, business documents, operational data	
Manage expectations		Management doesn't buy courses; they buy the expectation of improved performance.	Be mindful of and manage the expectations of customers to ensure that they are in line with what can realistically be delivered.

Where does one start? I realized I needed a template to follow that would:

1. Be an outline of the 6Ds
2. Ensure proper communication of the concept in client meetings
3. Serve as a tool for staying true to the process and incorporating all the required steps

So I set about creating a quick and thorough cheat sheet of the 6Ds, which, when used in conjunction with the checklists and other resources in the book, ensures a comprehensive and effective process design.

What We Did

The process I followed to develop the tool was as follows:

1. Thoroughly studied *The Six Disciplines of Breakthrough Learning* highlighting key features
2. Summarized all the chapters into headings, subheadings and notes—trying to include all essential elements in concise language
3. Created an Excel® workbook of 6Ds—one sheet per chapter and one sheet for linked resources
4. Inserted page references for all essential information and resources

I ended up with a document that looks like the one in Exhibit I.3.1.

Results

The outcome of my efforts is a document that is easy to access and outlines the essential elements of the 6Ds. I peruse through it before presenting the 6Ds process to a potential client. I also use it, in conjunction with the resources in the book, to create a learning experience from scratch as a job-support tool. It has been an invaluable external memory aid for promoting and designing the 6Ds learning process.

In my first client encounter, I was (with a few months of instructional design experience behind me) meeting with the national vendor and marketing manager and learning solutions sales consultant of one of Australia's largest RTOs (combined industry experience of about thirty-five years). By reviewing the tool before the meeting, I was able to go in speaking with expertise, capture their attention, and gain real interest in the product.

Advice to Colleagues

- Keep the content clear and concise.
- Make sure to stay close to the process and wording, as per the book.
- Use the tool as an extension of the book through links and references.

Case I.4

How We Are Lighting Up the Fire of Continuous Improvement for Our Lean Sigma Green Belts

Alberto Massacesi, ChiChung Chan, Debra Modra, Eric Haddon, John Resing, Joshua Ebert, Susan McDermott

Lean Sigma Master Black Belts at Underwriters Laboratories PLC

Background

UL is a global independent safety science company with more than a century of expertise innovating safety solutions, from the public adoption of electricity to new breakthroughs in sustainability, renewable energy, and nanotechnology. Dedicated to promoting safe living and working environments, UL helps safeguard people, products, and places in important ways, facilitating trade and providing peace of mind. UL has a global footprint, with more than ten thousand people in 131 locations worldwide.

UL certifies, validates, tests, inspects, audits, advises, and educates. We provide the knowledge and expertise to help navigate growing complexities across the supply chain from compliance and regulatory issues to trade challenges and market access.

For UL, training and people development are foundational elements, so we created an internal university staffed with seventy people working full-time to support it. We are proud of being part of this incredible team.

Since the end of 2005, UL has embarked on a Lean journey. As a one-century-old company, we needed to transform from being a transaction-centric organization to a process-oriented organization.

We also needed to continuously improve in order to keep pace with an always-changing reality. The stewards of this change are the Green Belts and Black Belts who are working to adapt and improve our processes continuously.

When we reviewed our Green Belt training, however, we realized that the trained Green Belts, who valued the class itself, were not applying the learning back in their daily work. This was a big warning sign for us. Are we really delivering the bottom-line results that the company expected from these intensive classes?

In this case report, we share the approach we used to solve the problem highlighted by this compelling question.

Actions

The need for a change to the approach to Green Belt training was evident to all of us. What was less evident was what approach we should follow in order to bring more bottom-line results to the company by training Green Belts. In other words, how could we increase the number of Green Belts actually working and applying the learning when back at their daily jobs?

Acknowledging a problem is a first step toward a solution. In December 2012, we called a meeting for a redesign of the class based on the feedback collected from the classes hosted earlier that year. In parallel, two other factors entered into play:

1. We received the outcome of a study aimed to identify the root causes why the continuous improvement culture was not taking off as planned;
2. The whole redesign team of Master Black Belts was offered the opportunity to attend the 6Ds training.

The synergy of these three elements made it possible to identify the approach that we used to redesign the new class.

Define Business Outcomes: Following the 6Ds, we interviewed the main stakeholders from the business side and secured the needed agreement about what success would mean to them. This can be summarized as follows:

- Have the trainees use the scientific approach for problem solving (DMAIC) instead of the usual firefighting "jump-to-conclusions" mode;
- Have the trainees work effectively across siloes in kata, Kaizen, and projects;
- Have the trainees use the new Lean and Six Sigma glasses to look at our processes in order to remove both waste and variability.

The three "soft" goals above enable Green Belts to complete more continuous improvement initiatives. These initiatives immediately resulted in higher throughput and hence revenue, less inventory, lower lead times, as well as cost savings, as documented by each of those projects.

Design Complete Experience: The challenge was to create a new design of a complete experience. How could we move the finish line so that the training didn't end until the Green Belt shows the new expected behavior on a daily basis? Exhibit I.4.1 highlights a comparison of the old approach with the newly designed approach.

We can identify some key differences:

- The roles (champion, mentor, and trainee) need to be understood before the class, so we created dedicated briefing sessions.

Exhibit I.4.1. Comparison of Green Belt Course Before and After Implementing the 6Ds

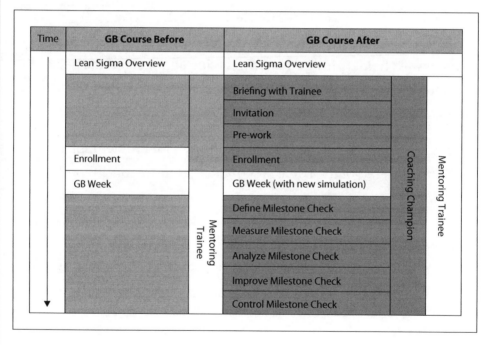

Time	GB Course Before	GB Course After		
	Lean Sigma Overview	Lean Sigma Overview		Mentoring Trainee
		Briefing with Trainee	Coaching Champion	
		Invitation		
		Pre-work		
	Enrollment	Enrollment		
	GB Week	GB Week (with new simulation)		
		Define Milestone Check		
		Measure Milestone Check		
		Analyze Milestone Check		
		Improve Milestone Check		
		Control Milestone Check		

(Mentoring Trainee — under GB Course Before column)

- People have different levels of knowledge about statistics and business fundamentals.
- We wanted to keep the amount of hands-on practice during the week at greater than 50 percent.

These conditions required that we assign some pre-work (six to eight hours) to the trainees. In order to document this, we created a "Green Belt Learning Path" that includes prerequisites, core-curriculum, and post-class project work on our LMS (Exhibit I.4.2).

Exhibit I.4.2. The Green Belt Learning Path Includes Prerequisites, Core Curriculum, and Post-Class Project Work. Course Listing from LMS Is Shown.

Course Name
Project Charters
Eight Wastes of Lean
Introduction to Statistics for Lean Sigma Green Belt Training
Flow Concept - Part 1
Flow Concept - Part 2
Flow Concept - Part 3
Lean Sigma Green Belt Training
Green Belt Practical Requirements Accreditation
UL Internal Lean Sigma Green Belt Examination

During the week of the class, students run an internally designed capstone simulation. Their goal is to turn a business (a car factory, Exhibit I.4.3) that is losing money into a profitable one by applying what they have learned about DMAIC, Lean, and Six Sigma.

In order to keep the momentum going we also created milestone checks after the class (Exhibit I.4.4). These are expected to encourage learners to work on their real-world project when back in the office. They are requested to attend and present their results.

Exhibit I.4.3. The Production Plant Layout Used in the Capstone Session

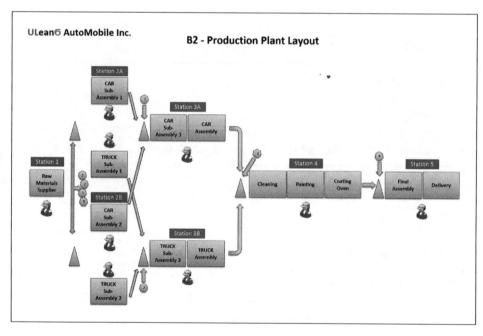

Exhibit I.4.4. Example of Checkpoints Following Green Belt Training

Attendee	Checkpoint 1 Define 11/02/2013	Checkpoint 2 Measure 09/04/2013	Checkpoint 3 Measure 2 07/05/2013	Checkpoint 4 Analyze 21/05/2013	Checkpoint 5 Improve 11/06/2013	Checkpoint 6 Control
			Attendance to follow-up			
1	Yes	Yes	Yes	Yes Not Present		
2	Yes	No progress	Not Present Progress?	Not Present No Progress		
3	Yes	Yes	Yes	Yes Not Present		
4	Yes	Project Changed	Yes	Not Present No Progress		
5	Yes	Yes	Yes	Not Present No Progress		
6	Yes	No Progress	Yes	Yes		
7	Yes	Yes	Yes	Yes		
8	Yes	Yes	Yes	Yes		
9	Yes	No Progress	Yes	Yes		
10	Yes	Yes	Yes	Yes		
11	Yes	Not Present	Not Present	Not Present		
12	Yes	Not Present	Yes	Yes		

A Master Black Belt will coach the champions and mentor the learners along the way.

Deliver for Application: We identified three key elements, as follows:

- We are working to have the champion (direct supervisor) coached to become a coach.
- The exercises executed and the new simulation performed during the Green Belt week will allow at least 65 percent hands-on time for the trainees.
- We defined additional activities to support people after the class that will help them apply what they learned so that we will be able to check their understanding.

Drive Learning Transfer: This is at the center of the new approach. In fact, we defined a new approach as a consequence of our root-cause analysis, as shown in Exhibit I.4.5:

Exhibit I.4.5. Triangle of Continuous Improvement Green Belt Fire

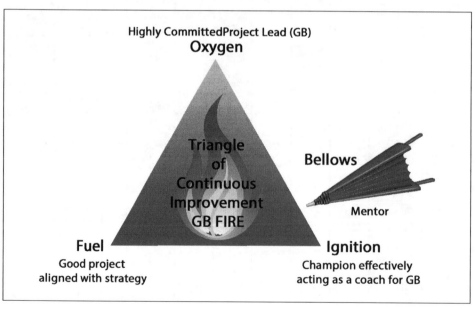

This is what we called "The Triangle of Continuous Improvement Green Belt Fire." Just as in fire science, where three elements (fuel, ignition, and oxygen) are needed simultaneously to have a fire, we need to have three elements in place at the same moment to have the Green Belt apply learning:

- **Fuel:** A good project that the champion cares about and that is well aligned with corporate strategy;
- **Ignition:** A manager of the trainee willing to act as a coach; and
- **Oxygen:** A capable and highly committed trainee.

A fourth element is also needed when the "fire" becomes weaker: the Master Black Belt, or Black Belt acting as a mentor for trainee, or as coach for the champion, which is the **bellows** in our analogy.

Deploy Performance Support: This took the form of:

- Provide mentoring to the trainee as project lead when he or she will be working on the assigned project.
- Provide feedback to the champion (direct supervisor) about his coaching to the Green Belt trainee as project lead.

Document Business Results: We will consider the results of the continuous improvement projects as direct results of the training. In addition, the less tangible results requested by the main stakeholders will become much more evident:

- People using the scientific approach for problem solving instead of jumping to solutions;
- People will better collaborate as focused teams in kata, Kaizen, and projects;
- We will also see a different mindset/culture that results in using the Lean and Six Sigma glasses to look at our processes.

Results

So far we have deployed classes using the new approach in Europe, North America, and Asia; additional classes are scheduled.

The feedback from the students has been positive. What is really interesting is the progress that people showed on their projects in the follow-up checks. While in the past only around 10 percent to of students were able to apply the learning to their project, based on the data available so far we have 66 percent of the students who are on track up to the Analyze phase of their project. This means that, assuming that only 50 percent are certified by completing their projects, there has been a big improvement to the baseline. Of course, we also need more data from the other classes, so it is still too early to claim victory, but the preliminary results are very positive.

On the other hand, we also received feedback on needed improvements. We need to work on our champions. Many supervisors are not ready to act as real coaches. The following analogy describes our current situation: our trainees are like soldiers asked to cross a bridge between their current mindset and a new mindset. Their champions are like machine gunners who are preventing the soldiers from crossing the bridge by shooting at them.

Advice to Colleagues

- Most training is aimed at teaching people a different behavior to use in their daily jobs. This is very true for the Green Belt training. In fact, the main challenge is not related to the technical content; it is logical and flows very well. The real challenge is the existing behaviors of the trainee, and especially the supervisor. If these are not eliminated and "delearned," they will hinder the application of new approaches. So in order to have the trainee apply the learning, we need to work hard to create a safe environment where he or she can actually apply it.

- Coaching by champion is a key in our new process. How many managers today are good coaches? In most companies managers are currently formed and selected based on:

  - Their ability to solve problems quickly, which means they are good firefighters;
  - A strong ego (otherwise they will not climb the ladder much), so they want to own the solutions themselves in order to show results to get promoted; and
  - A command-and-control style rather than a coaching- and enabling-others style.

  As a result, it is rare to find a supervisor willing to act as a coach. For those who are willing, it will be difficult for them to behave as coaches, since no one has coached them. This element needs to be factored in so that a specific action can be deployed at least to mitigate those effects.

- There is no endpoint to the improvement of our teaching process. Continuous improvement needs to be applied along the way. For example, we designed a completely new simulation, but then we needed to adapt and change it multiple times based on the feedback gathered from the trainees and the instructors regarding its effective usage.

- Moving part of the content before or after the class was very effective. Nothing is more true than the concept that "less is more" while teaching. We are still considering what we can remove or move out of the week of the class so that the main focus will be on learning some basic behaviors, applied using specific tools and concepts.

Case I.5

How We Used the 6Ds Framework to Redevelop Our Sales Leader Curriculum

Cecil W. Johnson, III

Director, Management Development, Janssen Pharmaceuticals

Background

Janssen Pharmaceuticals, Inc., a pharmaceutical company of Johnson & Johnson, provides medicines for an array of health concerns in several therapeutic areas. Our goal is to help people live healthy lives. We have produced and marketed many first-in-class prescription medications and are poised to serve the broad needs of the healthcare market. Headquartered in Titusville, New Jersey, Janssen is named for Dr. Paul Janssen, a leading Belgian researcher, pharmacologist, and general practitioner. Dr. Janssen led a group of researchers to discover a medicine that helped change the way mental health patients were treated.

Janssen Pharmaceuticals remains guided by Dr. Janssen's values of excellence and innovation.

In 2011, the management development team undertook a complete review and revision of our sales leadership curriculum, with the goal of creating a comprehensive and coordinated series of learning experiences that would provide a career developmental ladder from management development candidates all the way through to experienced regional business directors.

The business objectives of the revision included:

- Improving sales leadership at all levels
- Improving identification and qualification of management development candidates
- Shortening the time to proficiency of newly appointed district managers
- Enhancing the business results of both new and experienced sales managers
- Increasing the quality and bench strength of our talent pipeline

What We Did

We created teams of learning, sales professionals, and HR to tackle each of the four developmental stages of sales leadership:

1. High-potential sales representatives prior to promotion to district manager
2. New district managers
3. Experienced district managers
4. Regional business directors

In my role as director, management development, I served as overall strategic lead of the work streams and met both formally and informally with the teams and team leaders. All of my skilled senior managers were team leads and had strategic input into the plans and accountability for execution.

We used the 6Ds to provide an overall framework for the design and engaged a 6Ds consultant to independently review the work and make recommendations.

Results

The 6Ds proved to be a very useful framework for thinking about not only individual courses, but the multi-year sales curriculum as a whole. The focus on business outcomes (D1) in particular was especially helpful in presenting proposals to management and getting their buy in. I always included the expected business outcomes and benefits as the second or third slide in the deck for whatever aspect of the curriculum we were discussing (Exhibit I.5.1 is an example). This helped secure the business leaders' attention and focus the discussion on the best ways to achieve the desired outcomes.

Exhibit I.5.1. An Example of a Slide Linking the Training Initiative to the Business Outcomes

---

Business Outcomes and Objectives

- Improving the effectiveness and efficiency of Regional Business Directors (RBDs). As a result of elevated management and leadership competencies and behaviors, RBDs will:
  - Drive business results and performance in their regions
  - Increase the successful execution of regional business strategies for business growth
  - Increase the engagement, retention, and teamwork of their regions through increased leadership skill and behaviors
  - Increase the quality and bench strength of their talent pipelines

---

Using the 6Ds as a touchstone for each program and for the sales leadership curriculum as a whole helped us consider the whole learning path required to achieve proficiency and to think beyond "training events." Even so, we found it challenging to design meaningful follow-through that would ensure learning transfer and to design effective but efficient evaluation. Those areas continue to be part of our own developmental journey as learning professionals.

In the end, we were able to present a coherent and comprehensive sales leadership development plan that was accepted by management and has since been implemented. We are now in the process of continuous improvement (one of the concepts of D6), but we are already seeing the positive benefits of the new approach:

1. Key product insights developed from the director training program were used in marketing brand strategy and increased impact of selling conversations.

2. The regional business director training program resulted in an increase in team impact and role performance and produced an increase in customer focus and engagement.

3. Regional business directors tell us that newly appointed and new-to-the-organization district managers are coming up to speed more quickly, have a higher success rate in integrating with their teams, and are more independent than in the past.

4. Experienced district manager training produced plans to increase effectiveness of product launches, resulting in greater synergy and alignment of marketing/sales partnership.

5. District manager training resulted in an on-the-job increase in engagement of direct reports and an increase in frequency and quality of coaching.

6. Emerging leaders new to the district manager role come on board with business planning skills that accelerate market performance.

7. Strategic thinking skills developed in the tenured manager track have produced improved district and regional performance.

> **Advice to Colleagues**
> - Always engage business partners in the discussion regarding business objectives and expected benefits to the business of any training proposal.
> - Teach your teams the 6Ds and use them as a framework for evaluating both individual courses and whole curricula.
> - Consider engaging an independent 6Ds consultant for strategic projects to add external perspective and best practices from other firms to the discussion.
> - Recognize that shifting the focus to business outcomes for a learning and development function can be a cultural change for the function and the business leaders in the organization. Change and transition management plans are important for sustained success.

Case 1.6

How We Introduced the 6Ds to Our Team

Ted Joyce

Adjunct Professor, Rouen Business School and Visiting Professor,
Université Paris 1, La Sorbonne

Background

Deloitte globally has nearly 200,000 professionals with a single focus: serving our clients and helping them solve their toughest problems. Deloitte provides services in four key business areas—audit, financial advisory, tax, and consulting—but our real strength comes from combining the talents of those groups to address clients' needs. *Fortune* and *BusinessWeek* consistently rank our organization among the best places to work, which is good news for our talent and our clients alike.

As a professional services firm, Deloitte invests heavily in training and development to keep our professionals at "the cutting edge." In 2012, I was part of the Global Tax and Learning team and was the Americas tax and legal regional leading leader with oversight of learning and development for all tax and legal professionals in the Americas. I had attended a workshop on the *Six Disciplines of Breakthrough Learning* sponsored by the firm and became convinced that these principles applied to all learning programs for Deloitte. I wanted to make sure that these principles were introduced to all members of our global learning teams as well as the learning professionals in all the firms that we supported.

What We Did

We started by purchasing a copy of the *Six Disciplines of Breakthrough Learning* for each member of our team. Then, as part of our weekly team calls and monthly regional calls, we would discuss the assigned chapter(s) in the book to determine how to drive best practices through to our global and regional stakeholders so as to deliver the best learning programs for our tax and legal professionals around the world.

As part of our weekly team calls we also introduced an additional element of fun and a slight degree of competitiveness to the process with a photo contest focused on finding the most exotic or interesting place in the world to be reading the *Six Disciplines of Breakthrough Learning*—"where in the world have you been reading 6Ds?" True to the high-performing nature of the members of our team, we received amazing entries, including pictures of people reading the book in Hong Kong, near the Golden Gate Bridge in San Francisco, by the World Trade Center in New York, from a precarious boulder high in the mountains of Norway (Exhibit I.6.1) and while swimming in Turkey (Exhibit I.6.2).

Exhibit I.6.1. The Winning Entry. Andrea Kahudova Takes the *Six Disciplines* to New Heights in Norway.

Photo by Jan Zobal, used with permission.

By adding elements of fun and competitiveness, the photo contest helped maintain interest and engagement. We subsequently attended a two-day workshop led by one of the authors that provided additional insights, reinforced core concepts, and gave us opportunities to practice application as an intact team.

Exhibit I.6.2. A Strong Contender. Alban Le Nech Takes a Brisk Dip into the *Six Disciplines* in a Mountain Lake at Three Thousand Meters in the Taurus Mountains of Turkey.

Results

Having a common language and understanding of this framework for designing, delivering, and evaluating training helped us work more effectively as a team, constructively critique plans, and share best practices.

Advice to Colleagues

- Train the whole team on the 6Ds; there is synergy in a common understanding and vocabulary.
- Don't try to tackle the whole book at once; work your way through the chapters with time for discussion after each section.
- Have some fun with the task—such as our photo contest—learning should be enjoyable!
- Although the book is very complete, we found it helpful to also attend a workshop as a group to gain additional insights and have time practicing application to our specific programs. The ability to apply our knowledge of our organization and our professionals to the learning from the book really helped us jump-start the process of transferring the learning to our daily tasks.

Editor's Note

Where have you been reading the *6Ds Field Guide*?

Send your photo to photos@the6Ds.com. We will post them on the 6Ds website and include those that receive the most votes in future editions.

Case D1.1

How We Moved from Order Takers to Business Partners

Patricia Gregory and Steve Akram

Senior Director and Director, North American Sales

Force Development, Oracle

Background

Oracle simplifies IT and powers innovation with hardware and software engineered to work together. With more than 390,000 customers—including all one hundred of the Fortune 100—and with deployments across a wide variety of industries in more than 145 countries around the globe, Oracle offers an optimized and fully-integrated stack of business hardware and software systems.

North American Sales Force Development is responsible for the training, curriculum, and development of the North American sales force for this $37 billion global technology leader. Our responsibilities include preparing the sales force in all aspects of the sale process, including sales presentations, product knowledge, messaging and communications skills, negotiation and demonstration skills, and—because many of our products involve enterprise-wide solutions—executive-level engagement skills.

Historically, the sales force development group offered a broad catalog of courses that covered the gamut of knowledge and skills required to sell our products and services. Business units and individual representatives selected among the courses, depending on their needs and interests. We were essentially "order takers." We would present the catalog of courses available to the heads of sales and ask, "How much of each do you need?"

At the time this project began several years ago, about 70 percent of our courses were open enrollment and only 30 percent were specifically sponsored by a vice president of sales.

After we learned about the 6Ds—in particular, D1—we became convinced that we could provide greater value by taking a more proactive role in defining the business needs and prioritizing the training time and offerings to match.

What We Did

We changed our approach so that we start with the business needs. As a result we now have much more meaningful business conversations. Instead of offering a catalog of courses, we start with a question: What sales skills or knowledge do you need to improve to meet your sales targets?

We probe for whether there will be new products that will require training, new pricing structures that must be explained, or new markets that we want to penetrate. We take much more of a consultative approach. We ask about how many sales representatives will be hired, whether they will be experienced or new to the field, and therefore what they will need to know. We ask, for example:

- Are our representatives successful in getting to the C-suite?
- If so, are their discussions with executive management as productive as they should be?
- How will we know whether the training is successful?

Throughout the conversations we keep the focus on the business results that need to be achieved. Only after these are clear do we identify or create the programs required to meet them.

About twice a year, we meet with top-level sales management to optimize the planning process and ensure we have prioritized the training investment—especially where the reps are spending their time—in a way that will produce the greatest value for the organization.

Results

The statistic that most tellingly demonstrates the value of this approach is this: when we began the initiative to shift our focus from courses to business needs, 70 percent of the sales training programs were open enrollment and only 30 percent were VP-sponsored. Now, several years into the process, the ratio has completely reversed: 70 percent of the courses are VP-sponsored and only 30 percent are open enrollment.

Another telling metric is that requests for training have actually *increased* as a result of doing a better job of addressing business needs up front, as well as reporting the impact of training on the job (see Case D6.4: "How We Use Success Stories to Communicate Training's Value").

Finally, as training directors, we are now viewed much more as business partners than simply training providers. We are brought into discussions earlier, we receive greater management support for training, and our opinions are more highly valued.

Advice to Colleagues

- Always start any discussion of training needs with a discussion of the business's strategic and tactical objectives and the skills that will be required to achieve them.
- Stick with it; the change won't happen overnight. It has taken us several years to move from order taker to strategic business partner.
- Clarify how the sponsor defines success—which is almost always application on the job that achieves some business purpose—and then gather evidence that this is happening.

Case D1.2

How We Turned a "Feel Good" Training Program into a Successful Business Transformation

Dr. Sujaya Banerjee
Chief Talent Officer and Senior Vice President, HR, The Essar Group

Tahseen Wahdat
Senior Manager, Learning and OD, The Essar Group

Anand Justin Cherian
Manager, Learning and OD, The Essar Group

Background

The Essar Group is a diversified infrastructure conglomerate with interests in steel, oil and gas, power, projects, shipping, and business process outsource (BPO) among other industry sectors. With group revenues of US $27.3 billion and more than 75,000 employees globally, Essar is among the leading business houses in India. The last seven years have witnessed concerted efforts to transition the group from a predominantly family-run enterprise to a professionally managed global multinational corporation. Among the key initiatives undertaken as part of this transformational agenda was the creation of the Central Learning and OD Team (Learning Team).

The Learning Team, since its inception, has served as the change engine for the group, working on key levers such as culture, capability building, people processes, leadership development, strategic talent management, and career development, among others. The team is strategically positioned to leverage specialist expertise and economies of scale (with group-wide deployments), while ensuring connection to business-wise ground-level realities through active liaising with the CEOs and business heads. Dedicated key account managers for each business provide ongoing support and ensure that the Learning Team stays focused on business priorities.

The initiative in question was designed for the Steel Hypermart Business Unit, the retail sales arm of the Steel Business Group. Hypermart is an innovative business extension aimed at capturing greater value and margins, with Essar being the first major steel producer to venture into retail sales in India. The need for a learning intervention was felt, however, when the unit initially failed to deliver projected results in spite of its first-mover advantage and pan-India presence. The stakeholders realized something was not going right, but pinpointing the specific problem had proven to be a challenge.

What We Did

The Learning Team was approached by the business HR team. Their need identification had concluded that the front-line sales executives were wanting on effective negotiation skills, which are essential to build and maintain relationships with customers at ground level. Additionally, it was felt that the front-line sales personnel were unable to adequately convey the different product characteristics and advantages in a convincing manner to the end-customer, who was invariably price-sensitive. Thus, communication skills was added as another module in the program brief requested by HR.

Keen to pursue the 6Ds, the Learning Team, while accepting the preliminary brief from HR, contacted some of the senior line leaders from the Hypermart Business. We were surprised to find ambiguity about what the program was supposed to accomplish. One leader candidly told us: "We just need a training session to create better engagement among front-line sales executives."

Convinced that the answers sought by the rigor of D1 were still far from clear, the Learning Team developed a proposed approach based largely on negotiation and communication skills and presented it to a panel comprising the Hypermart CEO, HR, and a few senior line leaders. Our goal was to create a forum in which to pose D1 questions (the Planning Wheel) to the group in order to gain greater clarity on the brief. Fortuitously, the president of strategy and global markets (manager of the CEO) walked into the meeting and saw the shallowness of the initial brief. First he, and then the CEO, questioned the basis for the training needs as identified and engaged in an animated discussion that soon engulfed all members of the audience, lasting for the better part of two hours!

The open brainstorming, discussion, and debate—aided by D1 questions from the Planning Wheel—ended with all participants being convinced that the true need was not a behavioral training session, but a fundamental re-look at the entire sales process that was the foundation for all the other business processes of the unit. A rigorous adherence to D1 saved all concerned from the futility of (yet another) good-to-have, but ineffective, training program. Instead, we were able to acknowledge and identify a more real, deep-rooted concern for their business.

At this stage, the exact sales and business model needed to achieve the business goals was not yet completely defined and articulated. It was felt that expert input from external consultants would help analyze and address the situation from a much-needed outside-in perspective.

The Learning Team set about scouting for consultants and learning partners with relevant expertise in the commodities marketing and retail field. After much research and proposal exploration, AchieveGlobal was identified as an ideal learning partner for this evolving business transformation project. After a detailed interaction with the CEO and president of strategy and global markets, the AchieveGlobal team visited several Hypermart locations to assess first-hand the factors impacting sales effectiveness and performance. Involving the learning partner in an extended D1 stage reaped rich dividends. Their findings, when presented to the president and CEO, were found to be in consonance with the realities experienced within the business.

AchieveGlobal's recommendations included creating a detailed sales manual, launching of a comprehensive know-your-customer (KYC) initiative (with requisite forms, templates and training/ orientation), and instating key account managers (KAMs) across locations. Following approval of the proposal, the AchieveGlobal team worked closely with the Learning Team to create the documents and training modules that would support this massive change intervention, with input from leaders as required. The president and CEO approved the sales manual that was created, as well as the KYC program, and supporting documents and templates before we concluded the design phase and prepared for D3. With the go-ahead on the program definition and design, the project moved to the delivery phase, which would cover 135 personnel across eight locations in the country.

Being experts in sales training, AchieveGlobal worked closely with us to ensure that all training was application-oriented, made relevant with case studies close to real pain points, and supported with job aids that would actually be used by the sales team on the job.

Further, we included one-level senior managers as key account managers. This was critical not just for the implementation of the key account manager approach to sales, but also to support (D5) the application of learning imparted to the front-line sales force. Performance support was also extended by way of the redefinition of performance itself; balanced scorecards were developed for all sales executives and KAMs.

Driving Learning Transfer (D4) was supported by the Learning Team but was predominantly the responsibility of the BD managers as ensured by the CEO. The completion of KYC forms was tracked centrally and reviewed by the CEO for the initial few months to ensure alignment to the plan and the celebration of early wins. In addition, participants were sent weekly nuggets on different aspects of the training and the newly adopted sales model. Here, too, the team partnered actively with AchieveGlobal for creating relevant material in order to reinforce key ideas and insights from the program.

Results

The targeted focus on addressing fundamental business issues impacting performance meant that the intended change was sustained across the country, with real ground-level improvements in customer orientation and sales effectiveness. The detailed Know Your Customer initiative now enables key account managers to better predict the consumption patterns of key customers, versus the ad hoc nature of sales in the former way of doing business.

As a result of the discipline and enhanced perspective injected by this initiative, Hypermart turned around performance in a tough business environment, with revenues growing 5 percent in the very next quarter. Gross margins for fiscal year 2012–2013 were nearly four-fold over the previous year, bolstered by the sharper focus on aligning value-added product offerings with specific customer needs. While improvements in other aspects of the business (such as supply chain, regional segmentation, enhanced alignment with upstream operations) have certainly contributed to this performance uplift, the role of the change intervention with the redefined sales model and enhanced customer orientation has been openly acknowledged and accepted by all.

Advice to Colleagues

- Pursue the *real* sponsor of the program to clearly articulate what the real business challenges are and how the program will impact desired business outcomes.
- While inputs from multiple sources help add more perspectives to your understanding, it is important to find the overarching direction as defined by the principal sponsor as the pole star for all decisions moving forward. This has the added advantage that once the business head or manager has bought into the learning intervention, a positive learning transfer climate is ensured.
- Using the Define stage effectively leads to driving an intervention as opposed to just putting on a program. Therefore, dwelling on D1 is a good idea; laboring through D2 is also very important to ensure D3 hits bull's eye by generating the D6 business impact.

- Training for performance improvement is our credo and it has been our persistence and perseverance through associated areas (scorecards, career ladders, role definitions), which made this a joyous journey of change and gratification for all involved. "Learning can make a business impact" is an important experience for creating development-savvy leaders.

Endorsement by CEO, Essar Hypermart

Essar Hypermart, a $750 million company that provides steel solutions to small and medium enterprises across India, operates eighty company-owned stores and over 250 distributorships. With a workforce of over one hundred key account managers (KAMs) scattered across the country, we were facing several challenges in regard to maintaining a uniform image of the company across the country, educating our workforce on institutional selling, and most importantly, teaching our KAMs on developing long-lasting relationships with our clients. With the Indian economy slowing down, the need for creating a competitive edge with our sales force became all the more imperative.

Essar Hypermart used the 6Ds approach to Breakthrough Learning with our KAMs in 2012. The leadership team first consulted with the learning team on precisely identifying the business challenges that faced the company and defined the measures for success. The company also identified which people would lead the effort so as to maintain consistency between planning and execution. Once the objectives were identified, the team developed a plan of execution. It placed special emphasis on following through with quantifiable results after the completion of the learning program, which is where many programs fail to achieve results. The program commenced with three-day workshops held across the country for the entire sales force, including their supervisors. The content of the workshops was created in order to resonate with the KAMs' daily working environment. It was important that the learning program was found to be unique rather than routine. Feedback on the course content and its relevance was obtained after each session so that improvements could be incorporated into subsequent seminars.

I personally visited almost all sessions across the country to emphasize that this new approach was designed not only to create better sales, but also to develop the professional skills of the KAMs in their redefined roles and make them operate on a much higher level than they had so far been operating on. I also obtained informal feedback on the efficacy of the program, which was very positive.

I was delighted to hear that the 6Ds approach was welcomed by the KAMs as path-breaking and extremely intuitive. The 6Ds approach allowed them to channel their thoughts in a cogent and cohesive manner, which clearly translated into a better trained and much more enthusiastic workforce. The 6Ds approach was able to make the goalposts clear and also allowed for the learning team to follow through months after the classroom sessions to assess business results. I was particularly impressed with the way the approach took us to many other areas that needed change.

The 6Ds unique approach to breakthrough learning helped Essar Hypermart develop its sales force into a cohesive nationwide organization with a unity of purpose and a desire to excel.

Ashok Bajpai
CEO, Essar Hypermart

Case D1.3

How We Defined Business Outcomes and the Learning Continuum for *iteach*

Hemalakshmi Raju and Anjali Raghuvanshi

Assistant General Manager, Learning and Development, and Program Manager, *iteach*, Tata Motors, Ltd.

Background

Tata Motors Limited is India's largest automobile company, with consolidated revenues of US $32.5 billion in 2011–1012. Established in 1954, it is the leader in commercial vehicles and among the top three in passenger vehicles with winning products in the compact, midsize car, and utility vehicle segments. Its vision is to be "Most admired by our customers, employees, business partners, and shareholders for the experience and value they enjoy from being with us."

To support the business objectives of Tata Motors Limited, our Human Capital Strategy emphasizes learning and capability development. Tata Motors Academy, the corporate university of Tata Motors Ltd., was established in 2011 to bring focus and depth to learning in a way that helps the business achieve results. In 2012, Tata Motors was named "best learning organization" in Asia by the L&OD Roundtable.

In the past, although substantial investments were made in training employees, the organization relied very heavily on external experts for delivery. This approach failed to take advantage of all the tacit knowledge and expertise our leaders have as the result of many years of experience in the organization. Hence the need was strongly felt for a program to prepare internal trainers.

This led to the launch of *iteach*—our internal facilitator's program. The focus of *iteach* is skill building for internal trainers through a structured train-the-trainer program.

What We Did

We began with "the end in mind" by mapping the desired business outcomes based upon inputs from both HR as well as business leaders.

Business outcomes were structured around the four questions of the Outcomes Planning Wheel (Figure D1.3.1).

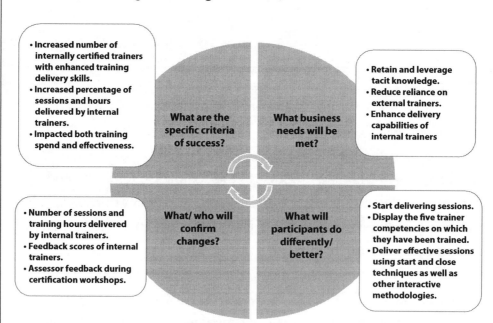

Figure D1.3.1. Desired Business Outcomes for *iteach*

Learning continuum. The learning continuum defines the complete learning experience of a participant in the *iteach* train-the-trainer certification course. There are five phases in this journey, as depicted in Figure D1.3.2.

Results

In its first year and a half, 710 employees have participated in the *iteach* train-the-trainer program and 238 of them have completed the entire learning journey and have been certified.

1. In the most recent fiscal year, 38 percent of the senior leaders have facilitated sessions and 52 percent of learning hours were delivered by internal trainers, compared to less than 10 percent before *iteach* was created.
2. The preparatory phase benefits both the participants and the facilitator by ensuring that the participants are better prepared; it has been widely appreciated.
3. Providing post-program support in the form of a mentor helps participants transfer their knowledge, understand their strengths and areas for improvement, and become better at facilitation.
4. Delivering sessions in the presence of a mentor/assessor gives participants an opportunity to practice their skills with feedback.
5. After completing the course, the learners have a sense of achievement as they are feted in the presence of senior leaders.
6. The rigor built into the process has ensured creation of high-quality trainers, as reflected in their feedback scores.

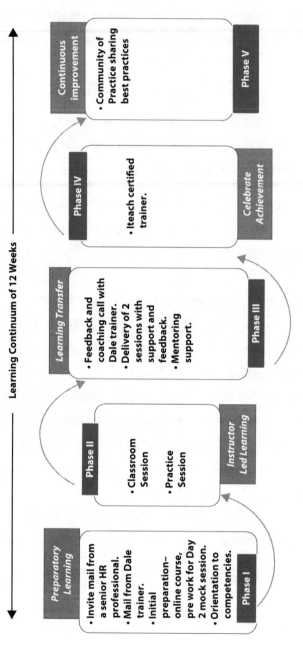

Figure D1.3.2. The Five Phases of *iteach*

Advice to Colleagues

- Return on investment is a key question that learning professionals often face from business leaders. Use of the Planning Wheel can be the first step toward ensuring business impact; it ensures partnering of learning with business and their active involvement.
- Involve leaders as teachers to capitalize on their tacit knowledge, experience, and expertise.
- Following a structured approach enhances the credibility of the learning function.
- Learning cannot be looked at as a one-time event. It has to be built as a journey with specific milestones. This also gives a better structure and focus to the process.
- The preparatory phase ensures better preparation and the post-program phase is essential to ensure transfer of learning.
- Recognition at the end of the learning journey adds to the sense of completion and also acts as a trigger to move forward.

Case D1.4

How We Used In-Depth Analysis to Design the Right Intervention to Achieve Business Objectives

Russell Evans and Clive Wilson
Managing Director and Deputy Chairman, Primeast Ltd.

Background

Primeast is an international learning development consultancy that has been providing services in leadership, organizational change, and teamwork since 1987.

Cape plc is an international leader in the provision of essential non-mechanical industrial services, principally to plant operators in the oil and gas, power generation, chemical, minerals, and mining sectors and major engineering and construction contractors.

Cape's 21,000 people deliver *safe, reliable* and *intelligent* solutions both onshore and offshore. International coverage extends across the UK, Europe and CIS, Middle East and North Africa, and Asia Pacific. Cape shares are traded on the main market of the London Stock Exchange. Reported revenues 2012 were £749.4 million.

In a highly competitive market, Steve Connolly, then head of Cape's UK onshore business, recognized the need to spend more time on strategy and key commercial relationships. He realized that he was spending 80 percent of his time in one-on-one problem solving with the direct reports who formed his senior management team. His primary aim was to reduce this time allocation to 50 percent, giving him "headroom" to focus on his other priorities.

In consultation with Alex Spence, his UK HR director, Steve deduced that this could be achieved by improving the senior team's capability through empowerment, self-sufficiency, resilience, and interconnection. Alex recommended engaging Primeast to design and facilitate a suitable intervention.

What We Did

1. We consulted with Steve and Alex to understand the challenge, the root causes, and local dynamics, rather than just the immediate, presented problem.

2. We explored the organizational context, Cape's people strategy, and its learning and development framework using our PrimeFocus™ model (Exhibit D.1.4.1).

3. Specifically, we used our PrimeFocus model as a map to help Steve describe what was happening in his team against each of the eight PrimeFocus elements:

- Purpose
- Vision
- Engagement
- Structure
- Character
- Results
- Success
- Human talent

Exhibit D1.4.1. PrimeFocus™ Model Showing Relationships Among the Eight Critical Elements

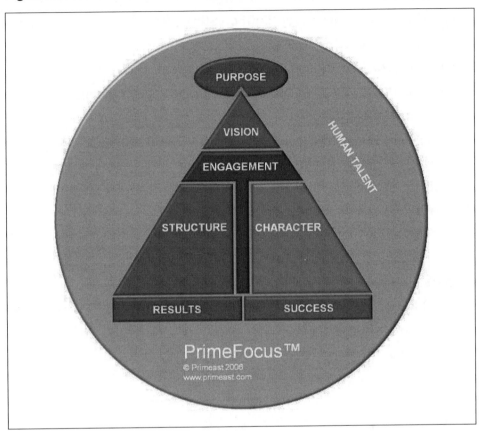

4. We discussed the desired state for each element that would be achieved at the end of the intervention, including measures of tangible results and personal success for Steve and his team members.

Key Insights from Using PrimeFocus

- A dependency mindset existed among Steve's team members so they deferred problem solving and decisions to their boss
- A lack of ownership of the team's purpose and vision by senior managers in the team
- Low recognition and use of team members' personal talents to achieve and exceed business objectives

How These Insights Helped Us

- These insights supported the design of a thorough-going intervention (D2), which put the spotlight on Steve's leadership and his vision for the future.
- They helped us be clear about the required business outcomes (D1).
- PrimeFocus helped us understand the breadth and depth of contributory factors and root causes (D1).
- PrimeFocus also provided a framework for the design (D2) and delivery (D3) of the intervention by ensuring that the solution was totally aligned to delivering Steve's vision and was reflected in measured results (D6) and personal success factors.
- PrimeFocus helped us consider eight critical elements (shown in the exhibit above) when defining the business outcomes (D1) required from a successful organizational learning intervention.
- Coaching support was provided to senior managers to focus and motivate learning transfer (D5) and facilitate the delivery of stretching commitments.

Results

- Steve achieved his goal of getting his time back to invest in strategy and key commercial relationships (D6).
- Steve's team made a strong connection between their personal strengths and the business strategy, enabling them to be more impactful day to day.
- By focusing on enabling the team, rather than supporting Steve in isolation, the team members personally committed to the implementation of a plan to deliver approximately £20m to the bottom line (D6).

- In addition, Steve's subsequent attention to strategy and key commercial relationships secured the delivery of challenging profit targets for the year and a platform for subsequent gains (D6).
- A follow-up intervention was staged to review and celebrate outcomes (D6) and personal successes.

Advice to Colleagues
- Thoroughly defining business outcomes (D1) is the foundation for success. Do not neglect this step in any way!
- Be rigorous on the measurement of business results and personal successes (D6). This provides the business case to embed this type of intervention as an ongoing strategic alignment process. In turn, it allows all senior leaders to remain strategic rather than being subsumed by tactical issues.
- In the same way that 6Ds provides clarity and a common language for driving high-impact learning, it is important to use an organizational framework (such as PrimeFocus) to drive performance improvement in leadership, organizational change, and teamwork.
- Align the corporate communications plan for the business to celebrate the gains made by managers as a means to leverage cultural development (D6).
- Deploy performance support (D5) by ensuring that there are suitable ongoing flexible learning opportunities for managers to further leverage their personal strengths in support of identified business objectives.
- Ensure there is sufficient one-on-one coaching (D5) for managers to fully deliver on their commitments when faced with ongoing challenges of "business as usual."

Case D1.5

How We Incorporated the 6Ds into Our Learning Services Tool Box

Richard Low

Senior Specialist, Learning and Development, Merck & Co., Inc.

Background

Merck, known as MSD outside the United States and Canada, is a global research-driven pharmaceutical company that discovers, develops, manufactures, and markets a broad range of innovative products to improve human and animal health, directly and through its joint ventures. Merck's headquarters is located in New Jersey, USA.

Within Merck there are several divisions, each of which has a supporting training group. Merck Research Laboratories is one such division that focuses on discovering and developing novel medicines and vaccines. Merck Research Laboratories are supported by The Merck Polytechnic Institute through services that include strategic partnership, design and development of curricula, course design and development, training consultation, and measurement and evaluation.

The use of the 6Ds was prompted by several challenges experienced in our training projects:

- The business person who originally had written the objectives and outline of the course was no longer available.
- A new business team was in place.
- Current business needs were not formalized and documented.
- Learning objectives were not fully defined and there were questions as to whether the current objectives met the business needs.
- The course content outline had not yet been approved by the new team in place.

What We Did

I have found the implementation of the D1: Define concepts to be the most valuable and easiest to apply of the 6Ds. D1 can be thought of as a tool to align and calibrate understanding between the training organization and the business about what business needs will be met.

We have implemented the actions and concepts defined in D1 on projects just starting, as well as those in progress. The results have been positive in all cases.

During one of our projects, we implemented the 6Ds Outcomes Planning Wheel, a tool within D1 that outlines four questions centered on documenting:

1. What business needs will be met?
2. What will participants do differently and better?
3. Who or what can confirm these changes?
4. What are the criteria for success?

The training team took the following steps in implementing the Planning Wheel:

- We introduced the Planning Wheel to the new business manager and described its intended purpose.
- We discussed each of the four questions associated with the Planning Wheel with the business manager.
- The manager in turn provided answers representative of the current state of the business.
- As a team, we performed a review and comparison of the original scope of the project and objectives with the answers obtained from the Planning Wheel discussion.

All parties agreed that:

- A new set of business needs will be incorporated in the scope of the project.
- A new course outline will be developed along with revised course objectives that are in line with addressing the business needs.
- The design and delivery of course and training materials will be refined based on the business needs.

Original Business Needs
- Business needs were not fully identified at the time. The basic needs identified were to understand methods and share best practices.

New Business Needs
- Formalize training: at present, the business does not offer any formalized or organized training on this topic.
- Create a baseline of knowledge: introducing a formalized training session will institute a baseline of knowledge among audience members.
- Provide best practices on making the best selection that can be implemented consistently throughout the targeted business area.

- Provide answers to commonly asked questions in a central forum easily referenced by all.
- Interest in building a set of standards across groups to create uniformity in the business.

Results
- Achieved consensus among team members on what the business needs were
- Focus and attention to items requiring additional work
- Provided the information needed to align the course outline and objectives to address the business needs
- Introduced a structured approach that facilitated discussions around training needs
- Reinforced basic training principles already learned, but organized the information and principles in a manner easily referenced and implemented

An unexpected outcome of sharing the Planning Wheel with the business manager was that the manger found value in using the concepts of the wheel for internal business needs. The manager was being asked at the time by senior management to identify current training needs of the group. After reviewing the Planning Wheel, the manager highlighted how useful the tool would be to help answer questions being asked and facilitate discussions regarding training needs.

Advice to Colleagues

- Utilize the 6Ds D1: Define concepts to validate or re-validate what the expected business needs are. This should be applied for both new and ongoing projects.
- Share the 6Ds Outcomes Planning Wheel with your business clients and encourage them to use the tool in their internal decision process for evaluating training needs prior to contacting training.
- Never underestimate how others will use 6Ds tools once they have been presented. 6Ds tools and concepts can serve business purposes outside of just training.
- On a related note, but not directly associated with the Planning Wheel, much can be learned from the design and content structure of the 6Ds Workshop manual with its supporting documents. It provides an example of conveying information in a manner that invites repeated use and reference.

Case D2.1

How We Increased the Volume and Variety of Learning Solutions While Decreasing the Time to Develop Them

Kaliym A. Islam
Vice President, DTCC

Background

The Depository Trust & Clearing Corporation (DTCC) is the world's largest post-trade financial services company. Through its subsidiaries, DTCC provides clearance, settlement, and information services for equities, corporate and municipal bonds, unit investment trusts, government and mortgage-backed securities, money market instruments, and over-the-counter derivatives. It also manages transactions between mutual funds and insurance carriers and their respective investors, as well as clearing, settlement and information services for equities, corporate and municipal bonds, government and mortgage-backed securities, money market instruments and over-the-counter derivatives.

The DTCC Learning Group is the team responsible for delivering learning solutions to the employees of the financial industry firms that are the participants or customers of DTCC. These solutions include instructor-led classroom and web-based training, help files, user guides, podcasts, webcasts, e-learning courses, and product simulations.

At the beginning of this project, the DTCC Learning Group was composed of four teams: the learning business consultant group, responsible for all internal customer interface and business analysis; the learning program management group, responsible for delivery of all instructor-led programs; the learning application development services group, responsible for designing and developing all learning solutions; and the learning analytics and technologies group, responsible for all learning technology infrastructure and analytic reporting.

Like most training organizations, the Learning Group employed the ADDIE model for training development. The business consultant group would conduct an initial feasibility or business analysis to ensure that training requests received could be solved via a learning intervention. If the business team felt that a learning intervention was required, the findings would be passed on to applications development, who would conduct a learning analysis and make recommendations for learning solutions. If their recommendation was approved by the internal customer, the application development services team would then build the learning solution. The learning program management group would become involved if instructor-led training was one of the recommendations, and finally, the analytics and technologies group would support all technology requirements and provide usage and survey results.

Over the years, this approach to learning product development had earned DTCC numerous industry awards, including the CLO Learning Elite Top 25, and the Society of Technical Communications International Award. Nevertheless, DTCC Learning Group employees felt that the methodology was too process-oriented and that the ADDIE process limited creativity.

Although internal customers (product managers) consistently rated their satisfaction with the learning group at close to 100 percent, there were whispers that it was taking too long for the organization to deliver learning solutions. Finally, a review of the solutions that the team had actually delivered during the previous year was limited to virtually one type of solution, user guides.

The management team of DTCC Learning Group was unanimous in the belief that the team needed to both adapt its organizational structure and development methodology in order to better meet the needs of the business and address employee engagement issues. As a result, the DTCC learning team adopted Agile as its methodology for developing learning solutions to better enable rapid and iterative development, quick reaction to change, and closer customer collaboration. Implementing Agile necessitated concomitant changes in the organizational structure.

The Agile approach originated in software development. It is based on iterative and incremental development, rather than extensive up-front planning. Requirements and solutions evolve through a series of short development cycles in which continuous feedback and collaboration among cross-functional teams and customers are used to successively develop and refine solutions.

What We Did

The Announcement. The leadership team of DTCC Learning Group knew that organizational restructuring and process reengineering were both major changes that needed to be managed. They felt strongly, however, that both had to be done. It was thus decided that the announcement of the organizational change and the process reengineering would occur at the same time.

Agile Structure		
	Depository Services Learning Domain	**Clearing Services Learning Domain**	**Dedicated Business Learning Domain**
---	---	---	---
Team Structure	• Domain Lead / Product Owner • Instructor / Facilitator • Designer • Develop • Consultant	• Domain Lead / Product Owner • Instructor / Facilitator • Designer • Develop • Consultant	• Domain Lead / Product Owner • Instructor / Facilitator • Designer • Develop • Consultant
Areas Supported	• Asset Servicing • Securities Processing • Settlement • Cross Organizational • NIC Oversight	• Equity Clearing • GSD • MBS • International	• Derivative / Service • Loan / Service • Wealth Management • Insurance • Risk
Technology Services		

Figure D2.1.1. The New Agile Structure of the Learning Group Includes Three Cross-Functional Teams

The first step on the road to improvement was to restructure the organization from one in which designers reported into one silo, instructors into another, and business analysts into a third. The new structure (Figure D2.1.1) consists of teams of designers, instructors, analysts, and technologists for each of the three learning domains. Each team is responsible for all learning support for its specific line of business.

The leadership team was also in agreement that the ADDIE waterfall approach to learning product development was limiting the team's ability to react as quickly as needed to a rapidly changing business environment. With the agreement in place, the date of the reorganization and timing of the agile training were decided.

A mandatory "all hands" meeting was held and the rationale for the changes was communicated to the organization. Without prompting, team members began asking questions. Most were about workflow and process issues. It was explained that the new approach would be one in which each team would decide for themselves how to get the work

done as opposed to our current methodology that was largely engineered by management and pushed down to employees.

The Training. The next step in the process was to ensure that all team members had the tools that they would need to implement this new approach. A vendor was commissioned and everyone in the organization was trained in the Agile methodology via a program that was tailored to the specific needs of DTCC Learning Group.

The Agile Beginnings. Once the DTCC Learning staff completed Agile training, the organization immediately began to implement the approach. While some employees struggled with the transition, most of the training staff embraced the new freedom and flexibility. There were, however, challenges with the transition that included:

- How to translate a language and approach that was meant for software development into something that made sense for learning solution development
- What to do with work that was already in progress
- How to handle work that is not specific to any one line of business

As the teams became more familiar with Agile, these challenges became non-issues. Language that made sense in a learning development environment was substituted for the words that were more appropriate in software development. In-progress work immediately moved under the responsibility of the corresponding learning domain. Team members agreed that as cross-functional requests came into the organizational backlog, the team with the greatest capacity at the time would be responsible.

Results

The early results of the Agile implementation exceeded expectations. The average number of learning assets delivered to customers increased from about twenty per month to thirty-five per month, translating into a 75 percent increase in total learning solutions delivered compared to the same period the previous year (see Figure D2.1.2).

The feedback from both internal customers and DTCC Learning employees has also been glowing. One internal customer praised the "quick turnaround" and "quality of work," another related that his post-Agile experience has been "nothing short of positive."

Eight months after the Agile implementation, the improvements were even more profound. Nearly one hundred more learning assets were delivered to customers after implementing Agile, compared to the number delivered during the same time period of the previous year (Figure D2.1.3).

Monthly Comparison

	Duration	Assets Delivered	Monthly Average	
Pre Agile implementation (Waterfall)	7 Months	139	19	
Post Agile	2 Months	69	34	75% Improvement

Figure D2.1.2. Pre- and Post-Agile Implementation Results

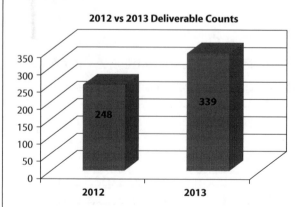

2012 vs 2013 Deliverable Counts

(Bar chart: 2012 = 248, 2013 = 339)

Figure D2.1.3. Almost One Hundred More Learning Assets Were Delivered in the Same Time Period After Implementing Agile

Not only were more learning assets delivered, but the learning assets were larger in terms of the number of work units they contained. Figure D2.1.4 shows that the number of work units delivered from year to year increased almost ten times, from 394 in Q1 2012 to 3,604 during Q1 2013.

Perhaps the most telling result of the Agile adoption was the year-over-year comparison of the types of learning assets delivered. In Q1 2012, the teams almost exclusively delivered articles or procedural documentation as learning assets to customers. During the same period in 2013, the teams delivered a much more diverse set of learning solutions, including webinars, webcasts, product simulations, and instructor-led training (Figure D2.1.5).

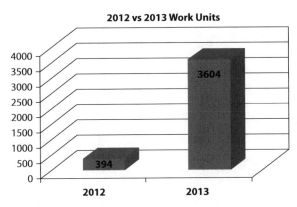

Figure D2.1.4. Work Units Delivered in Q1 2013 (Post-Agile) Versus Q1 2012 (Pre-Agile)

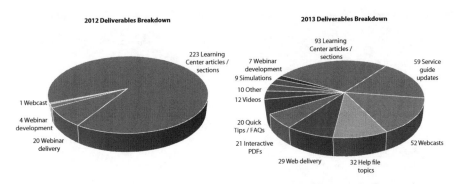

Figure D2.1.5. Comparison of Types of Deliverables Before and After Agile Implementation

The quantitative results from the year-to-year comparisons indicated that the Agile approach for learning product development worked well, dramatically increasing both the number and variety of solutions provided by the same size team.

Bottom Line. The DTCC Learning Group has substantially increased the number of learning solutions that it has been able to produce as a result of adopting Agile as a development methodology. At the same time, the team has decreased the amount of time required to deliver these solutions. Moreover, the feedback from customers and employees since the transition has been extremely positive.

Advice to Colleagues

- Ensure that the learning organization is structured in a way that best supports an Agile approach. Functional silos can make an Agile implementation difficult or impossible.
- Make the change immediately. Phasing in Agile will cause the team members to revert back to old habits.
- Resist the impulse to help. Stepping in to help teams as they try to understand and adapt to Agile may undermine what you're trying to accomplish.
- The team must know that they are empowered to make decisions and that they ultimately have ownership for the results.

Case D2.2

How We Use Alumni to Help Set Expectations for New Program Participants and Their Leaders

Wanda J. Hayes

Director, Learning and Organizational Development,
Emory University

Background

Emory University, a top-ranked national private research institution, comprises nine schools and colleges. The main campus in Atlanta, Georgia, is home to Emory College of Arts and Sciences, the Laney Graduate School, and six professional schools. Emory maintains an uncommon balance for an institution of its standing: our scholars and experts generate more than $500 million in research funding annually, while also maintaining a traditional emphasis on teaching. Emory has more than 14,000 students, and more than 13,000 faculty and staff (not including the Emory Healthcare employees).

The Learning and Organizational Development (LOD) department is part of the human resources division and provides numerous development and training opportunities for the university's faculty and staff. In addition to the general enrollment courses, LOD provides several programs that target specific employee groups (e.g., executive leaders, managers, supervisors, and administrative professionals). Participants are nominated and/or apply for acceptance into the programs and move through them in cohort groups over an eight- to ten-month time frame, during which they participate in sequenced classes and assessments and in action learning projects.

In order to help the participants and their leaders make the commitment required by the program, it is important for them to understand what they can expect to gain as well as what is expected of them. We wanted participants and leaders to understand that the programs were more than a series of classes in which they could learn new skills and tools; the programs are also an experience that will require them to enhance their level of self-awareness and apply the skills and tools they obtain.

What We Did

We enhanced the orientation sessions that we offered to participants and their leaders so that they would have a clear understanding of the level of commitment required and the type of achievements they could expect. One example of how we have expanded on the orientation process is the website we developed for the Excellence Through Leadership program, which targets high-performing, high-potential director-level and above administrative leaders.

On the Learning and Organizational Development website we provide information about the program, including the areas of focus, how it supports the university's mission, and expectations of the leadership development activities (Exhibit D2.2.1). A "Program at a Glance" is also available for review.

Exhibit D2.2.1. Overview of the Excellence Through Leadership Program from the LOD Website

Having conducted success case interviews with alumni of the program, we also knew that some of the best information about the program was the positive impact that it had had on prior participants. In order to capitalize on their experiences, we videotaped testimonials from two previous participants and added the links to our website (Exhibit D2.2.2). We also incorporate the videos into the orientation sessions prior to the start of the program.

Exhibit D2.2.2. An Example of a Testimonial from a Prior Participant on the Website

One of the critical aspects of the Excellence Through Leadership program is the action learning project. For each cohort of participants, there are typically two strategic-level group projects. The projects have a university-wide focus and are designed so that they can be implemented, in whole or in part, within the program timeframe. The projects provide the participants with a means to incorporate and demonstrate what they have learned in a manner that can have a lasting impact on the university and also give the participants significant visibility.

Excellence Through Leadership action learning project presentations are videotaped and are also provided on the program website (Exhibit D2.2.3). These presentations are yet another mechanism for demonstrating to upcoming participants and their leaders what is expected as a result of their learning and application in the program. The videos are also used by current participants as they prepare their

Exhibit D2.2.3. Learning Project Presentations Are Posted on the Program Website

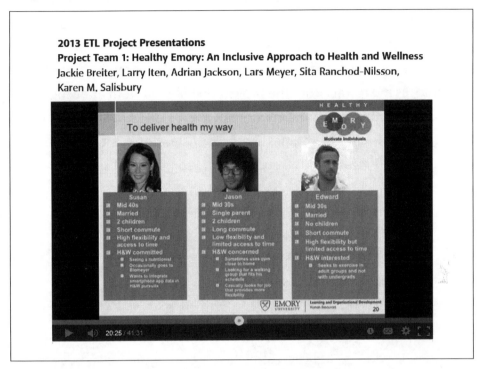

own presentations, as a way of understanding how to scope projects, examples of previous research, and how to present their findings.

Results

We have found that "a video is worth a thousand words." While we in Learning and Organizational Development can set the stage for expectations of individuals coming into our programs, the testimonials of actual past participants provide a richness and authenticity that cannot be matched. The videos set an expectation of what a participant can hope to gain and what a participant's leader can expect as outcomes from the program.

Additionally, by placing action learning project presentations on the website, potential participants can see a realistic preview of the type of work that will result from their participation in the program. It also provides guidance to those who are in the program as they work on their projects.

Participants and their leaders have indicated that the testimonials help them understand that application of the program's content is expected, as are results from the project and impact from applying the concepts after the program. Testimonials are utilized similarly for our Manager Development Program, Supervisor Development Program, Administrative Professionals Development Program, and Mentor Emory.

Advice to Colleagues
- Capture stories of success and achievement from past program participants.
- Add video testimonials to your orientation sessions.
- Make videos easily accessible to new and potential participants and to their leaders.
- Share videos of achievement and results, such as project presentations.
- Prepare new participants to take action and to expect to achieve results.
- Measure results and share them with leaders.

Case D2.3

How We Build Enterprise High-Potential Talent at Agilent

Mike Girone

Director, Global Learning and Leadership Development,

Agilent Technologies, Inc.

Background

As the world's premier measurement company, Agilent offers the broadest range of innovative measurement solutions in the industry. With revenues of $6.9 billion, our 20,500 employees serve the needs of customers in over one hundred countries. Agilent's singular focus on measurement helps scientists, researchers, and engineers in the electronics and bio-analytical industries address their toughest challenges with precision and confidence with products and services that make a real difference in the lives of people everywhere. One of our critical success enablers is our ability to develop best-in-industry leadership, as measured by our employees and business results.

Agilent's Global Learning and Leadership Development team works to accelerate and deepen the development of successful leaders at all levels who drive our business strategies and culture forward. A key development program for Agilent is our Emerging Leaders Program (ELP), implemented in 2011. The ELP is a six-month leadership development process designed to identify Agilent's emerging leaders and prepare them for a trajectory of future high-impact leadership.

Agilent has a history of high-quality, accelerated development programs. In 2008, in the midst of the economic downturn, we paused to rethink and refocus our accelerated development programs, with a specific focus on "What are the most critical business requirements for future leaders?" Up to that point, we had been developing a high-potential talent pool either for promotional opportunities or expanded roles based on the individual's aspirations and past performance. With the Emerging Leaders Program, we narrowed that focus to promotable high-potential individuals based on strategic business need. This means that our business strategy is now the key driver for where we place our talent development investments.

What We Did

We instituted several actions to ensure that we met our stated intention for the Emerging Leaders Program.

Active Senior Sponsorship. We wanted to ensure that nominees for the ELP program had sponsorship at the highest levels of the organization. The nomination process was designed such that, in addition to the nominee's direct manager, there must also be a senior leader sponsor. This senior leader must endorse the nominee as a high-potential candidate, having the ability, engagement, and aspiration to rise to and succeed in a future leadership role.

Exhibit D2.3.1. Part of the Nomination Process Form Highlighting the Need for Senior Leader Sponsorship

Emerging Leaders Program – PARTICIPANT NOMINATIONS
*Submit summary of the **business need** for talent and identify the nominees for ELP.*

NOMINATION CRITERIA			
Business Need	**Promotable**	**Sponsorship**	**Aspiration for Promotion**
1. Describe the **strategic business need.** Use SPR to identify critical initiative. 2. How was the nominee identified (e.g. through Leadership Supply / LOR talent review / other)?	**The potential next assignments* that you could envision for this individual (in the next 12–24 months).** **with promotion and job level change.*	**Name of Sr. Mgr. or Exec who endorses participant as Hi Po candidate,** i.e., with the ability, engagement, and aspiration to rise and succeed in a more senior, critical leadership role. **Sponsor meets bi-monthly with participant for career guidance.**	Has the employee demonstrated behavior or expressed the desire for promotion and broader responsibility? *[Yes, or have not asked yet].*

As shown in Exhibit D2.3.1, the senior leader sponsor not only plays a role at the time of nomination, but is expected to stay actively engaged through bi-monthly meetings with the participant for career guidance.

The nomination process is carried out by the businesses, with a review by the leadership team of each operating unit, and a final review by the CEO, COO, and senior vice president of HR. This further ensures a

Exhibit D2.3.2. An Excerpt from the Commitment Form for Emerging Leadership Managers and Coaches

---

Agilent Emerging Leaders Program
Manager and Sponsor Commitment Form

The ELP program is a journey for the both the participant and the participant's manager supported by the sponsor. Leadership development programs yield the highest impact for participants, the organization, and Agilent when they are all engaged in the process.

We will partner with you to achieve this goal and will provide detailed information throughout the program as needed. Contact the Next Generation Leadership team with any questions or concerns.

Commitment and actions throughout the program

. . .

---

level of sponsorship among the executive team for these high-potential candidates.

Manager and Senior Sponsor Commitment. Both the direct manager and the senior leader sponsor are asked to review and commit to a series of actions via a Commitment Agreement (Exhibit D2.3.2) that details their role in supporting the participant before, during, and after the formal ELP program. Responsibilities include active support and coaching, meeting and check-in frequency, methods to increase the participant's visibility within the business, and reward and recognition ideas.

Direct Manager Candidate Enrollment Checklist. Once a candidate is accepted into the ELP program, the direct manager begins specific conversations around aspirations, development goals, and career objectives. A Candidate Enrollment Checklist (Exhibit 2.3.3) guides the manager in these initial conversations.

Exhibit D2.3.3. Excerpt from Emerging Leaders Program Checklist

---

This checklist is specifically for those who have been selected to be part of the Emerging Leaders Program.

Program Participation Checklist

❏   1. **Review** the <u>ELP Overview Presentation</u> about the program
❏   2. **Review** the <u>Participant Commitment Handout.</u>
❏   3. **Meet with your manager:**

    ○ Have a development conversation and review your aspirations, development goals and career objectives.
    ○ Discuss how the program would enable your possible career objectives and readiness for roles you might play in Agilent's business needs.

Business Sponsor/Liaison. Another key component of the ELP program is the business project (Exhibit D2.3.4). Designed as an action-learning project, the business project is based around a current business challenge with an active project sponsor. This project sponsor and project liaison, in addition to the senior sponsor and direct manager, play integral roles in the development process, providing coaching and feedback in the context of the overall business situation.

ELP Board of Directors. The senior sponsor, business sponsor and liaison, and the direct manager all form members of the ELP participant's "board of directors" (Exhibit D2.3.5). This model helps to solidify the ongoing coaching and support that is needed as the candidates progress through the Emerging Leaders Program as well as into their ongoing careers.

Exhibit D2.3.4. An Example of the Timeline for the Emerging Leaders Program Business Project

ELP 2012 Project Purpose, Timeline and Roles
Purpose of ELP Business Projects

The purpose of Business Projects in the ELP program is to provide an **action learning opportunity** to practice strategic and leadership skills, gain knowledge about Agilent businesses and contribute to Agilent's **results.**

Business Driven Action Learning Projects focus on achieving "best in class" or **competitive differentiation** in a specific area, process, or business, and provide an opportunity for ELP participants to learn skills required of integrating managers.

Projects Timeline

	MAY *LAUNCH*	JUNE *MEET LIVE*	JULY	AUG	END SEPT *RECOMMEND*	OCT *RESULTS*
TEAM FOCUS	Launch projects Select leader Create team charter	Attend **Strategic Leadership Week** in Santa Clara (June 11–15) Refine charter and do stakeholder analysis	Team working sessions	Teams present progress to date at Virtual Project Reviews (**VPRs**) (not for Liaison / Sponsor)	Team presents recommendations to Sponsor and other stakeholders	Team presents results to ELP judges at **Strategic Innovation Week** October 8–12 in Santa Clara
LIAISON & SPONSOR SUPPORT	Meet with team and/or members as needed to develop charter Provide information for charter	Meet with team in Santa Clara If available, June 14 for dinner and June 15 AM panel and working session	Continue to support team with regular* meetings and feedback *Liaison on weekly basis and with Sponsor monthly		Attend presentation, provide feedback, and identify key execs to include for the meeting	Support team by attending presentations and debriefing project learning / process. Santa Clara October 11 including dinner

Exhibit D2.3.5. An Excerpt from the ELP Participant's Guide Illustrating the Personal Board of Directors

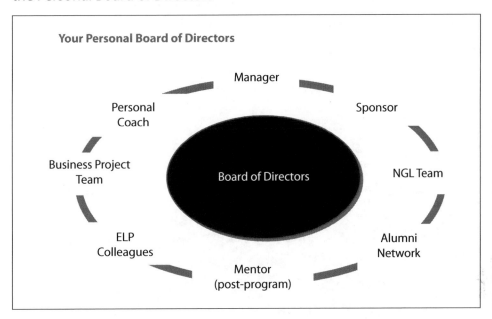

Results

Since the program is designed to create a strategic pool of high-potential leaders ready to step into new or expanded roles, a key measure of its success is the rate of such promotions. Every quarter, we report on ELP participant promotion to the business, with a stated goal that ≥ 85 percent of participants will be promoted within twenty-four months of completing the program. By early 2013, 55 percent of the 2011 cohort had been promoted, as well as 19 percent of the 2012 cohort. Emerging Leadership Program participants are promoted into management positions at six to eight times the rate of managers in the company overall.

Tracking and reporting the progress of our high-potential talent in the businesses on a quarterly basis has increased the focus and added value to our overall talent conversations.

Finally, we conducted a post-ELP program survey to capture feedback from participants. In response to the question "I was given support by my manager or organization to participate fully in the program," 81 percent strongly agreed and another 13 percent agreed.

Advice to Colleagues

- When building a program to support accelerated talent development, alignment to strategic business needs is critical.
- Active engagement of the senior executive team in reviewing and tracking the emerging leadership participants before, during, and after the program is key.
- While the support of the direct manager is essential, a broader support structure, or "board of directors," helps ensure visibility and sponsorship for future opportunities as well as continued coaching and development for each high-potential candidate.
- HR can provide data on the mobility of the ELP participants, but the talent is owned by the business and must be actively managed by the business.

Case D2.4

How We Moved the Finish Line for Leadership Development

Justin Keeton

Manager of Organizational Effectiveness, Development and Training, Methodist Le Bonheur Healthcare

Background

Methodist Le Bonheur Healthcare is an integrated, not-for-profit healthcare delivery system based in Memphis, Tennessee. Our seven-hospital system includes home health services, outpatient surgery centers, minor medical centers, diagnostic centers, sleep centers, and a hospice residence. Rated as the number one hospital in the region by *U.S. News and World Report*, Methodist received accolades in twelve specialties. We have more than ten thousand associates in both clinical and non-clinical roles; over nine hundred are in leadership roles.

Employee engagement in a high-quality work environment is a high priority at Methodist Le Bonheur, because, as Len Berry, distinguished professor of marketing at Texas A&M University, succinctly put it: "The patient's experience cannot exceed that of the associates' experience."

We recognize that leaders are key to creating the positive work environment that produces outstanding care. For that reason, we closely monitor employee engagement on an annual associate feedback survey and we have been working hard to create a coaching culture throughout our organization.

A key component of that effort has been a two-day "Coaching Clinic" program for our leaders based on the Coaching Core Essentials™ program developed by Coach U. While our leadership classes got great post-class review, we never really knew if the information, knowledge, or skills were being transferred to the workplace.

What We Did

After learning about the 6Ds, we decided it was time to "move the finish line" for our leadership development programs. So we piloted a new finish line for our internal coaching certification program.

Historically, participants would "graduate" from this two-day course, pick up their certificates, and disappear into our organization as soon as the class ended. After becoming familiar with the 6Ds methodology, we realized that the simple act of picking up a certificate and graduating directly after the class communicated to our participants that they were finished learning. This couldn't have been further from the truth—they had only just begun!

What's different now? We use two main strategies to ensure that the knowledge and skills are transferred from the program to the workplace; that's our "condition of satisfaction."

First, prior to leaving the course, each participant establishes two goals for transferring and applying their learning to the workplace.

- These goals are then emailed to their supervisors, together with recommendations of how to support transferring the skills.

- Participants have to participate in a SharePoint discussion about their goals and progress with their course cohorts. This allows us to see how each participant has progressed toward meeting his or her goals, as well as how he or she has applied the skills. The SharePoint discussion group is open for three weeks following the course, allowing each participant to give and receive feedback and coaching.

The second requirement to receive credit for completing the program is for each participant to take a computer-based training module that reinforces key concepts. The module includes a learning assessment that tests knowledge of the coaching principles.

Only when both of these requirements have been met (SharePoint discussion and successful completion of the online module and test) does the participant receive his or her certificate, continuing education units, and coaching reference book—typically four weeks post-course.

Recognizing that the post-class activities took time and to underscore that they are really part of the program, we actually shortened the in-class time by half a day so that the total time commitment is similar. Culturally, this new finish line has been a huge paradigm shift for us, but one that has already begun to pay dividends.

Results

To gauge whether the program and follow-through were having an effect, we analyzed the results from the annual associate feedback survey. When we compared the pre- and post-training results for leaders who had participated in the Coaching Clinic (with the new finish line), we found statistically significant improvement in the ratings related to coaching competencies. The program is having a measurable effect on the associates' work environment.

Further evidence that the change is having an effect include the change in enrollment. Given the nature of the material, we limit each coaching clinic to sixteen participants. Previously, we typically had eight to ten participants per class. Since we established the new finish line and publicized the effect it was having on engagement scores, we now fill each class and usually have a waiting list of six to ten. Demand is such that we recently asked for, and received, funding to certify additional facilitators.

Additionally, we were pleasantly surprised and gratified when the COO listed the Coaching Clinic as one of the organization's top five leader accountability and development initiatives during a recent five-hundred-person quality leadership meeting.

Advice to Colleagues
- Rethink the finish line for your key strategic programs.
- Stop sending people the wrong message ("you're done") by awarding credits and certificates at the end of class.
- Engage participants' managers and support them in practicing new skills back on the job.
- Be patient with these and other changes. Changing leaders' attitudes about new finish lines for learning won't happen overnight. Explain the "why" and the benefits of feedback.

Case D2.5

How We Enhanced and Stretched Our First-Level Managers' Learning Experience

Christopher Goh Soon Keat

Director, Global Learning and Leadership Development, Agilent Technologies, Inc.

Background

As the world's premier measurement company, Agilent offers the broadest range of innovative measurement solutions in the industry. With revenue of $6.9B, our 20,500 employees serve the needs of customers in more than one hundred countries. Agilent's singular focus on measurement helps scientists, researchers, and engineers in the electronics and bio-analytical industries address their toughest challenges with precision and confidence with products and services that make a real difference in the lives of people everywhere. One of our critical success enablers lies in our ability to develop best-in-industry leadership, as measured by our employees and business results.

In 2007, a significant leadership gap was identified among the first-level manager population. On average, each manager manages ten employees. However, without future promotion to higher levels of leadership, the opportunities for continuing their development were scarce. These leaders were not keeping pace in their development with middle- and senior-level managers.

At that time, there was already a core leadership program in place to develop our middle- and senior-level managers, but there was no core leadership program to develop our first-level managers, who are accountable for managing and influencing the results of sixteen thousand employees across Agilent. To fill this gap, we designed a three-month leadership development program that has since been delivered across Agilent with great success.

What We Did

Instead of looking at training as just being a one-time learning event, we wanted to enhance and stretch our participants' learning experience, especially in allowing time for them to apply and transfer what they have learned back to their workplace after they have completed their classroom training.

We shifted our thinking and approach from designing a one-time training event to three phases of learning (see Exhibit D2.5.1), including pre-event, three-day classroom training, and post-event activities. As the figure illustrates, we utilize a variety of learning approaches to deliver a high-impact blended development experience and also to accommodate the various learning styles of our participants.

Exhibit D2.5.1. The Agenda for the Complete Learning Experience for First-Level Manager

First Level Manager Program Design at a Glance

Pre-Event	Day 1	Day 2	Day 3	Post-Event
• **Kick-off Webinar** 3 weeks prior. • **Hold conversations with team members** regarding past learning and growth. • Contract with manager to **select a Leadership Challenge** you are facing that is important to your organization's customers. • Complete **Financial Acumen e-Learning modules.**	The role of the First Level Manager at Agilent *(Senior Leader)* Collaboration to solve Leadership Challenges ——— How to build the Voice of the Customer into your work and the work of your team Improving speed and effectiveness of decision making ——— Creating and building winning teams	***Driving Business Results*** Year 1 Simulation Know-how session: *Profitable growth within Agilent's Operating Model* Year 2 Simulation Know-how session: *ROIC Drivers* Year 3 Simulation Actions to embed Agilent Operating Model in your work	The Art of MBO in the midst of change: Aligning team objectives to Strategic Intent Talent management: How to develop the right set of skills to achieve results ——— Personal plan for action and peer support structure ——— Share Key Insights ——— Kick off post-event program	**Post-Event** • **Collaboration groups** meet 5x/10 weeks; accountable for supporting each other to achieve stated objectives • **Meet with your team** to review insights and objectives • **FMP "Virtual Collaboration Space"** • **Meet with your manager** to assess progress toward meeting stated objectives

Before the three-day classroom training, participants attend a kick-off webinar in which the facilitator discusses the program's intentions, design, and learning objectives. He or she also explains the pre-event assignments they need to complete before coming for the classroom training. The pre-event assignments include completing some e-learning modules and selecting a significant leadership challenge to discuss with their managers and bring to the classroom training. We have found that these pre-training activities have helped to build intentionality and create greater learner focus and motivation for the training program.

For the classroom training, we have designed a variety of learning experiences, which include simulations, group discussions and presentations, dialogue with Agilent's senior leaders, feedback sessions, and personal action planning. Throughout the entire three-day training, participants are continually reminded of how they could apply what they have learned to resolving their personal leadership challenges.

To ensure transfer back to the workplace, we create a post-training collaboration structure in which participants who share similar leadership challenges will be grouped together in "pods." These pods continue to meet for the next ten weeks to help each other resolve their common leadership challenges. We also use Microsoft SharePoint to support the pods' collaborative activities and provide post-training resources to the participants. Exhibit D2.5.2 shows our SharePoint site for this program.

At the end of the ten weeks of collaboration, the program facilitator brings the program to completion by facilitating a closing webinar in which each of the pod groups is asked to share their learning, insights, actions taken, and results achieved for the past ten weeks. Many participants have commented that the collaboration has helped cement what they have learned from the program.

Exhibit D2.5.2. A Screen Capture from the SharePoint Site for the First-Level Managers Program

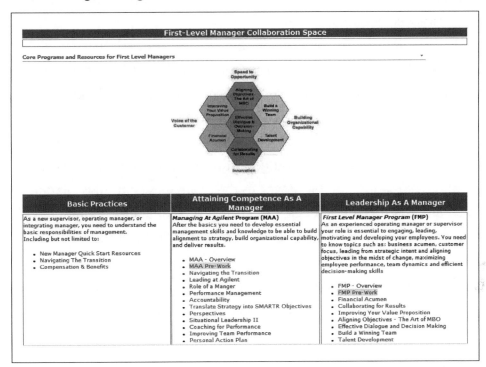

Results

We measure the outcome of our efforts through the following approaches:

1. An online Level 1 evaluation survey following the three-day classroom training
2. An impact report collected from all the pod groups at the end of their ten-week collaboration to measure behavioral change and business results
3. An organization-wide "leadership audit" survey, which is also used to measure the bench strength of our leaders

The scores from our organization-wide leadership audit survey are one of Agilent's four measures of success. Since 2007, the organization has seen a rise in all the indexes found in the leadership audit survey, especially in the areas of customer orientation, speed and decisiveness, and employee engagement.

For example, the employee engagement index has risen from approximately 65 percent in 2007 to 90 percent in 2012. Given that our first-level managers directly manage over 80 percent of the total employee population, and that the first-level managers program is aimed at driving the behavioral indicators covered in the leadership audit, this program has contributed significantly to the improvement in employee engagement. Moreover, as the program's content is aligned to our leadership competencies, the first-level managers program has also helped our organization build critical capabilities to ensure our current and future success.

Other anecdotal evidence we have collected are exhaustive and cannot be represented here in their entirety, but below are some representative success stories (direct quotes from participants):

- "Completed project and calculated savings of $17.2 million over three years."
- "The biggest benefit that I see is that there is a real collaborative effort from all my peers, different points of view but same bottom line, which is quality orders for [our] customers. This has sparked 'out of the box'" thinking. When we hear 'that's how we always did it'. . . that statement is an indicator to start asking 'Why?'"
- "I took my second-level manager to visit two global accounts to discuss customer needs in their global business environment. I discussed my leadership challenge with this manager and suggested for key global accounts we set up a team quota and team selling. He has taken this to the worldwide staff for review. More directly, I have set up a rigorous approach to working with global accounts. I have set a higher bar for myself and my team to communicate early and often. I

have put a stake in the ground to set expectations about what work is needed in the U.S. and to get commitment that the Asia team agrees that we need to work together."

- "Increasing market share, got the word out fast, stayed focused on the goal, and we started getting competitive orders that would have slipped by. Last count, was four (sales) for certain totaling $500K."

Advice to Colleagues
- Design your training program as a continuous learning process rather than a single learning event.
- Stretch your participants' learning experience by building in pre-training, actual training, and post-event activities as part of your program design.
- Where possible and appropriate, incorporate various learning approaches so as to enhance your participants' learning experience and to accommodate the different learning styles of your participants.
- Leverage available social learning technology to foster knowledge sharing and collaborative learning.

Case D2.6

How We Bring Employees Up to Speed in Record Time Using the Learning Path Methodology

Steve Rosenbaum

President of Learning Paths International and author

of *Learning Paths: How to Increase Profits by Reducing the Time It Takes to Get Employees Up to Speed*

About Learning Paths

Learning Paths is a proven process improvement methodology that dramatically reduces the time to proficiency. It has been applied to more than four hundred different functions in eight countries. In each instance, time to proficiency was shortened by 30 percent or more. The Learning Paths Methodology (Figure D2.6.1) identifies and drives out time and waste and reduces variability by applying accelerated learning best practices.

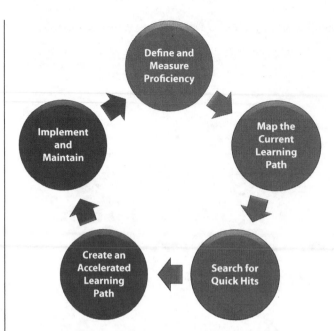

Figure D2.6.1. The Learning Paths Methodology

Background

An example of the application of the Learning Paths approach is illustrated by an initiative developed by a partnership that included AXIS Minnesota, Learning Paths International, the Minnesota Department of Economic Development, and Century College. AXIS Minnesota provides residential care for the severally disabled, including twenty-four-hour nursing care in Ramsey County, Minnesota. The initial project focused on support service aides who provide daily care for residents with a wide range of both medical and social challenges.

The goal of this initiative was to speed up the on-boarding and training of new employees to meet the growth plans set out by AXIS Minnesota's leadership. At the start of this initiative, it took around nine months for support service aides to become fully proficient. Proficiency was defined as providing the required level of care for range of clients with different needs. Proficiency was measured through direct observation by superiors who were considered experts.

In addition, there was a strong desire to reduce turnover which, at the start of the project, exceeded 50 percent in the first year. High turnover had a negative impact on resident care, hiring and training costs, and on the willingness of the staff to train new hires. When the existing staff wasn't convinced a new hire would stay, they were less willing to spend time training him or her on the job, which increased the probability that the person would leave. In our experience, the faster employees are up-to-speed, the more likely they are to stay because they gain the confidence that they can do the job and they fit in better with their co-workers.

What We Did

1. The first step was to form a "learning path team" of the key stakeholders, including HR, supervisors, and managers. This team was then trained in the Learning Path Methodology and worked together on this initiative. The team provided the content and expertise required for the project. In addition, involving the key stakeholders from the onset created the buy-in and ownership required for success.

2. The second step was to build a proficiency definition, which included a series of statements that described the measurable results and observable actions that define proficiency (the ability to perform independently to an appropriate level of quality for the position). The proficiency definition also served as the ongoing assessment tool. The proficiency definition was based on the tasks the support service aides performed. The team identified more than ninety-seven distinct tasks performed by support service aides.

3. The third step involved quantifying the current time to proficiency to provide a baseline for improvement. This was done through reviewing historical data and interviewing key staff and managers.

4. The fourth step was to map out a current learning path. In other words, mapping all the learning activities from day one to proficiency, which took around nine months. Learning activities included both formal and informal learning. The learning path at the beginning of the project was a very traditional approach that consisted of classroom training for required medical topics, a corporate orientation, followed by unstructured hands-on training provided by supervisors and co-workers.

5. The fifth step involved searching for quick hits. Quick hits are improvement ideas that can shrink time to proficiency through changes to the learning path. Quick hits are usually low cost and require limited development. Altogether, the team identified more than fifty quick hits, the most important ones involved:

   • Structuring and formalizing hands-on training
   • Integrating the proficiency definition as an on-the-job assessment tool
   • Reorganizing the path so that medical topics were delivered just in time in order to dramatically increase retention
   • Finding ways to make new hires immediately helpful for existing staff so that they were more likely to help in the training
   • Providing more real-time experience earlier so that new hires could determine whether they really wanted to do the job

6. The sixth step was to map a new learning path that included the quick hits structured around an organizing principle. An organizing principle allows training to be more like how people really learn versus what's easy to teach. In this case, the learning path was changed from a topic-by-topic approach to one organized by resident type. For example, on the old path you would learn about helping residents with showering. Then as you went from resident to resident, you would have to remember or figure out what to do in each case. In reality, helping a person shower is very different

with a fully ambulatory resident who could talk compared to a paraplegic resident who is unable to speak.

On the new path, new hires start with the relatively simpler situation: a resident who was fully ambulatory and can talk and learn each of the care tasks for that kind of patient. When they reached proficiency with that resident, they move on to the next level of resident. The task force defined four levels of patients, from the easiest to assist to the most challenging. A support service aide was considered fully proficient when he or she could correctly perform all the key tasks on all four levels of patient (see Table D2.6.1).

7. The seventh step was to create an implementation and maintenance plan that installed the new learning path, measured results, and provided a process for ongoing improvement. A key part of

Table D2.6.1. An Example of a Proficiency Checklist for Support Service Aides

Task	Level 1	Level 2	Level 3	Level 4
Showering				
Feeding				
Medication				
Transportation				
IV Infusion				
Meal Preparation				
Hygiene				
Safety				
Communicating (Family)				

developing new training was to provide an instructionally sound method for on-the-job training that made sure that training was consistent no matter who delivered it.

Results

Results were measured using the proficiency definition as the assessment tool. This assessment tool was integrated into the daily care plan for each resident that the new support service aide would work with. The time to proficiency for new hires at the start of the project was compared to the time to proficiency for new hires as they completed the revised learning path.

The results were dramatic. Using the learning path methodology to redesign the complete learning experience for new hires, the team was able to reduce the time to proficiency from nine months to less than two months—the probationary period for new hires.

Simultaneously, retention improved from approximately 50 percent to over 95 percent. The cost savings were significant. Most importantly, shortening the time to proficiency contributed to better resident care. The satisfaction of the residents' families with the care provided also improved.

Keys to Success

- Involve a team of stakeholders and subject-matter experts to reduce research time and to gain support and consensus for the project.
- Start with a proficiency definition and then build the training to reach proficiency as fast as possible.
- Move away from topic-by-topic design. Find an organizing principle that integrates how the job is really done; incorporate accelerated learning principles.

- Involve a team of stakeholders to provide critical information and to build ownership.
- Eliminate the "nice to know" and even the "need to know"; teach people to do what they need to do.
- Ensure that there is a plan for all the essential learning activities (such as hands-on training by more experienced workers); leave nothing to chance.

Advice to Colleagues

- Learning is a process rather than a one-time event. Once you map out a learning process, you can apply process improvement tools to reduce time, waste, and variability.
- Knowing and doing are two very different things. The most valuable learning happens when you focus on doing.
- Retention goes way up when you make training just in time and get employees up to speed faster. This means training people when they are going to use it, rather than when it's convenient to teach.
- Ask top performers *how* they learned, not just *what* they learned. They often have a unique perspective that is very different than a typical teaching process.
- If you don't have the training or experience to do valid measurements, involve others in your oraganization who are trained in measurement and statistics. You can usually find them in the quality department.

Case D2.7

How We Designed a Complete Experience for Our Signature Induction Program "SteerIn"

Ishita Bardhan and Kanika Sharma

Assistant General Manager, Learning and Development, and Senior Manager, Learning and Development, Management Development Centre of Excellence, Tata Motors Academy

Background

Tata Motors Limited is India's largest automobile company, the world's fourth largest truck manufacturer, and the world's third largest bus manufacturer. In 2011, Tata Motors articulated a new Human Capital Strategy to help us achieve our aspirations in an ever-more-competitive global market. One of the key levers of that strategy is talent and leadership development. Tata Motors Academy was established to prepare employees to meet the challenges of the future and achieve the strategic objectives of the organization.

The absence of a uniform induction program for new employees was identified as one of the biggest gaps in our efforts. Inductions were conducted sporadically and independently by various departments.

These were more of an orientation to that particular function, rather than to the company as a whole. Failing to provide new employees with a complete view of the organization, its values, and its business fostered a "siloed" culture that negatively impacted performance.

We designed a company-wide, signature induction program called **SteerIn** that included a distinctive logo (see Exhibit D2.7.1) and branding to give it a strong identity in the organization.

Exhibit D2.7.1. A Distinctive Logo and Brand Were Created to Give the Program a Strong Identity

The underlying requirements of SteerIn are

- New employees should be proud that they have joined one of the Tata Group's flagship companies. The Tata Group is one of the oldest and most-respected business houses in India, with a rich heritage and history.
- The new employee needs to understand the automobile industry and the auto business in India.
- The new employee needs to appreciate how the various key functions, like manufacturing, research, and commercial operations, contribute to the shared success of the organization.
- The program must be interesting and emotionally engaging to anchor the employee to the company.

This signature program had to be designed to the last detail. Every element—from content, to giveaways, activities, seating arrangements, and so forth—had to be standardized and checklist-driven to ensure that every part of the organization would conduct it in the same manner and as intended.

What We Did

We used the 6Ds Planning Wheel to understand the business objectives of the program for identifying the instructional strategy, method, and media for the program (Exhibit D2.7.2).

Exhibit D2.7.2. Summary of Planning Wheel for SteerIn Induction Program

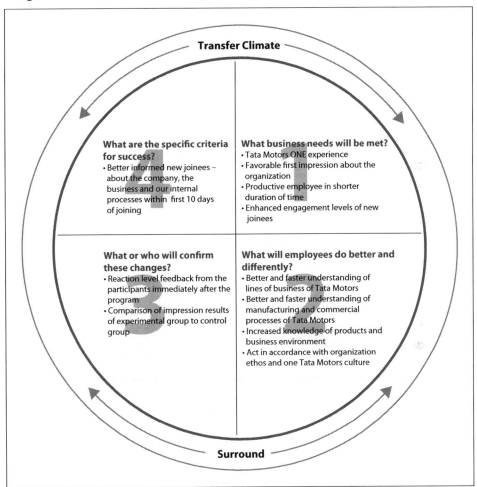

The required job performance expected from the induction was mostly around enabling new employees to be productive as quickly as possible. We followed the steps outlined below to deliver the content in

a way that not only enhanced their recall, but also facilitated their ability to apply it.

The entire induction program was broken down into logical clusters of information and modules.

1. The instructional objectives for each module were defined based on the desired business outcomes.
2. Appropriate instructional strategies were chosen for each module, based on the learning and performance objectives expected.
3. Finally, a list of instructional modalities, exercises, experiential learning, and support required was drawn to enable application (Exhibit D2.7.3).

Exhibit D2.7.3. The Four Modules of the SteerIn Induction Program

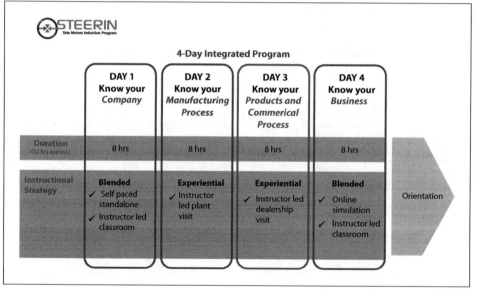

The key objectives and elements of each module are described below.

Module 1: Know Your Company

1. Creating an emotional connection of the new employees with the organization so that they appreciate the history /ethos that defines the Tata Group.

2. Establishing pride by equipping the new employees with basic information about the organization, the norms, values, some HR policies, and processes.
3. Instructional methods include various puzzles, such as matching of names of subsidiary companies with their functions, that provide an element of kinesthetic learning for participants.

Module 2: Know Your Manufacturing Process

1. Equipping new employees with basic information about the manufacturing processes.
2. Giving them a first-hand overview through a guided tour of a manufacturing facility.
3. The tour is made more competitive and interesting by giving participants a set of questions that require them to dig out the answers during the tour. A collaboration game is used as an exercise toward the end of Module 2 to impress upon the new employees the criticality of collaboration in a complex manufacturing facility.

Module 3: Know Your Products and Commercial Processes

1. Helping the new employee appreciate the impact of the sales event and the role of our channel partners.
2. Helping improve product knowledge. Several games (puzzles and Housie [the Indian version of bingo or tombola]) are included to ensure that we are involving as many senses as possible in learning about our products. These games are also used to induce a certain level of healthy competition among participants.

Module 4: Know Your Business

1. Enhancing the understanding and appreciation of key business drivers for the automobile industry.
2. Building an appreciation of the importance of all parts of the organization and their criticality in being able to sell in the market.

3. Convincing employees to look at Tata Motors as their own business, and not just as a job in a department where they are hired.

Module 4 is the showstopper in the whole curriculum. This is the only induction program we know of in India that uses a business simulation with new hires. The participants operate in teams that represent different auto manufacturing companies. They compete with each other a simulation of the actual market dynamics. The company team that makes the most profits wins.

Not only is this a high-energy and high-engagement activity, but it leaves the new employees wowed as they begin to understand the nuances of the industry in a very hands-on manner. This has proven to be an amazing, cost-effective, and impactful module with which to complete the induction program.

Results

At Tata Motors, we strongly believe that participants' perceptions of the program's *utility* is a key predictor of its overall quality. To measure and track the perceived relevance of this program we asked participants to rate the following statements at the end of the instruction:

- The program was relevant and helped in development of skills that facilitate work.
- I will be able to apply and implement the learning from this program.

Our participants have immensely appreciated the overall structure of the program. Most of the reaction-level feedback indicates that trainees find the experiential design of the program unique. The other aspect that most trainees find commendable is the right mix and balance of the information that is given directly and that is learned through activities. One of the most highly rated modules is "Know Your Business," which helps a new employee learn about the business drivers of the auto industry through a game-based simulation.

We also use a number of web-based modules during these four days and after for SteerIn. Some of these are also available to other employees to enable learning anytime/anywhere. An internal survey revealed that one of the courses used in the induction program—Basics of Automobiles—is the most visited e-learning module on the LMS.

Advice to Colleagues

- Instructional methods, media, and exercises should be designed with the "end in mind" as defined in the first two segments of the Planning Wheel.
- Select an appropriate instructional strategy first, followed by method of delivery.
- Use a variety of instructional methods to facilitate on-the-job application.
- Use neuroscience while designing programs. Instructional methods should give the learner intellectual stimulation as well as opportunities to use as many as possible of his five senses to create greater engagement in learning the content and higher retention.
- Use Bloom's taxonomy to identify the instructional goal and method. An ideal method should maximize application.

Case D2.8

How We Made Learning Relevant to Deliver Business Impact

Raymond Phoon and Jonathan Low

Managing Partners, PowerUpSuccess Group

Background

PowerUpSuccess is one of Asia's leading HRD and learning development organizations with specialization in organizational change, sales and revenue optimization, leadership development, EQ in cultural revolution, and transformational training. Our training and human capital development solutions help individuals, managers, and teams work at their best and operate productively within high-paced, performance-driven market environments in places like Malaysia, Singapore, Thailand, Indonesia, Philippines, China, India, and the Middle East.

In this case study, we report work we did with Visual Solutions, a market leader in HR software and services, to deliver a comprehensive learning and development solution to help in their business transformation journey. Visual Solutions had recently executed a management buyout from a much larger organization, spinning off into an independent entity. The result was a leaner, but emotionally drained and disillusioned workforce that lacked key competencies needed to achieve their business plan.

What We Did

A comprehensive learning and development solution was put in place (Exhibit D2.8.1), spanning two years and incorporating the following key activities:

1. Base-lining of current organizational challenges, sentiments, and staff proficiencies
2. Comparative gap analysis against business goals and objectives
3. Development of learning activities for various levels of the workforce
4. Creation of task force and performance-management processes
5. Mini-projects to implement and apply acquired skills
6. Intermediary coaching and mentoring efforts
7. Ongoing assessments to document results (business results, climate survey, attrition rate, skills analysis, etc.)
8. Improvement strategies and enhanced intervention measures

Results

It was truly encouraging to see how many areas within the organization were impacted by the learning solutions and performance support implemented during the two years. Some of the significant contributions were

Empirical Results

- Revenues went up by 20 percent after the first year.
- Attrition rates were reduced by half.
- Employee engagement index doubled.

Exhibit D2.8.1. The PowerUpSuccess Approach for Delivering Business Impact

Our Talent Empowerment & Learning Transfer Approach

Base Lining
- **Situational Assessment**
  - F2F interviews | Mystery Shopping | Climate Survey
- **Comprehensive Reporting & Recommendations**
  - Determining gaps | Appropriating role based and proficiency level solutions

Leadership Empowerment
- **Alignment**
  - Focused Areas | Approach | Timeline & Milestones of Intervention
- **Readiness**
  - Equipping Leadership | Aligning Expectations | Functional KPIs | Performance Management Tools

Team Revolution
- **Imparting Best Practices**
  - Pre-determined enhanced processes
- **Action Learning & Development**
  - Motivation & Personal Mastery | Functional Competencies | Team Improvement Influence

Application & Monitoring
- **Implementation & Execution**
  - Deploying mini-projects | Utilizing new knowledge in real sales scenario
- **Focused & Aligned Mentoring**
  - Buddy system | 1 x 1 coaching | Group Engagement |

Validation
- **Onsite evaluation & coaching**
  - Post-Assessment of Climate & Proficiencies | Mystery Shopping | F2F Interviews
- **Tracking Performance**
  - Performance Management Reporting | Quality Assessment

Anecdotal Results

- Employees wanted to be more involved in ongoing changes.
- Employees no longer viewed performance reviews as a challenge and "punishment."
- Managers wanted to take responsibility of staff performance and be directly involved in helping to close gaps.

Lessons of Experience

- It was key to ensure that classroom learning was delivered in ways that made it easy to apply at the workplace.

- Post-class application was essential, not only to help with learning retention, but to deliver business results; the staff's continually enhanced competencies clearly drove significant business impact.
- In the future, there is opportunity to tighten up learning activation and better track and document expected activities across various functions.

Keys to Success

- Management buy-in was crucial to the success of this project; there were several occasions when it could have stalled if not for sponsorship influence.
- Collection of base-lining information to support management feedback/concerns was essential in defining the reality of the situation.
- Recruitment of the mid-management team to take ownership and drive post-class activities helped maintain momentum and achieve key milestones.

Caution

- Avoid making assumptions on issues. Solicit feedback at ground level and mid-levels of performers, influencers, and under-performing staff to corroborate management views.

Advice to Colleagues
- Base-line current performance versus future goals to determine relevant gaps.
- Set learning goals that support specific business goals (not just overall big picture).
- Develop specific learning solutions that are relevant to roles and staff proficiencies.
- Avoid generic learning topics and focus on key outcomes that support business goals.
- Ensure that objectives of each learning module are clear and associated training actions connect with good fit.
- Provide a platform for application of learning at the workplace beyond the training class.
- Establish one-on-one engagement opportunities, for example, coaching, mentoring, a buddy system, etc.
- Check transference of learning by regular assessment (empirically as well as anecdotally).
- Check back against impact to business bottom line on a quarterly basis.

Case D3.1

How We Use Experiential Learning to Engage Learners' Hearts as Well as Minds

Praise Mok

Principal Consultant, ROHEI Corporation Pte Ltd

Background

ROHEI Corporation is a learning and development consultancy that specializes in creating highly contextualized learning experiences for non-technical corporate training in industries such as finance, service, aviation, education, and government.

Founded in 2007, the team is made up of thirty-two full-time consultants from seven different countries with diverse professional backgrounds. We have trained adult learners extensively on topics such as emotional intelligence, building high performance teams, resilience, change management, and values alignment.

One of our clients, a leading provider of food solutions in the Asia-Pacific region, came to us with very specific needs. Having recently re-launched their core values after a major organizational restructuring, they needed their staff to work in a cohesive way to increase engagement and improve business outcomes. They realized that, while the internal communication on core values were ongoing, it was mainly lip service and very few staff truly embraced the core values and even fewer understood what they meant in action in the work context.

Some specific requirements we were given including:

1. A large number of employees had to be trained within a short period to meet organizational timelines. This required conducting the training in groups of about one hundred.
2. The employees needed to apply training to their workplace immediately.
3. The training had to impact people's hearts as well as their heads. The staff had already been made aware of the core values. They had acquired relevant knowledge, but the communications had little impact on their attitudes and thus their behaviors at work.

What We Did

We recognized that, to produce a lasting change, we had to create an experiential learning environment that would engage participants' emotions as well as their intellect. A purely cognitive approach would fail. Designing an effective and experiential approach required in-depth knowledge of the audience, the current culture, and the performance gaps that had to be closed.

We followed a four-step interactive and iterative process to create a successful learning experience (Exhibit D3.1.1).

Exhibit D3.1.1. Our Four-Step Process for Ensuring a Successful Learning Experience

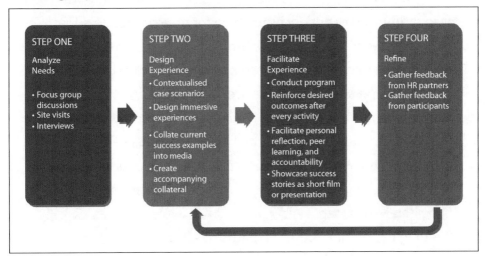

The process is iterated many times until the experience is deemed to be optimally aligned to facilitate the intended outcome. A train-the-trainer program is then conducted to create a more standard program that can be rolled out on a larger scale or over an extended period.

Key elements of the approach we used to address this client's specific challenge included:

1. In-depth study of the organization through focus-group discussions and site visits to understand the organizational culture and the composition of the staff

2. Investing many man-days to work with key client staff to better understand scenarios that would link the learning to the workplace and ensure immediate application

3. Practicing continuous improvement by collaborating with the client between program runs to refine the contents and implementation until all parties were satisfied with the results

4. Understanding that changes in attitudes are more likely to be "caught than taught," which required ensuring that there was sufficient time and experiences to allow for meaningful personal reflection. We also provided action planners and job aids to help participants remember the learning encounters, and more importantly, their personal takeaways from each

5. Keeping in mind that the debriefing is the most powerful and crucial component of experiential learning, we paid special attention to ensuring effective facilitation of reflection by the learners and made sure that sufficient time and attention were allocated to this step

6. Keeping the number of participants small enough so that learning is not compromised; our solution was to break the large groups that the client wanted to train simultaneously into smaller training subsets of twenty to thirty participants each

7. In deciding how to frame the training, we drew our inspiration from a theme park experience. Elements of a theme park experience that we wanted to incorporate included:
   - A variety of experiences in one large venue
   - Each experience makes a strong and lasting impression
   - Each experience evokes different feelings and thoughts
   - All the experiences share an overall theme and thus can be remembered collectively

Using the theme park frame, we created a "Learning Carnival" in a large venue with a number of different training rooms. Each training room provided a unique, but thematically coherent, experiential learning experience that incorporated different sensory elements including the use of light, sound, taste, touch, and smell.

Exhibit D3.1.2 is a sample of the posters that we used for different stations within the Learning Carnival. Each poster was designed with a distinctive theme to keep the learners engaged and curious. Each station provided an immersive and varied learning experience. In the Learning Carnival design, the learning points are packaged in highly experiential, engaging, and compact segments with short breaks in between for learners to reflect.

Every time participants entered a new room, they entered a different experience, although one that reinforced the overall message and attitudes we hoped to instill. As they walked through the assigned tasks, they were encouraged to formulate their own thoughts about the experience. A debriefing with facilitators helped cement their learning and connect the learning experience to their experiences at work.

Exhibit D3.1.2. Posters Used for Different Stations of the Learning Carnival

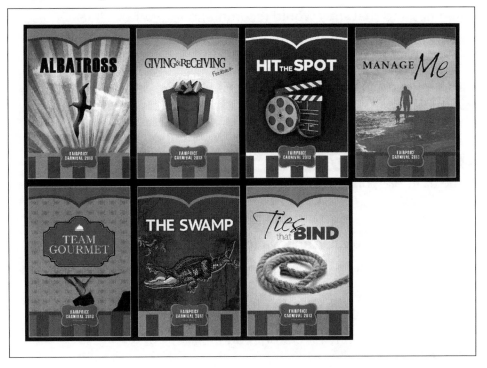

For example, in the "swamp" experience, the participants walked into a set-up resembling a swamp and were quickly orientated into performing a deceptively simple team challenge that required all participants to move to a common destination from their different starting points. In the course of this facilitated activity, they are provoked to question their definitions of "team," as well as the concepts of trust, goodwill, giving a second chance in building teams, and collaboration. At the same time, because they are immersed in the learning experience, they are able to process their immediate and actual thoughts and feelings.

Results

The Learning Carnival format has received very favorable reviews. On post-course evaluations, more than 96 percent of participants have indicated that the format was effective in achieving its intended outcomes and that they would recommend it to others. In a recent survey conducted three months after a Learning Carnival, 89.1 percent of respondents indicated that they have applied at least one thing that they learned at the program back at the workplace.

Participants have also shared many of their thoughts in their evaluation forms both immediately after the experience and months later. Some examples, drawn from various learning carnivals, are included below:

- "I apply this core value (innovation) by being involved in the evaluation team for the assembly line project. Besides improving productivity, it will help us to reduce human errors."
- "I've incorporated part of what I've learned in the safety module in reworking the safety induction program."

- "Previously, I did planning and execution all on my own. Now I'm sharing my plan with others to get more ideas to plan and execute my deployment. It works; I have more ideas and solutions to execute in deployment."
- "I can't wait to go home every day to practice what I have learned with my family. Not only have I gained insights at my workplace, but I am gaining them as a person. The past two days have had me saying nice things to my girls, which has caused them to wonder what I have learned at this program."
- "The stations that were designed for me can relate so much to my working life. This made me have a positive outlook on life."
- "I've gone to many training programs. I must say that this is something different and more meaningful."
- "ROHEI catered all these training programs to trigger reflection not just on workplace events but personal life as well."

Keys to Success
- A commitment to work with clients to truly understand their organizations and their people and a healthy respect for the clients; that they know their people best. The learning experience should be designed with a clear idea of the participant demographics, especially when they are from a range of departments and of different educational levels.
- Not beginning to design until we have clarity about agreed-on learning outcomes; they are often not clear at the start. When the goals are clear, key learning points can be made into short, pithy statements that help participants remember the point.
- The design of the learning space should, as far as possible, incorporate elements that engage all the senses and emotions as well as intellect.

Advice to Colleagues
- When designing the experience, ask more and tell less, both for the clients as well as for the participants.
- Leverage off the power of reflection that adult learners possess and work on building strong debriefings.
- When creating an experience, identifying and compressing the key elements helps to heighten the experience (for example, doing X task in Y timeline).
- The foundation of all design should be to encourage the participants and to engage them in a way that preserves/highlights their value as individuals.
- To change attitudes and behaviors, you have to engage the heart as well as the head, which means people need visceral, not just cerebral experiences.

Case D3.2

How We Improved the Signal-to-Noise Ratio to Transform the Presentation Culture at KLA-Tencor

Glenn Hughes
Director of Global Learning, KLA-Tencor

Background

KLA-Tencor Corporation, a leading provider of process control and yield management solutions, partners with customers around the world to develop state-of-the-art inspection and metrology technologies. These technologies serve the semiconductor, LED, and other related nano-electronics industries. With a portfolio of industry-standard products and a team of world-class engineers and scientists, the company has created superior solutions for its customers for more than thirty-five years. Headquartered in Milpitas, California, KLA-Tencor has dedicated customer operations and service centers around the world.

In 2009, KLA-Tencor decided to change its presentation culture. Like many high-tech companies, presentations at KLA-Tencor tended to be heavily laden in jargon, charts, and bullet points. This method of "non-communication" led to inefficient meetings, confusion, and misinformation.

What We Did

We recognized that the current communication style was a deeply entrenched habit and that a simple one-off training program would fail. To fix this problem, the company took six actions:

1. Worked with communication design expert Nancy Duarte, author of *slide:ology: The Art and Science of Creating Great Presentations*, to create a customized presentation workshop that addressed the needs of KLA-Tencor and our customers
2. Designed a simple, clear rubric to measure success
3. Built an achievement story, using an early pilot group
4. Used senior management as change agents
5. Provided extensive long-term coaching to participants
6. Developed pre- and post-event communications for both participants and their managers

We mapped these actions against the 6Ds to ensure that we had a robust and thorough-going solution (see Exhibit D3.2.1).

D1: Defined Business Outcomes: At D1, we took great care to define our outcomes in a way that would resonate with our leaders and workforce. Too many slide design courses focus on "arty" concepts or technical tools. Our company did not want or need a course that showed employees how to animate charts.

We aimed to reduce presentation waste by eliminating:

- Inefficient meetings
- Confusing outcomes
- Frustration while creating slides
- "Death by PowerPoint"
- Unclear or non-existent messages

Exhibit D3.2.1. Map of the Complete Solution

	D1 Defined Outcomes	D2 Designed Complete Experience	D3 Delivered for Application	D4 Drove Transfer	D5 Deployed Support	D6 Documented Results
Success Criteria	Improve meeting communication efficiency and improve decisions and actions by increasing signal and reducing noise in visuals.	Created "Glance Test" to measure signal-to-noise ratio (SNR) in slides or still media. Set target at 4:1 ratio of signal-to-noise.	The Glance Test is demonstrated, taught, and practiced in the session.	Criteria-based certification.	Coaches identify 'good' slides in public forums.	Signal-to-noise scores from audits and certification are tracked and reported. Senior leaders report improved meeting efficiency.
Slide:ology Design		Designed slide:ology@ KT with presentation guru Nancy Duarte. Included pre- and post-training elements.	Senior trainers delivered all sessions. Participants bring slides to improve to sessions.	Business leaders are taught to use Glance Test and encouraged to rate the presentations they see.	Post-training coaching built into design.	

Exhibit D3.2.1. (*Continued*)

	D1 Defined Outcomes	D2 Designed Complete Experience	D3 Delivered for Application	D4 Drove Transfer	D5 Deployed Support	D6 Documented Results
Achievement Stories	Identified pilot group (improve SNR for critical customer training presentation).	Built pilot achievement story into training design.	**Achievement story from pilot group is delivered in the session.**			**Achievement stories are tracked and reported.**
Senior Management Engagement	Secured sponsorship from director.	Built executive quotes from pilot into training. Delivered exec-only slide:ology summit to gain sponsorship.	**Executive quotes are built into training.**	**Senior managers recognize and reinforce good/bad signal-to-noise ratios using Glance Test.**	Senior managers help reinforce good/bad slide criteria in real time.	Follow up with senior leaders validated the meeting efficiency outcome was met.

Long-Term Coaching	Ensured successful application by providing access to coaches post training.	Designed workshop experience with 90-day support and criteria-based certification.	Use of 90-day support through coaching is promoted in session. Free re-enrollment is announced.		**Participants are invited to re-attend slide:ology @ KT for free anytime. Coaches available for 90 days and beyond.**	
Pre/Post-Event Communication	Create learning intentionality and encourage follow-up through communication.	**Designed pre / post communications to manager and employee: "what you'll learn" and "what you learned." 30 / 90-day evaluations of behavioral frequency.**	**References to pre/post communications, evaluation criteria, and certification in the session.**	**30 / 90-day surveys were run to track the frequency of critical behaviors.**	Reminders.	**90-day evaluations from managers of attendees showed the session "provided high ROI to 100% of attendees."**

The most important actions are in boldface.

Doing so would improve meeting efficiency and increase the number of successful decisions and actions as a result of presentations.

Working with Duarte, we defined our performance outcome as increasing the signal-to-noise ratio (SNR) of presentation slides. The terminology, "signal-to-noise," is a basic design principle familiar to our engineering audience. Signal-to-noise can be thought of as the difference between a clear, strong signal on a radio and one marred by the distracting sound of buzzing or competing stations (noise).

During D1, we also identified a pilot group with a strong and visible leader. The group had a compelling use case—they were designing training for a key customer, but the training materials were cluttered, confusing, and uninspiring.

Exhibit D3.2.2. The Glance Test

Glance Test	signal	NA	noise
Did it pass the glance test?	○		○
One Message (one point vs. many)	○	○	○
Audience Relevance (resonant content vs. inapplicable)	○	○	○
Visual Elements			
Background (supporting vs. distracting)	○	○	○
Text (scannable vs. document)	○	○	○
Color (system vs. random)	○	○	○
Photo (simple vs. involved)	○	○	○
Data (emphasis vs. non-emphasis)	○	○	○
Diagram (shapes clarify relationships vs. confuse them)	○	○	○
Arrangement			
Contrast (clear prioritization vs. indistinct)	○	○	○
Whitespace (open space vs. cluttered)	○	○	○
Hierarchy (identifiable parent|child vs. no relationship)	○	○	○
Unity (structured grid or look vs. unstructured)	○	○	○
Flow (clear path for eye vs. meander)	○	○	○
Proximity (intentional placement vs. random)	○	○	○
Animation (intentional meaning vs meaningless distraction)	○	○	○
	⬭	vs	⬭

D2: Designed the Complete Experience: During D2, we created a simple rubric (see Exhibit D3.2.2, the Glance Test) to measure signal (the number of elements on a slide that clarified the core message) to noise (the number of elements on a slide that distracted from the core message) and measured hundreds of slides. We found that successful slides (see Exhibit D3.2.3) have a SNR of 4 to 1 or higher, while unsuccessful slides (see Exhibit D3.2.4) have SNR ratios of less than 4 to 1.

Exhibit D3.2.5 provides an example of a completed glance test, in this case for the poor slide in Figure D3.2.4

This rubric and the content of Duarte's *slide:ology* became the foundation of a slide:ology@KT workshop. This workshop was designed to teach KLA-Tencor's employees the concepts and tools that increase signal and reduce noise. The pilot group used these methods to improve the SNR of their slides from 3:6 before training, to 9:1 after training.

Exhibit D3.2.3. Slide with High (Good) Signal-to-Noise Ratio

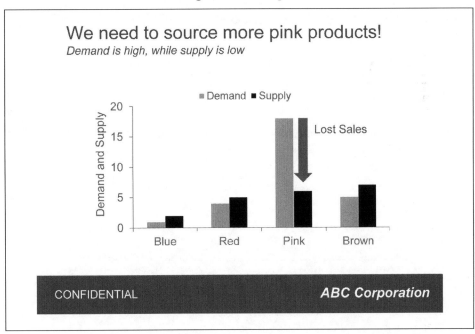

Exhibit D3.2.4. Slide with Low (Poor) Signal-to-Noise Ratio

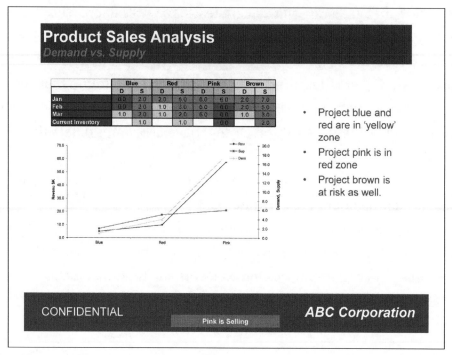

Figure D3.2.5. Glance Test Scorecard for "Noisy" Slide in Exhibit D3.2.4

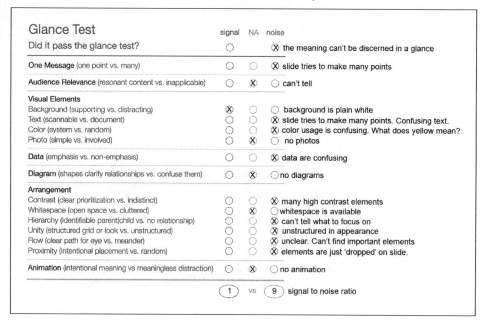

More importantly, the customer found the training so compelling that they awarded KLA-Tencor with a certificate of appreciation.

As we refined the slide:ology@KT workshop content for a corporate-wide rollout, we realized that, despite the pilot program's success, concepts and tools would not be enough to change a presentation culture that has been in place for more than thirty years.

To design the "complete" experience, we added five support systems:

1. We built the pilot group's success story into the training, showing the before/after slides that were relevant to the audience.

2. We ran an executive-only workshop. Executives spend much of their day looking at slides, basing important decisions on what they see and hear. In this accelerated session, the executives learned the language of slide:ology. They were encouraged to recognize and reinforce slides that displayed high SNR and to ask presenters who showed low SNR slides to attend slide:ology@KT.

3. We added a ninety-day "aftercare" program to the course, which included free coaching on slide design and a new certification program. Participants were asked to send us three redesigned slides. If the slides passed the "glance test," students received a custom slide:ology@KT certificate designed by DuarteDesign.

4. We designed pre-workshop communications, which are sent seven days before class to remind both the manager and employee of the workshop objectives. We inform them that there will be thirty- and ninety-day surveys about how often they practiced the skills taught in the workshop and we encourage them to discuss how the employee will immediately practice the skills learned in the workshop.

5. We designed post-workshop surveys that were sent to the manager and employee thirty and ninety days after the workshop. The surveys collected quantitative data. For example, in one item, the

employee completes the sentence, "I created X number of story-boards in the past thirty days," while the manager completes the sentence "My employee created X number of storyboards in the past thirty days." This quantitative approach encourages participants and managers to put the new skills into action.

D3: Delivered for Application: To deliver for application, we supplemented the performance objectives in three ways:

1. The "glance test" is demonstrated, taught, and practiced by the students to reinforce the practical application of signal-to-noise in their daily slide design.

2. The before and after images from the pilot group are displayed and discussed in the workshop as a case study. This shows how the tools work in our environment. Additionally, participants improve the signal-to-noise ratio of a real engineering slide as a workshop exercise.

3. Executive quotes and stories are built into the workshop to reinforce the impact of both good and bad slides on meetings and decisions.

D4: Drive Learning Transfer: We drove learning transfer in three ways:

1. We leveraged senior management by encouraging them to ask presenters whether they had attended slide:ology@KT. Leaders who had attended the executive-only session drew attention to slides that met or failed the glance test.

2. We provided "criteria-based certification" and supported it with ninety days of free coaching.

3. We used the thirty- and ninety-day surveys and reminders to encourage participants (and their managers) to put the training into action.

D5: Deploy Performance Support: Performance support was provided through the previously mentioned mechanisms: senior leaders providing feedback on slides in public presentations; and the Corporate Learning Center (CLC) providing free coaching for ninety days after workshop attendance. Additionally, with the release of slide:ology@KT, KLA-Tencor's CLC implemented a new policy: any participant of a CLC workshop can re-attend that workshop for free, as many times as he or she wants, forever. Our company mission is to improve performance, not count heads. We believe that if an employee feels he would benefit by attending multiple sessions, we should facilitate that. A number of students took advantage of this policy, attending slide:ology@KT as many as five times.

D6: Document Results: Learning transfer was documented and reported in four ways:

1. The signal-to-noise scores were tracked from three sources—the certification program, private coaching. and random audits of meeting presentations.
2. Achievement stories were tracked and reported.
3. Anecdotal evidence of meeting efficiency gains were collected from senior leaders.
4. Thirty- and ninety-day surveys were collected to track the number of times critical behaviors were performed by attendees and seen by managers.

Results

As a result of taking a 6Ds approach to the design, delivery, and follow-through to this workshop, KLA-Tencor was able to transform a deeply engrained presentation culture to be more engaging and efficient. Achievement stories allowed leaders and employees to see and articulate what successful presentations looked like, removing fear and enabling workplace application. Additionally:

- The terms "slide:ology" and "signal-to-noise" have entered the corporate lexicon.
- Teams and individuals that attended slide:ology@KT saw—and continue to see—gains of 3X to 10X in signal-to-noise of their slides.
- Numerous achievement stories, from participants and leaders, have been documented throughout the company.
- One hundred percent of all managers surveyed after the first year of the program responded that they saw a high ROI from sending their employee or team to slide:ology@KT.

Advice to Colleagues

- Alignment is critical. Clear business and workshop outcomes ensure that instructors, managers, and participants all understand what the course is designed to achieve.
- Having a successful, credible pilot group that is willing to advocate for the program is like strapping a rocket booster to your initiative. Our pilot group gave the program visibility, integrity, and outstanding content for the workshop.
- Teaching executives the basic concepts of your workshop can turn them into a legion of auditor/advocates. We didn't teach the senior leaders how to make great slides; we taught them how to recognize great (and not-so-great) slides. They could then reinforce presenters who had done great work and send the others to us.

Case D3.3

How We Designed a Complete Experience to Deliver Business Results

Diane Hinton, Mary Singos, and Lauren Grigsby

Director of Corporate Learning, Learning Professional, and Learning Coordinator, Plastipak Packaging, Inc.

Background

Plastipak Packaging, Inc., is a global, privately held, $2.5 billion manufacturer of rigid plastic containers. To enable the company to meet the challenges and opportunities of rapid growth, the company launched Plastipak Academy in 2006. Its mission: deliver targeted learning solutions aligned with current business needs, equipping leaders enterprise-wide to grow the business.

In late 2012, a site manager recognized a problem in a large production area at his plant. The team was not achieving key manufacturing targets and turnover was increasing. The root cause was strained relationships among team members in an expanding and competitive local labor market. In order to resolve the problem, the site manager looked into a variety of interventions.

The regional leadership development manager linked this problem, in part, to skill gaps in using effective communication skills among the team. Subsequently, she invited the production manager to take part in a corporate pilot of the VitalSmarts Crucial Conversations program. The Plastipak Academy team, regional leadership development manager, and production manager debriefed after the pilot and it became clear that this training initiative would be used as a key tool to begin to improve target numbers and increase retention in the problem production area. In light of tight production deadlines and plant scheduling, we determined that the program would have the most impact when delivered via spaced learning to an intact team.

Starting with a serious business problem and the involvement of top management at this plant, we developed Tools for the TOUGH Talks, a five-week spaced-learning program based on key concepts from VitalSmarts Crucial Conversations. We delivered this training program to twenty-one top production leaders at this plant, including intact teams on both the day shift and the night shift. Our audience was a group of highly technical guys under an immense amount of pressure, with no formal training or effective management models. They are well-intentioned, hard-working, and extremely knowledgeable about production issues, but under-skilled in managing people.

What We Did

To exploit the program for achieving business results, we designed the complete experience, not as a training event, but as a learning process inside a change initiative. These are some of the key design elements that contributed to the success of the program:

Prepare

- We developed an Impact Map (Exhibit D3.3.1) for the program based on interviews and approvals from the site manager and production manager. They identified metrics for their business goals of safety, retention, and performance.

Exhibit D3.3.1. Impact Map to Create Learning Intentionality for the Tools for TOUGH Talks Program

Impact Map—Tools for the TOUGH Talks
Targeting My Learning to Achieve Business Goals

Plastipak **ACADEMY**
Personal Growth • Industry Leadership

LEARN	DO	GET RESULTS	ACHIEVE GOALS	
I'll learn how to do these things when I actively participate in the program.	*I'll be able to do these things better when I practice and apply what I learned.*	*I'll get these results when I improve how I hold crucial conversations.*	*I'll impact these business goals when I hold effective crucial conversations.*	Name: _____ Discussed with Leader: ___/___/___ (date)
○ Identify the conversations you need to have to improve results	○ Open up and improve communication channels with my peers and associates	○ Stronger team ○ Increased morale ○ Increased engagement	○ Safety: _____ ○ PPM: – Injection: _____ – Blow molding: _____	**TO USE THIS IMPACT MAP:** ❶ **Review each column.** Note how the items in each column drive the fulfillment of items in the next column.
○ Hold yourself and others accountable by stepping up to difficult conversations	○ Listen and evaluate rather than get defensive when my associates speak up	○ Increased productivity ○ Increased interactions between direct reports and leaders	○ UPE: – Injection: _____ – Blow molding: _____	❷ In the two leftmost columns, **mark the top few things to LEARN and DO** that you most need to focus on during
○ Identify your role in contributing to the results that you don't want	○ Make it safe for my associates to bring up concerns and issues without feeling like they'll get penalized for doing so	○ Improved interpersonal skills of leaders	○ Associate Retention: _____%	your learning experience. If you think of additional items that you want this program to help you DO better that aren't listed,
○ Create a safe environment to dialogue with anyone about anything	○ Step up and talk about the hard stuff, the things that are holding us back from getting results	○ Accelerate the spread of productive communication skills among associates	○ _____ ○ _____	write them in the space provided.
○ Identify the stories we tell ourselves that create emotions that undermine your crucial conversations	○ Be a role model for holding high-stakes conversations that lead to positive results and relationships	○ _____	*Note: We have removed specific metrics from this Impact Map for confidentiality purposes.*	❸ In the last two columns, **mark the RESULTS and GOALS** you think you'll impact by improving your crucial conversation skills.
○ Use skills that will help you focus on facts and listen better to others	○ _____	○ _____		Feel free to add additional RESULTS and site-specific GOALS you want to impact with this program.
○ Make decisions to commit to actions with others that will lead to better results	○ _____	○ _____		

Revised: 1/3/13

- The site manager approved our proposal of engaging the top leadership team as change agents for the initiative. We designed and executed a change team pre-program discussion one month prior to the first learning event to provide an overview of the program and learning process, its purpose and objectives, and their role as change agents in the learning process.

- We developed a thirty-minute kick-off session for the production manager to present during team meetings two weeks prior to the first learning event. The session included a video of the program facilitator introducing the program and some initial content, and an activity for preparing for the first learning event and finding out what was in it for them and their part of the business. Participants were given personalized packets with a program schedule, impact map, and pre-work assignments.
- Participants and their leaders marked up the impact map and held individual pre-training discussions to agree on a personalized learning focus.

Learn

- The program facilitator is a seasoned leadership development manager who has established deep relationships with the leadership team and many of the participants. She not only served as the program facilitator, but also as a coach throughout the learning process; leaders and participants felt comfortable talking with her during and between learning events.
- The site manager, production manager, and talent manager selected twenty-one top production leaders from the same department, who all have similar job responsibilities and direct reports, to participate in the same program. The rosters were split into day shift participants and night shift participants.
- We used a spaced learning approach. The course was split into five learning events. We implemented one learning event per week on Wednesday evenings, back-to-back for each of the two groups. We designed email communications and skill application assignments for participants to complete between sessions (Exhibit D3.3.2), which included both learning and teach-back components.

Exhibit D3.3.2. An Example of an Intersession Learning Assignment

Tools for the TOUGH Talks

With Key Concepts from Crucial Conversations

MODULE 3: MASTER MY STORIES

Commitment assignment

DUE January 23, 2013

WATCH

Watch for stories presented as facts. Online, TV, radio, newspapers, meetings, your own stories, etc. Have two examples to share for the next training session.

1.

2. _____

DO

Between now and the next training session, **meet with your learning partner** and discuss a key relationship where your emotions make healthy conversation difficult. Share the following prompts.

Who is it? What are the tough conversations typically about? Did you tell yourself any Victim, Villian, or Helpless stories? How were your feelings impacted by these stories? How did your actions influence others in ways that confirmed your stories? What stories could others tell themselves about you based on your actions? Did paying attention to your stories help in any way?

Notes: _____

TEACH

Introduce someone to one of the three clever stories and the questions to ask in order to master your stories.

Clever Story (circle one):   Victim   Villian   Helpless

Who: _____   When and Where: _____

Transfer/Achieve

- The final learning event included a celebration and achievement recognition hosted by the site manager.

- Leaders and participants held post-training meetings to discuss how to apply what they learned in the training on the job to achieve the business results in their areas (Exhibit D3.3.3).

Case D3.3: How We Designed a Complete Experience to Deliver Results

Exhibit D3.3.3. Action Plan to Move from Learning to Results

Focus: My Next Steps
Moving from Learning to Doing

Name: _____

1 Results I'm seeking:

2 Actions I'll take which lead to those results:

What: When:

Carry out the plan for my TOUGH talk.

3 Obstacles I anticipate:

What might get in the way of performing those actions?

When you meet with your designated leader, discuss how you'll remove obstacles, and the help you'll need.

4 Other support I need:

Are there other forms of support you need to seek in order to carry out this action plan (such as additional tools, coaching, etc.)?

To be completed by leader:
Things I will do to help this learner achieve results. (Examples: provide coaching, on-the-job support, etc.)

Look at the Learn column on your Impact Map. What are the **top two or three results** you'll aim for as you apply your learnings?

How will you work to achieve those results?

Name up to three specific actions you'll take, and by when, in addition to the one that's listed for you. For additional ideas, see the Do column of your Impact Map - but **be as specific as possible** about how you'll demonstrate those behaviors.

2/13/2013   Tools for the TOUGH Talks.
My Journey to Results - Page 2

Leader Initials: Learner Initials: Date:

- Participants were required to meet with their leaders and complete an online self-assessment one month after the final learning event. Upon completion of the assessment, participants received a certificate of recognition and the postcard they had filled out at the final learning event.
- We designed and held a post-program discussion with the change team one month after the final learning event to go over their roles as change agents in skill application and reinforcement, and to walk through a reinforcement plan.
- We designed and executed a three-month reinforcement plan to help participants move their new skills from the workshop to the

workplace. For each business goal (safety, retention, and performance) we provided:

- A change team email communication
- A fifteen-minute team meeting activity and an in-house-produced video of the program facilitator tying content to our workplace for leaders to present during regularly scheduled meetings, and
- A participant e-newsletter

The purpose of the reinforcement plan was to keep key content and language fresh, link participants to resources and support, and make the skills relevant to their development needs and their area's business needs.

Results

Quantifiable and Anecdotal Evidence of Success. We conducted an online self-assessment to collect both quantifiable and anecdotal evidence of the short-term impact of this program on our top three metrics: safety, retention, and performance. We continue to strengthen this evidence of success by implementing the Tools for the TOUGH Talks Reinforcement Plan.

In response to a series of "mark all that apply" questions on the online self-assessment:

- Sixty-four percent of program participants indicated they have impacted safety
- Seventy-nine percent have contributed to increased engagement
- Fifty-nine percent indicated that they have increased productivity
- Thirty-five percent indicated that they have impacted retention as a result of applying their new skills from the Tools for the TOUGH Talks program

Select anecdotal responses from program participants, in their own words, are as follows:

- **Safety:** A program participant explains his renewed focus on safety: "As a result of this course, I have let everyone know that safety is our number one goal and we should all look out for ourselves and each other."
- **Retention:** "I've been able to contribute to each result by showing a positive new approach with new employees and allow open communication with both new and old employees."
- **Performance:** "Just recently I had a few new associates who were having issues that were affecting their performance. I held one-on-one meetings with them. Changes in their abilities and efforts greatly improved. The technician on my shift who has filled the role as a mentor to our new hires had a talk with me yesterday. He notes how much they improved when I took the time to talk with them one-on-one."
- **Teamwork:** Program participants have also described a heightened sense of teamwork when troubleshooting defects: "By talking through tough issues with mutual respect, associates feel they have contributed more to helping find solutions."

Successful Team Dynamic. By working together on this training initiative, Plastipak Academy and the change team were able to establish a strong relationship that was dynamic and business-oriented, yet playful, as we tackled tough issues and challenging content. This was never more evident than during the post-program discussion that ended with the production manager saying, "The group down here is in awe of what you produced. The videos, the emails, and the handouts were all very professionally done. You guys just do a great job." The site manager subsequently made a joke about a long-standing NCAA basketball rivalry. It was a success for Plastipak Academy to cultivate a relationship and become a trusted resource for a group of top management leaders at our company.

Lessons of Experience

A specific insight that we had during this process is that, when training an intact team where tensions run high, it is crucial to employ a variety of methods that increase engagement and influence the participants' motivation to learn.

The first method employed is leader as teacher. Our program facilitator is a leadership development manager at Plastipak, who has years of experience working directly at our manufacturing sites. Given the sensitive content of the program, the trusted relationships she has cultivated were vital to the program's success. The top leaders at this plant hold her in high regard, while still finding her accessible, and this was communicated to the participants of the program. Ultimately, she was able to successfully create a safe environment, where program participants sought her out for advice. An outside facilitator, however skilled, would not have had the same level of trust and credibility.

To strengthen engagement from the beginning, we designed a kick-off session led by the production manager and ensured that each participant had a pre-training meeting with a leader. The result was that participants showed up to the first learning event motivated to learn and viewed this training initiative as a priority. To sustain learner motivation, the production manager attended each of the learning events as an active observer during the five weeks.

Throughout the program, and specifically during the learning events, we made the material relevant to our participants by bringing in content from the workplace. We identified opportunities in the content where this would have the most impact and used case studies, showed relevant videos, and created activities using real Plastipak situations. This made it much easier for our participants to engage with the material and see its relevance and application to their own work. They practiced realistic on-the-job application of the new communication skills, without being distracted by examples that didn't look or sound like a typical manufacturing environment.

All the communications that program participants received from Plastipak Academy were branded with a unique logo and color scheme. This design choice enabled program participants to immediately identify the communications as content from the Tools for the TOUGH Talks program and prioritize it accordingly. Creating a strong brand identity helped maintain a high level of engagement and carry the learning forward from the events to the post-training environment.

Keys to Success

- The biggest key to our success was viewing Tools for the TOUGH Talks not as a stand-alone program but as a change initiative. We had sponsorship from leaders at Plastipak, specifically the site manager and production manager. They set expectations and modeled the behaviors. These leaders were personally involved and continuously sent the message to the participants that this was a high-level priority. Their visible and sustained support had a positive impact on learner engagement.

- The second key to success was that we were agile in the development of the program. We continuously asked for feedback from both the leaders and program participants. Based on this feedback, we were able to implement thoughtful changes to materials and activities as we went. As an additional result, participants voiced ideas that added to the value of the program. For example, in our second learning event, a participant in one group mentioned that he would like an additional review session with the team to discuss the homework assignments and keep the content alive between spaced learning events. Another participant agreed and volunteered to lead this meeting. For the rest of the program, this group met between learning events for an organic review session.

Cautions

- Try to minimize distractions so learners can concentrate on the material. A pitfall of the Tools for the TOUGH Talks program was the location of the learning events. In an effort to accommodate the plant schedule and minimize the program participant's travel time, we chose to hold the learning events in a meeting room with large windows adjacent to the production area. This proved to be extremely distracting to the program participants as they struggled to focus on the content rather than the production noise. For example, during one learning event an alarm sounded from a machine at a line next to the room. The line leader, a program participant, became noticeably agitated and stood by the window to supervise his crew until the issue was resolved and the alarm deactivated.

- Be cognizant of internal tensions and conflicts, especially when teaching this kind of material. Given the nature of the course content and tensions among the intact group, we learned it would have been beneficial to spend additional time understanding the interpersonal group dynamics and identifying local support systems including the plant talent management team.

- Be aware of the demands that agile development creates. From a workload perspective, agile program development is a buzz saw that makes it difficult to forecast the time and resources that should be allocated for the project. Our experience has shown that designing on the fly often takes an unexpectedly large amount of time. In response to feedback from program participants, our team would often work to design custom resources under a tight deadline, even while the program was in progress. Ultimately, this resulted in a great product for Tools for the TOUGH Talks, but it stretched the timelines for other projects in the department in order to accommodate the additional time and resources needed.

Case D3.3: How We Designed a Complete Experience to Deliver Results ■ **397**

Advice to Colleagues

- Benchmark with other companies for best practices. Before designing this program, we benchmarked with another company that shared their tips and tools that they use for spaced-learning programs.

- Don't rely solely on packaged content from a vendor. Always start with a content package from a top-notch training vendor, such as VitalSmarts! In addition, pull resources and examples from a variety of sources—particularly company-specific examples—to enhance the content. Doing so ensures that participants will be able to connect with the concepts and gain a better understanding of how the content relates to them.

- Build humanity. Develop interpersonal relationships and a good reputation through working history. Become a trusted resource for your company whom leaders feel safe reaching to when they first begin to experience a performance problem. This is important. If they wait until the problem is out of hand, it may be too late to design an effective solution in the "heat of the battle."

Case D3.4

How We Increased Leadership Effectiveness by Delivering for Application

Melanie Brunet Relyea and Michelle Cooper

Training and Development Manager and Training Supervisor,
Oneida Nation Enterprises, LLC

Background

Oneida Nation Enterprises, LLC (ONE) was established in 1990. Since the opening of Turning Stone Resort Casino in 1993, ONE has grown to 4700+ employees across fourteen enterprises, including convenience stores, marinas, health care, recreation, video production, and the Indian Country Today Media Network.

Rapid growth resulted in promotions from within for much of the management staff. Although we provided basic management training, two observations led us to conclude that the approach of stand-alone classes was not driving adequate learning transfer or skill application:

1. The high number of managers turning to employee relations to handle basic employee performance issues such as attendance and low performance and

2. The number of employees seeking assistance for situations normally handled by a manager.

We knew we needed a new approach that would address these issues, so we created and deployed The Leader Learning Circle, an eight-week program in which core leadership skills were taught and applied immediately on the job.

What We Did

The Leader Learning Circle uses the book *Monday Morning Leadership* by David Cottrell as its basis. The leaders read a chapter each week and set goals to change one of their behaviors as it relates to the book.

They report back on their successes and challenges in class the following week. Recognition is given for even small, incremental change and suggestions for overcoming their challenges are discussed by the group. A new goal is set each week based on a new chapter; the process is repeated for the eight weeks of the circle.

At the conclusion of the eight weeks, the leaders set future goals for continuing to apply the skill sets and behaviors they have learned. After sixty to ninety days they are surveyed to measure the effectiveness of their continued efforts, and after six to nine months their managers are surveyed for their perceptions as well. In addition, monthly leadership articles are sent to graduates and class reunions are held annually. Graduates are also encouraged to seek out the facilitator for help with challenges and to report successes.

The eight chapters of the book drive the weekly class content:

- **Week 1**: *Drivers vs. Passengers*: Leaders learn that they give up the freedom of "being along for the ride"; they're "responsible for everything," including the actions of their people.
- **Week 2**: *Keep the Main Thing the Main Thing*: Leaders learn that failing to set clear expectations, goals, and priorities creates

demotivated, disengaged, and frustrated employees. "People quit people before they quit companies," so if a leader is not clear and consistent in communicating expectations, employees move on.

- **Week 3—*Escape from Management Land*:** Leaders learn that they have to get out of their offices and get in touch with their people to be sure that employees understand what's expected of them, to show that they care, to build trust, and to learn who is really performing and who is not.

- **Week 4—*The Do Right Rule*:** Leaders learn that, although hard, they must address performance and behavior issues immediately, that not doing so puts their integrity as a leader at risk.

- **Week 5—*Hire Tough*:** A company's most important asset is having the *right* people on your team. When you have the wrong people, you spend all of your time trying to fix them. Leaders learn that hiring a warm body to fill a position is not in the best interest of the team or the company. They learn how to hire tough to have a strong and effective team.

- **Week 6—*Do Less or Work Faster*:** Leaders learn that their time is *their* responsibility. They need to find a way to either do less by delegating and eliminating unnecessary tasks, or work faster by prioritizing, limiting interruptions, and effectively managing meetings.

- **Week 7—*Buckets and Dippers*:** Leaders learn that employees are motivated to do their best when they know *what to do, how to do it, and whether or not they're doing it well*. They also learn that, as leaders, they are responsible for making sure that the things that "dip into buckets" and cause morale and motivation to diminish—such as negativity, gossip, cynicism, and fear—are stopped as soon as they start.

- **Week 8—*Enter the Learning Zone*:** Just as our organization learned that taking classes without follow-up and reinforcement did not lead to performance improvement, our leaders learn that their efforts must continue beyond our eight classes. They create action plans to continue their learning and their efforts toward achieving the goals set each week in class.

Class reunions are held periodically and leadership articles are regularly sent to graduates. In addition, the language and skill sets are reinforced in all of our other leadership programs and are echoed by our COO in his new leader and quarterly leadership team meetings.

Results

Monday Morning Leadership was created to increase the effectiveness of leaders across the organization in three critical areas:

1. Setting clear performance expectations
2. Addressing performance issues
3. Accountability for increasing performance

Managers of seventy-five Leader Learning Circle graduates from January 2011 to January 2012 were surveyed to identify our success in increasing effectiveness in these areas. Survey data of skill application before and after the program indicate significant increases in the effectiveness of leaders across the organization in all three of the critical areas targeted for improvement (Figures D3.4.1 to D3.4.3).

Today, the Leader Learning Circle continues to be a foundational course for new and existing leaders. As one of our graduates put it:

"I have had the opportunity to attend many classes here with a number of management techniques and styles. The Leader Learning Circle is unique in that it presents some very basic concepts in a straightforward fashion with the end result of challenging you as a leader to take immediate and specific steps to put these concepts into practice. You start with many ideas that can be categorized as common sense, but you soon realize they can produce powerful and lasting results."

Dan, Director, VIP Services

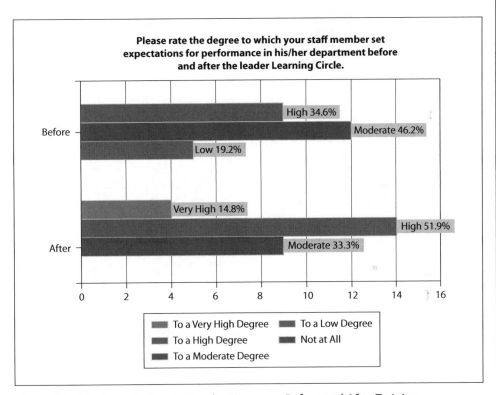

Figure D3.4.1. Expectation Setting by Managers Before and After Training

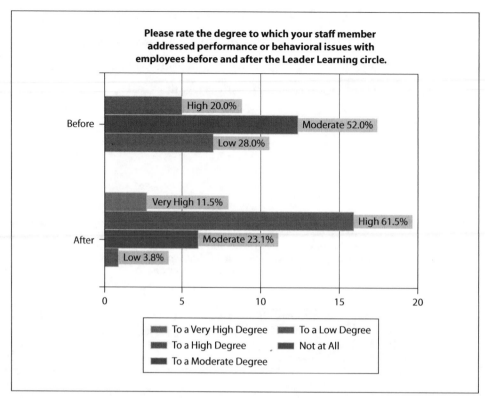

Figure D3.4.2. Addressing Performance Issues by Managers Before and After Training

Lessons of Experience

Lesson 1: Buy-in from senior leadership is critical to the success of this program. That did not come immediately for us. We worked diligently to encourage senior leaders to complete the program and encourage (or require) their direct reports to attend. Over time, the word spread and the program increased not only in popularity but in effectiveness, because directors were then teaching and holding their managers accountable, and so on down the line to supervisors and leads. In future

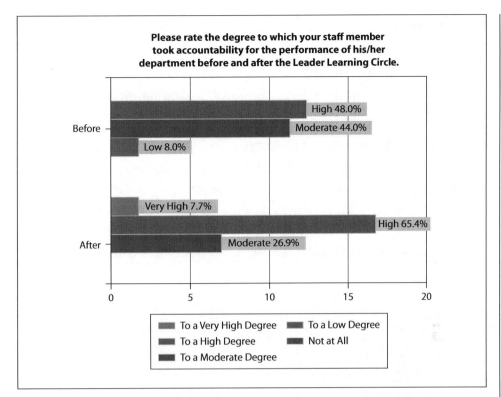

Figure D3.4.3. Accountability for Performance by Managers Before and After Training

program rollouts, we will engage at the senior leadership level first and then deploy in a systematic way to the other levels of leadership.

Lesson 2: Follow-up is key to drive learning transfer. Desired skills and behaviors must be practiced during the learning, and plans to ensure application on the job afterward must be in place to ensure success. We are currently in the process of redesigning the program to "move the finish line" to ensure that skill application continues for all "graduates" once the program is over.

Keys to Success

- Clearly defined objectives based on desired business outcomes, not necessarily stated "needs"
- Clear communication of how the program will benefit the learner, the department, and the business
- Periodic communication of successes to senior leadership
- Timely communication of the measurement outcomes

Caution

- Don't assume anything. Always do a thorough assessment.

Advice to Colleagues

- Design the entire learning experience up-front based on desired business outcomes.
- Don't allow the "day-to-day" to get in the way of delivering the entire experience.
- Celebrate your successes in a meaningful and visible way, crediting learners, business partners, and anyone else who contributed to the success of the experience.

Case D3.5

How We Turn Front-Line Supervisors into Safety Leaders

Rebecca Nigel

Manager, Marketing Communications, BST

Background

BST is a global safety consulting firm that pioneered behavior-based safety and has established a reputation for innovation and thought leadership since 1979.

Among the greatest opportunities for our clients to improve safety performance is strengthening the role and influence of front-line leaders. When supervisors and managers learn to do the right activities in ways that build a strong safety culture, not only do they improve on-the-job safety, but they also learn leadership skills they can use to drive improvement in production, quality, and other critical performance areas.

Yet many organizations are frustrated because typical safety training doesn't produce the results they're looking for—even with the most dedicated supervisors. The problem is that traditional safety "training"

is so far removed from what site leaders do day-to-day that its lessons often have no relevance to the work being done.

That's why we focus on developing leadership skills around the most essential safety activities that supervisors do every day. We call these activities "moments of truth" because they are unique opportunities for supervisors to strengthen the safety culture in real time without taking a lot of time.

What We Did

We develop front-line supervisors by using an approach that enables them to practice leadership skills while also building competence in core safety activities. Rather than doing one or the other in isolation, this approach enables front-line leaders to execute the safety activity more effectively while learning how to actually use leadership practices—all without adding to their workload.

We distilled safety activities into five categories (Table D3.5.1) that provide supervisors with critical "moments of truth" they can use to

Table D3.5.1. Key Supervisor Activities and Their Effect on Safety Culture

Activity	Effect
Safety contacts	Provide reinforcement and guidance, understand safety issues
Job safety briefings	Strengthen exposure recognition and use of mitigation measures
Physical hazard identification	Assure safe working conditions and equipment
Safety procedure verification	Improve consistency in use of key safety procedures
Incident response and root cause analysis	Care for injured, focus prevention efforts

Table D3.5.2. Key Supervisor Activities and Their Links to Leadership Practices

Activity	Leadership Practice(s)
Safety contacts	Feedback
Job safety briefing	Communication, collaboration
Verification audit	Accountability
Physical hazard identification	Action orientation
Incident response/root cause	Credibility

shape their safety culture and simultaneously build leadership best practices (Table D3.5.2).

Understanding the five critical activities is the first step in developing the skills to seize the "moments of truth" and build a stronger culture of safety. Performing these activities in a genuine, consistent, and effective way is essential. This is known as skill fluency—understanding the activity so well that you can teach it to others.

Training or workshops aren't enough to create fluency with critical safety leadership skills; learning must move from the classroom to the workplace. We begin by conveying to supervisors the underlying concepts, the organization's objectives, and the benefits the practice will provide them. We then teach them how to integrate each safety activity with its corresponding leadership skill. We reinforce the training with in-field coaching, and track progress with metrics. Through this process, supervisors see their growth, hone their skills through practical application, and realize peak safety performance.

Results

- Organizations that have used this approach have achieved improvement both in safety and leadership metrics.

- Supervisors report better relationships and communication with their teams.
- Supervisors are especially happy to learn this approach because it works and it doesn't add to their already full plates.

> **Advice to Colleagues**
> - The best leaders are both task-oriented and relationship-oriented.
> - Developing quality leaders means cultivating both of these areas.
> - Supervisors become better leaders by honing leadership skills while engaging in core activities that build the safety culture.
> - Learning must move from the classroom to the workplace; training can't stop at the classroom door.

Case D3.6

How We Fostered a Proactive Approach to Leader Development

Colonel Bernard B. Banks

Professor and Department Head, Department of Behavioral Sciences and Leadership, United States Military Academy at West Point

Background

The United States Military Academy (USMA) at West Point was founded in 1802. The mission of the Academy has always focused on the development of character-based leaders for the U.S. Army, the nation, and the military forces of the United States' allies. The Academy's 4,400 cadets are drawn from all fifty states and thirty-six other countries.

A hallmark of West Point's rigorous four-year undergraduate educational process is its core curriculum. Every cadet is required to successfully complete a minimum of forty semester-long courses. Of these, thirty are prescribed in order to ensure broad exposure and competency in math, science, and engineering; the humanities and social sciences; and physical, leadership, and character development.

West Point has thirteen academic departments that are responsible for the effective delivery of the core curriculum and maintaining the standards of the academic majors. The Department of Behavioral Sciences & Leadership houses five majors (management, psychology, sociology, engineering psychology, and leader development science) and delivers two core courses (PL 100–General Psychology for Leaders and PL 300–Military Leadership) to ensure that every cadet understands the science of leading and the issues associated with the human dimension of influencing behavior. The Military Leadership (PL 300) course is taken by all cadets during their junior (third) year.

After learning about the 6Ds (especially D4), the Department of Behavioral Sciences & Leadership elected to pursue a change in how it conducted PL 300 in order to more proactively drive attainment of the course purpose and its two main goals.

What We Did

Prior to the 6D intervention, the PL 300 course purpose was stated as:

> As a result of this course, cadets are capable of integrating new knowledge, experiences, and reflection to lead soldiers and military organizations more effectively in a culturally diverse, changing world. *In short, cadets leave this course as better leaders.* To achieve this, PL 300 has two main goals:
>
> - Cadets are better, more self-aware leaders who are capable of reflecting on and learning from their life and leadership experiences;
> - Cadets *can* apply relevant frameworks, concepts, and theory to leadership situations.

But we had insufficient reinforcing mechanisms to ensure the cadets actually demonstrated they were *better* leaders as a result of their studying the course material.

One experience, in particular, highlighted the weak linkage between our desired outcomes and actual practice. The PL 300 course instructors conducted an after-action review with some senior (fourth year) cadets who had participated in a summer internship in Mexico. The internship had involved a team of graduate students from the University of Michigan and three West Point cadets. The team was working in concert with Procter and Gamble to deliver water purification systems to rural areas. The task was fairly unstructured; consequently, original thought and leadership were required to address the team's various challenges.

However, when we asked cadets: "To what extent did you rely on the material you learned in PL 300 to help you address the leadership challenges you encountered in Mexico?" the answer was almost always: "I hadn't thought about doing so." We realized that our actual outcomes were falling short of our stated purpose; the cadets had fallen prey to the learning transfer dilemma. Consequently, we decided to change PL 300's purpose to place much greater emphasis on application.

In the fall of 2011, we changed the wording of one of the two main goals of PL 300 to: "***Cadets <u>will</u> apply relevant frameworks, concepts, and theory to <u>current</u> leadership situations***" (rather than <u>can</u> apply). Although we only changed two words in the purpose, moving from "can apply" to "will apply" and adding "current" to leadership situations changed the way both the instructors and students approached the course. It required new tools and procedures to ensure application in addition to education.

An online learning transfer support system (*ResultsEngine*®) was integrated into PL 300 as a proactive tool to propel application and provide empirical evidence of a cadet's improvement as a leader. We provided the following information to cadets about the tool and expectations for the course:

> To support you in the application of your PL 300 learning, you will be given a web-based tool called *ResultsEngine®*. During each application period, *ResultsEngine* will ask you to respond to five questions:
>
> 1. What framework, concept, or theory did you apply from PL 300?
> 2. Describe the situation and outcome from the application of this learning.
> 3. How has this experience improved you as a leader?
> 4. Characterize your progress (pick one from: Just Starting, Early Win, Visible Application, or Valuable Improvement).
> 5. How will you use what you learned from this experience going forward to become a better leader?
>
> On the last update (after seven weeks), you will be asked to tell the Achievement Story of your leadership development by answering the following questions:
>
> 1. Reflecting on your development as a leader during the last seven weeks, what application actions and improvements are you most proud of?
> 2. Have others commented or reacted to the change in your leadership? Give an example.
> 3. How will this experience help you spot or create opportunities to apply leadership learning in future situations?
> 4. How will this experience help you in the future to develop your soldiers' individual strengths, capabilities, and/or talents?

Results

The end-of-course feedback results reflected some significant changes in cadet behavior. For example, three feedback questions demonstrated statistically significant improvement compared with the prior semester (before the change in purpose and focus on application):

1. Strong expectation to apply course concepts
2. PL 300 provides process to apply and report use of course content
3. Ability to share clear/detailed examples with my course mentor

Other application feedback questions also reflected improvement. Instructors also noted an enhanced ability to assess application of theory to experiences. Additionally, they cited increased engagement in classroom discussions because of the students' ability to tie material to recent life events made salient by the use of *ResultsEngine*.

Advice to Colleagues

- Always start the design of a developmental experience with the end in mind and ensure the appropriate linkages are present.
- Ensure you are incorporating learning transfer. Hope is not a method.
- Ensure that the purpose emphasizes application (*will* use) as opposed to just learning (*can* use).
- Measure your results and adjust the approach when multiple measures indicate a failure to achieve your stated aims.

Case D4.1

How We Implemented an Immediate Application Checklist to Ensure Learning Transfer

Calhoun Wick
Founder, Fort Hill Company

Background

The Fort Hill Company is a pioneering leader in learning transfer. Our goal is to move the finish line of learning from the delivery of a course to improved workplace performance that delivers business results. In 1999, we invented the first learning transfer support system, now called *ResultsEngine®*. It has been used by more than 200,000 trainees in more than sixty countries. Our research was instrumental in the identification of *The Six Disciplines of Breakthrough Learning* (Wick, Pollock, & Jefferson, 2010).

Recently, the learning leader of a global, high-technology business asked me to look at a new program he had designed. He is passionate about having learning deliver business impact and wanted ideas for improvement. I was impressed; the design was brilliant—an innovative approach that can be led by local managers.

The business sponsor had asked for a program that would enhance leadership effectiveness (D1) by requiring his managers to recollect and use the great leadership development they had received over the last several years in the context of the situations they face in their work as leaders. The design (D2) consisted of monthly discussions built around a powerful one-page case study. Each month's case presents a different leadership or business challenge in a compelling way.

Participants are broken into teams and challenged to consider which of many options they could use to solve the issue presented in the case. Each team then presents its solution and rationale to the whole group for discussion and feedback. An innovative feature of these monthly sessions is that they are designed in a way that a local leader at a site can facilitate each session; no learning and development instructor is required.

From the perspective of the sponsor and participants, the pilot was a roaring success. So the program was slated to be rolled out globally and enterprise-wide.

But after reviewing the program process and materials, I asked the learning leader, "Where is the immediate application to the real work of participants?" The design was brilliant in every way except for the transfer step. It occurred to me that if such a skilled and committed learning leader could miss building in an explicit transfer process, then he and others could benefit from a job aid to be sure that this critical element is not overlooked. I likened it to a preflight checklist. Even the most experienced pilots use a checklist before takeoff to ensure that nothing critical is overlooked. We should do the same before we launch a program.

What We Did

I first considered what caused the transfer step to be overlooked. I concluded that three things had blindsided the learning leader:

1. The cases and discussions were so engaging that it felt as if learning were being applied to real work situations, when in fact no actual transfer step was built in.
2. The reactions to the course were so positive that they obscured the fact that something was missing.
3. It was not clear how to immediately apply some of the case studies to the leaders' day-to-day work. For example, the first case study in the pilot session concerned a massive time crunch across an organization to meet a delivery deadline. It was the kind of thing that might only happen once a year. The learning leader assumed that, since such an experience was uncommon, there was no immediate application for the learning.

I was an instrument-rated pilot for more than twenty years with more than a thousand hours of flight time. Even though I had made hundreds of takeoffs, I always ran a pre-takeoff checklist; I always pulled out my laminated checklist, called out each item, confirmed it, and then said "check." I took the time to do this every time because the consequences of missing an item just once—because I was distracted or preoccupied—could have been fatal.

Likewise, no matter how many programs we have designed, we should stop and run an Immediate Application Checklist (Exhibit D4.1.1) before launching a program to ensure that we have not missed anything that could be fatal to its success.

EXHIBIT D4.1.1. IMMEDIATE APPLICATION CHECKLIST

Immediate Application Design Checklist

❏ **SITUATION:** The workplace challenges that learning will solve are well understood.

❏ **LEARNING:** Learning is tailored to turn workplace challenges into application opportunities.

❏ **CONNECTION:** Participants are shown opportunities for immediate application and are provided adapters to help them make connections between learning and practice.

❏ **APPLICATION:** Application is made easy by example, practice, job aids, and process.

❏ **EXPECTATION:** Improved participant workplace performance is the condition of satisfaction.

❏ **ALL GO:** Ready for launch!

Immediate Application Delivery Checklist

❏ **SITUATION:** Delivery is in the context of the participants' work, not just course content.

❏ **LEARNING:** The criterion for teaching effectiveness is learning's application on the job.

❏ **CONNECTION:** Connectivity between work situations and learning is constantly switched on. Learners are provided adaptive tools and processes to help them see opportunities.

❏ **APPLICATION:** Application made easy by example, practice, job aids, and process.

❏ **EXPECTATION:** Improved participant workplace performance is the condition of satisfaction.

❏ **ALL GO:** Ready for launch!

Results

The use of these Immediate Application Checklists caused three important changes in the program:

1. First, the learning leader built examples to show participants where they would find similar situations in their work on a weekly or monthly basis. The case study remained a blockbuster example, but connections were actively made between the dynamics the case highlighted and situations in which participants could immediately put what they learned to work. The learning leader said this intentional focus on participant *situations,* rather than just delivering content was a breakthrough in thinking that is now being applied to other programs.

2. Second, these checklists led to the realization that we need to provide "connection adapters" for participants who are literal learners. This came to light when a participant commented, "I will never experience the exact situation presented in the case study so I do not see how I can use what I learned." Connection adapters are like an adapter for a different kind of electrical plug. They help the participant plug the learning into situations in their own work. The most agile learners make these connections on their own; others need help to see the connections.

3. Third, participants are now challenged to find opportunities between the case study sessions to apply what they learned. Each case study session after the first now begins with participants reporting their workplace application actions and "lessons learned" before they dive into the next case study. This not only underscores the expectation for application, but it also harnesses the powerful effect of "spaced learning" to solidify and reinforce prior sessions (see review by Thalheimer, 2006).

Much to the sponsor's delight, these changes ensured that not only do managers and leaders receive stimulating learning through the case study process, but they also are delivering improved workplace performance. As the revised program, with its monthly report-outs, is expanded enterprise-wide, the learning organization will have literally hundreds of examples monthly that illustrate learning being applied in ways that improve performance.

Advice to Colleagues

- Don't launch a training program without completing an Immediate Application Checklist.
- Before you push the throttle forward, make sure that the learning you will deliver is well connected with the workplace situations your participants face.
- Check that your participants have the opportunity to immediately apply what they learn to their work.
- Provide your participants with a clear destination of improved performance.
- If all the checks are "Go," you are ready to launch and cleared for learning transfer takeoff.

Case D4.2

How We Achieved Lean Improvements with Learning Transfer

Alex Jaccaci and Charlie Hackett
Corporate Improvement Training Facilitator and Corporate Improvement Team Leader, Hypertherm Inc.

Background

Hypertherm designs and manufactures advanced plasma, laser, and waterjet cutting systems. Hypertherm's technology and products are used in industries such as shipbuilding, manufacturing, agriculture, transportation, and industrial construction. An associate-owned company, Hypertherm has headquarters in New Hampshire and manufactures nearly all of its products in the United States.

Hypertherm has several training teams, including:

- Organization development responsible for associate development
- Hypertherm technical training to train CNC machine operators
- Customer training, which trains Hypertherm partners
- Corporate improvement team

The corporate improvement team is responsible for facilitating the global adoption of Hypertherm's hyperformance practices including Lean and Six Sigma to promote a culture of continuous improvement and operational excellence.

Hypertherm has pursued lean manufacturing as a corporate philosophy and strategy for approximately sixteen years. In 2010, Hypertherm established a model of lean principles and standards as a roadmap for achieving operational excellence. The authors, management, and the operations team leaders identified the opportunity to engage all 650 production associates in a learning program to advance operational excellence and achieve continued growth.

The corporate improvement team, with support from consultant Kevin Duggan, created the Lean Principles and Standards for Operational Excellence Learning Program. The program was designed to provide associates with an opportunity to learn about and then *apply* the ten lean principles through improvement projects within their production setting.

What We Did

The Lean Principles and Standards for Operational Excellence (Lean P&S) Program was designed utilizing *The Six Disciplines for Breakthrough Learning* (Wick, Pollock, & Jefferson, 2010) for guidance to achieve learning transfer and business results. The Lean P&S initiative was implemented as a thirteen-week engagement with intact teams across the Hypertherm manufacturing facilities.

The objectives of the program included supporting associates to gain an understanding of the lean principles and then to transfer their learning into business value by applying lean improvements in targeted areas of production. The initiative was designed with four phases of leadership and participant engagement. Following are the four phases of the initiative and the primary activities that were incorporated into each phase.

Phase 1: Preparation (forty days)

Aim: to engage team leadership through outcomes planning and prepare the participants for the program; steps included:

1. Corporate improvement team (CIT) facilitated leadership planning meetings to define targeted outcomes and measures for the initiative.
2. CIT and team leaders conducted gap analyses comparing current state to desired state of incorporating lean principles into the value streams.
3. Team leaders defined improvement priorities and identified participants for project teams.
4. Team leaders met with participants to introduce the Lean P&S learning process and objectives.
5. CIT invited participants to join the initiative and provided pre-training reference materials.
6. CIT trained team leaders on "best practices for learning transfer and achieving results" to support leaders to create an environment of learning transfer and to prepare leaders to serve as improvement project sponsors.

Phase 2: In-Class Training (eight hours)

Aim: to provide participants the opportunity to gain familiarity with the lean principles through an application-oriented learning experience; steps included:

1. Senior management sponsor opened each session with an overview of the business case for pursuing Hypertherm's lean principles and operational excellence.
2. CIT shared the ten lean principles and foundational concepts.

3. Associates participated in a manufacturing simulation using Legos® to gain experience in applying the lean principles in three simulated rounds of production.

4. Participants toured production areas, observing lean principles at work and discovering opportunities for application.

5. CIT shared examples of the lean principles at Hypertherm and invited project teams from prior implementations to present their projects as examples of successful applications.

6. Participants worked with their project teams to complete initial planning for their improvement projects during the classroom session.

7. Participants completed a classroom evaluation assessing whether the training met their learning session expectations.

Phase 3: Application (forty-five days)

Aim: to extend the learning for the participants and practice applying lean principles through on-the-job improvement projects; steps included:

1. Participants worked with project teams of three to four associates on projects aimed to integrate lean principles into their value streams.

2. Each project team created a four-panel project plan, received endorsement, and then coaching and support from their project sponsor throughout the project.

3. Project teams employed the plan, do, check, act method of problem solving to define their project objective, solution, and evaluation of project success.

4. The larger team created a visual measurement board located in a central location to display progress of all projects in achieving their milestones.

5. CIT provided coaching and support to project teams in application of lean principles and to leaders in project sponsorship throughout the project period.

6. Teams completed their projects and reported on their results and learning to all members of their teams at a change of shift meeting.

7. Participants completed a Lean P&S knowledge test to verify their understanding of key content and process elements.

8. CIT facilitated the Phase 3 team leadership meeting to review progress of projects and prepare leaders for Phase 4 activities.

9. Participants completed a program evaluation on their project results and experience in transferring their learning.

Phase 4: Achievement (twenty-one days)

Aim: to evaluate the learning and improvement results, to recognize participants' accomplishments, and to plan for continued improvement.

1. CIT gathered data and analyzed initiative results, including: Phase 2 and Phase 3 evaluations; percent of participants who completed course requirements (attending classroom session, passing the test, and completing their project within fort-five days); percent of associates who reported that they transferred their learning to create business value; percent of improvement projects completed; data on participant engagement; and success factors and barriers of the initiative.

2. CIT facilitated the Phase 4 team leadership meeting focusing on lessons learned and planning for continued improvement for the team and continuing the momentum achieved in the program.

3. Participants received a reward of a Lean P&S T-Shirt for completing course requirements.

4. CIT facilitated team celebrations and report-outs that included presenting the results of the initiative to the team and invited guests throughout Hypertherm.
5. Several highlighted improvement projects were presented during the team celebrations.
6. Team leadership created and initiated an improvement plan to continue momentum of their Lean P&S journey.

Results

As of this writing, three teams that comprise a total of 248 participants have completed the Lean P&S learning initiative. The results of the initiative to date were measured in several ways and are listed below:

1. Course Completion. Ninety-eight percent of the participants completed the course requirements (attended the class session, passed the test, and completed their project—the new finish line).

2. Learning Transfer Self-Reported. Ninety percent of participants reported that they applied their learning and made an improvement to add value to the business. Ninety percent of participants reported that they used their learning to create a positive impact for their teams and Hypertherm.
3. Learning Transfer Measured Through Improvements Applied. Ninety-five percent of the participant project teams completed their improvement projects within the project period of forty-five days.
4. Associate Engagement/Participant Self-Report of Engagement. Ninety-one percent of participants reported that they were motivated to keep applying what they learned to make improvement for their team.

5. Qualitative Success Factors. The top success factor that was identified by participants was that they utilized and appreciated teamwork on their team to learn and make improvement.

The results of the initiative to date suggest that the model of the *Six Disciplines for Breakthrough Learning* created an effective framework for achieving learning transfer and improvement for the company. The next steps for the Lean P&S program are to continue to implement with the remaining Hypertherm production teams and build on the learning and results archived to date.

Another related result of the Lean P&S program is that the corporate improvement team, and now other learning departments at Hypertherm, are incorporating the six disciplines and learning transfer as a best practice for training and development.

Advice to Colleagues
- Begin with the end in mind—identify the business and improvement outcomes desired by team leaders and design the program to achieve these outcomes.
- Create a parallel leadership development track in the program that trains and supports leaders to support their associates to transfer their learning and achieve improvement.
- Establish and build on the leadership alignment through all levels to establish priority and focus for the learning and improvement activity.
- Define learning transfer as a goal of the program and communicate the rationale and approach to achieve learning transfer to leaders and participants.

- Define and include measure(s) of learning transfer and share the results with participants and stakeholders.
- Design the classroom learning to be as practice- and application-oriented as possible to assist the participants to gain experience putting their learning to work. (The design in this case study had an approximate allocation of 65 percent time dedicated to practice-orientated activity and 35 percent time dedicated to lecture.)
- Define action learning projects or assignments prior to the training that extend participant learning after the classroom session into a period of learning transfer.
- Report the results that the team achieved back to the team and stakeholders.
- Use the *Six Disciplines for Breakthrough Learning* as an effective roadmap to achieve learning transfer and improvement results for your company.

Case D4.3

How We Implemented a Low-Cost, Low-Effort Follow-Up

Rob Bartlett
Corporate Trainer, DirectWest

Background

DirectWest, a wholly owned subsidiary of SaskTel, is the exclusive provider of mysask411 solution, Saskatchewan's choice for local search. The company continues to help connect buyers and sellers with new and innovative products and services based on Saskatchewan's best source for local information, the print, online, and mobile SaskTel telephone directory. We are located in Regina, Saskatchewan, Canada, and have one hundred employees. Our training organization consists of one person.

A department in our organization had a need to improve communication. We did a workshop on examining your own communication preferences. Outcomes were for each team member to pick one thing to focus on to do differently or better to improve their interpersonal communication.

What We Did

We knew that for soft-skills training, in particular, follow-up was essential to ensure learning transfer. Given the size of our training department (me), we needed an efficient solution. So I used a weekly email reminder to the group asking them to respond by answering three questions based on the Friday5s® model. I also included a tip of the week, such as a short graphic or illustration that supported the material.

A sample email is shown is Exhibit D4.3.1.

Exhibit D4.3.1. Example of a Reminder Email to Participants

Subject: Communication Skills Reminder

As promised, here is your Friday reminder.

A great technique for building new skills is continually reflecting and planning. With that in mind here are three questions for you (that should take no more than five minutes to answer).

1. Last week I tried _____ and it went well.
2. Last week I tried _____ and it went not so well.
3. Next week I am going to _____.

Communication tip of the week:

"How to _____ "

Results

Eighty percent of participants followed up with the trainer with requests for coaching on a specific item following the training. Previous training efforts had no after-training follow-up.

Lessons of Experience

- I would start the emails in the three-week period before asking what people would do, to get them to start imagining the change they might make.
- I would also have the reminders come from the sponsor rather than from the trainer. Strong sponsorship from the leader is critical to success.

Advice to Colleagues

- Do something after training to cause recall of the information.
- It doesn't have to be perfect; you just need to help participants recall what they learned and how they planned to use it.

Case D4.4

How We Used Spaced Learning and Gamification to Increase the Effectiveness of Product Launch Training

Duncan Lennox
CEO, Qstream

Background

The pharmaceutical industry is one of the most highly regulated industries in the United States. Drug companies must work diligently to mitigate financial and compliance risk by ensuring that their medical science liaisons and sales teams have the level of knowledge they need to sell effectively—and safely. Representatives must possess not only a thorough understanding of product attributes and competitive positioning, but also of multiple disease states and the complexities of the regulatory and healthcare systems.

One of the world's largest pharmaceutical companies was preparing for the launch of a new drug for chronic obstructive pulmonary disease (COPD). The challenge was to prepare the 3,000+ member U.S. sales team for the competitive and regulatory challenges it would face.

Instilling the required level of knowledge was a critical task for the product brand manager. Ensuring its long-term retention by the sales team posed an even more monumental challenge. Research conducted by 19th century German psychologist Hermann Ebbinghaus demonstrated unequivocally the existence of the "forgetting curve" (Figure D4.4.1).

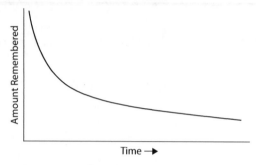

Figure D4.4.1. Forgetting Curve (after Ebbinghaus, 1885)

What Ebbinghaus discovered is that the human brain starts *forgetting* information immediately after it is learned. The forgetting curve is initially very steep such that, without subsequent reinforcement, by thirty days people retain only roughly 20 percent of what they've learned, no matter how compelling or effective the initial training was. Combating the forgetting curve requires a program of "spaced education" that combines recall, repetition, and active engagement.

Given the importance of this product launch, the company could not risk having its representatives operating on 20 percent or less of the critical medical and regulatory information they had been provided. So the company turned to Qstream, a pioneer in the development of technology solutions for increasing engagement and knowledge retention long after sales training has been completed.

What We Did

Calling on the experience of its training team, the pharmaceutical giant began the process of educating its field force on the new drug using typical sales-readiness approaches that included a formal plan of action (POA) and launch meetings, online learning and assessments, as well as sales management mentoring and coaching.

In the face of an ever-more-challenging regulatory and competitive landscape, however, the brand managers had to be certain reps could recall and apply the critical information. The training team considered traditional reinforcement paths such as offering more e-learning, building richer, interactive content, and even convening more face-to-face meetings. They quickly concluded that incremental improvements such as these would not be sufficient and that they needed a "game changer."

The company contacted Qstream to explore the use of its mobile, game-based learning and analytics system. Developed originally at Harvard, the solution combines personalization, social engagement, and gamification with a patent-pending "spaced education" approach that reinforces core messages and skills in the form of questions, answers, and rewards. Delivered to any laptop or mobile device, Qstream requires less than three minutes a day. Nevertheless, in controlled clinical trials, the approach has been shown to increase long-term retention and comprehension of medical concepts and information (see Kerfoot & Baker, 2012).

Following the early success of the first-phase pilot for 150 medical science liaisons, the company rolled out a twenty-five-question "refresher course" to more than 2,500 respiratory field reps.

Every other day, the system would send users two short questions about the material they had studied (Exhibit D4.4.1), which they could answer through their laptops or mobile devices.

Exhibit D4.4.1. Example of Qstream Question

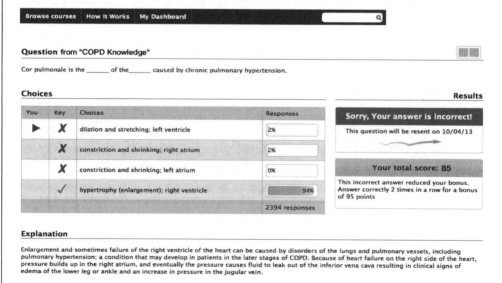

| Browse courses | How It Works | My Dashboard | [🔍] |

Question from "COPD Knowledge"

Cor pulmonale is the _____ of the_____ caused by chronic pulmonary hypertension.

Choices

- ○ dilation and stretching; left ventricle
- ○ constriction and shrinking; right atrium
- ○ constriction and shrinking; left atrium
- ○ hypertrophy (enlargement); right ventricle

[Submit]

Reps could instantly see how their peers answered the same question, as well as concise explanations for each answer whether correct or not (Exhibit D4.4.2). After a rep could answer the same question correctly twice, the question was "retired," and the next question

Exhibit D4.4.2. Example of Feedback on Answer

| Browse courses | How It Works | My Dashboard | [🔍] |

Question from "COPD Knowledge"

Cor pulmonale is the _____ of the_____ caused by chronic pulmonary hypertension.

Choices   **Results**

You	Key	Choices	Responses
▶	✗	dilation and stretching; left ventricle	2%
	✗	constriction and shrinking; right atrium	2%
	✗	constriction and shrinking; left atrium	0%
	✓	hypertrophy (enlargement); right ventricle	94%
			2394 responses

Sorry, Your answer is Incorrect!

This question will be resent on 10/04/13

Your total score: 85

This incorrect answer reduced your bonus. Answer correctly 2 times in a row for a bonus of 95 points

Explanation

Enlargement and sometimes failure of the right ventricle of the heart can be caused by disorders of the lungs and pulmonary vessels, including pulmonary hypertension; a condition that may develop in patients in the later stages of COPD. Because of heart failure on the right side of the heart, pressure builds up in the right atrium, and eventually the pressure causes fluid to leak out of the inferior vena cava resulting in clinical signs of edema of the lower leg or ankle and an increase in pressure in the jugular vein.

delivered. The process continued until the representative mastered the content.

Results

Prior to implementing Qstream's game-based sales reinforcement approach, the company's training director was consistently frustrated by the low levels of retention of essential knowledge in the field—despite the wealth of resources made available.

"The bottom line is that there was a lot of noise in the field. Our reps were bombarded with product emails and resources and just screened them out."

By embracing the mobile platform, the company was able to take advantage of the well-established principle of spaced learning by pushing relevant product information to the field automatically in small chunks over an extended period. And by capitalizing on reps' competitive nature through leaderboards and a point-scoring system that allowed them to see their own score relative to other users or teams, they were able to boost engagement rates to more than 80 percent.

According to the company's training director, "The reps totally love it. 'Addictive' is the word I hear over and over again. Reps would set their alarms for 4 a.m. so they could answer the question faster than the others." At the end of the COPD launch reinforcement program, the company brought the top ten reps on stage at the company meeting to recognize their achievements in the program.

Overall, retention increased by 150 percent, while the flexibility to reuse existing, approved content simultaneously increased training efficiency by nearly 40 percent. The company has already extended use of the platform to two other divisions and sees clear applications for use of the platform beyond sales.

Success Factors

To speed the rollout, the brand team needed to be able to re-use content from e-learning modules that had already been cleared through the company's medical and legal regulatory process. They also required a diversity of question types and the flexibility to embed graphics and videos. Given the complexity of the material, some explanations included reference links to the company's learning management system (LMS).

Qstream's powerfully simple user experience—combined with a point-scoring system, leaderboards, and answer blogs—helped keep the learners engaged. An onboard analytics engine offered the company's brand managers unprecedented insights into engagement, mastery, and retention, and—at the same time—highlighted critical knowledge gaps in the field.

Advice to Colleagues

- Planning for pull through is critical. The ideal time to roll out a reinforcement solution is after your initial knowledge transfer programs are completed; the timing can vary by company. While solutions such as Qstream can be used to teach anyone anything in just three minutes a day, the primary benefit to an organization is long-term retention of sales-critical messages and skills that impact revenue.
- Users, particularly on-the-go sales representatives, enjoy the learning experience more when given simple tools with game elements. Adding leaderboards, and even prizes, can

appeal to the natural competitiveness of a sales team and increase engagement.

- Keep the overall number of questions relatively low (ten to twenty-five), course timeframes short, and emphasize the most relevant, scenario-based information. When reps are bombarded with too many training resources, they tend to screen them out, viewing your efforts toward knowledge retention as just more corporate noise without real value.

- While reinforcement programs are ideal for reuse of existing content—such as material created for e-learning modules or assessments—it's easy and fun to create material using different question types to achieve different results. If you are creating a reinforcement program for the first time, start by asking yourself what information you want rolling off the tongues of your sales team. And remember, if you can effectively put these core messages and skills in the form of a question, you can create a course out of it!

- Use the results to demonstrate training's effectiveness and provide insights into the capabilities, trends, and knowledge gaps of your teams. However, be sensitive to how this data is distributed and used. If the performance results are used for punitive purposes, engagement and the quality of the feedback will decline precipitously.

- Experiment! Even small changes to your approach can dramatically improve engagement and retention. Seek systems with onboard analytics and simple browser-based authoring tools that will give you the flexibility you require, including the ability to update live course content and questions on the fly.

Case D4.5

How We Develop Managers to Leverage Learning Transfer

Geoff Rip

Research Director, Institute for Learning Practitioners, Australia

Background

Our research and experience have led us to conclude that:

- Since training's aim is to achieve specific standards of on-the-job performance, training effectiveness and value ultimately depend on learning transfer to the workplace.
- Transfer is essential to complete the learning process and achieve competence and proficiency. Learning and transfer go hand-in-hand.
- For most organizations, the weakest link in the training process is transfer of learning. Too often, application is either not attempted or quickly abandoned.
- Employees often rate training highly, but then fail to apply their new learning on return to work. This is like saying, "The operation was a success but the patient died."

- Without transfer, any money invested is a waste (negative ROI). There are also significant opportunity costs, especially related to people's time.
- Lack of transfer has a significant negative impact on the credibility and reputation of training. When training fails to deliver, it's the learners and L & D function that tend to be blamed.
- Transfer is influenced by individual, training design, and workplace factors. Inhibitory forces in the workplace tend to dominate unless deliberately counteracted.
- The factors that cause a negative or toxic transfer climate also result in employee demotivation and disengagement.
- The dominant influence on transfer is the immediate manager of the learner. As one learner put it, "What interests my manager fascinates me!"
- Most managers don't understand their fundamental role in the training process and/or they lack the know-how to effectively leverage transfer of learning.
- Expressions of support are not enough. Managers need to use their influence as leaders—before, during, and after training events—to maximize learning transfer.

What We Did

Recognition of the above need led to the development of the Leveraging Results from Learning program. This is a unique, research-based training program for managers whose staff will be attending off-the-job training (synchronous or asynchronous).

A key design principle was that the program would act as a model of effective training. In other words, both the content and the process would create experiential learning and understanding of what it takes to ensure learning is successfully applied in the workplace.

The following are key features of the program design:

- *Four Phases:* The program consists of four phases: (1) preparation, (2) workshop, (3) transfer, and (4) application story (Figure D4.5.1). Managers are informed in advance that Leveraging Results from Learning is an eight-week program and only concludes when they have submitted an application story.

Figure D4.5.1. Four Phases of the Program

- *Positioning:* Pre-training communications about the program positions it as leadership skills development, focusing on how to get the best results from money invested in off-the-job training. Ideally, pre-training communications are sent through the participants' managers.
- *Preparation:* Participants complete a "results map" for one or more members of their staff who will attend training during the next two months, thereby introducing them to this tool and raising perceived relevance of the training.
- *Workshop facilitation:* We determined that a half-day, classroom-based workshop, delivered in-company by accredited trainers would be most effective. When in-company learning practitioners facilitate the workshop they are demonstrating their expertise, creating a shared experience, underscoring relevance, and building a partnership approach with the managers.

    The workshop consists of four sections:

1. The Transfer Problem
2. Motivation to Transfer
3. Strategies for Transfer
4. Planning for Transfer

Participants gain practical models and ideas that can be easily implemented after the workshop. The workshop demonstrates activity-based, high-engagement training using methods that basically guarantee the planned learning outcomes.

- *Support site:* The participants are given immediate access to an online support site that includes strategies for self-managed transfer, copies of job aids, and additional information on learning transfer and transfer strategies.
- *Application story:* The application story (more recently referred to as a proficiency story) provides evidence of successful application and targeted leadership in action.

Results

Companies that have implemented the Leveraging Results from Learning program have reported numerous benefits, including:

- Appreciation of the need to manage learning transfer
- Practical understanding of how to improve training results
- Managers seen to be encouraging and assisting transfer
- Learners who feel more supported by their managers
- Enhanced motivation and commitment to transfer learning
- Improvement in transfer climate assessment scores
- Greater transfer of learning and learning from transfer
- Increased training effectiveness, value, and ROI
- Enhanced credibility and reputation of training
- Reinforcement of leadership development programs

Application of the participants' learning produces a triple win. Transfer is improved on courses targeted by the managers during their training, the transfer strategies can be applied to all future courses, and the leader behaviors have a positive influence on employee engagement.

Keys to Success

- Position the training as the development of leadership ability/skills. Clarify the benefits from a leadership perspective.
- Keep it practical and straightforward. If influencing transfer looks too hard or time-consuming, managers will just give it lip service.
- Help the participants' managers to set the right example. Make sure they demonstrate the behaviors that are the focus of the training.

Advice to Colleagues

- Be proactive in harnessing management involvement and influence on transfer.
- Provide training so that managers understand their crucial role and have the know-how to leverage results from learning.
- Use the program to role model training best practices and strengthen your partnership with managers.

Case D4.6

How We Engage Managers to Acknowledge the Achievements of Leadership Program Participants

Mike Schwartz
Learning Program Manager, Cox Media Group

Background

Cox Media Group (CMG) is an integrated broadcasting, publishing, direct marketing, and digital media company that includes the national advertising rep firms of CoxReps. Additionally, CMG owns Cox Target Media, which operates Valpak, one of North America's leading direct marketing companies, and Savings.com, a leading online source for savings. In 2013, the company's operations included fourteen broadcast television stations and one local cable channel, fifty-seven radio stations, eight daily newspapers, more than a dozen non-daily publications, and more than one hundred digital services.

One of our key development initiatives for high-potential middle managers is the Cox Media Group Leadership Program. Each leadership program class consists of twenty participants drawn from all CMG business units. Two classes run simultaneously during the year.

The seven-month program includes:

- Three multi-day visits to corporate headquarters in Atlanta for instructor-led leadership and management training
- Group projects between corporate training sessions
- 360-degree feedback
- Use of an online goal-setting and progress-reporting tool

What We Did

Prior to "graduation," we ask the managers of participants to submit acknowledgments in which they highlight observable performance improvements. The acknowledgments are read aloud in front of the class during program closing ceremonies and participants receive copies.

Results

These concrete acknowledgments have significant impact in two ways:

- For the participant, it is public recognition of his or her progress. The acknowledgment reinforces the connection between participant and manager. It also clearly demonstrates that the participant's progress was observable and noticed by his or her manager.
- For the program, they are a powerful affirmation of the impact the program has on participants and their growth. The manager's

perspective as a separate but involved observer gives considerable weight to the program's impact on its participants.

Here are two samples that demonstrate the quality and value of the acknowledgments:

Sample 1

"In the past I've heard you speak of doing your best and being your best. Well, you have done them both. Due to your hard work and training, I've seen you go from being a great team member to an even greater team leader. Your training has allowed you to develop even better skills at remaining calm under sometimes difficult circumstances, taking control of the situation rather than letting the situation take control of you. Calmness is your strength and will serve you well. To simply say congratulations is not enough but it is appropriate. Congratulations."

Sample 2

"It has been such a pleasure to watch your professional growth as part of the Cox Media Group Leadership Program. The timing of the program was excellent in that we were undergoing significant reorganization that elevated your role and immediately tested your developing skills. During this anxious period you were put on the spot, and time and time again you demonstrated a tremendous grasp of the facts and poise under pressure. In both small and large groups, and under some degree of pressure, you presented with both confidence and a calming style. In addition, as part of the reorganization, you faced several tough decisions. I think participation in the Cox Media Group Leadership Program helped you balance many influences and make the smart and tough decisions. You have developed a keen analytical sense that will serve you well. You are quickly developing into a strong media executive, and it is programs like this one that will allow us to develop our stars of the future."

Advice to Colleagues

- Give the manager notice at the beginning of the program that you will seek an acknowledgment of the participant's progress.
- Give the manager plenty of advance time to prepare the acknowledgment.
- Give the manager samples of previous acknowledgments as a guide.
- Set a deadline to receive the acknowledgments well in advance of the 'graduation.'
- Have the acknowledgment read at 'graduation' by another participant in the program.

Case D4.7

How We Sustain Priority-Management Training

Marc Lalande

President, Learning Andrago Inc.

Background

Our approach to training can be likened to a GPS. We first help clients assess where they are now (current performance) by triangulating information, confirming the cause of performance gaps, and identifying the execution obstacles. Then, based on their goals (desired performance), we propose a route that will help them get where they want to be, stay there, and document the impact of changes. Like a GPS system, we suggest the path to follow to accelerate the speed to competency and to evaluate ROI.

By way of example: One of our clients was experiencing challenges keeping their sales representatives focused on the most important business priorities. Rather than take the predictable—and dead end— route of running a priority-management course with limited transfer outcomes, we agreed to take the representatives on a blended-learning journey that included support for learning transfer as an integral part of the plan.

What We Did

We started the journey by assessing the representatives' everyday attitudes and paradigms about priority management in the field using a web-based anonymous questionnaire. A short preparation reading assignment was prescribed next, prior to attending a classroom hands-on workshop.

The one-day workshop began with a simulation experience during which participants had to prioritize items to survive a plane crash. During debriefing participants reflected on their learning, including the simulation experience, recent reading, personal experience, and the needs assessment results.

Participants were then tasked to create their own priority ranking criteria. The second simulation exercise enabled participants to apply their own new priority ranking system to real business tasks and activities.

But the learning journey did not stop there. We knew that to produce the desired business results, the training had to be sustained and transferred to the representatives' day-to-day work.

The pillar of the transfer strategy was the action-planning session at the end of the workshop. Participants were asked to complete a *"commitment to apply contract"* to capture the elements of intention to change. Participants were instructed to write, using action verbs, what they intended to "start doing, stop doing, improve, do differently" on an NCR form that created three copies (Exhibit D4.7.1).

Once the action-planning session was completed, the participants folded one copy and slipped it in an envelope to be mailed back to them in two weeks as a reminder of their commitment. Another copy was collected by the facilitator for further analysis. The final copy was folded and inserted into a tennis ball (previously cut half open). Participants gently tossed the balls to each other so that they could randomly pick someone else's contract copy for future instructions.

Exhibit D4.7.1. The Commitment-to-Apply Contract (Bilingual Template)

Priority Management Ideas

START DOING / COMMENCER	STOP DOING / CESSER
IMPROVE/AMÉLIORER	DO DIFFERENTLY/ FAIRE DIFFÉREMMENT

We provided our client with a transfer plan that included suggested initiatives to keep the learning alive, support changes, and encourage the use of the new priority ranking criteria. The transfer plan included:

- The general manager of the company provided everyone a copy of the new priority-management criteria (job aid) by email in the first week.
- We conducted a frequency analysis of the content of all contracts collected during the hands-on workshop. This provided guidance to our client on a number of aspects that would turn out to be useful during the transfer period:
  - The level of commitment to change and apply
  - The main aspects that representatives intended to start or stop doing

- The focus of the application efforts
  - The range of obstacles representatives anticipated to come across
- Participants received their own copies of their commitments to apply change within two weeks.
- The director of marketing developed an Outlook-compatible template to ensure that the priority ranking criteria will live on.
- Sales managers started follow-up discussion in the third week to explore what assistance was required from them.
- Head office also provided the signal for participants to directly contact the owner of the contract form that they received during the tennis-ball-throwing exercise (buddy system).
  - This initiated a series of informal discussions across the entire sales force about priority management, what people had done, and what had worked.
  - The goal of these peer-to-peer conversations was to have representatives verbalize their motivation to apply and to discuss recent successes. Change and improvements are more sustainable when you do not feel alone.
- The client started to sprinkle various communications and initiatives to keep the focus alive on priority management and support the change and application efforts of the sales representatives.

Results

- We elected not to use a Level 1 questionnaire at the end of the one-day workshop. The first measure of success came from the commitment-to-apply contract. Participants scored 8.4 (+ 1.4) on a scale of 10 to describe the importance of their commitment. Their confidence to apply the desired changes also scored 8.4 (+ 1.4) on a scale of 10.

- Every participant was highly involved in the creation of the "commitment-to-apply contract" and, on average, each participant captured 7.4 actions per contract.
- The most frequent mention in the "start doing" section was the intention to perform a regular priority review. This was one of the critical behaviors desired by the client. Aligned with this finding, the most frequent mention in the "stop doing" section was to "stop being reactive."
- Two months after the workshop, we had a conversation with the client to confirm the place that priority management occupied in the representatives' daily reality. They were very happy; the message and the behaviors were still very much alive.
- Unfortunately, the client did not provide a budget to more formally document the level of behavior changes (Level 3) or impact on business (Level 4).

Lessons of Experience

- Learning concepts such as priority management should be addressed with an experiential approach. I was able to convince the client to refrain from using a didactic approach to the topic. In my opinion, this contributes to "walk the talk" from the first minute of the workshop and paves the way to higher transfer and application.
- I am using learning transfer plans as much as possible to encourage clients to keep the learning alive. As they may not necessarily know how to best support learning transfer, I find that if I provide a list of suggested steps, they end up doing more.
- Sadly, few clients see the value in spending additional money to document the outcomes after a workshop. What we would do differently the next time is to build a single price for conducting the attitude questionnaire before and after the workshop. That way we would collect more evidence of lasting change.

Keys to Success

- In my opinion, the learning transfer plan is essential. Having regular points of contact with the client to keep them motivated to execute the plan is critical. When I do not support the transfer plan from the outside, it is quickly forgotten and the transfer conversations are overwhelmed by the day-to-day business tasks.

Cautions

- If you are an external service provider, you must be careful not to come across as telling the client what to do. As much as transfer requires frequent reinforcement, this could easily become an annoyance. Be sure that you have management buy-in for the concept and moderate your approach.

Advice to Colleagues

- If you want training to stick, commit to do it right or stay away from it. We should not compromise on where the finish line should be.
- In practicing the first discipline (D1), discuss or agree on the transfer terms before the project starts. People are too busy with other pressing priorities after the training.
- The transfer plan is like the exercising sequence you get when you enroll in a gym. It makes the routine a lot easier to follow and to stick to.
- Secure permission to pursue the transfer plan ahead of time with the various stakeholders and participants. If you omit this part, the energy you will display to drive follow-through (D4), and deploy active support (D5), may not be so well received after the training is delivered.

Case D4.8

How We Turn Learning into Action

Emma Weber

Founder and Director, Lever Learning–Australia

Background

Moree Plain Shires Council is one of the largest local government areas within New South Wales, Australia. It is responsible for all local services and governance in the region.

One of the major issues the council faced was that, as an organization, they were not performing well enough when it came to managing the performance of staff. This was not just about the annual performance review process, but more importantly, about managers' day-to-day actions and conversations to ensure appropriate behavior and productivity—a challenge shared by many organizations.

A one-day performance management program was delivered by a tried and trusted training provider that the Council had worked with for a number of years. It was a great program that always had good end-of-the-day reviews.

The learning outcomes of the program included:

- Knowing how to conduct effective everyday performance conversations
- Understanding the link between leadership, behavior, and performance and how to create a high-performance culture through role models, setting expectations, effective feedback, and identifying strategies to enhance individual performance

The real challenge was not whether people knew or understood the concepts at the end of the program, it was whether they actually did anything with the knowledge and skills back in the workplace.

This is where Lever Learning was bought in. Our specialty—Turning Learning into Action®—was needed to ensure what the participant had learned in the training was transferred back into behavioral change in the workplace. Our clients include multinationals across automotive, IT, financial services, and manufacturing and a similar methodology is used whether it is a one-thousand-person leadership training global rollout or a departmental sales training.

We have chosen to report this small project to laser in on and demonstrate our approach, learning transfer methodology, and evaluation process.

What We Did

We partnered with the current training provider to deliver real change back in the workplace. In our view, transfer of learning is the missing link between effective learning and business impact. Turning Learning into Action (TLA) is a proven learning transfer methodology that solves the problem through a series of specific, structured, and accountable one-on-one conversations at intervals *after* the training event.

In its simplest form, our TLA methodology is in three key parts:

- Preparation
- Action
- Evaluation

The first stage of TLA is *preparation.* At the end of the one-day program, the facilitator worked with the group to capture specific action plans. These were then copied to the coach and the participants' managers.

The participants created individual action plans, which they aligned with their key learning from the program and the challenges or opportunities they were facing in the workplace.

We gained commitment and confirmed understanding of the follow-up process by having the individual sign a learning agreement, including confidentiality and process. Schedules were created for three thirty-minute follow-up telephone conversations with a TLA specialist over a twelve-week period.

Every individual left the training event with three thirty-minute telephone calls locked in their calendars, a clear understanding of immediate actions to take, and an action plan to work on for the next three months.

The process was communicated to key stakeholders, including managers of the participants and program sponsors.

An example of a typical action plan from the performance management program is shown is Exhibit D4.8.1.

Exhibit D4.8.1. Example of a Typical Action Plan

Action Plan	Program Name: PERFORMANCE MANAGEMENT		Date: Dec 2012

Participant Name: Ian Smith .... Email: .... TLA Coach: Phenella Lill ....

Telephone: (landline) .... (mobile) .... Role: Landfill Facility Manager ....

Session 1: Date: 18th January 2013 Time: 2pm   Session 2: Date: 8th February 2013   Time: 1.15pm   Session 3: Date: 8th March 2013   Time: 3.30pm

TO USE BACK IN THE WORKPLACE			NOW	PLAN
What do you want to achieve? What specifically will you implement from the program and by when?	Why is it important to you? What does it mean to you personally? Why is that important to you?	Measures / Success indicators How will you know you have been successful? Describe by seeing, feeling & hearing success.	What is your current status? Where are you now with this action on a scale of 1 (low) to 10 (high)?	Next steps What actions can you take within the next 48 hours? What are the future steps?
Have regular one on one meetings with my team, starting by mid January	Allow me to see how staff are progressing, make them happy in their work environment	By determining how each staff member is travelling to maximise productivity	1 2 3 **4** 5 6 7 8 9 10	Start planning one on one meetings Book first meetings in the calendar
Schedule monthly team meetings with staff	Increase communication, feedback and recognition of tasks performed	Meetings held	1 **2** 3 4 5 6 7 8 9 10	Set dates and send out invitations
Confirm expectations and manage use of personal phones	To maximise staff time and job productivity	Staff become more proficient in their roles and less stress on other employees	1 2 **3** 4 5 6 7 8 9 10	Personal phones to stay in lockers until breaks

Please sign: I, _____, have read and understood the learning agreement outlined overleaf.

Contact details for your session Telephone: Europe / UK +44 333 301 0714   Asia / US / Australia +61 2 8221 8833   Email: phenella@ieverlearning.com

The second stage of TLA is the three thirty-minute *action conversations*—what is actually happening in the workplace following the training. As the name suggests, the focus of these conversations is on *action*—the changes participants are going to make between the follow-up conversations to progress each of their stated objectives.

These powerful conversations were delivered by phone over a period of several weeks to encourage inward self-reflection. The real goal is to get the participants to have conversations with themselves, rather than just an external discussion with a coach. This is the process that actually moves a participant from A to B and it's about questioning, to get the individual to take the ownership for the changes they are going to make.

The conversations follow the flow of our ACTION methodology illustrated in Exhibit D4.8.2.

Exhibit D4.8.2. ACTION Methodology

ACTION Conversation

ACCOUNTABILITY

CALIBRATION

_____

TARGET

INFO

OPTIONS

NEXT STEPS

Accountability

Calibration

Target

Next steps

Info

Options

The ACTION Conversation Model is an acronym for the stages that the conversation must pass through to successfully facilitate transfer of learning and behaviour change:

A = Accountability: Setting up the context of the process and the TLA relationship.

C = Calibration: Calibrating a score for where individuals are now, and the scores for where they want to get to for each goal on the TLA plan.

T = Target: Where is the individual trying to go? What's the target for the session?

I = Information: Gather information about what is happening in the workplace.

O = Option: What options do individuals have in this situation? What could they do?

N = Next Steps: How is the individual going to commit to action and move toward the target?

As an example, one of the participants set the goal of holding regular one-on-one meetings with his team. He started with a score of 2 of 10, as he had held only occasional meetings in the past with his team of four people. Initially, he shifted quickly to a 5 of 10 and felt he was making good progress. Through discussion with his TLA specialist, however, he realized that he was rescheduling the difficult people each month. Thoughtful probing helped him identify what made those people difficult and what he needed to do to overcome this perception. He committed to preparing for the conversations before the meetings and, by the end of the twelve-week period, they had become habitual. Importantly, he could see the benefits that the regular meetings were having. Transfer was achieved by having the TLA specialist hold the individual accountable to putting into place what he wanted to achieve.

Finally, stage three is *evaluation*, once people have followed through on their TLA plans. In this phase, we gather information about what the participants have actually done since the training event and through the TLA conversations. Typically, this information is gathered online three months after the initial program.

Results

Every participant completes an online Progress Review form that collects information based on their initial action plan and tracks the progress against each goal. These are collated into a learning dashboard (Exhibit D4.8.3)

The dashboard is in six sections (refer to Exhibit D4.8.3).

1. *Program Details (Top Left)*. The program details box offers the reader an immediate overview of the program the dashboard relates to. Where the client is familiar with net promoter score (NPS) the dashboard also includes this popular metric. For those familiar with the Kirkpatrick/Phillips methods of evaluation, this is all Level 1 data:

Exhibit D4.8.3. An Example of an Impact Dashboard

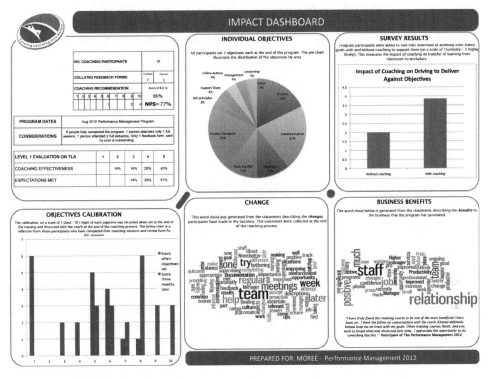

capturing the reaction. Seventy-two percent of participants scored the process a 4 or 5 out of 5 for effectiveness.

2. *Individual Objectives (Top Middle).* At the end of a training program, every participant commits to three actions, which they detail in their TLA plans. The pie chart on the dashboard is a visual representation of the distribution of objectives by topic or area to give stakeholders a quick snapshot of the key themes or types of actions that participants have focused on implementing.

3. *Survey Results (Top Left).* In the feedback process we ask all the participants from the TLA process to answer two questions:

   • On a scale of 1 to 5, to what level did you meet the objectives that you set at the end of the program?

Case D4.8: How We Turn Learning into Action   **465**

- On a scale of 1 to 5, what level do you think you would have met on those objectives without coaching?

    These questions help participants to reflect on how far they have come in the TLA process and also what they think would have happened had they not had that coaching support.

4. *Objectives Calibration (Bottom Left).* This graph captures a self-report based on a score for each objective: where they were before they began implementing the changes from the program and then three months later. The client had the option to cross-reference these scores with the view of the participants' manager but, in this instance, was happy to leave this as a self-report.

5/6. *Change (Bottom Middle)* and *Business Benefits (Bottom Right).* In this section we generate word clouds around all the anecdotal information we receive in the feedback forms. Participants are asked, "What changes have you put into place?" and "What benefits have your changes created?" Their responses generate the word cloud. The importance of each "word" is shown in terms of size or colour, depending on how frequently it is in the selection of data. We use www.wordle.net to generate these.

As you can see here, the key benefits' themes for the performance management program were "positive," "relationships," and "staff."

In addition to the learning dashboard, we also create an individual case study from one of the participants to capture a learning story that could be used across the organization (Exhibit D4.8.4). Within this case study format, we document the challenge the individual was facing, the solution, and the results by interviewing the participant by phone.

Exhibit D4.8.4. Example of an Individual Case Study

Moree Council - Performance Management Program
Case Study: Leadership drives productivity and engagement

Manager, Landfill Waster Management Facility

The participant runs the Moree Landfill Waste Management Facility, one of the most environmentally and technologically sophisticated waste management sites in Australia. He attended the Performance Management Program in 2012.

Challenge	Solution	Result

• To increase productivity by engaging staff
• To enable the team to contribute ideas for improving the way work gets done
• To leverage the leading position of this facility to drive innovation
• To improve happiness and well-being at work among employees who were often unhappy and unmotivated
	• John has got more involved with staff to understand their concerns and try to proactively resolve problems
	  • Regular 1-to-1 communication
	  • Observe and act on feedback
	  • Fit tasks to staff preferences
	  • Manage own and others emotions
	  • Support team by providing feedback to supervisor
	• John uses 'toolbox meetings' every week to enable staff to propose ideas for resolving problems and improving work
	• He set weekly goals outside core tasks
		• Daily tasks are completed quicker so that the team have time to work on improving the site environment and preparing new disposal areas at the facility
		• Team are contributing ideas to improving the way things are done at the facility
		• Significant decrease in leave being taken (both annual leave and sick leave)
		• Team are happier at work and take pride in their workplace (mowing lawns, tidying customer drop-off areas)
		• Team are rediscovering their drive to contribute to improving the environment

Business Impact
- **Improved productivity** enables the team to complete daily tasks and work on improving and preparing the site
- Staff are more engaged so are **contributing new ideas to improve how work gets done**
- Team are happier and more engaged so **absences are reduced**

Keys to Success

A number of factors are especially important to the success of such a program:

- Consider who is best placed to be the person working with the participant on TLA. Regardless of whether you use a fully-trained internal manager, L & D professional, or external TLA specialist to conduct the TLA conversations, everyone involved must understand these are a very different type of conversation. They are focused interactions designed to elicit change; as such, they require the managers or L & D professionals to "change their hats" from their normal role and communication style. For the external TLA specialists, this is their sole role, which is why, in many cases, they are the most effective choice.

- Keeping the program facilitator and the TLA specialist separate. The participant will have become used to seeing the facilitator as a knowledge expert and may want answers rather than the coaching necessary to effect real change.
- Consider how to engage the participant's manager in the process. We encourage our participants to talk to their managers about the action plan and vice versa. Be realistic about the time that the managers can invest in learning transfer. Consider whether they are truly skilled in this area or if they should just provide encouragement.
- Consider your logistics plan to support the process before you start. Logistics are key to the success of the program and the evaluation; ensure you have processes in place that will help you deliver a scalable one-on-one process. We broadly follow the same methodology whether we are working with a group of twelve or a group of one thousand; smooth logistics are essential to delivering the results.

Advice to Colleagues

- Bite the bullet with learning transfer. Do a small pilot, learn from it, and keep trying.
- Remember it is the participants who will make the change. Having them engaged, committed, and held accountable is more important than engaging the manager.
- Utilize the telephone as a powerful secret weapon.
- Have a methodology that you follow to secure results.
- Share the results with the key stakeholders to demonstrate the value you have delivered.

Case D5.1

How We Engage Key Contributors to Disseminate Corporate Culture

Conrado Schlochauer

Partner, AfferoLab

Background

Promon Engenharia (www.promonengenharia.com.br) is a Brazilian engineering company with more than fifty-two years' market experience and special competencies in engineering, management, procurement, construction and assembly, and information technology. Promon has one of the largest portfolios of projects completed by any Brazilian engineering firm and more than half a billion U.S. dollars in revenue annually. Promon operates a set of independently managed companies that are aligned by the overall strategy, policies, and guidelines established by Promon Group.

Promon's special organizational culture is key to its success. The internal relationship model is a community of professionals; its shareholders are the professionals who make up the group. Promon engaged AfferoLab—the leading provider of corporate learning programs in Brazil—to develop a mentoring program to help strengthen its culture among the professionals who make up the consortia in which the organization operates.

The objectives were to:

- Spread the Promon culture and values consciously
- Provide career planning
- Encourage organizational networking among professionals

What We Did

At AfferoLab, we seek to boost value through innovative methodologies that generate in-depth learning, support knowledge transfer into practice, produce a change in behavior, and ultimately increase bottom-line results aligned with the strategic goals of the organization.

Recognizing the importance of cultural knowledge transfer through people (social learning), we developed a custom mentoring process for experienced professionals at Promon to help them strengthen and disseminate its unique culture and values. We utilized the 6Ds framework (Exhibit D5.1.1) to help us develop an effective program.

Additional Highlights

- Successful mentoring requires the right match between mentors and mentees; a poor match can often be worse than no mentoring at all. The personal skills and expertise of the mentors are of vital importance in ensuring post-instruction impact. Mentees, too, need to be open to the mentoring process and be willing to commit to and learn from their mentors.

Exhibit D5.1.1. Key Design Elements and the 6Ds

Case Exhibit D5.1.1

D1: Define the business outcomes	Worked with sponsor to clarify the objectives: **"To disseminate Promon Culture among contributors and provide organizational development and career paths to professionals."**
D2: Design the complete experience	Created a learning experience that included: ○ Mini curriculum (mentors) ○ Formation training ○ Agenda of meetings ○ Evaluation survey
D3: Deliver for application	Provided training for both mentors and mentees on their roles, expectations, and how to maximize the value of the program. ○ **Mentors:** Formal training for role (8 hours) ○ **Mentees:** Communication meeting (2 hours)
D4: Drive learning transfer	○ Chat script ○ Individual Development Plan (new approach) ○ Two-way appraisal
D5: Deploy performance support	○ "Learning Plaza" (best practice exchange based on daily experience)
D6: Document results	○ Evaluation survey: participants' testimonials after six months

- To ensure that both mentors and mentees were prepared for the mentoring process and could maximize the benefit of their time together, we designed a complete learning experience:
    - An opening seminar for candidates discussed the benefits of the process for those involved and for the company.
    - Once they were accepted to participate, mentors were given access to a website designed specifically for this mentoring program.
    - After that they received emails with teasers and readings.

- Mentors participated in an eight-hour foundation course that included basic training, the mechanism of the program, and the opportunity to talk to former mentors.
  - Finally, during the process, they participated in meetings called "Praça de Aprendizagem" (Learning Plaza), where they discussed issues and shared their best practices and insights.
- We let mentees know the professionals designated to be their mentors. We ensured a communication strategy between mentors and mentees that clarified expectations and enforced alignment of desired behaviors and actions during the learning experience.
- We set a four-hour, two-way appraisal process meeting ("Learning Plaza") to foster greater exchange among contributors and to facilitate best practice sharing.
- With the agreement of Promon management, we removed the requirement to share the results with HR to increase openness and *place the responsibility for developing the participants in the group itself.*
- The objectives of an individual development plan were defined between mentors and mentees. At the first meeting, they aligned their expectations about the process and scheduled their meetings. The IDP works as a roadmap throughout the mentoring process for them to check accomplishments and/or change the objectives if necessary.
- The mentor has access not only to training, but also to examples of others, so that they can improve their *repertoire* in this field. They don't have to share the IDP with HR.

Results

Participants' declarations confirmed that the process of mentoring was effective in disseminating Promon culture and fostering the development of professionals.

Lessons of Experience

- Matching the mentors and mentees is a crucial success factor.
- Mentors and mentees benefit from a level of training and familiarization prior to the commencement of the mentoring relationship.
- Affinity mapping helps the entire process.

Advice to Colleagues

- Understand the context and your client's strategic needs.
- Establish the success criteria from the start.
- Utilize appropriate tools.

Case D5.2

How We Use Proficiency Coaching to Improve Performance

Geoff Rip

Research Director, Institute for Learning Practitioners, Australia

Background

The dominant view of training is as an event. People say, "I was sent to training" or "I attended a course on . . .," indicating that they consider the training finished when the event comes to an end.

As learning professionals, we know this is not the case. Training is fundamentally an influence process. The purpose is to influence workplace performance through learning-based interventions. The real finish line of training is the successful achievement of performance outcomes/standards.

Learning transfer is a critical link in the causal chain from training to the results the organization needs (Exhibit D5.2.1).

Exhibit D5.2.1. Causal Chain from Training to Business Results

In today's competitive environment, line managers need employees who are not just competent, but proficient in their jobs. Proficiency is "fluent, masterful performance." Someone who is proficient in a skill is able not only to perform correctly, but also quickly and without hesitation. Participants rarely, if ever, achieve proficiency during training events. There simply is not enough time to unlearn old behaviors and practice enough to habituate new ones. Moreover, real proficiency is contextual; it can only be developed in the real work setting.

Viewed from the perspective of proficiency, training events are merely "warm-ups." Together with pre-course communications, they provide a foundation for additional action learning on the job that is required to achieve competence and proficiency.

The training effectiveness equation, then, is

$$\text{Initial Learning} \times \text{Action Learning} = \text{Results}$$
$$\text{(off the job)} \quad \text{(on the job)} \quad \text{(proficiency)}$$

What We Did

To ensure that learning did not stop at the classroom door and that participants engaged in action learning and proficiency development, we implemented a process we call proficiency coaching.

Proficiency coaching adds two critical phases beyond the "training event": proficiency development (workouts) and proficiency story, so that the complete learning experience includes:

- **Phase 1: Preparation.** Pre-work is used to raise perceived relevance and importance of the training.

- **Phase 2: Course/Workshop (Warm-Up).** Phase 2 can consist of a blended combination of live workshops, e-learning modules, or virtual sessions.
- **Phase 3: Proficiency Development (Workouts).** Phase 3 consists of the necessary 'workouts' (action learning) for achieving proficiency. This phase should incorporate at least three proficiency coaching sessions.
- **Phase 4: Proficiency Story.** Participants have completed the training only when they have submitted a proficiency story (also called an application story, success story, or achievement story).

It is essential that participants be informed, in advance, of the program structure and be provided summary details of each phase. Using terms like warm-up and workouts helps convey the message that the instruction (Phase 2) isn't the main event and crucial learning occurs during Phase 3.

Proficiency coaching can be delivered by:

- Other participants
- Past participants (who have successfully completed the full program)
- Facilitators
- Managers of participants

The best practice is to have participants "buddy up" and provide each other with proficiency coaching; both the coach and coachee benefit. If a participant isn't available to coach another, then consider using past participants, facilitators, or managers as the primary proficiency coach.

Provide proficiency coaching know-how through a short face-to-face or e-learning session that covers the rationale, methods, success factors, responsibilities, and benefits. Content of that session should include:

- Meaning and importance of proficiency coaching
- How top performers benefit

- Why workouts (action learning) are so important to personal development
- The value of deliberate practice, guided reflection, and feed forward
- The Proficiency Coaching Wheel and Reflection Framework job aid
- Powerful questions for turning experience into learning
- Dealing with personal emotions from moving out of one's comfort zone
- The role and responsibilities of a proficiency coach
- Use of proficiency stories to reinforce learning and demonstrate success

Research has shown that the immediate managers of participants have the most dominant influence on transfer of learning in the workplace. For this reason, it's vital that managers of participants actively support the proficiency coaching initiative and Phases 3 and 4 of the training.

One way to encourage line manager support is to provide them with an overview of proficiency coaching, with particular attention to their crucial role in its success. The overview session should also explain proficiency stories and how they should be used.

Results

Companies adopting the proficiency coaching model have identified the following benefits:

- The process clearly communicates the importance of learning transfer.
- Participants and their managers find it an intuitively sensible/logical approach.
- Participants learn more about coaching, guided reflection, and experiential learning.

- It increases predictability of achieving performance outcomes.
- It increases transfer of learning, proficiency development, and training effectiveness.
- It has real business impact: meaningful and measurable outcomes in the workplace.
- It helps to create a culture in which continuous personal growth is highly valued.
- It positively influences a number of key drivers of employee engagement.
- It provides evidence of training benefits and effectiveness.

Keys to Success

- It is important that participants be informed in advance of the overall structure of the program and given summary details of each phase.
- Be sure to prepare both the proficiency coaches and the managers of participants for their roles.
- Follow up with the participants and their managers and "work the process."

Advice to Colleagues
- Treat training as a process rather than an event.
- Use peer proficiency coaching to extend learning back into the workplace and ensure the practice necessary to achieve proficiency rather than merely familiarity or capability.
- Make submitting a proficiency story the criterion for completing the training.

Case D5.3

How We Engage Participants for Optimal Learning Transfer

Ishita Bardhan and Kanika Sharma

Assistant General Manager, Learning and Development, and Senior Manager, Learning and Development, Management Development Centre of Excellence, Tata Motors Academy

Background

Tata Motors Limited is India's largest automobile company, with consolidated revenues of US $32.5 billion in 2011–2012. It is the leader in commercial vehicles in each segment, and among the top tier in passenger vehicles. It is the first company from India's engineering sector to be listed in the New York Stock Exchange.

One of the critical levers of our human capital strategy is talent and leadership. Tata Motors Academy was established to address Tata's current and future leadership needs and to prepare employees to achieve the strategic objectives of the organization.

Leaders' ability to provide constructive feedback and coach employees towards higher levels of performance is essential to the success of the performance appraisal process. Effective coaching helps individuals to build and grow in their careers and contributes to Tata's overall performance. We identified a need for more effective performance appraisals and coaching, so we developed a program called Coaching imPACT (PACT being the acronym for our Performance Appraisal and Coaching Tool).

We recognized that for our training to deliver on its promise of producing improved performance, the skills had to be transferred and applied on the job. We knew that numerous elements of the transfer climate would influence the outcome. We also understood that our employees are busy. So it was important to propose a solution that would be easy to understand and use, that was time-efficient, and that had a strong business case for acceptance.

The entire continuum of the program was developed to facilitate the participants' ability to use the training, as well as to ensure support from the work environment.

What We Did

Our program is composed of five phases (Exhibit D5.3.1) that include self-directed pre-learning, two classroom sessions separated by a thirty-day application period, and culminating in ongoing, on-the-job learning.

Learning transfer is built into the process through:

1. Coaching mirror as a tool for feedback
2. Three field exercises
3. Use of application planner
4. Coaching simulation

Exhibit D5.3.1. The Five Phases of the imPACT Program

LEARNING COTINUUM

TATA MOTORS ACADEMY

Finish line : Annual Coaching Olympics

Phase I

Pre-learning — 3.5 hrs

- Attempt online coaching simulation "Coaching with Confidence" in the test mode
- Identify coaching situations at work place
- Answer questions on coaching

Phase II

Classroom session — 8 + 4 hrs

- Contact setting & icebreaker
- Understanding coaching
- Introduction to GROW & coaching capsule
- Coaching mirror
- Mindset to coach – Believing in others
- Skills to coach – Establishing trust and showing respect
- Skills to coach – active listening
- Mindset to coach – coaching presence
- Wrap up

Phase III

Next 30 days plan — 2 hrs

- 3 field exercises
- Use of application planner

Phase IV

Classroom session — 8 hrs

- Recap icebreaker
- Skills to coach – powerful questioning & how to use it in GROW
- Skills to coach – performance evaluation & direct communication (feedback)
- Structure coaching conversations
- Action plan

Phase V

On the job learning — 3 hrs

- Coaching buddy meetings
- Virtual connect with leaders on coaching
- Revisit online coaching simulation "Coaching with Confidence" in the explore mode

Case D5.3: How We Engage Participants for Optimal Learning Transfer   **483**

Coaching Mirror as a Tool for Feedback　During the first instructor-led session, the participants complete a questionnaire called "Coaching Mirror" that helps gather self and peer feedback on the competencies required to be an effective coach at Tata Motors. The participants are also given a brief report of how they were rated on the Coaching Mirror.

This serves a dual purpose:

- It provides an opportunity for the participants to recognize their current levels of proficiency and the areas on which they must focus to become competent coaches.
- It augments social motivation by making peers capable of encouraging the right behaviors at Tata Motors.

Three Field Exercises　Between the first and second classroom sessions, participants are required to complete three field exercises in order to practice and become comfortable in applying the skills. Participants cannot register for the second classroom session until they have completed all three exercises. Here is a brief outline of the structure of field exercises:

- Participants are divided into random triads at the end of the first instructor-led session.
- Each participant is asked to practice in turn being the coach, coachee, and observer during the three rounds.
- The person acting as coachee is responsible for bringing a real-life coaching issue for discussion. The coach is expected to practice the skills taught, and the observer provides feedback.
- Each triad is expected to complete three field exercises lasting one hour each, during which the person acting as the coach has two thirty-minute opportunities to practice.

- The observer is provided with a checklist to help identify strengths and the areas that need additional effort.

This process not only enables the participants to practice the new skills in a safe environment, but it also shifts the onus of learning onto the participating employees. When intact teams experience the program together, it provides a solid foundation for the manager's involvement, thus enhancing the prospects of a successful transfer.

Use of Application Planner   During each field exercise session, the trainee enacting the role of a coach uses an application planner to reflect on how he or she is developing the specific skills and mindsets of effective coaches and to plan next steps (see Exhibit D5.3.2). The application planner helps to reinforce the key concepts, provide participants with a sense of progress, and underscore the expectation of continued development.

Coaching Simulation   The coaching simulation is an online simulator that presents situations to the participant and asks him or her to decide how to react. The scenarios are typical people-related issues that occur between a manager and his or her direct reports. The simulator provides participants with the opportunity to practice coaching skills in a safe, non-threatening environment that resonates well with them.

Results

Our participants have appreciated the approach of the program, which encourages them to practice their skills at intervals along the way. They also specifically value having their peers as practice

Exhibit D5.3.2. The Coach's Application Planner Used in the Field Exercises

MINDSET OF A COACH		
	Situation where I applied it	
	How did I prepare?	
1. Believing in others 2. Coaching presence	What did I do?	
	My reflections on how it went	
	Reviewed the reflections with	

partners. We observed that retention of the course content is enhanced by the spaced learning effect: principles, concepts, and methods are repeatedly revisited and reinforced throughout the five-phase process.

In the mid-process connect calls we did with our participants, we found that the majority of trainees made efforts to complete the field exercises and share feedback with others on their gaps. We also found that participants were forthcoming about skills they found challenging to apply/practice during the field exercises and that they were open to suggestions on how to improve their performance.

Advice to Colleagues

- Use different sources of influence (social motivation, social ability, and personal ability) to create a positive transfer climate.
- Support the transfer process by reinforcement and measurement.
- If intersession assignments are part of the program, make completing them a requirement for continuing the course.
- Provide support to strengthen learning and assure participants that they are manifesting the desired new competencies that produce business value.

Case D5.4

How We Deployed Performance Support for a Technical Capability Building Initiative

Hemalakshmi Raju and Sumita Menon

Assistant General Manager, Learning and Development, and Divisional Manager, Learning and Development, Tata Motors, Ltd.

Background

Tata Motors Limited is India's largest automobile company, with consolidated revenues of US $32.5 billion in 2011–2012. Established in 1954, it is the leader in commercial vehicles, and among the top three in passenger vehicles, with winning products in the compact, midsize car, and utility vehicle segments. Tata is the world's fourth largest truck and bus manufacturer.

The company has a well-defined vision: "Most admired by our customers, employees, business partners, and shareholders for the experience and value they enjoy from being with us." To support the vision and the business objectives of Tata Motors Limited, our human capital strategy emphasizes learning and capability development.

The automobile industry in India is experiencing heightened competition from both global as well as domestic players. In a market in which buyers have many choices, superior product quality is an important source of competitive advantage. For this reason, our leadership places great importance on creating a culture that focuses on product quality. Initiatives are in place at our manufacturing locations to ensure that we build consistently world-class quality products.

In early 2012, we launched *autonova TX*, a large-scale technical capability building intervention for the commercial vehicle business unit to help it achieve its mission of *"zero defects and zero rejections."*

What We Did

Specific product lines were selected to bring razor-sharp focus to the initial autonova TX deployment. The aim was to use autonova TX to create role-model lines and subsequently replicate the process on other product lines.

For initial deployment, we selected the product lines for which improvement would have the greatest impact on the business and customer base. Once the product line was identified, we identified the relevant participants by:

- Identifying all the functions that impacted product quality directly or indirectly across the various stages of manufacturing
- Mapping individuals within those functions who had a performance gap in any of the five essential domains of expertise
- Having the head of department validate and sign off on the target audience

To ensure that training produces a change in on-the-job behavior, and to hold employees accountable for the end result, each participant is required to fill out a template at the end of training that clearly states the project he or she will execute within a defined timeline. A tracker was developed by the L & D team to consolidate the project details. Regular communication to the participants on project progress was initiated.

The success of autonova TX is ultimately its impact on product quality. To ensure that learning from the training would be implemented and monitored on the shop floor, we developed and deployed performance support.

A key element of the support was a check sheet of critical-to-quality (CTC) parameters that needed to be assured at every station. The check sheet traveled with the cab, clearly reminding the participants who work on the shop floor what needs to the checked and how to capture defects at his/her station.

A cross-functional team of CX (Center of Excellence) owners, line managers, manufacturing QA, and central QA was formed to develop the check sheet, using the five W and one H methodology:

1. **Why:** The need to check CTC parameters for recurring defects
2. **Where:** The location where the inspection needs to be done or defect identified (on the product/station/line/buy-off gate)
3. **What:** What parameters need to be checked/inspected (gaps/flushness/spots/sealant application, etc.)
4. **Who:** Who does the inspection (operator/officer)
5. **When:** The frequency of inspection
6. **How:** Method of inspection (gauges/visual inspection/touch and feel)

The check sheets included labeled photographs as well as text to ensure the operator knew exactly where to look and what to look for (Exhibit D5.4.1). The checklist enabled process adherence as well as monitoring of defects on a daily basis. The check sheet consisted of a

Exhibit 5.4.1. An Example of a Performance Support Check Sheet

		BIW CHECK SHEET		DATE:		BIW NO.		
TATA MOTORS, PUNE				SHIFT:		MODEL :		
Sr. No.	CHECK POINTS		Specifi-cation	Gauge Used	OK/ Not-OK	Inspected by	IMAGE	
6	**Rear door Setting**							
a	Sidewall to rear door gap		6±2 mm	Taper gauge				
b	Between LH & RH rear door centre gap		8 ±2 mm	Taper gauge				
c	Ensure crease line matching between rear doors and sidewalls		±2 mm	Scale				
d	Ensure flushness with sidewall		±2 mm	Scale				
e	Ensure sealing gap on D pillar		9(+2,-1) mm	Scale				
g	Ensure tightening torque		4.8 ±0.7 Kgm	Torque wrench				
7	**Front Door door Setting**							
a	Ensure front door to B pillar gap (A, B)		6±2 mm	Taper gauge				
b	Ensure front door to side bonnet gap (E, F)		6 ±2 mm	Taper gauge				
c	Ensure crease line matching between Front Door and Side bonnet		±3 mm	Scale				
d	Ensure crease line matching between Front Door and B pillar		±2 mm	Scale				
e	Ensure flushness with sidewall (A,B)		±2 mm	Scale				
f	Ensure flushness of front door to side bonnet (E, F)		±1 mm	Scale				
g	Ensure tightening torque		4.8 ±0.7 Kgm	Torque wrench				
8	**Sealant Application, Roof stiffener tightening & Sliding door Fitment**							
a	Ensure thumb sealant application as per sealant plan		————	Visual				
b	Ensure mastic sealant application in roof stiffeners as per sealant plan		No Unfilled gap	Sealant Gun				
c	Ensure sliding door is positioned on jig in straight position		————	Visual				
9	**Bonnet centralization & side bonnet setting**							
a	Align the bonnet centre with side bonnet outer with Equal gap on both side (D)		Max. taper gap of 2mm	Scale				
b	Alignment with top line of side bonnet Location **C**		± 2 mm	Scale				

maximum of thirty parameters (an average of three parameters per station) on an A4 size sheet. This was a dynamic check sheet in which the parameters were modified depending on the frequency of occurrence and severity of defects.

A RACI matrix (who is responsible, accountable, consulted, or informed for the various activities and deliverables) was developed for implementation of the check sheet and signed off by the plant head.

The production supervisor had the primary responsibility for implementing the check sheet. His or her immediate superior was accountable for ensuring that it was done. Data from the check sheet was consolidated by the quality team at the quality gates and shared with the center of excellence manager. The deviations in the critical-to-quality parameters were then taken up for improvements. Implementation and data analysis was audited monthly by head-manufacturing, head-quality, and L & D team members to ensure 100 percent process adherence.

We recognized that participants would probably encounter some difficulties when they tried to apply new knowledge/skills for the first time. They would require regular support and feedback during this phase. Therefore, for each autonova TX topic, two functional mentors were identified. These functional mentors were senior leaders specializing in a core area of production specific to the topic who had contact with the target audience on a day-to-day basis. Mentors were responsible for monitoring the progress each participant had made in his or her post-program project and for providing constructive inputs, assistance, and coaching.

A dashboard was developed for each of the product lines to monitor and review the business impact of autonova TX programs. It included the critical-to-quality parameters, their current status, and the improvement targets taken. The critical-to-quality parameters were co-jointly identified by CX owners and the quality team and finally signed off by shop quality heads for the respective product lines. This dashboard was then reviewed to monitor the progress made and devise action plans.

The success of any learning intervention depends on the extent to which business participates and co-owns the initiative. For autonova TX, this was ensured through the Learning Advisory Council (LAC), the learning governance body at Tata Motors, with the primary objective of ensuring alignment of learning with business.

Autonova results were reviewed on a monthly basis by the plant-level LAC, which included the local plant head, manufacturing head, quality head, and their sub-teams. The program was reviewed quarterly by the central LAC, including the vice president of manufacturing, plant heads, manufacturing heads, and quality heads of each manufacturing location. The progress made on each of the product lines was reviewed and a forward action plan was devised. Learning Advisory Council meetings also served as a platform for cross-location knowledge and best-practice sharing.

Results

Huge momentum has been generated by this initiative. Focusing on specific product lines ensured quick coverage of identified participants. The training, combined with performance support and implementation monitoring, have already had a measurable and significant impact on business outcomes.

Some of the early wins achieved include:

- *Product Quality:* Overall success rate increased from 70 percent to 95 percent first-shot-ok in five months
- *Cost of Rework:* The number of employees focusing on rework was reduced by 75 percent in five months

> ### Advice to Colleagues
> - Post-program performance support is the key to success for any training intervention.
> - Measuring business outcomes rather than learning outcomes is essential for buy-in from senior leadership.
> - Involving business leaders in the entire learning journey will ensure their ownership and support.
> - Reviews need to be built into the process.

Case D6.1

How We Guide Our Clients to Design with the End in Mind

Peggy Parskey
Strategic Measurement Consultant with Knowlege Advisors

Background

KnowledgeAdvisors is a leading learning and talent analytics company that enables organizations to better allocate human capital investments through practical learning measurement guidance and strategies. Their analytics system, Metrics That Matter®, helps organizations measure and improve their talent development programs, driving improved productivity, reduced administrative costs, and increased return on learning investments through data-driven decision making.

KnowledgeAdvisors' clients represent many of the world's leading organizations, including four of the five largest accounting firms, three of the last five winners of Training's Top 125 Award, the world's largest company, and the prestigious U.S. Defense Department University.

All organizations need scalable and repeatable processes for measuring their programs. Strategic and costly programs require special treatment though. These highly visible programs are under greater scrutiny, not only to ensure a high-quality learning experience, but equally importantly, to ensure that they make a difference, that is, impact a business outcome. The challenge for many of our clients is that they don't sufficiently clarify the success indicators during the D1 (Define) stage or the chain of influences among a set of inputs (e.g., resources to design, develop, and deliver a solution), the outputs (e.g., people trained), the short-term impact (improved job performance), and finally, to the ultimate goal of improving customer satisfaction, market share, or profitability.

I have two goals as a consultant guiding clients through the process of designing with the end in mind:

1. To make explicit the linkage between program inputs (resources, funding, and technology), program activities (assessments, training, collateral, coaching), outputs, short-term results, and ultimate outcomes.
2. To demonstrate the importance of systematically embedding this up-front activity into an end-to-end training solution development lifecycle.

What We Did

To make a stronger connection between the program and ultimate outcomes, I leverage a standard methodology used in program evaluation. This methodology is not specific to training, but rather employs a process to make the link between a change initiative and its ultimate impact. The process itself is straightforward and is known as logic modeling.

Simply put, a logic model is a logical chain that depicts program connections and the expected accomplishments of the program. The logic model consists of a series of "if-then" relationships that, when implemented as intended, lead to the desired outcomes. The logic model identifies the resources that are invested in the program, the activities that are undertaken, the direct outputs (or deliverables of the program), the short-term and medium-term results (e.g., new knowledge, skills, or behaviors), and finally, the business outcomes (see Exhibit D6.1.1 below).

With logic modeling as a foundational process, I add three components to the front end:

- Identify the stakeholders and what they believe to be credible evidence of impact.
- Describe the solution and all the components that contribute to the outcome.
- Document other contributors or inhibitors to success (for example, performance incentives, other skills training, organizational changes, and so forth).

Exhibit D6.1.1. Logic Model for Training

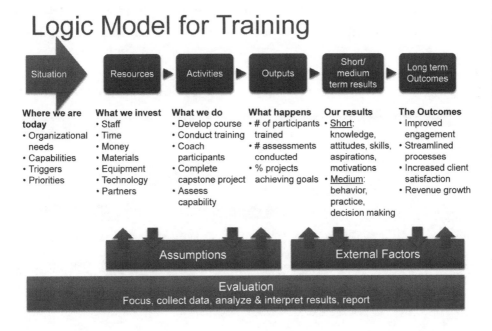

Together with the logic model, this process not only characterizes what the program is intended to do, but ensures that stakeholders will believe the results when they are ultimately presented.
I start by establishing the basic hypotheses of the training:

- Why are you doing this?
- What do you expect to happen as a result of the training?

This discovery process is best handled through the use of mind mapping where the client can brainstorm the expected results and out-comes. When a client has not distinguished between short-term result (e.g., increased knowledge), a medium-term result (demonstrated com-petency), and visible impact (improved client retention), the brainstorm-ing process helps sort out how the pieces of the program fit together. An example of a branch of the mind map for a hypothetical management development program is depicted in Exhibit D6.1.2.

After completing the mind map, I then guide the client through a pro-cess of identifying the key measures for each link in the chain of influences:

- If the program is scheduled to train fifty new managers in the next six months, when will these attendees complete all components of the program?

Exhibit D6.1.2. Mind Map for a Management Development Program

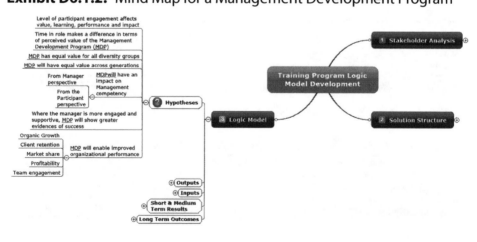

- How long will it take for their managers to see new behaviors in coaching, planning, and executing on the job?
- And finally, how long will it take to see an impact on employee retention, increased customer loyalty, and year-over-year sales?

This discussion results in a more meaningful answer to the question: "What does success look like?" and, equally important, it answers the question: "When will we see it?" This portion of the discussion is critical because it often triggers the realization that:

- D2: Designing the complete experience may require pre-work or pre-assessment to ensure participant readiness to engage.
- D4: Driving learning transfer will require more visible management support and perhaps a formal coaching program to help participants overcome barriers and create accountability for application.
- D5: Deploying performance support will necessitate tools and perhaps a social network to enable participants to learn from each other.

In our hypothetical example of the management development program, the sponsor realizes that the elapsed time between the start of the training and evidence of all business outcomes is thirteen months (Exhibit D6.1.3). At this point, she has a clearer picture of other critical activities required to ensure full learning transfer.

Exhibit D6.1.3. Time Line from Training to Results

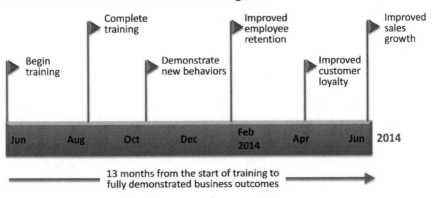

Cautions   Logic modeling has the greatest impact when used in the early stages of solution design. Unfortunately, as a consultant, I often find myself employing the process after the fact, in some cases months if not years after the program was initially deployed. So logic modeling becomes a reverse engineering effort that can have multiple benefits but also a few risks.

The single biggest risk is that the logic model surfaces gaps in the design. With one client, I asked the team to describe the desired behaviors from the program and how these aligned with the expected behaviors for the role. "You mean, like a competency model?" the client asked. The discussion resulted in them pausing program development to align program outcomes with the competency model for the role.

With another client, the logic model highlighted that the program would not contribute to the anticipated business benefits. The program was intended to build leadership bench strength. However, it was predominantly knowledge- versus skills-based. So while the program would increase awareness of new behaviors and some new skills, it would be unlikely to materially contribute to the quality of the leadership bench.

Surfacing gaps in a program design, particularly for a long-running program, can undermine the credibility of the program lead and cause leadership to question the value of the investment. So my advice is to set expectations about this process in advance and help the program lead to position logic modeling as a process enhancement and a long term benefit for L & D.

Results

All my clients exposed to logic modeling experience an aha moment. They realize that they lack a well-defined "chain of influences" between the training and the business benefit. The missing links will make it difficult for them to conduct a meaningful impact analysis or credibly demonstrate the contribution of the program to business outcomes.

The most powerful result that my clients have experienced is the opportunity to build different relationships with their business partners. Discussions with key business stakeholders not only create mutual accountability for results but help focus the solution. Clarity on what is to be achieved and agreement on specific outcomes has enabled clients to produce higher-quality solutions more efficiently and effectively.

This understanding of the power of logic modeling has led several of my clients to commit to embed the logic model framework into their initial discussions with their sponsors. My clients who have embraced performance consulting have integrated this additional step into the business needs analysis as well as the client contracting process. Several are beginning to set specific performance goals for the program. They realize that it's not enough to indicate that sales will increase from the management development program, but specifically that it will contribute 5 percentage points to the planned 20 percent increase in sales in the next fiscal year.

Simply put, logic modeling provides more rigor to the front-end discussions and changes the conversation with the business, not just after the fact, but through the entire training solution development lifecycle. This structured and repeatable process has enabled clients to design higher quality programs that deliver the expected outcomes and demonstrate the value of L & D to the business. For L & D practitioners wanting to have a seat at the table, this process gets them a lot closer.

Advice to Colleagues

While logic modeling is not a new process, few L & D functions have embraced it. As with any change, I suggest you start small and then grow. Also, while you can use logic modeling for any program, it is most useful for strategic, costly, or visible programs.

To start, I recommend the following:

- Learn the process. There is a lot of free material on the web and dozens of high-quality books on the topic.
- Practice the process with one key program, even if it's after the fact. Involve a small group of colleagues and stakeholders who have been engaged in the program design, development, and/or deployment of the program.
- Identify where you can embed this process into your end-to-end solution design process. Pilot it in specific areas, for example, leadership development or sales skill programs.
- Identify early adopters who can execute this process and have the skills and confidence to engage the sponsors in business-oriented discussions.
- Communicate successes achieved by using a new approach. Build support for logic modeling across L & D.
- Learn, expand, and evolve. The more widespread the use of the process, the more impact it will have on changing the conversation with the business.

Case D6.2

How We Used Measurement to Drive "SOAR—Service Over and Above the Rest"

Joyce Donohoe, Paul Beech, Karen Bell-Wright, Jim Kirkpatrick, and Wendy Kirkpatrick

Manager, Strategic Commercial and Service Initiatives, Emirates Group Learning and Development College; Manager, Emirates Global Contact Center; Vice President, Emirates Retail and Contact Centers; and Consultants, Kirkpatrick Partners

Background

Emirates Airline (Exhibit D6.2.1), headquartered in Dubai, United Arab Emirates, is part of The Emirates Group, which manages more than 68,000 employees. Founded in 1985, the airline is the world's largest by scheduled international passenger kilometers flown. The Emirates Group has its own learning and development unit, which trains the majority of business units within the corporation.

Exhibit D6.2.1. Emirates Airline Is One of the World's Top Ten Airlines

As the Group's growth trajectory continued and accelerated in 2012, the rapid growth increased pressure on resources. This pressure created an immediate need to review processes and practices to identify opportunities to work more effectively and efficiently.

The training group was confident that the services they provided added value to the organization, but they often lacked tangible evidence to support this. In response, Emirates Group Learning and Development, with the assistance of Kirkpatrick Partners, initiated a bold transformation, moving from a model of "effective training" to one of "training effectiveness."

The Emirates Global Contact Center's *Service Over and Above the Rest* (SOAR) program was selected as the major global initiative to pilot Group Learning and Development's new business partnership approach to learning and performance. This cooperative initiative was selected for two reasons:

1. The two functional areas had a good history of working together. Importantly, Paul Beech and his boss, Karen Bell-Wright, were

open-minded about undertaking a new learning and performance methodology. Active, collaborative participation by all parties greatly increases the likelihood of success.

2. This high-profile strategic program, once successfully executed, would set the stage for similar cooperative global initiatives.

What We Did

The program was rolled out initially in Dubai, Mumbai, Melbourne, Manchester (United Kingdom), and New York, with a plan to expand to Guangzhou (China) during the following fiscal year.

To ensure "training effectiveness" in addition to "effective training," a great deal was done before and after the actual two-day SOAR training event.

A policy statement detailing Emirates Group Learning and Development's approach to learning and performance formed the foundation for this initiative and served as the guiding light. Relevant details are as follows:

Who We Are. The Emirates Group Learning and Development faculty are learning and development professionals dedicated to helping employees at all levels enhance their individual performances, collectively leading to true competitive advantage for all of Emirates, and Dnata, (a combined air services provider at Dubai International Airport).

What We Believe. It is not enough to be world-class training providers. Our employees and business partners deserve more:

- To become true strategic business partners, we must identify and implement innovative, worldwide best practices while leveraging current core competencies.
- Learning is a process, not an event. Our purpose and our jobs extend beyond the walls of our college facility. Collaboration with business leaders at all levels is critical to corporate success. Much of our work will include providing advice and support to those who have the

power to enhance a culture that encourages ongoing learning and on-the-job application of training.

- A business partnership approach to learning, performance, and results is the best way to maximize each initiative. This begins with building collaboration, internal bridges, and trust with our internal customers.
- The ADDIE (analyze, design, develop, implement, and evaluate) model is fundamentally sound, but we will supercharge it with enhancements to each component. Critical to modernizing ADDIE is to plan for training by starting with targeted business results and working backward through the Kirkpatrick model.
- A variety of targeted interventions, including formal training, collectively serve to maximize on-the-job application and business results.

Pre-SOAR Preparation

1. Key leaders from both the learning and business sides of the initiative were taught the Kirkpatrick foundational principles:
   - The end is the beginning.
   - Return on expectations (ROE) is the ultimate indicator of value.
   - Business partnership is necessary to bring about positive ROE.
   - Value must be created before it can be demonstrated.
   - A compelling chain of evidence demonstrates your bottom-line value.

2. Specific measures of success were determined, and the subsequent required level of effort was defined. A memorandum of understanding was drafted detailing key processes and roles, required drivers of critical on-the-job behaviors, and evaluation methodology.

SOAR Formal Training: In this program, participants understood their role as service-excellence professionals responsible for creating a memorable experience for all customers who call Emirates contact centers globally. Over the course of the two-day program, participants were taken through the new Emirates brand identity, "Hello tomorrow."

Additionally, the new service style for Emirates contact centers was unveiled to achieve internal and external alignment of a service culture aligned to the brand.

Out of thirty service criteria, approximately ten were selected as critical behaviors. Data regarding these behaviors were used to generate a dashboard for ongoing tracking.

Call center consultants and their team leaders were trained on the new service model. Each team leader supervises a small number of consultants (direct reports) as well as a number of consultants (indirect reports) who are not necessarily part of his or her team. Team leaders also received a two-day leadership training program called "Coach to Perform."

Follow-Up to SOAR Training: The business partnership model was underpinned by the well-established fact that training alone will not generate significant performance and results. Therefore, a robust effort was made after training to ensure maximum application. The following methods were used to leverage the formal training and constitute the comprehensive package for learning and performance success:

- Continual on-the-job training
- Coaching by supervisors and L & D staff
- Formal and informal recognition
- Executive role modeling
- Monitoring of phone conversations with customers by internal quality staff, who refer to a quality audit sheet containing criteria
- Mystery shopping performed by BPA, an external marketing company
- Participant and supervisor survey assessments of service application
- Customer survey and phone interview assessments of service application
- Monthly dashboard to track significant metrics along the way
- Ongoing performance data analysis and subsequent adjustments

Results

The monitoring of critical behaviors post-training clearly demonstrated that the business partnership model of training was working.

The data in Figure D6.2.1 show that there was significant improvement in the demonstration of the service behaviors by call center consultants during the months after the formal SOAR training compared to the before-training benchmark.

Further evidence of the positive impact was the decrease in the number of customer complaints after the SOAR training (Figure D6.2.2).

	BENCH MARK	May	June	July	August
DX BCC	52.58%	⬆ 58.30%	⬆ 59.73%	⬆ 61.74%	⬆ 63.65%

Service Pillars	BENCH MARK	May	June	July	August
Calm And Assured	58.89%	⬇ 57.23%	⬇ 54.79%	⬆ 59.95%	⬆ 67.23%
Cosmopolitan	33.87%	⬆ 37.79%	⬆ 39.98%	⬆ 41.58%	➡ 41.07%
Empathy And Warmth	54.86%	⬆ 61.36%	⬆ 64.32%	➡ 64.83%	➡ 65.39%
Recognise And Respect	79.01%	⬆ 87.76%	➡ 88.22%	⬆ 89.94%	⬆ 91.83%

→ The results are based on 10,366 call evaluations

Figure D6.2.1. Leading Indicators of Change by Service Pillar

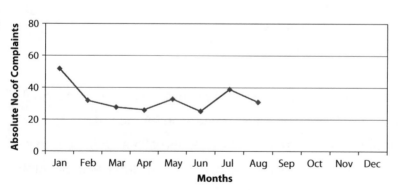

Figure D6.2.2. Number of Customer Complaints About Call Center Service Following SOAR Training

Reactions to the training by call center staff were positive because the training was clearly linked to a larger business strategy and emphasized application. Typical comments included:

- From Mumbai: "After delivering SOAR, one really feels so happy and content that you were able to talk so positively about the organization and at times transform people and their thoughts. I am so glad that I am a part of this. St. Francis de Sales said, 'Be what you are and be it at its best' and I guess SOAR is all about that."
- From Dubai: "SOAR made me shift my way of thinking and brought back the human in me. SOAR is not just understanding what we went through during the training, but also to believe in it and really use it."

The feedback solicited from customers also provided evidence that the business objectives were being met:

- From Mumbai: "I am a Skywards Gold member for many years, based in Singapore. We recently had a service need regarding a redemption ticket, and Lloyd Fernandez in India gave us SPECTACULAR service. This note is to say THANK YOU to Lloyd, and to encourage Emirates to give him a well-deserved 'pat on the back.'"
- From Dubai: "You asked me if I ever had feedback on Emirates to send it to you. Just recently I have had to go through changing some flights we had booked for Christmas as sudden things came up at work and I have to say the experience of dealing with your call centre has been a delight! I found both the staff members I talked to polite and very helpful and I was someone with difficult issues. Please feel free to pass this information on as I know that sometimes people only get negative feedback. I am a very satisfied Emirates customer!"

The continuous monitoring of behaviors had another important benefit: it allowed the organization to identify and document an

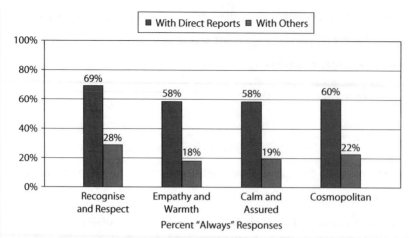

Figure D6.2.3. Application of Service Pillars by Shift Team Leaders with Consultants

important problem area and opportunity for further improvement. Team leaders did an excellent job of providing support and role modeling the customer service style internally with their own direct-report consultants, always exhibiting the behaviors 60 percent or more of the time. But during a shift, those same team leaders struggled to support consultants who did not report to them, with "always" scores dropping below 20 percent (Figure D6.2.3).

It was only by measuring and monitoring on-the-job results that the learning team was able to identify this pain area. When these data were presented to senior business leaders, they were in complete agreement and supported the changes recommended to address the issue.

Final Word

The partnership has truly allowed training to move beyond the walls of the classroom and into the business. The business stakeholders and the Group L & D team worked together for over a year, monitoring and measuring, and today they are able to celebrate their success stories. In this process, the Group Learning and Development team has built credibility within the entire business and developed stronger relationships; they continue to work with their business partners in a continual improvement process.

Advice to Colleagues
- Prior to any mission-critical training initiative, meet with and draft a memorandum of understanding among all parties, spelling out critical roles and steps along the way.
- Offer a learning and performance package approach to any major business need, as opposed to just a training initiative.
- Monitor critical behaviors and other important metrics during the execution stage. Make adjustments along the way based on the data.

Case D6.3

How We Used NPS to Track and Improve Leadership Impact

Sylvain Newton

Senior Leader for Business and Regions, GE Crotonville

Background

General Electric is one of the best-known and most widely respected companies in the world, with more than $150 billion in annual revenue and over 300,000 employees worldwide.

An important factor in GE's continuing success has been its commitment and investment in leadership development. Indeed, the name "Crotonville"—GE's original leadership development campus in New York—has become synonymous with excellence in corporate leadership development.

Its reputation notwithstanding, GE knows that it cannot rest on its laurels, but must continuously improve everything it does to continue its success—including how it trains and develops its future leaders.

In 2008, I was leading the Crotonville EMEA team—the leadership development organization at the time for Europe, Middle East, and Africa. During one of our offsite meetings, I challenged my team with the question: "How can we increase our impact?" So far, our discussions had been centered around "activity" metrics (number of programs, participants) or "satisfaction" metrics ("happy sheets"). It was clearly time to reconnect more strongly with the business objectives. This simple question led to a passionate discussion and led us to realize that we could improve the way we measure the impact we are driving for, for the people we train and for GE as a whole. What metrics did we have?

We had good data on consumer satisfaction, that is, the reactions of the participants in our programs—and these were consistently outstanding. But those did not gauge whether the programs were truly impacting their leadership: Were we changing their behaviors and, as a result, increasing their performance? We needed data from our *customers*—in this case, the managers who sent their high-potential candidates to us. Were they, in fact, observing beneficial impact?

As a company, GE has no patience for bureaucracy; we are driven to find efficiencies in everything we do. We needed to find a robust, simple (but not simplistic), and credible measure of training's success that did not cost more to collect than to teach the program in the first place.

Then the team had a breakthrough: We decided to use the Net Promoter Score, then in common use across GE, as a summary measure of the extent to which we were meeting customer needs. The Net Promoter Score (NPS™) was introduced by Fred Reichheld in his 2003 *Harvard Business Review* article "One Number You Need to Grow." Customers are asked whether they would recommend a product, service, or company on a scale of 0 (extremely unlikely) to 10 (extremely likely). To calculate the net promoter score, the percent of those who give a rating of 6 of less (detractors) is subtracted from the percent who give a rating of 9 or 10 (promoters).

What We Did

Every quarter, we surveyed managers whose direct reports had attended our leadership program three months previously. We asked them, on a scale of 0 to 10, how likely they would be to recommend our leadership training to a peer or another high-potential candidate *based on the impact they had observed on their direct report's leadership.* We then calculated the NPS.

This "manager's NPS" score was clearly a much tougher measure than the one we collected from participants at the end of the program. First, the metric was collected not at the end of the program when participants are on a "high," but three months after the class, after the reality of leadership has had some time to set in. Second, the NPS was not linked to a measure of satisfaction but with an evaluation of impact.

After collecting a few months' worth of results, we decided to set ourselves a stretch goal to improve this NPS by 20 points during the coming year. At the time, we did not know how we were going to achieve that or even if it were possible, but we put a stake in the ground to challenge ourselves to think big and creatively, rather than just about small incremental improvements.

From the literature and the *Six Disciplines*, we knew that managers have a big impact on learning transfer. We reasoned that engaging managers more actively in the process would improve impact and the NPS. So we began experimenting with ways to involve managers more. Some ways worked better than others. We kept the successful practices and modified or replaced the less successful.

In the end, the most successful practices included:

- Sending the manager an email prior to the class the direct report was going to attend. The email included a brief overview of the program and its objectives; a one-page document (including questions to ask) for a brief pre-training discussion; and recommendations on ways to link the training to the participant's most recent performance review.

- We also sent follow-up emails after class that included a brief and specific template for a post-training discussion.

Last, we decided to see whether we could also engage the manager during the program itself. We did that in two ways:

- By encouraging the participants to send their managers brief "status reports" mid-week: "Here is where we are, here is what we have covered, here are my key takeaways so far."
- We also asked the facilitator to send all managers of participants a brief mid-course report outlining class progress, the key topics discussed, and the topics remaining, which encourages the managers to send a short note of support to their candidates.

While our intuition, and the *Six Disciplines*, told us that those measures would increase the managers' involvement in the learning process and, as a result, enhance our impact, we wanted to test it statistically. We therefore took a full year's worth of data and compared the "manager's NPS" to whether the manager and participant had had a pre-course discussion, a post-course discussion, or both.

Results

The first and most important finding is that the actions we took to involve managers more in supporting their direct reports produced an overall increase in the impact as measured by the NPS. That's important because the greater the number of "promoters" among business managers, the more likely they will be to support continued investment in leadership development.

The correlation analysis was even more interesting. As we predicted, there was a strong statistical correlation between having a pre-training discussion and a high NPS (based on impact) from managers three months later. There was also, as expected, a strong statistical correlation between having both a pre- and post-course conversation between the manager and the attendee. Surprisingly, having *only* a post-course discussion did not correlate to a higher NPS.

The positive influence of the pre-course conversation likely reflects Brinkerhoff's concept of "learning intentionality" (Brinkerhoff & Apking, 2001). When participants have discussions about the training with their managers in advance of the program, they arrive with a more positive mindset and a more focused and stronger intent to learn. The course facilitators noticed a qualitative change in the tenor of the discussions at the beginning of the class after we instituted the emails to facilitate pre-meetings. Participants were much more engaged and focused than in the past.

Bottom line: Engaging managers—especially prior to the training itself—was instrumental in driving the impact of this critical leadership program.

Keys to Success
- Having a stretch goal based on a quantifiable measure
- Optimizing for impact as perceived by the customer (managers of participants) rather than just the consumers (the participants themselves)
- Getting managers more engaged in the process, especially prior to the training
- Providing simple "how-to" documents enabling managers to engage easily and effectively in the learning process

Advice to Colleagues

- Define a stretch goal with a measurable target. Make it so challenging that it forces you to think "out of the box."
- Bring in ideas from the outside; don't feel you have to invent everything yourselves.
- Ask a lot of questions; read widely. Adopt good ideas from other companies and industries—including your competitors!
- Don't expect everything to work the first time. Indeed, if you aren't having some failures, you aren't stretching enough. We tried a lot of things and measured the results. Those that worked, we kept; those that did not, we improved or replaced.

Case D6.4

How We Use Success Stories to Communicate Training's Value

Steve Akram and Patricia Gregory
Director and Senior Director, North American
Sales Force Development, Oracle

Background

Oracle offers an optimized and fully integrated stack of business hardware and software systems to its more than 390,000 customers—including all of the Fortune 100—with deployments across a wide variety of industries in more than 145 countries around the globe.

Sales Force Development is responsible for the training, curriculum, and development of the North American sales force for this $37 billion global technology leader. Our responsibility includes preparing the sales force in all aspects of the sales process, including sales presentations, product knowledge, messaging and communications skills, negotiation and demonstration skills and—because many of our products involve enterprise-wide solutions—executive-level engagement skills.

While our programs have always been well received, we struggled in the past to effectively assess and communicate their business value to management. One of the key things we took away from the 6Ds Workshop was the need to capture feedback after participants had had time to apply the training to their work.

What We Did

- Instead of focusing solely on the training "event," we now build pre- and post-training activities into the process:
- Before training we create learning intentionality by triggering participants and their managers to have conversations about the program and set some goals for its application.
- Three months after the program, we prompt the managers and their employees to meet again and briefly review what has been accomplished.

Three months post-training we use an automated system to collect success stories. We survey participants and ask them to provide, if possible, a specific example of how they used what they learned in the training to achieve a positive outcome.

We then collate these stories into an easy-to-read and visually appealing report to managers that they can quickly scan to gain a sense of how the training is being applied in the field.

Results

For virtually every program we run, participants are able to relate specific instances in which applying what they were taught helped them close a sale or move it along to the next step. Although the response rate is not as high as we would like, the examples are often very compelling and credible to senior management. Management's reaction has been positive and these reports have helped increase their interest and involvement in training.

The three-month follow-up has also helped support continuous improvement by identifying some issues that needed attention. For example, we identified that salespeople speaking to C-level customers needed much more specific information about particular industries and applications than they had previously received. While this was not a "training problem" per se, it indicated an opportunity to improve the overall selling process; we would not have been able to identify and address it if we had stopped with end-of-class evaluations.

> **Advice to Colleagues**
> - Don't stop with end-of-class evaluations; gather data after employees have had the opportunity to apply the training in the course of their work.
> - Success stories can provide credible and compelling evidence that the program is helping achieve business outcomes.
> - Have the leaders who sponsor these programs help drive them.
> - Ensure that your team has business savvy as well as technical and instructional design skills; expertise in both business and instruction are needed to deliver business impact from training.

Case D6.5

How We Created a High Impact Mars University Brand

Maria Grigorova
Marketing College Director, Mars University

Robert Moffett
Customized Learning Director, Mars University

Background

In 1911, Frank C. Mars made the first Mars candies in his Tacoma, Washington, kitchen and established Mars' first roots as a confectionery company. In the 1920s, Forrest E. Mars, Sr., joined his father in business, and together they launched the MILKY WAY® bar. In 1932, Forrest, Sr., moved to the United Kingdom with a dream of building a business based on the objective of creating a "mutuality of benefits for all stake-holders." This objective serves as the foundation of Mars, Incorporated, today.

Based in McLean, Virginia, Mars has net sales of more than $33 billion and six business segments, including Petcare, Chocolate, Wrigley, Food, Drinks, and Symbioscience. More than 72,000 associates world-wide are putting its Five Principles of quality, responsibility, efficiency, mutuality and freedom into action to make a difference for people and the planet through its performance.

The Mars Five Principles are the foundation of the Mars culture and its approach to business. They unite Mars across geographies, languages, cultures, and generations.

Mars has always taken the development of our associates seriously, and has pioneered approaches to training and development in many of our markets. In 2004 a decision was taken to launch the Mars University, a virtual corporate university that brought together all our strategic investments in leadership development and functional learning into ten colleges within the university.

Mars historically has prized local freedom to operate and autonomy, with limited top-down direction and a pragmatic approach to deployment. For the University, this meant starting with the best of what existed and building from there. It also led to a very diverse approach to the visual identities for all of the ten colleges, not to mention region-to-region and market-to-market variations. Each college was proud of its identity and looking for ways to differentiate itself from the others.

As Mars continued to experience significant growth and a large increase in the number of associates with limited exposure to this culture, as well as a move to organizing into global segment businesses, this led to a re-evaluation of the strategic role and effectiveness of the Mars University. The conclusions were to significantly tighten up the focus and to create a single "one Mars University" experience.

What We Did

Faced with a legacy of multiple branding styles and different focuses of the colleges, we decided to apply our knowledge of building powerful global brands and apply them to the Mars University.

Using our strategic review as a base, we clarified the promise that Mars University would make to the business and to our associates: to provide globally standardized, unique to Mars, learning across our various businesses and geographies. Our goal: to improve our associates' UNDERSTANDING about who we were and what we did.

With a sharper focus we were able to clarify what we stood for and what we would and would not do. We turned our strategy in a talk-able story format that would grab people's attention, engage hearts and minds of all associates, no matter what their roles in the business are. This would help to get us NOTICED.

Finally, we developed a clear and distinctive look and feel for the Mars University (Exhibit D6.5.1)—one that broke with all the legacy brand images and went beyond visuals to encompass a "tone of voice" to create a holistic brand experience.

To do all this, we set up a tight project team and carried out an "archeological dig" to uncover the history of the brand, as well as its role and meaning within the business. We then used these insights to craft our "brand story." Using an agency partner with strong design credentials, we developed the brand experience and created deployment materials, including comprehensive brand guidelines and usage guides to help promote consistency across our business. We then undertook an engagement program inside the Mars University to share our brand story, create meaning, and ensure a full understanding of the Brand Guidelines and standards across all the colleges and regions. Finally, we

Exhibit D6.5.1. The Mars University Logo

sought a commitment and a timeframe to achieve a full cascade of the new identity across our business.

Results

Today the Mars University brand is a powerful and well-respected brand you can find in offices across Mars. It is featured on our company website and has been attributed with improving our attractiveness as an employer, because it is a tangible demonstration of the commitment Mars makes to each associate's development. We have leveraged the power of the brand to improve the cohesion of the Mars University teams and drive more standardized approaches to our curriculum structure and our competence frameworks that continue to raise the bar.

Most important for us is the feedback and stories we receive from the individuals and teams we support about the impact of our programs and offers on their work and in their lives.

Advice to Colleagues
- Sponsorship is key; be sure you secure it before embarking on the branding journey.
- Creating a strong brand requires creativity initially, then discipline to stay the course.

Case C.1

How We Are Incorporating the 6Ds Methodologies into Our Culture, One Step at a Time

Tom Stango and Jon Hurtado
Learning Consultant and Senior Learning Consultant, Coventry Workers' Comp Services

Background

Coventry Workers' Comp Services (Coventry) offers workers' compensation cost and care management solutions for employers, insurance carriers, and third-party administrators. The mission of the learning and development department is to provide learning solutions that support strategic operational outcomes. We accomplish this by maintaining responsive, consultative partnerships, enabling success with stakeholders, and connecting employees' roles with business goals.

In January 2012, we realized that our training was not aligned with the company's business goals and performance support. It was our practice to measure the effectiveness of our training programs at the Kirkpatrick Level 1 (Reaction) and Level 2 (Learning) only. Therefore, we formed a subcommittee, known as the Metrics Team, charged with researching and implementing the policies and procedures allowing us to measure Kirkpatrick Level 3 (Behavior) and Level 4 (Results) and ensure that transfer of learning occurred.

After months of research, we learned about the 6Ds Company and agreed as a team to use their methodologies as the foundation for our culture change.

What We Did

We began by incorporating the 6Ds methodology into our needs analysis process. The five 6Ds Outcomes Planning Wheel questions were inserted into the needs analysis form used by our learning consultants for initial stakeholder interviews. In doing so, our learning consultants and stakeholders became familiar with the questions, and that began to change the way we approach training projects.

Next, we reviewed all of the training programs that were in the design phase to identify opportunities for updating with the 6Ds methodology. One program in particular, the Service Group Training project, was determined to be a good candidate. We met with the learning consultant on the project, presented our ideas, and agreed to make the following changes to the program:

- Meet with the stakeholders to redefine their original expectations of the course and clarify the criteria used to measure the training program's success.
- Incorporate "transfer of learning" checklists to engage the participants and their managers throughout the learning process and to encourage the participants to use their newly learned skills on the job.

- Revise the course's learning objectives to ensure they aligned with business outcomes and included discrete, measureable behaviors.
- Modify the course to include exercises and activities that mimicked the true work environment as closely as possible, so the learning experience would be seamless for the participants as they moved from training to the job environment.
- Collaborate with the quality assurance department and managers to provide timely feedback to the participants.

Results

Adding the 6Ds questions to the needs analysis form has allowed us to change the way we and our stakeholders approach training requests by:

- Establishing a mutual understanding with our clients of each other's expectations,
- Remaining focused on the goals and behaviors that need to change, and
- Creating effective programs that meet or exceed our stakeholders' expectations.

As a result of the changes made to the Service Group Training program:

- Eighty-eight percent of the respondents said they felt confident they could apply the skills on the job, and 100 percent were committed to applying the skills on the job.
- Post-training evaluations and quality assurance data confirmed that participants were using the skills they learned in class on the job.
- Within three months post-training, the stakeholder confirmed a 76 percent increase in expense savings to our customers, due in large part to the skills learned in training!

Advice to Colleagues

- Be prepared if your stakeholders are reluctant to answer the Outcomes Planning Wheel questions, especially if they are not accustomed to them. You may need to help them understand why you're asking the questions before they will share the information you want.
- Establishing a partnership with stakeholders is paramount. Without the support of the stakeholders, it is impossible to ensure that training will result in behavioral changes on the job.

![PART IV]

How-to Guides

This section contains practical "how-to" guides for using 6Ds tools and implementing other highly effective learning strategies. Additional details and information are available in the references cited.

H2 D1.1

How to Use the Planning Wheel to Clarify Business Purpose

Introduction

"The *only* reason that learning functions exist is to drive business outcomes" (Smith, 2011, p. 10). A prerequisite for successful training, therefore, is to understand the business purpose of the training and the business leader's definition of success. Training professionals who focus on business needs move into the roles of performance consultants (Robinson & Robinson, 2008) and trusted advisors to the business (Maister, Green, & Galford, 2000).

The 6Ds Outcomes Planning Wheel™ (Figure D1.1.1) has proven to be a useful aid for clarifying the business rationale behind a request for training. Its questions help structure the discussion with business managers.

Guidance

1. When you receive a request for training, ask the business manager to meet briefly to discuss the request in more detail. Stress the benefit to him or her of clarifying the desired results and your genuine interest in providing training that adds business value.

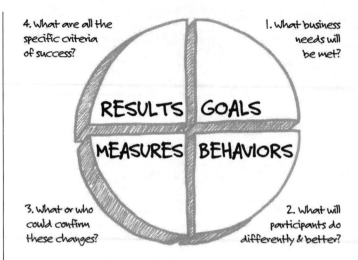

4. What are all the specific criteria of success?

1. What business needs will be met?

RESULTS | GOALS

MEASURES | BEHAVIORS

3. What or who could confirm these changes?

2. What will participants do differently & better?

Figure H2 D1.1.1. The 6Ds Outcomes Planning Wheel™

2. Prior to the meeting, review relevant material, such as prior discussions regarding training and the unit business plan.

3. Open the meeting by stating the purpose and value, proposing an agenda, and checking for agreement.

4. Work your way through the four questions using the following guidelines:

- Ask open-ended questions.
- Probe for deeper understanding. Two helpful techniques are to ask for examples or to use the phrase "Help me understand . . ."
- Practice active listening skills; restate what you have heard frequently and ask for confirmation that you have understood the point.
- Reframe as necessary to keep the conversation focused on the results the business is seeking rather than solutions (a training program).

- Don't be too rigid about the order of questions and answers. If your business partner provides an answer to question 4 in response to your question 1, just note it there and follow up as appropriate. Indeed, one of our 6Ds partners, Conrado Schlochauer, finds it productive to start with quadrant two first: "What do you want people to do better and differently?"

5. When you have answered the four central questions, ask one more: "If we really want people to perform the actions you have described, what else needs to be in place? I am thinking of things like incentives, recognition, support from managers, etc." Your goal is to help your business colleagues understand that training is only *part* of the solution and that the work environment (transfer climate)—which they control—will make or break the success of the initiative.

6. Finally, following the meeting, summarize the results in a memorandum like the one in Exhibit H2 D1.1.1 to thank the leader for his or her time, confirm your understanding, and "contract" for the deliverables as well as roles and responsibilities in achieving them.

Key Success Factors

- Genuine interest in the business and in understanding the sponsor's goals.
- Good listening skills.
- A consultative attitude and style.
- Willingness to try a new.
- Openness to different points of view.
- Follow up to ensure agreement.

EXHIBIT H2 D1.1.1. SAMPLE MEMORANDUM OF UNDERSTANDING

Dear _____ ,

Thank you for your time yesterday to discuss the
_____ program. I am writing to confirm my
understanding of the needs and deliverables for the program.

The underlying business need that the training is designed to
address is _____. Therefore, the desired business outcomes include: _____.

If the training and on-the-job reinforcement are successful, then
the learners will do (more / less) of _____
and (more/less) of _____ in their work. The
following elements, in addition to the training, need to
be in place to support these behaviors and achieve the
business objectives: _____,
_____, and _____.

The results will be apparent to _____ and will
be measured by _____. You will consider the
program to be a success when _____.

Please let me know if I have correctly summarized our discussion or
if any changes or additions are needed. Thank you again for helping to ensure that we design a maximally effective program.

Sincerely,

_____

H2 D1.2

How to Decide Whether Training Is Necessary

Introduction

In *Transfer of Training*, Broad and Newstrom wrote: "Training is expensive to design and deliver; it should be the *last*, not the *first*, intervention the HRD professional and the organization should consider in order to improve employee performance" (1992, p. 5).

Unfortunately, many business managers try to use training as the first response to a host of performance issues for which it was neither designed nor can succeed.

But how do you differentiate between performance issues in which training is an essential part of the solution (it is never the whole solution) and performance issues for which training will have no effect, or could even make the situation worse?

Guidance

Assuming that the performance gap is real, and that closing it will provide sufficient value to justify the cost, then the critical question is whether or not the underlying cause is a lack of skills or knowledge. There are many other potential impediments to performance (Figure D1.2, p. 15). Training can only impart knowledge and skills (and to a small degree influence attitude). If the real cause is something other than insufficient skill or knowledge, then training won't help and could do harm.

Mager and Pipe (1997) proposed that the acid test for whether the cause was a lack of knowledge or skill was: "Could they still not perform the task to the required standard if their lives depended on it?" Performance standards should include quality criteria as well as acceptable time for completion or process requirements, if appropriate. If, in a "do or die" situation, people would still be unable to perform at an acceptable level, then training and/or a job aid needs to be part of the solution (Figure H2 D1.2.1).

If, on the other hand, people are *able* to perform as required, but they are not doing so on the job, then the impediment is something other than a lack of skill or knowledge, and training—at least of the workers themselves—is unlikely to improve the situation. As Mager and Pipe went on to say, "If a genuine lack of skill is not the problem, then you can forget training as a potential solution" (1997, p. 93). Your task, then, becomes identifying the true impediments to performance and persuading management that those need to be addressed *before* or in addition to training.

A decision tree is provided in Tool D1.2 (page 175).

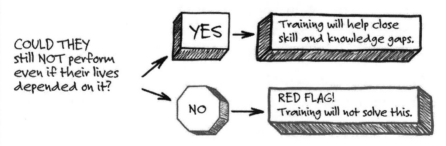

Figure H2 D1.2.1. The Acid Test for Whether Training Is Needed

Key Success Factors

- Making sure there really is a performance issue and that it is worth addressing.
- Identifying the root cause as a lack of skills or knowledge (on the part of the proposed trainees!).
    - If it is, complete the needs analysis, design and deliver relevant training, *and* ensure the work climate will support the use of what is being taught.
    - If workers *are able* to perform to standard, but are not currently doing so, then identify the true impediments to performance and address them directly.

H2 D1.3

How to Use (and Not Use) Learning Objectives

Introduction

Learning objectives are a critical link between the identification of a training need and the delivery of training to meet that need (Garavan, Hogan, & Cahir-O'Donnell, 2003, p. 182). They serve three vital purposes:

- To define specifically what a successful learner will be able to do as a result of the instruction
- To guide the selection of content, methods, and exercises
- To establish criteria for determining whether or not the instruction was successful.

Instructional objectives require three elements to fulfill these purposes (Mager, 1997, p. 47):

- *Performance.* The objective clearly communicates what the learner must be able to do or produce to be considered competent.
- *Conditions.* The objective specifies important conditions (if any) of the performance, such as location, time constraints, audience, etc.
- *Criteria.* The objective clearly defines the criteria of acceptable performance.

541

Well-crafted learning objectives are essential to guide instructional design decisions. Indeed, Hodell (2006) argues that "Almost all design problems start with sloppy or non-existent objectives" (p. 45).

We agree. Failure to plan is planning to fail. Instructional objectives are essential to communicate the desired outcomes to instructional designers. But—and this is a very large but—they are a poor way to communicate with business leaders and learners in corporate training. Although some texts on instructional design refer to learning or instructional objectives as "performance objectives" (for example, Rothwell & Kazanas, 2008, p. 169), they only specify how the learner will be able to perform at the end of training, not the standards of performance on the job. Moreover, learning objectives tend to be formulaic ("at the end of this module, the learner will be able to . . .), full of learning jargon, and, frankly, boring.

Most importantly, learning objectives fail to answer the questions adult learners are *actually* interested in:

- What's in it for me?
- Will this help me in my job, my responsibilities, my success?
- Will it be worth my time?

Likewise, because they only specify what will be *learned*, they don't directly address what the business sponsors and learners' managers want to know:

- What is the connection between this training and our business imperatives?
- Will this improve performance? How?
- Will it be worth the investment of time and money?

Guidance

1. *Define the business objectives of the program first* (see H2 D1.1).
   Business objectives are the bedrock on which any training program

should be built. They are the ultimate reason for its existence—indeed for the existence of the training function in the first place.

2. *Define learning objectives clearly, concisely, and completely.* Learning objectives are the blueprint that instructional designers need in order to select the appropriate methods, exercises, assessments, and timing of instruction. Make sure they conform to best practices for instructional objectives. Use the checklist for learning objectives (Exhibit H2 D1.3.1) below to confirm.

3. *Follow Julie Dirksen's advice: "just say no to learning-objective slides at the beginning of the course"* (2012, p. 73). And, we would add, "in course descriptions and invitations." Instead, apply the principles of motivating communication (see H2 D2.1: "How to Communicate to Motivate"). Explain how the training relates to current business challenges, or to the learners' job responsibilities. Do so in a way that is interesting and that builds their confidence in the relevance and utility of the training, such as by including testimonials or success stories from previous attendees (see Case D2.2).

Key Success Factors

- Having an in-depth understanding of the business drivers and the on-the-job performance required.
- Writing detailed and well-crafted learning objectives based on the performance requirements to communicate *within the design team*.

- Crafting credible and compelling statements that answer the "What's in it for me?" question for participants and their managers, distinct from the learning objectives.

EXHIBIT H2 D1.3.1. CHECKLIST FOR LEARNING OBJECTIVES

❏ Each objective uses a verb that describes how the learner will demonstrate proficiency.
   ❏ The verbs are specific and observable (list, analyze, explain) rather than vague and unmeasurable (know, appreciate).
   ❏ The verbs are relevant to the job performance (apply, calculate, construct) rather than mere tests of memorization (list, define, label).
   ❏ It is immediately apparent how proficiency could be assessed.
❏ Objectives contain the criteria that define acceptable performance.
   ❏ Process criteria define how the learner should perform the task ("conforming to company safety procedures" or "within ten minutes").
   ❏ Product criteria define the quality required of the output*("to the client's satisfaction," "With 100 percent accuracy").

❏ Objectives define the working conditions under which the learner must demonstrate proficiency.
   ❏ If these are the same for all the objectives, than the conditions are included in the preamble to avoid tedious repetition.
   ❏ So far as possible, the conditions relate to real job performance rather than to the training environment or "to the satisfaction of the instructor."
   ❏ The conditions focus on essential elements rather than long laundry lists of equipment, and so forth.

❏ Objectives are concisely stated; unnecessary words or phrases have been eliminated.
❏ The language is clear and understandable and eschews jargon.

H2 D2.1

How to Communicate to Motivate

Introduction

Motivation is an energizing force. Motivated people are creative, take on challenges, and produce more and better work. Motivated employees are more willing to learn and to apply what they learn. Thus, improving motivation improves training outcomes.

Many factors affect motivation, external as well as internal. External factors include expectations of performance, reward structures, and organizational ethos. Internal factors include confidence, a feeling of belonging, trust, and a drive for self-efficacy.

Motivational messages have been shown to enhance performance in studies of learning in a variety of contexts and settings (Visser, 2010, p. 516). Thus, providing motivational messages, especially prior to training, is an important part of designing the complete experience and maximizing training's impact.

Guidance

Messages that motivate address the four key elements in Keller's ARCS model: attention (A), relevance (R), confidence (C), and satisfaction (S) (Keller, 1987).

Strategies to get the learner's *attention* include:

- Asking a thought-provoking question
- Stating a surprising statistic or using attention-grabbing visual or medium
- Emphasizing the individual's value to the organization and its willing-ness to invest in his or her development
- Increasing the feeling of belonging to a group that does important work
- Having a senior and respected leader discuss the importance of the training, or better, lead it

Strategies to emphasize the training's *relevance* include:

- Showing the links between the training and the job requirements
- Capitalizing on people's intrinsic desire to achieve
- Giving concrete examples of what prior participants have achieved
- Providing testimonials from participants' peers
- Showing how instructional goals support performance expectations
- Providing examples of how the learning can be applied in useful and valuable ways
- Connecting to people's beliefs and values

Strategies to enhance the learner's *confidence* include:

- Sharing examples of how others have succeeded
- Expressing confidence that they, too, can succeed
- Encouraging collaboration and teamwork ("you are not alone")
- Recognizing improvements, even small ones
- Giving learners some control over pace and level of difficulty

Strategies to give the learners *satisfaction* include:

- Designing for success early on ("small wins")
- Providing testimonials or examples of prior participants' satisfaction
- Giving positive feedback whenever appropriate
- Recognizing sincere effort, even when results are not yet significant
- Offering further opportunities for personal growth
- Making sure excellent work is called to the attention of others, especially managers

Communications in general, and about learning opportunities in particular, are motivational to the extent that they gain attention, emphasize relevance, express confidence, and predict satisfaction, provided they are sincere and believable. Communications demotivate learners when they are cold, impersonal, bureaucratic, or insincere. Learning professionals can enhance the effectiveness of training by reviewing their communications and revising them to incorporate ARCS principles.

Checklist

Review the communications about your training program. Check off which criteria of the ARCS model it satisfies. Aim for at least three of the four.

Criterion	Explanation
☐ Attention	☐ The communication includes something to attract the learner's attention very near the beginning, such as a provocative question, surprising fact, humorous statement, cartoon, etc.

☐ Relevance ☐ The communication clearly links the training to the person's job responsibilities and the business's strategic objectives.

☐ Confidence ☐ The communication includes elements that help boost the readers' confidence, such as testimonials from prior participants and/or descriptions of the kind of support they will receive.

☐ Satisfaction ☐ The communication suggests ways in which the learner will be satisfied with the outcome, such as a sense of personal mastery, recognition by others, or improved performance. It may cite examples of positive results or statements of satisfaction from prior participants to support the claim.

Keys to Success

- Knowing your audience; try to put yourself in their position.
- Designing the message so that it is on target with an attention-getting first sentence, visual, etc.
- Reading the communication carefully and considering how you would react to such a message.
- Trying out the message on a few people.
- Avoiding boring buzzwords, hyperbole, and expressions of fake interest.
- Distributing a message that would please and motivate you personally.

H2 D2.2

How to Create Results Intentionality

Introduction

A central theme throughout the 6Ds is that learning and development initiatives need to produce *business results*. The first link in the value chain—learning—is strengthened when participants come to training programs with clear goals and expectations to learn—something Brinkerhoff and Apking (2001) termed "learning intentionality."

Learning intentionality is created when participants actively think through how the training will benefit them and what they want to get out of it. The process is facilitated by course descriptions and invitations that stress program benefits and applicability (See H2 D2.1: "How to Communicate to Motivate") and when participants have a pre-training discussion with their managers.

Learning intentionality is important to jump-start the process, but learning is not the ultimate goal; it is only a step in the causal chain leading to results. Training's effectiveness is increased when learners develop "results intentionality" from the onset. Employees with results intentionality have a perspective that extends past the training to how they will apply what they learn and the benefits it will produce. They understand the ultimate goal of the program and they expect to be held accountable for applying the training to their work.

Results intentionality is fostered by:

- Making the business purpose of the training clear from the onset
- Emphasizing the WIIFM (What's in it for me?) for the participant before and during the training
- Having managers underscore the expectation for application before and after training
- Having participants set goals for learning before the training as well as goals for its application afterward

Guidance

The process of converting training to business results occurs in four phases (Figure H2 D2.2.1). The most effective training programs facilitate results intentionality in all four phases as described below.

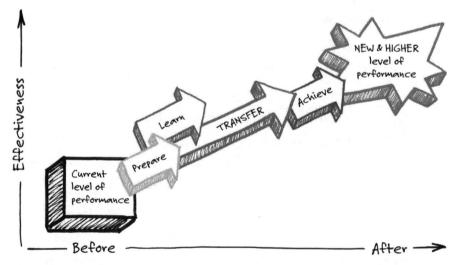

Figure D2.2.1. The Process of Transforming Training into Results Involves Four Phases: Preparation, Learning, Transfer, and Achievement.

Phase 1: Preparation

1. Describe the training in ways both the learners and their managers clearly understand the expected performance and the job impact the program is designed to achieve.

2. Utilize the success of prior participants to create interest and excitement about the program. (See Case D2.2: "How We Use Alumni to Help Set Expectations for New Program Participants and Their Leaders.")

3. Facilitate a discussion between the attendee and his or her manager in advance of the program focused on expected results. Tool D2.2 provides a sample "learning contract" that can be used to guide the discussion and create a record to underscore its importance. See Jefferson, Pollock, and Wick (2009), *Getting Your Money's Worth from Training and Development*, for additional information and guidance.

Phase 2: Learn

1. Continually reinforce the business objectives of the program and the WIIFM during the instruction and how the learning relates to the actual work the participants do on the job.

2. Use company- and job-relevant examples and stories.

3. Start exercises by explaining their rationale and how they relate to the work of the participants (see H2 D3.6: "How to Introduce Exercises").

4. Have participants bring a real work challenge to the instruction and use it to generate specific action plans for application.

5. Give participants time and guidance to reflect on how they can apply what they are learning at several points during the training.

6. If appropriate, have participants develop a written plan for application. Alternatively, give them specific goals for application to achieve in the first few days and weeks after training.

Phase 3: Transfer

1. Sustain the participants' intentions to produce results by periodically reminding them (see H2 D4.1: "How to Remind Learners to Apply Their Training").

2. Engage their managers by:
   - Reminding the managers of the business goals of the program and their role in helping achieve them
   - Providing short, specific guidance on how to maximize the return on the training investment
   - Sending managers copies of their direct reports' goals and action plans if appropriate

Phase 4: Achieve

The final phase of converting training into results is to provide a sense of achievement.

1. Reset the finish line by awarding credit or certificates of completion only when participants have demonstrated application to their work (see H2 D2.4: "How to Move the Finish Line for Learning").

2. Remind their managers of the importance of recognition and engage them in the process (see Case D4.6: "How We Engage Managers to Acknowledge the Achievements of Leadership Program Participants").

Keys to Success

- Fostering *results intentionality* before, during, and after the program
- Making the business results the training is designed to deliver explicit to both participants and their managers
- Facilitating pre-training discussions between participants and their managers to create learning intentionality

- Ensuring that managers and facilitators reinforce the message of relevance and the business impact
- Playing back the success of prior participants to create excitement and anticipation among future attendees
- Setting expectations for on-the-job application and engaging managers in the process

H2 D2.3

How to Start Learning Before Class to Improve Efficiency

Introduction

Pre-work—or what we prefer to call Phase I learning—is an important element of the complete learning experience. It serves a variety of purposes, including:

- Securing the learner's attention
- Generating learning intentionality
- Stimulating interest in the topic or a "need to know"
- Establishing a common understanding of concepts and terminology
- Gathering data to use during training

For Phase I learning to be effective, five conditions must be satisfied:

1. There must be a sound learning rationale for including it.
2. Its purpose should be clearly and convincingly communicated to participants.
3. The amount must be reasonable for the time available.

4. It must be engaging and thought-provoking.

5. Subsequent instruction should depend on and build on, but not repeat, Phase I learning.

Guidance

1. *Make Phase I learning a required part of any instructional design.*

2. *Clarify its purpose.* Explain to participants how, why, and when it will be used.

3. *Explore alternatives to reading assignments.*
   - There are many interesting and effective ways to learn before class besides reading—from e-learning to experiential (see Tool D2.4: "Purposes and Examples of Phase I Learning").
   - As in planning any instruction, strive for methods that involve active learning and require thinking.

4. *Find the minimum amount that will accomplish the instructional objective.* If participants perceive the amount of preparation to be impossible, they may not do *any*.
   - Challenge the design: Is this *really* necessary?
   - Eliminate any pre-work that is not essential for the subsequent instruction.
   - Provide an accurate estimate of how long it will take.
   - If there are several assignments, prioritize them.

5. *Make sure that the rest of the instruction builds on—rather than repeats—the Phase I learning.* A brief review may be appropriate, but if you cover everything that was in the pre-work again in class, you punish those who completed it and reward those who did not.

6. *Ideally, make completing the first phase of learning a prerequisite to attending the second phase, especially if the latter is instructor-led or expensive.* Some companies have initiated an "earn the right to learn" policy, and one has gone so far as to put people on a plane and fly them home if they have not completed the preparation.

Key Success Factors

- Knowing exactly what the Phase I learning is meant to accomplish and why.
- Requiring only as much preparation as is essential to achieve the training objectives.
- Selecting engaging, active learning activities whenever possible.
- Building on, but not repeating, the pre-work in class.

H2 D2.4

How to Move the Finish Line for Learning

Introduction

Training is a process that creates value for the organization and individual only when it is transferred and applied on the job. And yet, most training programs continue to reinforce the "event paradigm"—the mistaken notion that simply participating in the training is sufficient. To receive greater value from training, we need to "move the finish line" by redefining successful completion from attending class to on-the-job application.

Guidance

1. *Seek out and change wording and practices that reinforce the event paradigm.* Most training programs reinforce the event paradigm in many subtle and not-so-subtle ways. For example, describing the training as "one day" implies that the program is finished after that day. A better description might be "a three-week program that includes a one-day in-person workshop" or "a one-day, interactive workshop followed by three weeks of on-the-job application."

Training agendas and schedules also unwittingly reinforce the "showing up is sufficient" mentality when the last item reads something like "program concludes" or "graduation." Change it to "begin applying on the job" or a similar forward-looking sentiment.

2. *Redefine the requirements for completing the program.* Awarding credit or certificates of completion at the end of class sends the message "you have done all that is expected of you." Since the investment in training is repaid only when people apply it to their work roles, we need to send a much clearer message that "a change in behavior is required."

   One way to do that is to award certificates or credit only when, after a suitable period, there is evidence of application on the job. What kind of evidence is needed depends on the nature of the job and the criticality of the performance to the organization's success. In some cases, simple self-reports will suffice; they are certainly better than the current system of no follow-up at all. For closely supervised roles, the trainee's manager could be asked to sign off on "completion." For customer-facing roles, an interaction could be monitored and scored; in other cases, an improved work product (such as a piece of writing or a presentation) could be required.

   The key point is that "completion" must reflect progress toward the performance goals for which the training was created in the first place, not just "showing up" for the training.

3. *Harness intrinsic motivation by ensuring that learners have a sense of progress and accomplishment in the post-training period.* Numerous studies have demonstrated the power of intrinsic motivation. Two of the strongest intrinsic motivators are the satisfaction of making progress and of doing a job well. Harness these motivators by providing learners with feedback on how they are

doing during the application period. Learning transfer support systems such as *ResultsEngine®* include a progress meter for this reason. Case D4.4 describes Qstream, a software system that uses elements of game theory to encourage trainees to revisit topics and continue their learning. Self-evaluation and reflection are also effective; encourage people and score their performance a suitable period after training and compare it to their performance prior to training.

By way of example: we schedule a "capstone call" two to three months after our 6Ds workshops in which we ask participants to report:

- What I set out to do
- What I was able to accomplish
- What I learned in the process
- My advice to my colleagues

Announcing these calls as the finish line for the program motivates participants to have something to report. The calls give them an opportunity to take pride in what they have accomplished as well as to learn from the experiences of others. The calls have also proven highly motivating and rewarding to us as facilitators since we have the opportunity to hear and take pride in what our trainees have accomplished—something trainers otherwise rarely know.

4. *Finally, be sure that, when you "move the finish line" you acknowledge both effort and accomplishment.* Notify the trainee's manager and, ideally, have him or her recognize the employee (see Case D4.6).

Key Success Factors

- Consistency: making sure that course descriptions and practices all reinforce transfer and application as requisite parts of the complete learning experience.

- Changing your own internal paradigm from "events" to "process" and from "learning" to "performance."
- Providing learners with a sense of progress and accomplishment and recognize their efforts to apply what they learned.
- Getting buy-in from human resources and line managers for the new finish line concept and agreement to change policies, if necessary, to award credit only after learning transfer.

H2 D3.1

How to Use (and Not Abuse) PowerPoint

Introduction

PowerPoint® and its variants are ubiquitous in the business world. It's rare to attend a meeting or presentation that doesn't include some sort of projected slides. And while it is true that well-chosen visuals can enhance learning and retention, the misuse of slides is now so rampant as to have spawned the popular phrase "Death by PowerPoint."

While a full discussion of the use of visuals is beyond the scope of this book, application of a few principles will greatly enhance the effectiveness of training.

Guidance

1. *Avoid text-dense slides.* Garr Reynolds, in *Presentation Zen* (2008), calls these "slideuments." Human beings are very good at integrating pictures and spoken words; that is why presenting a relevant diagram, chart, or image together with a verbal explanation can boost learning and retention. On the other hand, it is very difficult to integrate two different forms of *verbal* information—listening to

a speaker and, at the same time, trying to read a long block of text. The two processes compete for the same mental machinery, leading to cognitive overload and decreased comprehension.

Prepare a handout so you do not feel compelled to cram everything into your slides. Use visuals to highlight and reinforce the message, not to carry it.

2. *Avoid endless series of bullet points.* Bullet points are just plain boring. A whole deck of them is stupefying. In *slide:ology*, Nancy Duarte (2008, p. 151) proposed the following "Bullet Laws":

- Protect your audience from the danger of bullets.
- Use them sparingly, if at all.
- Write as headlines.
- Use parallel structure in a list.
- Avoid sub-bullets whenever you can.
- Use relevant images.

The right image can help cement a point (by making it visually memorable) or lead to fresh insight (like illustrating the relationship between two variables). But the wrong image—such as a pretty but unrelated picture just to have something on the screen—is a distraction. Distractions divert attention and interfere with learning. If the image will not contribute to the understanding or recall of the topic, leave it out, or insert a black slide.

3. *Maximize the signal-to-noise ratio.* Garr Reynolds (2008) applied the concept of signal-to-noise ratio from engineering to visual presentations. The signal-to-noise ratio in this sense is the amount of useful information (signal) to the amount of irrelevant information or distracting elements (noise). Most slides contain a substantial number of elements (background images, decorative headers and footers, gridlines, unnecessary labels, etc.) that add complexity without providing useful information. Reynolds recommends: "If the item can be removed without compromising the visual message, then

strong consideration should be given to minimizing the element or removing it altogether" (p. 122). See Case D3.2: "How We Improved the Signal-to-Noise Ratio to Transform the Presentation Culture at KLA-Tencor" for an example of applying this principle in action.

A related concept is to reduce things to their essence. A simple line drawing is often better for instruction than a photograph or highly detailed drawing (Clark & Mayer, 2011, p. 164), presumably because it helps focus attention on the key elements (signal) while reducing the unnecessary details (noise).

4. *Show how things develop.* One advantage of an old-fashioned chalkboard was that the presenter had to slow down while he or she created a drawing, wrote an equation, or sketched a graph. Students were able to see how things developed—for example, the ratio of price to volume over a range of values—and had time to recreate them in their own notes. Nowadays, most charts and graphs are presented *fait accompli.* Because only the end result is presented, the sequence of events is not as clear, nor does the student have time to re-create the relationship (and therefore the understanding).

   Consider breaking sequences into a series of slides; for example, showing just the axes of a graph first and asking the students to anticipate what the plot of the relationship will look like. Indeed, there is evidence that a series of static illustrations is a more effective method than animating the same sequence (Clark & Mayer, 2011, p. 84).

5. *Turn off the damn projector now and then.* It is neither essential nor helpful to always have a slide on the screen. The greatest speeches in history were delivered without PowerPoint. The speakers used vivid language to paint pictures, arouse curiosity, and stir emotions. Edward Tufte does a very funny parody of Lincoln delivering the *Gettysburg Address* with slides to make this point.

Try turning off the projector, or presenting whole sections without slides; you and your learners will probably find the change refreshing. We know of several companies that have "no PowerPoint" rules for senior managers speaking in leadership programs. They come across as much more credible and sincere when they speak without the crutch.

Key Success Factors

- Using slides to illustrate and reinforce a presentation, not as a substitute for it.
- Avoiding text-dense "slideuments"; they undermine learning.
- Choosing images with care.
- Eliminating unnecessary details and decorative elements to maximize the signal-to-noise ratio.
- Not being afraid to turn off the projector; it is not necessary to *always* have something on the screen.

H2 D3.2

How to Gain and Hold Learners' Attention

Introduction

Gaining and then maintaining learners' attention is prerequisite to effective instruction. That's because people process, encode, and remember only what they attend to, and our attention span is strictly limited. The classic demonstration of the filtering effect of attention is the "dichotic listening task" (Anderson, 2010, p. 65). Participants were asked to listen to two different lectures simultaneously (one in each ear) but were instructed to *attend* to only one. Although they *heard* both lectures, they were able to recall information only from the one they actively attended to.

The relevance to instruction is that, unless learners are actively paying attention to the lesson (lecture, webcast, exercise, or discussion), they may *hear* it, but they won't *learn* it.

Attention tends to drift; "before the first quarter-hour is over in a typical presentation, people *usually* have checked out" (Medina, 2008, p. 74). The best evidence is that, unless there is something to rekindle interest, attention wanes after about ten minutes. Given the "gate-keeper" effect of attention on learning, instructional designs need to include specific actions to gain attention initially (the first of Gagne's Nine Events of Instruction) and then recapture attention at intervals.

Guidance

1. *Give audiences a break from the fire hose delivery of information every ten minutes or so.* Introduce some stimulus that will get through to their executive control and recapture their attention. Effective stimuli have two characteristics: they are relevant to the topic and they evoke some sort of emotion—laughter, anxiety, disbelief, surprise, puzzlement, and so forth.

2. *Use relevant attention-getting stimuli.* Relevance is vital. Telling a joke, for example, that has nothing to do with the topic at hand may give people a short break, but it is likely to interfere with learning rather than aid it, because it takes people's attention away from the task at hand. Be sure that whatever attention-getting device you use, it is appropriate for the audience and relevant to the topic.

3. *Engage learners' emotions.* Emotions are extremely powerful at capturing attention and in creating long-lasting memories—something you know from your own personal experience; memories of particularly emotional events persist for years and are easily recalled, even when you would prefer to forget them. All emotions—joy, sorrow, surprise—aid memory and recall. The practical application is that engaging participants' emotions as well as their reason will help them learn (see Case D3.1). That is why surprising outcomes to a simulation, engaging games, or an amusing anecdote that underscores a point are powerful teaching devices. Attention and emotions are two of the four key elements of the AGES learning retention model developed by the NeuroLeadership Institute (Davachi, Kiefer, Rock, & Rock, 2010).

4. *Use stories.* "Stories are easier to remember—because in many ways, stories are *how* we remember" (Pink, 2006, p. 101). As Patterson and his colleagues (2008) explained in *Influencer,* "A well-told narrative provides concrete and vivid detail rather than terse summaries and unclear conclusions. It changes people's view of how the world works because it presents a plausible, touching, and *memorable* flow of cause and effect" (p. 59, emphasis added).

5. *Make people think.* Effective learning requires active engagement with and encoding of the information. In other words, people have to actively *think* about the topic. You can use a variety of methods to actively engage learners, such as posing questions they have to answer, having them participate in a relevant game, explain a point to a colleague, or to discuss a topic. Bob Pike (2003) provides a number of useful methods.

6. *Mix it up.* Even the best re-engagement techniques lose their effectiveness when they are overused. Incorporate a variety of techniques throughout the session.

Key Success Factors

- Recognizing that attention wanders if it is not reactivated every ten to fifteen minutes.
- Building attention re-engagement activities into the instructional design.
- Using a variety of methods.
- Making sure that they are relevant and reinforce, rather than detract, from the instruction.

H2 D3.3

How to Re-Engage Learners After a Break

Terrence Donahue
Corporate Director, Training, Emerson, Inc.

Introduction

Breaks are important for learners' mental and physical well-being. But it can sometimes be challenging to get a group of learners to fully re-engage after a break, especially in the afternoon or toward the end of a multi-day program. Over the years, I have developed a fun, engaging, and stimulating exercise that I use after breaks. It takes only a few minutes, learners enjoy it, it raises the energy level in the room, and it brings participants back into a creative and active learning mode.

Guidance

1. Before the break, announce that there will be a table competition immediately afterward and name the starting time.
2. Start on time.
3. Project a slide of questions without answers (see examples).

4. Give the table teams two minutes to work together to answer as many as they can.
5. Call time after two minutes and go over the questions, asking the group to call out the answers before you project each one.
6. Have the tables keep a running score of the total number of correct answers across all the quizzes. You can (optionally) post the scores after each round.
7. [Optional] Award small prizes to the table with the highest total score.

You can easily create your own questions on any topic that interests you. I have created puzzles on everything from license plate slogans for the United States to match the flag to the country for international audiences. You can search Wikipedia or the Internet for topics like "national sports" or "which countries consume the most rice?" Animate the slides so that the answers are revealed one at a time.

Don't make the quizzes about the material you just covered. They are intended to give the participants a mental break. Sousa (2011, p. 99) found that it was easier to keep students on task during lesson segments if they went off-task between segments.

Key Success Factors
- Keeping the quizzes short, so they can be completed in two minutes or less.
- Making them fairly challenging so that people have to really think and pool their knowledge to come up with the right answers.
- Choosing topics that are appropriate for the audience, especially if you teach internationally.
- Writing questions that will take advantage of the diversity of the group.
- Incorporating humor—funny topics, questions, puns, or unexpected answers.

Here are a couple of my favorites (answers are given on page 574).

Candy Quotient: Name each candy described

1. Swashbuckling trio	10. Precursor to a black hole
2. Happy about nuts	11. A famous author
3. Red planet	12. What a bee makes
4. Favorite day of work week	13. A famous baseball player
5. Our galaxy	14. Twin letters
6. Two female pronouns	15. Superman's other name
7. Home of the movie stars	16. Sweet sign of affection
8. Round flotation devices	17. A dry cow
9. A quiet laugh	

Largest to Smallest

1. Largest island?	9. Highest mountain peak?
2. Smallest breed of dog?	10. Largest mammal?
3. Largest freshwater lake?	11. Largest ocean?
4. Longest mountain range?	12. Longest river?
5. Smallest continent?	13. Largest desert?
6. Largest snake?	14. Fastest animal on land?
7. Largest sea?	15. Smallest bird?
8. Largest country?	

Answers

Candy Quotient

1. Three Musketeers	10. Starburst
2. Almond Joy	11. Oh Henry
3. Mars	12. Bit O' Honey
4. Pay Day	13. Baby Ruth
5. Milky Way	14. M & M
6. Hershey	15. Clark
7. Hollywood	16. Kiss
8. Life Savers	17. Milk Dud
9. Snickers or Chuckles	

Largest to Smallest

1. Greenland	9. Mount Everest
2. Chihuahua	10. Blue whale
3. Lake Superior	11. Pacific
4. Andes	12. Nile
5. Australia	13. Sahara
6. Anaconda	14. Cheetah
7. South China Sea	15. Bee hummingbird
8. Russia	

H2 D3.4

How to Build Scaffolding

Introduction

The ultimate goal of training is to enable employees to perform proficiently in real time in real work environments. The more closely the training environment matches the performance environment, the easier it is for trainees to transfer and apply what they learned.

Experiential (immersive or whole task) learning approaches, in which people learn by tackling realistic work tasks and problems, have been shown to accelerate the development of problem-solving skills (Clark, 2010, p. 68). But most work environments and tasks are complex. Posing real-world challenges immediately to novice learners has the potential to overwhelm them with so many details that they fail to grasp core concepts. Imagine trying to learn to fly a plane for the first time in the cockpit of a 767.

The solution is to build "scaffolding" to support the learner and make the learning curve less steep (Figure H2 D3.4.1), rather than to abandon experiential learning. Just as scaffolding on a building allows construction workers to reach new heights and accomplish difficult tasks safely,

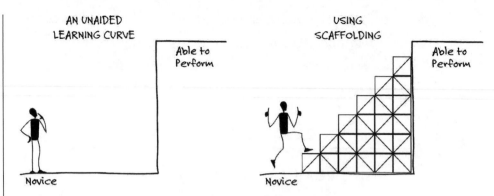

Figure H2 D3.4.1. Use Scaffolding to Make the Learning Curve Less Steep

scaffolding in a training program provides the support learners need to master complex tasks and reach new levels of competence.

Guidance

Build the training (whether live or virtual) around real scenarios and tasks, but help trainees up the learning curve by:

1. *Alternate demonstration with performance.* Demonstrate how to solve a problem or perform a task, then give the learners the opportunity to try for themselves. Repeat on subsequent and more difficult problems. We find it helpful to insert a step between demonstration and performance that we call discrimination. For instance, show an example (live or video) and ask learners what was done correctly and what could have been improved. The idea is that learners must be able to correctly classify techniques and approaches taken by others in order to be able to critique their own performance and, hence, improve.

2. *Start with relatively simple cases and work up to the more difficult.* Have learners begin with simple, yet still authentic, problems so that they gain practice and confidence with the basics before tackling more challenging or complex problems.

3. *Reduce the complexity initially.* Early exercises should have less complexity: fewer variables to consider, for example, or fewer non-relevant details. In teaching finance, for example, be sure students can correctly interpret a simplified income statement or balance sheet before introducing exceptions and advanced accounting principles.

4. *Provide lots of help and support early on and embedding job aids in the training.* The goal of scaffolding is to help learners build skills and confidence so that they continue to progress up the learning curve. It is especially important for them to achieve some success early on. So make support (job aids, hints, online help, or coaches) readily available and fairly prescriptive initially. As the training progresses, reduce the support so that learners develop the required level of independent competence their job requires.

   Do not withdraw all support, however. In particular, teach learners to use and depend on the kinds of aids that will be available to them on the job (checklists, computer diagnostics, databases, etc.) by incorporating those into the training. Require their use in cases where error could lead to serious adverse consequences; "Checklists seem able to defend anyone, even the experienced, against failure in many more tasks than we realized" (Gawande, 2009, p. 48).

Key Success Factors

- Making the training exercises and environment as close to the actual performance environment as possible.
- Supporting the learner with scaffolding early in the process, but gradually withdrawing support and increasing the level of challenge as the training progresses.
- Incorporating job aids and other kinds of performance support into the training to encourage their use on the job.

H2 D3.5

How to Build a Value Chain for Learning

Introduction

A fundamental precept of adult education is that adults want to understand why they should learn something before they will willingly undertake to do so (Knowles, Holton, & Swanson, 2005, p. 74).

The purpose of building a value chain as part of the process of program design is to ensure that there is a clear "line of sight" between what happens in training and what needs to happen at work. Michael Porter (1985) originated the concept of a value chain to describe the sequence of value-adding activities by which a company creates competitive advantage. Like Brinkerhoff and Gill's (1994) "impact maps," a value chain for learning illustrates the linkages between training and business results. It is similar to the logic modeling process described by Peggy Parskey in Case D6.1.

The value chain for training has three main links: the desired business outcomes, the skills and behaviors required to achieve them, and the learning experiences best suited to help employees master the essential skills and behaviors (Figure H2 D3.5.1).

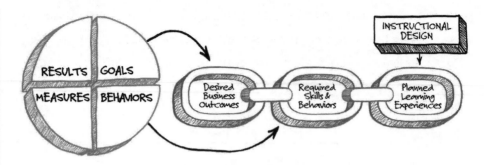

Figure H2 D3.5.1. Training Value Chain

The first link in the chain is the program's "reason for being"—its business goals—in accordance with Stephen Covey's famous dictum: "begin with the end in mind" (Covey, 2004). The second link is a causal link: it describes what employees must *do* to achieve the desired business outcomes. The third link is further "upstream": it describes the kinds of learning experiences (broadly defined) that are needed to generate the requisite skills and behaviors.

The value chain can be used in one of two ways:

- During program design, to help decide how best to teach so that learners are able to do what they need to be able to do
- For quality control of a proposed design

Guidance

To use the value chain chart (Tool D3.2) to aid in developing training:

1. Put the key business outcomes in the first column. If you completed the Outcomes Planning Wheel (Tool D1.1), then these will be in the first quadrant.
2. List the on-the-job behaviors and skills required to produce each result in the middle column (from the second quadrant of the Planning Wheel).

3. Use your knowledge of instructional design and this field guide to select the learning experiences that will most effectively generate the required capabilities. List them in the third column and connect them to the specific skill(s) or behavior(s) they teach.
4. Be sure to include the *complete* learning experience by considering what needs to happen before training as well as afterward in the work environment. Don't forget job aids and other kinds of performance support.

To use the value chain for quality control of an existing or proposed program:

1. List the key topics, exercises, and other learning activities in the third column.
2. Put the required behaviors and skills in the middle column and the business purpose in the first column
3. You should be able to draw a link between each topic/exercise and a required behavior or skill and between each of those and the desired results.
4. Answer the following questions about each topic or exercise you have mapped:
   - Does it have a clear relationship to one or more of the required behaviors/skills? If not, then either a) the D1 analysis was incomplete or b) this element of the training has no direct relevance to the aim of the course and should be eliminated.
   - If there is a strong link, will it be obvious to the participants? If not, how could the relevance be made more explicit?
   - Does the instructional approach match the required performance?
   - Is there enough practice to ensure that learners will answer, "Yes, I can," or is this like a lecture on how to ride a bike?

Key Success Factors

- Having a clear understanding of the business needs and the on-the-job actions required to produce them.
- Using a value chain, impact map, or logic model to make sure each topic and exercise has credible links to the business objectives.
- Selecting appropriate instructional strategies for the performance required.
- Not assuming that learners will deduce these links; making them explicit.
- Introducing each exercise with an explanation of how it relates to the employees' on-the-job performance.

H2 D3.6

How to Introduce Exercises

Introduction

Corporate training exercises are (or at least should be) designed with the end in mind—that is, how each exercise relates to building the skills necessary to achieve the business goals. But while that linkage is clear to the instructional designers, it is often lost on the participants. If they are unable to make the connection between the exercise and their job responsibilities, they won't be motivated to take it seriously, actively participate, and learn from it.

A significant contributor to the disconnect is the way in which exercises are typically introduced, whether in the classroom or online. The tendency is to go immediately to the *how* without explaining the *why*, what Margolis and Bell (1986) call the "administrative approach." A typical example in the classroom would sound something like this: "In the next ten minutes, I am going to break you into small groups. . . " or in e-learning: "In each of the following scenarios, pick the best next step."

The problem with introducing exercises in this way is that partici-pants begin thinking immediately about whether they will have enough time and whether they like or hate this kind of activity, rather than about its purpose and potential payoff; the thread to the purpose is lost and so are the participants.

The two questions that are on every employee's mind when asked (or required) to attend training are

- Will this be worth my time?
- What's in it for me?

Those same two questions come to mind about individual training exercises, especially the ones that are more work and less "fun," like role plays. For trainees to fully engage, they must be convinced of the exercises' relevance and utility.

Guidance

Margolis and Bell (1986, pp. 61–70) recommend that every exercise be introduced in a four-step process that follows the logic of learning and motivation:

1. *Explain the rationale.* "The introduction/ rationale [should be] always stated from the learner's perspective, not the trainer's or the organization's" (pp. 62–63). It should answer the fundamental question on each learner's mind: "Why should I enter into this task or experience?"

2. *Explain the task.* Explain the task such that the participants produce a product that aids their learning. The explanation should always include an action verb such as *identify, list, rank, solve,* and so forth, and usually include a phrase that defines the quantity and quality desired, such as "the five most important."

Adapted from: Wick, Pollock, and Jefferson (2010), pp. 123–124, used with permission.

3. *Define the context.* Margolis and Bell explain the third step as follows (p. 65): "The definition of context explains how learners will accomplish the task. The context for the task involves three elements:
   - The size of the working unit (individuals or subgroups);
   - The composition of the subgroups, if they are used; and
   - The amount of time allotted for completing the task."

4. *Explain what is to be reported.* The fourth and final step is simply a matter of telling participants what they are responsible for reporting to the group as a whole once their subgroups have completed the task; it need not include administrative details, which have a tendency to confuse rather than clarify. Reporting out enhances learning by allowing participants to review and summarize their discussions and by giving the instructor the opportunity to comment, embellish, and amplify key concepts and principles.

Keys to Success

- Always giving the rationale for the activity before describing the task, how it is to be done, and what will be reported. Don't assume learners will be able to connect the dots themselves.
- Remembering that a fundamental precept of adult learning is that adults want to know *why* they need to learn something before they will willingly undertake to learn it.
- Whenever you ask participants to produce something, making sure that the output will assist their learning and learning transfer in proportion to the time invested.

H2 D3.7

How to Improve the Predictive Value of Assessments

Introduction

Predictive value is a concept applied to diagnostic tests in medicine. The predictive value of a test is its accuracy. In other words, when the test is positive, what percent of patients actually have the disease? When the test is negative, what percent are truly disease-free?

Many training programs test participants to certify that they have mastered the material. Yet a common complaint among managers is: "How come they can pass the test, but cannot do the job?" That suggests that typical certification tests have a low positive predictive value: passing the test is not a good predictor of the ability to perform the job. Why is that?

The most common problem with certifying exams and other assessments of learning is that they focus too heavily on rote memory. Recall that in Bloom's taxonomy of learning objectives, knowledge (remembering) is the lowest level (Figure H2 D3.7.1). While higher levels of skill (applying, analyzing, and so forth) depend on a foundation of

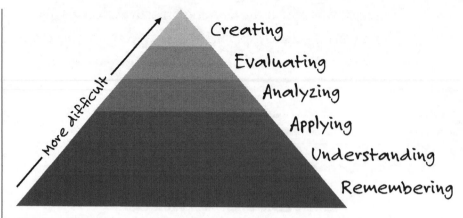

Figure H2 D3.7.1. Cognitive Processes of Bloom's Taxonomy of Educational Objectives (after Krathwohl, 2002)

knowledge, being able to remember facts, by itself, does not predict the ability to utilize them.

In a review of test items for the eLearning Guild, Shrock and Coscarelli (2007) found that "the vast majority of test items are written at the memorization level. In contrast, the vast majority of jobs require performance that is above the memorization level. This disconnect between testing practice and job performance is what often leads management to question the value of training and turns testing into a misleading indicator of performance" (p. 157). They concluded: "In general, the single most useful improvement you can make in writing test items is to write them above the memorization level."

To improve the predictive value of certifying examinations, we need to make them match much more closely the actual job performance required.

Guidance

1. *Ensure performance agreement.* "Performance agreement is the relationship between behavior and condition elements in objectives and evaluation tasks" (Hodell, 2006, p. 90). Agreement is necessary for the evaluation to be a valid measure of whether or not the

learning objective was met. If the learning objective specifies that the participant will be able to *explain* a particular concept to a prospective buyer, then the evaluation must test his or her ability to *explain*, not merely to regurgitate a definition.

2. *Write questions above the recall level.* The single most valuable improvement you can make to improve the predictive ability of tests is to write the questions above the recall level. Very few jobs require people to simply recall information. Moreover, nearly ubiquitous access to the Internet makes mere memorization less and less valuable. Since everyone has access to the facts, the distinguishing skill will be the ability to use facts appropriately. It makes no sense to test employees principally on their ability to recall facts. Why do most certifying examinations persist in testing mainly factual knowledge? Because factual questions are easy to write, they have an unambiguous right and wrong answer, and they are especially well suited to a multiple-choice format. The problem is that they do not predict performance.

   To address this issue, review your end-of-training examinations and score the cognitive process required to answer each question using Bloom's Taxonomy. If your organization is like most, 90 percent or more will be simple factual recall and most will fail the performance-agreement principle. Rewrite them to require higher mental processing and to mirror the learning objectives.

3. *Distinguish between the ability to recognize the right answer and the ability to generate an appropriate response.* The multiple-choice format prevalent in e-learning and certification testing evaluates a candidate's ability to *recognize* and select the right answer from among a number of distractors (Sousa, 2011, p. 114). Keep in mind, however, that it is much easier to recognize a correct answer than to generate the answer *de novo*. Also, for most multiple-choice questions, it is easy to eliminate one or more of the distractors without

any knowledge of the subject. Thus, multiple-choice tests may over-estimate a participant's true ability, especially for jobs like customer service, sales, or management, which require applying principles to generate answers in often novel situations.

If the training is for a job that requires unprompted recall (as opposed to the simpler task of recognition) or the generation of appropriate responses to novel situations, then the testing strategy cannot rely solely on multiple choice questions.

4. *Simulate the performance environment as closely as possible.* The focus of evaluation in instructional design should be on "measuring the student's ability to perform her or his newly constructed knowledge and skills in an authentic work environment" (Branch, 2009, p. 153), often referred to as "authentic evaluation" (Wehlage, Newmann, & Secada, 1996). That requires that the testing environment mimic the actual work environment as closely as possible, for example using actual equipment or a high-fidelity simulation.

The ultimate criterion, of course, is the ability to perform on the job in real time. Supervisors should be provided with checklists, scorecards, or rubrics, as appropriate, to assess on-the-job performance and provide feedback to both the individual and the training department.

5. *Use rubrics and scoring guidelines to improve reliability and the value of feedback.* Once you move beyond questions that test mere recall and that more closely resemble the actual performance required, then evaluation often becomes more qualitative than simply right/wrong.

When there are multiple raters involved—for example, when on-the-job performance is being assessed by supervisors—then ensuring consistency among evaluators becomes important.

You can improve consistency by providing scorers (as well as the participants) with rubrics, scoring forms, or checklists that make explicit what good looks like. An example is the Glance Test discussed in Case D3.2. For a discussion of how to create and use rubrics, see Wolf and Stevens (2007).

Key Success Factors

- Matching the assessment to the learning objectives and performance criteria.
- Making the assessment mimic the real work tasks as closely as possible.
- Designing tests that require participants to *use* their knowledge, not merely recall information.
- Requiring participants to *generate* acceptable answers, not just recognize them, if that is what the job entails (most do).

H2 D4.1

How to Remind Learners to Apply Their Training

Introduction

One of the most basic mechanisms to help improve learning transfer is simply to remind learners periodically after a training program.

The goal is to two-fold:

1. To keep the training and the need to apply it "top of mind"
2. To strengthen the neural pathways to the training concepts

The need to maintain "share of mind" is the reason that even the world's best-known brands (like Coca-Cola, McDonald's, and Apple) continue to spend millions of dollars annually on advertising. It seems counter-intuitive. If you are already well known, what is the point of continuing to advertise?

The reason is that companies have learned through bitter experience that in the absence of reminders, share of mind drops off and share of market follows. A similar phenomenon occurs after training. Employees leave a first-rate program motivated and committed to apply their training. But amidst the hundreds of demands for their attention daily, training quickly loses share of mind if there is nothing to remind them; share of effort soon follows.

The other reason to remind trainees periodically about the training is to reinforce neural connections to the material. Whenever we think about a concept, we elaborate and strengthen the neural pathways leading to it (Anderson, 2010, p. 73). The memory becomes both more durable, as well as easier to recall subsequently, part of the general phenomenon of spaced learning (Thalheimer, 2006).

Reminders can take many forms (see below). The key is to be sure that there *are* reminders and that they are an integral part of the design of the overall program to support learning transfer.

Guidance

1. *Build reminders into the overall program design.*
2. *In designing programs, or in reviewing program designs, ask: "What kind of post course reminders would help make this learning stick?"* Then make them part of the formal design.
3. *Aim for reminders that prompt active thinking.*
4. *Anything that brings a concept back to mind will help reinforce it.* Think about the variety of methods that advertisers use to implant their messages, from billboards, to jingles, to ads on airplane tray tables. A simple email reminder to keep using the material, a poster, screen saver, or an excerpt from the material covered in class will help bring the topic back to mind. Even better is providing new or slightly different material, like an additional tip on application, an interesting quote, or short snippet of a relevant article (see Case D4.3). Because the concepts and skills we want to reinforce following corporate training are typically more complex than simple brand association, techniques that require active processing of the information will lead to more elaborate and more durable neural connections.

Posing questions for learners to answer accomplishes this goal, especially if the questions are linked to some sort of scoring system that keeps track of the highest overall score (see Case D4.4). Learning journals—in which people record their efforts to apply what they learned and the results—can be especially valuable after soft-skills and executive programs. These journals can be paper-based or, increasingly, through electronic blogs or social media.

5. *Send enough reminders to help make the learning stick, but not so many that they become annoying.* In general, the more times a topic is revisited, the more effective spaced learning is. However, given most people's workload these days, it is important not to overload the user with too many reminders, too much information, or too frequently. Several iterations a few days to a couple of weeks apart probably strike the right balance. Be sure each reminder is relatively short, relevant to the learner's role, and useful.

6. *Vary the approach.* To avoid habituation and ensure active intellectual processing, use a variety of techniques—questions, tips, quotes, reflections—to encourage users to open, read, and think about the material.

7. *Automate the process to achieve scale.* It is impractical to try to manage reminders manually for a large number of trainees or programs. Online systems have been developed to address this need. Research and adopt one that meets your specific needs and budget.
   - Many email systems allow you to schedule messages to be sent on a future date.
   - Some LMS systems allow you to program reminders.
   - Specific learning transfer support systems have been developed, such as Qstream or Cameo for sending questions, and *ResultsEngine* and TransferLogix to support application.

Key Success Factors

- Making reminders an integral part of the overall design for learning and transfer.
- Starting reminders soon after training.
- Providing a number of reminders at intervals, but not so many or so frequently that they become annoying.
- Using reminders that require thinking or action—such as answering a question or posting a comment.
- Varying the approach to avoid habituation.
- Automating to manage a large number of trainees efficiently.

The Field Guide to the 6Ds

H2 D4.2

How to Engage Learners in Action Planning

Introduction

There is good research evidence that goal setting is positively correlated with learning transfer (Burke & Hutchins, 2007). So it makes sense to include action planning and goal setting in training programs. But how do you make the exercise engaging and meaningful?

Geoff Rip, director of the Institute for Learning Practitioners, Australia, developed the following technique—"Let's Roll"—as an engaging group activity to encourage participants to review their learning and think about application. It uses two kinds of questions: review questions to stimulate recall and elaboration of new learning, and application questions to underscore the importance of transferring learning to the workplace.

Used with permission of the Institute for Learning Practitioners, Australia.

Guidance

1. *When to use.* Use this activity at the end of a training course, especially if there is no formal application planning and if time is limited. It can also be used as a review activity any time during a training course.

2. *Materials.* You will need the following:
   - A pre-prepared list of twelve questions
   - A twelve-sided (dodecahedron) die, like those commonly used in role-playing games.

3. *Time.* The duration of the activity depends on the number of participants in the group and whether you complete one or two rounds of the game. Allow approximately half a minute per participant per turn.

4. *Introduction.* Ask the group to form a circle, preferably around a table. Then explain the purpose and rules:
   - The purpose is to review the course content and to start thinking about application.
   - Each person in turn will roll the die.
   - A volunteer will read the corresponding question, which the participant must then answer.
   - Although it is possible to run the activity without a helper/assistant, it works better to have a member of the group, rather than the instructor, read the questions. You may also want to post the twelve questions where everyone can see them, or print and pass them out for people to refer to.

SAMPLE INTRODUCTION

"I'm going to give [name of helper] a list of questions that relate to the course content and its application. [Hand the list to your helper.] Each of you will have a chance to roll this twelve-sided die. [Hold up the die for everyone to see.] Depending on your score, [name of helper] will read a question for you to answer. Please make sure you explain your answer, and when you have finished, pass the die to the person on your left."

If time allows, tell the group: "We will complete two rounds of questions; which means you will each have two turns. On the second round, if you roll the same number as before, roll the die again."

Start by handing the die to the person on the left of your helper. When the die has made it all the way around to the helper, you can let the helper read out his or her own question, or you can read it aloud.

If you have a large group, you can split them into two (or more) smaller groups to complete the activity simultaneously. Of course you will need an extra die and set of questions for each group.

5. *Suggested questions.* Here is a list of questions you can use, modify, or replace:

   Review Questions
   1. What is the most valuable insight you gained?
   2. What was your biggest "aha" moment?
   3. What is one thing that surprised you?
   4. What is one thing that really pleased you?
   5. Tell someone how he or she helped you during the course.
   6. What is one thing you were already doing that has been validated?

Application Questions

1. How are you going to start applying what you have learned?
2. What is one thing you intend to change as a result of this course?
3. What is one thing you intend to stop doing or do less of?
4. What is one thing you intend to start doing or do more of?
5. What is one insight that you will share with a colleague after today?
6. What is one obstacle you are likely to face and what can you do about it?

VARIATION 1: REVIEWING

To review learning during a course, use six review questions and a six-sided die. Alternatively, create a longer list of questions and use a die with the same number of faces. Eight-sided and ten-sided dice are also readily available, but are often numbered from zero.

VARIATION 2: TWO ROUNDS

This variation uses a standard six-sided die over two rounds. Use the existing review questions and number the application questions from one to six. The review questions are read out during the first round and the application questions during the second round. You can include eight questions in each list by using an eight-sided die.

6. *Wrap-up.* Thank the group for participating in the activity and sharing with each other. Highlight the significant benefits mentioned and emphasis the importance of applying the learning in the workplace.

How to Make the Business Case for Learning Transfer

Introduction

Learning transfer is a gateway that must be passed by all learners before there is any chance of seeing business impact. Increasing learning transfer improves business impact, but deploying strategies to drive learning transfer takes time and money. It requires either new resources or the reallocation of existing resources. Training organizations need to be able to make a *business case* that justifies investing resources to support learning transfer.

Guidance

Business leaders make decisions about resource allocation based on which investments will yield the greatest return in both the short and long term. Making a *business case* means describing the expected costs and benefits associated with a proposed investment (Vance, 2010, p. 8). To make an effective business case to invest in supporting learning transfer, you need to convincingly demonstrate that the expected return far outweighs the required investment.

1. *Establish the current rate of transfer.* This is the percent of trainees who apply what they learned well enough and long enough after training to improve their performance. Establishing the transfer rate requires having an agreed-on definition of "improved performance" and a credible system for assessing it.

2. *Establish the fully-loaded cost of training each participant.* "Fully loaded" means including all the costs, including salaries of the participants and facilitators, as well as travel, materials, training facilities, licensing fees, and so forth. The size of the figure will probably surprise you. If you have not done this before, get help from your finance department.

3. *Establish the financial value of improved performance.* This is what it is worth to the company when an employee improves his or her performance in the topic of the training. Obviously, this is easier for some training programs—such as those designed to reduce errors or improve sales—than for others, such as leadership training. Reasonable estimates can be obtained for even soft-skills training (such as the cost of replacing an employee) but unless you are an expert in finance, get help from the finance department. Your case will be a great deal more credible if you do.

4. *Use these values to show the incremental value of even a modest improvement in transfer rates.* An example is shown in the table below.

   The first column shows the current state in which the program is conducted with no special provision to ensure transfer. The second column shows the benefit of investing $200 per participant in learning transfer support (a 20 percent increase in cost), with no other change to the program or its content.

	Current Approach	**With Investment in Transfer Support**
# of Participants	100	100
Cost per participant	$1,000	$1,200
Transfer rate (% who truly applied the training)	20 percent	30 percent
Return per person who applied training	$6,000	$6,000
ROI* for program	$20,000/20 percent	$180,000/150 percent

*Return on Investment (ROI) = (return–cost)/cost

The business case is clear. Despite spending $200 more per participant, the total return realized increased significantly based on a change to only one variable: the investment in learning transfer.

Of course, the actual return will vary depending on the costs, transfer rates, and value created by a particular program. However, since the current transfer rate in most organizations is very low, investing in improving learning transfer almost always has a positive ROI.

The above illustration assumes that additional resources are available to invest. Of course, that is not always the case; the training budget may be fixed. In that case, you will need to reallocate resources in order to be able to support transfer. One strategy would be to train fewer people. While that may seem like heresy, you will find that when the transfer rate is low, it makes economic sense to train fewer people and invest the savings in support of learning transfer.

Do the math in the above example, but instead of changing the cost variable, change the headcount to keep the total cost constant. You will see that under the conditions of the example, it makes better economic sense to train eighty-three people with a 30 percent transfer rate than to train one hundred with a 20 percent rate. In many cases, it would be better to train fewer people well and support their efforts to produce results, rather than to train everybody and have less to show for it.

Key Success Factors

- Explaining to business leaders why transfer is such an important step in the process of getting value from training.
- Making a business case for investing in learning transfer.
- Showing the currently low transfer rates, preferably based on your own company data. If you don't have these, show industry averages.
- Calculating how much value is being lost.
- Explaining your strategy to address the issue and what it will cost.
- Projecting the incremental value you expect to generate.
- Rolling out your new program and measuring results.
- Reporting the findings to demonstrate the value of the investment.

H2 D5.1

How to Provide Performance Support for Managers and Coaches

Introduction

Managers significantly influence the success of training. A study done at Pfizer illustrated the profound impact managers have on whether training produces results (Kontra, Trainor, & Wick, 2007). The study assessed the effectiveness of an important leadership development program by conducting a second 360-degree assessment of participants a few months after training. The results were revealing. The training produced more effective leaders—as judged by their direct reports, peers, and managers—provided that the participant's manager was engaged in coaching and support. Those participants whose managers did not provide support and coaching showed significantly less, or no, improvement. These results have been replicated in many other studies.

Since managers are a critical success factor in training's effectiveness, the best training organizations deploy performance support not just for participants, but for their managers as well. Remember that the greater the cost of failure, the more important it is to provide performance support. Since the supervisors of trainees can "make or break any training initiative" (American Express, 2007), you risk failure when you leave their coaching to chance. Provide managers with support and it will pay dividends.

Guidance

1. *Create effective performance support for managers by including them in developing the solution.*
   - Convene a small working group or task force of managers whose employees are the target audience for the training.
   - Share the business outcomes that are the driving force behind the program.
   - Ask what they need to effectively coach in support of the specific curriculum.
   - Take that information and use it to create support tailored to their needs. You will find that managers who have had a say in designing the type of support they will receive will be much more willing to use it.
   - Create guides that are short, specific, and practical. Complicated or time-intensive procedures will never be tried or will be quickly abandoned.
   - Tools D2.1 and D2.5 are examples of coaching guides for managers from *Getting Your Money's Worth from Training and Development: A Guide for Managers* (Jefferson, Pollock, & Wick, 2009).

2. *If time and resources permit, provide specific training for managers of participants in advance of strategically important programs* (see Cases D4.5 and D5.3). The goal is to ensure that managers feel confident in their ability to coach—both in general and in support of the specific training—so that they use their influence to drive transfer and business impact.

3. *Given their impact on training, make support for managers part of every program design.* Managers are a critical success factor in whether or not the training produces business impact. Therefore, every important program should deploy performance support to enhance the manager's role as coach and mentor.

Keys to Success

- Being clear about the business needs being served.
- Asking managers what would help them support the specific curriculum.
- Using their feedback to create the appropriate resources.
- Choosing a support medium that is appropriate.
- Making sure the guidance is clear, concise, and useable.
- Collecting feedback from managers to understand what worked and what did not, then using their input to continuously improve.

H2 D5.2

How to Utilize Peer Coaching

Introduction

Peer coaches are a powerful and underutilized source of performance support—not just for introductory courses, but even at the highest levels of executive leadership. For example, at GE's famous Crotonville Leadership Center, Linda Sharkey reported that "when the leadership teams share their development needs with each other and use the coaching model, they often find three things: (1) they have similar issues, (2) they get great improvement suggestions from each other, and (3) they get support from each other to improve" (2003, p. 73).

Peer coaches can also help provide accountability and encourage each other to continue to make the effort to apply the training ("Will I?"). Peer coaching reinforces the learning for both partners; one of the best ways to learn is to try to teach.

Peer coaching can be used to provide support and facilitate transfer after any kind of training; it is especially useful for leadership and other soft-skills training that requires sustained practice over time to master. To be effective, however, peer coaching requires more than simply pairing people up in class. You also need to provide structure and support for the process.

Guidance

1. *Provide a coaching framework.* Most people don't know intuitively how to coach. Even those who do will benefit from having a model to follow, such as Marshall Goldsmith's feed-forward approach (Goldsmith, 2002), the ACTION conversation model described in Case D4.8, the proficiency coaching model described in Case D5.2, or another proven approach to the coaching conversation.
   The key to success is providing a consistent model for the coaching conversation that is easy to follow and engages partners as both coaches and coachees. Build at least one practice round into the training itself to allow peers to get familiar and comfortable with the model and each other.

2. *Prepare both the coach and the coachee.* Effective coaching requires a partnership. It is just as important for the persons being coached to understand their roles as it is for the coaches to understand theirs. Provide the coachees with specific instructions on their responsibilities and how to obtain the greatest benefit from the coaching interaction. Make certain that coaches understand the difference between coaching and providing advice (McDermott, 2011).

3. *Establish a schedule.* Coaching conversations are more likely to occur if a schedule is established in advance, during the training itself. Provide time for peer pairs or triads to coordinate their plans for weekly or bi-weekly calls before they leave the training. Establish a date for a final, group-wide sharing of experiences, progress, and insights (a new finish line) to increase the sense of accountability among participants. If appropriate, heighten the

importance of the final report-out by inviting participants' managers or members of the succession-planning committee to attend (see Wick, Pollock, & Jefferson, 2010, p. 189).

4. *Consider triads rather than pairs.* Although peer coaching is classically done in pairs, consider putting people into groups of three. The advantage is that if one member of the group is only weakly committed to following through, or feels overwhelmed by work and drops out, the other two can continue to provide support for each other. It is harder to skip a call or find excuses when there are two other people involved rather than just one.

For additional details, see "The Power of Peer Coaching" (McDermott, 2011).

Key Success Factors

- Preparing both coaches and coachees to maximize the value of the interaction.
- Providing a coaching structure or framework.
- Establishing a schedule and some form of accountability.

H2 D5.3

How to Develop Great Performance Support

Introduction

Performance support (job aids, checklists, help desks, and so forth) increase the return on investment from training by facilitating the effective transfer and application of learning to the work of the individual and firm. Performance support can also improve quality, reduce cost, and help avoid serious adverse consequences.

Great performance support is

- Developed to address a "felt need"
- Available when and where it is needed
- Specific to a task or situation
- Practical, that is, do-able with the resources available and skill level of the user
- Economical; contains only as many words and instructions as are needed. In addition, the delivery method is the most cost-effective that still achieves the goal
- Effective: It works

Develop performance support with these criteria in mind, then test it and improve it based on the experience in the field.

Guidance

1. *Make sure the performance support is developed in response to a felt need or one that can be anticipated based on past experience.*
   - Interview recent trainees and their managers to understand where they ran into difficulties applying the training.
   - Investigate the root causes of on-the-job errors. Try to identify ways in which they could have been prevented by better instructions, job aids, checklists, and so forth.
   - Use experiences from similar training in the past to anticipate the kind of performance support that will be valuable, and build into the overall course design and delivery.
2. *Ensure availability at the time and point of need by investigating when and how the performance support will be used, then selecting appropriate delivery vehicles.*
   - The working conditions at the time the job aid will be used need to be considered and may limit the choice of delivery vehicles.
   - A terrific computer-based job aid is of no value if employees won't have computer access at the time they need it.
   - If appropriate, post instructions in the needed location or build them into the operating system.
   - Make it specific. Limit the scope to one or a very few closely related situations.
   - If the support is in the form of a manual or online system, make sure each individual entry is brief and that they are well indexed and searchable so that the needed guidance can be quickly and efficiently located.

3. *Ensure practicality by considering the skill level and literacy of the user and what resources will be available at the time and place the support will be used.*
   - Employ terminology users can be expected to understand.
   - Use simple line drawings or photographs to illustrate physical objects and help the user locate critical components quickly (see Exhibit D5.4.1 in Case D5.4 as an example).
   - Test whether typical users can, in fact, understand and apply the guidance.
   - Make it economical. Strip out all unnecessary detail, steps, and words in order to "keep the main thing the main thing."
   - Engage a professional editor to help you make sure the writing is clear and concise.
   - Use the lowest-cost delivery that meets the criteria for availability and practicality. If a simple printed wallet card will suffice, use it.
   - Use the same illustrations, etc., as in the training. This improves recall and usability and simultaneously reduces costs.
   - Design the performance support as part of the overall instructional design; it is more efficient and produces a better product.
4. *Ensure effectiveness by testing the support in real time in real work situations by typical users.*
5. *Solicit feedback and use it to improve subsequent versions.*

Key Success Factors
- Applying instructional design expertise to the creation of job aids.
- Creating support as part of the overall design and incorporating it fully in the training itself.
- Applying the criteria of availability, specificity, practicality, economy, and effectiveness.
- Testing the support and seeking opportunities for improvement.

H2 D6.1

How to Ensure Your Measures Are Relevant

Introduction

The first guiding principle for effective evaluations is that the measures must be *relevant*. Relevant to what? To the reason that the training was created in the first place. If what you measure does not directly assess the outcomes that the training was designed to produce, then the evaluation will fail to answer the fundamental question: "Did it work?"

Guidance

1. *Clarify the claim.* Every training program, explicitly or implicitly, makes a claim: "Give us your people, time, and resources and we will improve performance in [fill in the blank]." The clearer you can be about what the claim is, the more obvious the relevant measures will be. In short, you must measure what you claim. Once the claim is clear, *what* needs to be measured is largely a matter of common sense (see below).

2. *Use common sense.* If the goal of a training program is to reduce the time it takes to process a claim, then the obvious measure of its effectiveness is the extent to which processing time was or was

not reduced. If the goal is to increase the quality of presentations, then you must assess presentation quality. If the goal is to improve safety, then you need measures of "safety" such as number of accidents, injuries, lost time, and so forth. How much people enjoyed the program, or even how much they learned, is not relevant to whether it achieved its purpose.

Notice that, at this point, we have said nothing about *how* to measure results; that may require special techniques or expertise, but such expertise is worthless without agreement on what is relevant to measure in the first place.

3. *Gain sponsors' agreement, in advance.* Always check with the sponsors to be sure they agree that the proposed measures are relevant *to them* (answer their questions about training's effectiveness), since they are the ultimate judges.

Key Success Factors

- Using a systematic process (such as the Planning Wheel, PrimeFocus™, Logic Model, or one of the other methods discussed in this *Field Guide*) to rigorously define the desired business outcomes.
- Applying common sense to ask, "What could we measure that would answer the question: 'Were the goals achieved?'"
- Engaging the business sponsors in the process and gaining their agreement on relevant measure *in advance,* ideally before the training is even designed.
- Postponing the discussion of method until after the relevant measures have been clearly defined; don't confuse "what" with "how."

H2 D6.2

How to Improve the Credibility of Evaluations

Introduction

To be effective, a program evaluation must be *perceived* as relevant, credible, and compelling by the target audience. We have italicized *perceived* because, while there are published guidelines for conducting valid and reliable assessments (see, for example, Russ-Eft & Preskill, 2009, and Babbie, 2010), credibility is ultimately a value judgment: "Do I believe this or not?"

Credibility is critical; if your audience doesn't believe your data, they won't believe your conclusions and they won't act on your recommendations.

What counts as credible depends on an organization's culture and the professional training of the target audience. For example, research scientists are likely to be more critical of issues related to experimental design and statistical analysis, while business managers are likely to focus on the financial claims and the data used to support them.

Nevertheless, there are some steps you can take (see below) that will improve the credibility—and hence impact—of any evaluation you conduct.

Guidance

1. *Get agreement beforehand.* Since credibility is ultimately in the eye of the beholder, it is critical to discuss the proposed evaluation strategy with the sponsors beforehand and gain agreement that they find the approach credible. It is a terrible waste of time, effort, money, and personal reputation to discover that the sponsors don't buy into your approach only *after* you have completed the study and are reporting the results.

2. *More data (up to a point) is better.* As a general rule, the more data points you have, the higher the credibility and the more confident you can be about the results. A poll of two thousand voters is a lot more creditable than a poll of six. Of course, there is a point of diminishing return at which the cost of collecting additional data exceeds its value in terms of insights or credibility.

   There are statistical methods to help you select the sample size needed that take into account the magnitude of the expected difference (see, for example, www.surveysystem.com/sscalc.htm#!). If your audience is likely to go into that level of detail, ask a statistician to help you (see number 3 below), but most business analyses don't require that level of precision. As a rule of thumb, include all the participants if the program is small (fifty or fewer). Sample a larger group. Fifty data points are usually enough, unless there is great variability in the results.

   If you do sample, do so with care. Seek expert advice if you don't have advanced training. Sampling should be truly random to avoid inadvertently introducing bias. For surveys, pay attention to response rates. If only a small percentage of the people you invite to participate do so, it is probable that they aren't truly representative of the larger group. For example, there is a tendency for people with extreme views (very positive or very negative) to respond, so that the results could be misleading.

3. *Use credible sources.* Be sure that when you gather survey data, the respondents are able to provide reliable information. In an effort to be helpful, most people will answer survey questions even when they are not really well-informed about the topic. For example, some evaluation methods rely on financial estimates provided by trainees. Will management accept that the trainees in question have sufficient insight and expertise to make credible financial estimates? If not, then any calculation of ROI based on those estimates will be rejected. Likewise, you might wish to demonstrate behavior change by asking managers to report on how often an employee has used a particular technique from training. That's fine, provided the managers are co-located with the trainees or otherwise have the opportunity to observe enough of their behavior to have an informed opinion. Otherwise, credibility suffers.

   If you use external comparators (like the average expenditure on training) or "the results of scientific studies" (like the relative efficacy of different kinds of training) be sure to cite your sources; it adds credibility. And use sources that your audience will be likely to believe—scientific studies in refereed journals, government statistics, or respected publications like the *Harvard Business Review.* Avoid, if possible, trade publications or "research" published privately by vendors.

   Whenever possible, use data collected by independent third parties such as the finance department, a regulatory agency, or independent consumer research agency. They are more credible than data collected by the training department because these other sources have no vested interest in the outcome.

4. *Use more than one source (triangulate).* Look for opportunities to buttress your findings with a second credible source of data. Credibility is enhanced when two or more independent sources of information point toward the same conclusion. For example, after

a sales training program, salespeople might report that they are doing a better job of answering questions. By itself, that finding is likely to be questioned, since most people overrate their own performance. If, however, a representative sample of customers also reported that, compared to their prior experience, the salespeople were doing a better job of answering questions, that would add substantial credibility to the self-reports.

5. *Get expert help.* You will increase the credibility (not to mention reliability and validity) of your evaluations by bringing in expert assistance and counsel when appropriate. There are entire textbooks and graduate programs on evaluation; there are complex issues of sampling, survey design, statistical inference, and so forth. Your company probably employs a number of people with expertise in relevant fields like market research, quality assurance, process improvement, and so forth. Use them. Explain what you are trying to accomplish and ask for their input.

   Likewise, as a learning professional, you probably do not have advanced training in finance and financial analysis. But many of the people in your target audience do. Again, you will increase your credibility (and reduce the risk of embarrassment) by getting help with the financial analysis—or better, having the analysis done by the finance department rather than training.

6. *Compare apples to apples.* Anytime you make the claim that the training improved, reduced, accelerated, and so forth, you are making an implicit comparison, usually to the state of affairs prior to the training or to the performance of employees who have not received training. The credibility of the evaluation depends on your choice of comparisons.

   In the laboratory, of course, you would set up a randomized control group. But we rarely have that luxury in corporate training and, for most business decisions regarding training, that level of rigor is not usually necessary. An alternative is to measure each trainee's performance before and then again after training so that each acts as his or her own "control." Even this can be challenged, of course, since some of the improvement—especially among new employees—may be due just to experience.

Comparisons are often made between two different groups—one that has been trained and one that has not. Credibility here depends on being sure that the groups being compared are truly comparable; you cannot credibly compare a group that is mostly experienced workers with a group of mostly new hires, or a trained group at one location to an untrained group at another that has a very different work environment.

There is no perfect comparison in real-world workplace studies. The key point is to protect your credibility by making the comparison groups as similar as possible and being forthright about the potential shortcomings of the design.

7. *Be up-front about the limitations.* You will improve your credibility—and the probability that your recommendations will be acted upon—if you are self-critical and mention the limitations of the analysis and conclusions as well as their strengths. We do not mean to heap ashes on your head or undermine the whole project, but simply to include a statement like:

   - "Given the size of the sample, we can't be entirely sure that . . ." or
   - "In retrospect, we probably should have conducted the study sooner . . ." or
   - "Given that these are mainly self-reports, it is possible. . . . nevertheless, . . ."

8. *Identify and propose ideas for continuous improvement.* You will also gain credibility by including an honest appraisal of shortcomings of both the program and its evaluation and by making recommendations to improve them.

Key Success Factors

- Discussing the proposed evaluation strategy with the key stakeholders *before* you conduct the evaluation.
- Using the largest practicable sample size.
- Triangulating findings if possible, especially if they are surprising or potentially controversial.
- Making sure comparisons are legitimate.
- Getting expert assistance rather than trying to do it all yourself.
- Honestly and candidly reporting the findings and pointing out the weaknesses of the analysis as well as its strengths.
- Using the evaluation credibility checklist (Tool D6.1) for quality assurance.

H2 D6.3

How to Make Your Evaluations More Compelling

"Most reports from development are too long, too dull, and just plain uninteresting."

—John Sullivan, *The Future of Executive Development*

Introduction

According to Bersin (2008) "The purpose of measuring any business process is to obtain *actionable information for improvement*" (p. 13). The purpose of evaluating training, therefore, is to generate insights that lead to informed actions by the training department and business managers to enhance the organization's competitiveness and results.

The third criterion for effective evaluation, then, is that it is *compelling*—it *persuades* the target audience to take appropriate action. This means that regardless of the magnitude of the result or the relevance, credibility, or elegance of the design, the evaluation is a failure if it does not lead to action. Appropriate actions range from expanding a successful initiative, to killing an unnecessary one, radically revamping a needed but unsuccessful program, or addressing the transfer climate if that proves to be the weak link.

An evaluation that receives a polite round of applause but leads to no action was a waste of time and money. An evaluation needs to be compelling.

Guidance

1. *First, make sure the results are relevant and credible*; they are the *sine qua non* of effective evaluation. A recommendation that is based on irrelevant measures or one whose credibility is in question will never be persuasive.

2. *Tell the whole story in the executive summary.* Business leaders are very busy people. Few will read, much less digest, your whole report. You must present your key data points and make your recommendations in the executive summary, as that is all most will read. Don't try to save the punch line for the last page; this is not a novel or a detective story. Lay everything out in front and keep the summary to a page or (preferably) less.

3. *Know your audience.* Audience analysis is just as (perhaps more) important in preparing your report and recommendations as it is in training. Are the stakeholders drivers who just want to get right to the point? Or are they more analytical and want to understand the details and nuances of the approach? Do they want to see slides or will they be bored to tears by yet more slides by this point in their meeting?

4. *Use the language of business.* Remember that the key decision-makers will be business leaders, not training professionals. Avoid using learning- or HR-specific terms (like "evaluation Level 3"). Use plain language and business terms. Seek first to be understood; don't try to impress them with training jargon. It will backfire.

5. *Use stories to make the numbers more memorable.* As learning professionals, we know how powerful stories can be in teaching. The same applies to presentations. In *A Whole New Mind* (2006), Daniel

Pink wrote: "Stories are easy to remember, probably because they are *how* we remember." Even if you have great statistics and impressive charts and graphs, be sure to illustrate your points with some examples of what people were able to accomplish as a result of the training, told in story form. They will be remembered (and retold) long after the charts have been forgotten.

6. *Make sure the evaluation makes a point and answers the "So what?" question.* Make clear, bold recommendations; don't waffle. We have all sat through far too many presentations that left us wondering, "So what? What was the point?" Be sure that you answer the so what question by making clear, bold, and unambiguous recommendations, such as:

   • "Based on these results, we recommend rolling this program out to all manufacturing sites."—or

   • "Based on the lack of support from front-line managers for any kind of follow-through activity, I suggest we kill this program and redeploy the resources to ones with a greater probability of producing results."

   Whether or not your recommendations are ultimately accepted, they'll be appreciated and you will earn a reputation as a clear thinker and person of action, which will boost your career prospects.

Key Success Factors

• Making sure your results are relevant and credible first; irrelevant or untrustworthy results will never be compelling, no matter how large.

• Understanding what your audience values and speaking to them in their language.

• Making the presentation memorable by using stories and examples to illustrate the key findings.

• Spelling out specific recommendations for action.

H2 D6.4

How to Conduct a Success Case Method Evaluation

Introduction

Training takes time and consumes resources. Business leaders want to know whether the investment was a good one, that is, whether it produced benefits commensurate with the cost. In today's competitive climate, they also want to know how the results could be further improved.

The Success Case Method was developed by Rob Brinkerhoff (2003) as a way to shift the focus from simply trying to *prove* training's value to *improving* its contribution. It takes into account two realities of training:

1. In any training initiative, there is always a wide range of application and results among the participants.
2. Training alone never fully accounts for the success or failure to achieve results.

The first reality—the wide range of application and impact—means that the "average" achievement is misleading; it overstates the value of the training for those who made no effort to use it and it understates the value of those who applied it diligently. The second reality means that you can never truly isolate the impact of the training from the impact of the transfer climate. Therefore, your approach to evaluation needs to assess the strengths and weaknesses of both.

Two elements must be in place prior to conducting an evaluation using the success case (or, for that matter, any other evaluation) method:

1. The business purpose of the training must be clearly understood (see H2 D1.1).
2. The causal links between training, on-the-job actions, and results need to have been mapped (see H2 D3.5 and Case D6.1).

Assuming that the business objective has been clarified as part of D1, and the linkage between training, behaviors, and results has been mapped, then the success case method itself has three steps (Figure H2 D6.4.1):

1. Survey participants to identify three groups: those who achieved clear success as a result of applying their training, those who had no success at all, and those in the middle.
2. Interview and document the results of the most successful participants and the impediments encountered by those who had no success.
3. Report the findings, conclusions, and recommendations.

Key points about each step are given below; for more complete discussions of the method, see *The Success Case Method* (Brinkerhoff, 2003), *Telling Training's Story* (Brinkerhoff, 2006), and "Success case methodology in measurement and evaluation" (Apking and Mooney, 2010).

| Triage | Interview | Report |

Figure H2 D6.4.1. Three Steps in the Success Case Method

Guidance

1. *Triage participants to identify the most and least successful.*
   - This is most efficiently done by surveying participants—either all, in a relatively small program, or a sample of a hundred or so in a large program—in order to have a large enough sample of responses.
   - Conduct the survey long enough after training for people to have achieved success if they were going to. The optimal timing depends on the kind of training. It may be as little as a few days for immediately applicable technical training to several months for soft-skills training.
   - Ask as few questions as possible to identify who did and did not apply the training and who did and did not experience a positive and verifiable benefit as a result.

2. *Interview a sample of the most and least successful candidates.*
   - The goal of the interviews is to verify—and, if appropriate, to quantify—the results of the most successful participants and to identify the obstacles encountered by the non-successful.
   - Interviewees should be randomly selected from the most- and least-successful pool.
   - Prepare structured interview outlines to ensure consistency.
   - For successful cases, the goal of the interview is to identify what was achieved in terms of both individual performance and organizational impact (if any) and to be able to relate it in story form.
   - For non-success cases, the goal of the interview is to understand *why* they did not apply what they learned or, having done so, did not produce the same kind of results that the more successful candidates enjoyed.
   - Make certain to independently confirm any success stories you plan to showcase.

3. *Analyze the results, prepare recommendations for improvement, and communicate them effectively.*

- Review the results of the survey and all the interviews. Summarize the findings along the following themes:
  - Examples of positive outcomes to which the training clearly contributed
  - The proportion of participants that achieved such successes
  - Factors in the training and transfer climate that contributed to success cases
  - Elements of the training and factors in the transfer climate that impeded success
  - Recommendations for improvement
- Prepare a report, but also communicate the results at multiple meetings and venues to be sure they are not overlooked.

Key Success Factors

- Understanding the business purpose of the training and the results that management is looking for.
- Making a sincere effort to identify "bad news" as well as successes, since understanding failures is the key to improving the process.
- Taking the time to confirm the success stories you plan to use as exemplars.
- Recognizing that both success and failure depend as much on the transfer climate (what happens before and after class) as they do on the training itself.
- Having the courage to report the results good, bad, or indifferent.

H2 D6.5

How to Write Better Surveys

Introduction

The widespread availability of online survey tools like Zoomerang®, SurveyMonkey®, and so forth, have made it much easier to use surveys to collect data. Anyone can create and send a survey in a few minutes. However, the ease with which one can create surveys has obscured the difficulty of creating *good* (valid and reliable) surveys. "Good survey questions are hard to write—they take significant time to develop and hone" (Russ-Eft & Preskill, 2009, p. 268).

Many of the surveys we see (including some from commercial measurement firms) contain questions that are difficult to understand or impossible to answer. "Even if they are the right questions, if they are poorly written the outcome is the same: decisions based on bad questions" (Phillips, Phillips, & Aaron, 2013, p. 19). And if the questions are bad, the decisions based on them are likely to be bad as well.

The following guidelines will help you write surveys that provide more relevant, credible, and compelling data.

Guidance

1. *Ask the fewest possible questions.* Response rate is inversely proportional to length; the more questions on a survey, the fewer people complete it. Response rate is important. The lower the response rate, the less credibility; you cannot be confident that the results of a very small sample are representative of the group as a whole. People who feel very strongly about a program (one way or the other) are more likely to complete the survey than those in the "middle of the road," which may skew the results.

   Avoid "throw-away" questions and only ask questions that will provide the insights you need to take informed action. Don't ask about things you can't or won't change and don't waste a lot of questions on demographics (gender, position, years with company, and so forth), unless you have reason to believe that analysis by these categories will produce meaningful insight.

2. *Use terms and language that the respondents will understand.* In an effort to be helpful, people often answer survey questions even if they don't fully understand them, especially if the answer is a rating scale. Obviously, the results are valid only to the extent that the respondents understand the questions. Keep the questions short; use plain language and simple constructions. Use only terms that you are confident will be understood and define any that might cause confusion. Avoid acronyms; don't assume everyone will know what they mean. Pilot test the survey with a sample from the target population to be sure (see below).

3. *Be sure the respondents can answer reliably.* Your evaluation assumes that the respondents are able to give valid and reliable answers. But many of the surveys we see ask people to answer questions about which they have no personal knowledge or about which they lack expertise. For example, it might seem reasonable to ask a manager how often he or she has seen a particular behavior by a

trainee. That assumes, however, that the manager has had a meaningful opportunity to observe the employee. With more and more employees working remotely, that might not be the case. Be sure to provide an "out" such as "No opportunity to observe" so that people do not feel compelled to answer when they do not really know. Likewise, be sure those being polled have the expertise to answer. For example, many surveys ask people to supply financial estimates of value. If the target population has no training or experience making such estimates, the results are likely to be unreliable.

4. *Avoid compound questions.* A common error in writing surveys—especially if you are trying to keep the number of questions low—is to combine one or more ideas in a single question: "Was the training interesting and useful to you?" While the two features may be related, they are not the same; a participant could agree with one and not the other. When you analyze the responses, if you were to find that the program was scored low on such a compound question, you would not know whether the problem was one factor, or the other, or both, and therefore it would not be clear how to fix it. Either break the question into two separate ones, or eliminate one of the terms (for example, "interesting") altogether if it won't lead to actionable insight. Avoid "and/or" questions for the same reason.

5. *Use consistent rating scales whenever possible.* You can improve the reliability of answers by using a consistent rating scale for a series of statements, (for example, "Rate the following statements using the following scale") rather than using a different scale for each. Be certain that the rating scale makes sense for the parameter being rated. For example, if you ask "How satisfied were you with the coaching you received?" then the scale must reflect the spectrum from "very dissatisfied" to "very satisfied." Conversely, if you ask people whether they agree with the statement "The coaching

I received was satisfactory," then the appropriate scale is "strongly disagree" to "strongly agree" since the question is about agreement.

6. *Don't lead the witness.* The credibility of your results will suffer if your survey contains questions that seem to try to suggest a particular rating or answer, such as:
   - "Don't you agree that . . ."
   - "Isn't it true . . ."
   - "Most people feel that we are not spending enough on training. How do you rate our current spending?"

7. *Pilot test and revise before distributing.* One of the single best things you can do to improve the quality of the information you collect by survey is to pilot test it with a representative sample of the target audience. Have them complete the survey and then interview them to obtain their reactions to the questions. Ask them to identify any items that were unclear or that they felt they could not reliably answer. It may be helpful to ask them to read the questions to you and explain their understanding to be sure they are interpreting it in the way you intended. Correct any issues identified before distributing the survey widely.

Key Success Factors

- Being clear about what you are trying to find out and how you will use the results before you start writing questions.
- Keeping the survey as short as possible.
- Using simple, clear, and understandable terms and constructions.
- Allowing people to skip or opt out of questions they feel they cannot answer.
- Pilot testing and revising the survey before disseminating it.

References

Amabile, T., & Kramer, S. (2011). *The progress principle: Using small wins to ignite joy, engagement, and creativity at work.* Boston, MA: Harvard Business School Publishing.

American Express. (2007). The real ROI of leadership development: Comparing classroom vs. online vs. blended delivery. Retrieved August 2013 from www.personnel decisions.com/uploadedfiles/Case_Studies/PDFs/AmericanExpress.pdf

Anderson, J. (2010). *Cognitive psychology and its implications* (7th ed.). New York: Worth.

Apking, A., & Mooney, T. (2010). Success case methodology in measurement and evaluation. In J. Moseley & J. Dessinger (Eds.), *Handbook of improving performance in the workplace: Vol. 3. Measurement and evaluation.* San Francisco, CA: Pfeiffer.

Ariely, D. (2010a). *Predictably irrational: The hidden forces that shape our decisions.* New York: HarperCollins.

Ariely, D. (2010b). *The upside of irrationality: The unexpected benefits of defying logic at work and at home.* New York: HarperCollins.

Babbie, E. (2010). *The practice of social research* (12th ed.). Belmont, CA: Wadsworth.

Barbazette, J. (2006). *Training needs assessment: Methods, tools, and techniques.* San Francisco, CA: Pfeiffer.

Bersin, J. (2008). *The training measurement book: Best practices, proven methodologies, and practical approaches.* San Francisco, CA: Pfeiffer.

Block, P., & Markowitz, A. (2001). *The flawless consulting fieldbook and companion: A guide to understanding your expertise.* San Francisco, CA: Pfeiffer.

Branch, R. (2009). *Instructional design: The ADDIE approach.* New York: Springer.

Brinkerhoff, R. (2003). *The success case method: Find out quickly what's working and what's not.* San Francisco, CA: Berrett-Koehler.

Brinkerhoff, R. (2006). *Telling training's story: Using the success case method to improve learning and performance.* San Francisco, CA: Berrett-Koehler.

Brinkerhoff, R., & Apking, A. (2001). *High impact learning: Strategies for leveraging business results from training.* New York: Basic Books.

Brinkerhoff, R., & Gill, S. (1994). *The learning alliance: Systems thinking in human resources development.* San Francisco, CA: Jossey-Bass.

Brinkerhoff, R., & Montesino, M. (1995). Partnerships for learning transfer: Lessons from a corporate study. *Human Resource Development Quarterly, 6*(3), 263–274.

Broad, M., & Newstrom, J. (1992). *Transfer of training: Action-packed strategies to ensure high payoff from training investments.* Cambridge, MA: Perseus Books.

Burke, L., & Hutchins, H. (2007, September). Training transfer: An integrative literature review. *Human Resource Development Review, 6*(3), 263–296.

Clark, R. C. (1986). Part I: Task-general instructional methods. *Performance and Instruction, 25*(3), 17–20.

Clark, R. C. (2010). *Evidence-based training methods: A guide for training professionals.* Alexandria, VA: ASTD Press.

Clark, R. C., & Mayer, R. E. (2011). *e-Learning and the science of instruction: Proven guidelines for consumers and designers of multimedia learning.* San Francisco, CA: Pfeiffer.

Clark, R. C., Nguyen, F., & Sweller, J. (2006). *Efficiency in learning: Evidence-based guidelines to manage cognitive load.* San Francisco, CA: Pfeiffer.

Corporate Executive Board. (2009*). Refocusing L&D on business results: Bridging the gap between learning and performance.* Washington, DC: Corporate Executive Board.

Covey, S. (2004). *The 7 habits of highly effective people: Powerful lessons in personal change* (2nd ed.). New York: Simon & Schuster.

Davachi, L., Kiefer, T., Rock, D., & Rock, L. (2010). Learning that lasts through AGES. *NeuroLeadership Journal, 3,* 53–63.

DeSmet, A., McGurk, M., & Schwartz, E. (October, 2010). Getting more from your training programs. *McKinsey Quarterly.*

Dirksen, J. (2012). *Design for how people learn.* Berkeley, CA: New Riders.

Dresner, M., & Lehman, L. (2009). The astounding value of learning brand: Learning brand is the learning organization's most valuable intangible asset. Retrieved August 2013 from http://documents.corpu.com/research/CorpU_Astounding_Value_of_Learning_Brand.pdf

Duarte, N. (2008). *Slide:ology: The art and science of creating great presentations.* Sebastopol, CA: O'Reilly Media.

Ebbinghaus, H. (1885). *Memory: A contribution to experimental psychology.* [Trans. Henry Ruger & Clara Bussenius (1913)]. New York: Teachers College, Columbia University. http://psychclassics.yorku.ca/Ebbinghaus/index.htm

Garavan, T., Hogan, C., & Cahir-O'Donnell, A. (2003). *Making training and development work: A best practices guide.* Cork, Ireland: Oak Tree Press.

Gawande, A. (2009). *The checklist manifesto.* New York: Metropolitan Books.

Goldsmith, M. (2002, Summer). Try feedforward instead of feedback. *Leader to Leader,* (25), 11–14.

Grossman, R., & Salas, E. (2011). The transfer of training: What really matters. *International Journal of Training and Development, 15*(2), 103–120.

Haidt, J. (2006). *The happiness hypothesis: Finding modern truth in ancient wisdom.* New York: Basic Books.

Hodell, C. (2006). *ISD from the ground up* (2nd ed.). Alexandria, VA: ASTD Press.

Holton, E. F., III (2003). What's really wrong: Diagnosis for learning transfer system change. In E. F. Holton III & T. Baldwin (Eds.), *Improving learning transfer in organizations.* San Francisco, CA: Jossey-Bass.

Holton, E. F. III,, Bates, R., & Ruona, W. (2000). Development of a generalized learning transfer system inventory. *Human Resource Development Quarterly, 11*(4), 333–360.

Islam, K. (2006). *Developing and measuring training the six sigma way: A business approach to training and development.* San Francisco, CA: Pfeiffer.

Jefferson, A., Pollock, R., & Wick, C. (2009). *Getting your money's worth from training and development.* San Francisco, CA: Pfeiffer.

Kahneman, D. (2011). *Thinking fast and slow.* New York: Farrar, Straus, and Giroux.

Keith, N., & Frese, M. (2008). Effectiveness of error management training: A meta-analysis. *Journal of Applied Psychology, 93*(1), 59–69.

Keller, J. (1987). The systematic process of motivational design. *Performance & Instruction, 26*(9), 1–8.

Keller, J. (2000). How to integrate learner motivation planning into lesson planning: The ARCS model approach. Retrieved July 2013 from: http://mailer.fsu.edu/~jkeller/Articles/Keller%202000%20ARCS%20Lesson%20Planning.pdf

Kelley, H. (1950). The warm-cold variable in first impressions of persons. *Journal of Personality, 18*(4), 431–439.

Kerfoot, B., & Baker, H. (2012). An online spaced-education game for global continuing medical education: A randomized trial. *Annals of Surgery, 256*(1), 33–38.

Knowles, M., Holton, E. F., III, & Swanson, R. (2005). *The adult learner: The definitive classic in adult education and human resource development* (6th ed.). Burlington, MA: Elsevier.

Kontra, S., Trainor, D., & Wick, C. (2007, September 12). Leadership development at Pfizer: What happens after class. Retrieved August 2013 from http://corpu.com/research/leadership-development-at-pfizer-what-happens-after-class/?t=3

Krathwohl, D. (2002). A revision of Bloom's taxonomy: An overview. *Theory Into Practice, 41*(4): 212–218.

Langley, G., Nolan, K., Nolan, T., Norman, C., & Provost, L. (2009). *The improvement guide: A practical approach to enhancing organizational performance.* San Francisco, CA: Jossey-Bass.

Mager, R. (1997). *Preparing instructional objectives* (3rd ed.). Atlanta: CEP Press.

Mager, R., & Pipe, P. (1997). *Analyzing performance problems: Or you really oughta wanna* (3rd ed.). Atlanta, GA: CEP Press.

Maister, D., Green, C., & Galford, R. (2000). *The trusted advisor.* New York: The Free Press.

Margolis, F., & Bell, C. (1986). *Instructing for results.* San Diego, CA: University Associates.

McDermott, L. (2011). The power of peer coaching. *Info-line, 28*(1106), Alexandria, VA: ASTD Press.

Medina, J. (2008). *Brain rules.* Seattle, WA: Pear Press.

Pallarito, K. (2009). E-mailing your way to healthier habits. *Health News.* Retrieved April 2010 from www.healthfinder.gov/news/newsstory.aspx?doci_627207

Patterson, K., Grenny, J., Maxfield, D., McMillan, R., & Switzler, A. (2008). *Influencer: The power to change anything.* New York: McGraw-Hill.

Paul, A. M. (2013). *The brilliant report.* Retrieved August 2013 from: http://anniemurphy paul.com/blog/

Petty, G. (2009). *Evidence-based teaching: A practical approach* (2nd ed.). Cheltenham, UK: Nelson Thornes Ltd.

Phillips, P.P., Phillips, J.J., & Aaron, B. (2013). *Survey basics.* Alexandria, VA: ASTD.

Pike, R. (2003). *Creative training techniques handbook: Tips, tactics, and how-to's for delivering effective training.* Amherst, MA: HRD Press.

Pink, D. (2006). *A whole new mind.* New York: Riverhead Books.

Pink, D. (2009). *Drive: The surprising truth about what motivates us.* New York: Penguin Group.

Plotnikoff, R., McCargar, L., Wilson, P., & Loucaides, C. (2005). Efficacy of an e-mail intervention for the promotion of physical activity and nutrition behavior in the workplace context. *American Journal of Health Promotion, 19*(6), 422–429.

Pollock, R. (2013). Training is not a hammer. Retrieved August 2013 from: www.hci.org/blog/training-not-hammer

Pollock, R., & Jefferson, A. (2012). Ensuring learning transfer. *Info-line, 29*(1208). Alexandria, VA: ASTD.

Pollock, R., Jefferson, A., & Wick, C. (2013). *The 6Ds workshop: Participant workbook.* San Francisco, CA: John Wiley & Sons.

Porter, M. (1985). *Competitive advantage: Creating and sustaining superior performance.* New York: The Free Press.

Reichheld, F. (2003, December). One number you need to grow. *Harvard Business Review.*

Reynolds, G. (2008). *Presentation Zen.* Berkeley, CA: New Riders.

Ries, A., & Trout, J. (2001). *Positioning: The battle for your mind.* New York: McGraw-Hill.

Robinson, D., & Robinson, J. (2008). *Performance consulting: A practical guide for HR and learning professionals.* San Francisco, CA: Berrett-Koehler.

Rosenbaum, S., & Williams, J. (2004). *Learning paths: Increase profits by reducing the time it takes employees to get up-to-speed.* San Francisco, CA: Pfeiffer.

Rossett, A., & Schafer, L. (2007). *Job aids and performance support: Moving from knowledge in the classroom to knowledge everywhere.* San Francisco, CA: Pfeiffer.

Rothwell, W., & Kazanas, H. (2008). *Mastering the instructional design process: A systematic approach* (4th ed.). San Francisco, CA: Pfeiffer.

Rouiller, J., & Goldstein, I. (1993). The relationship between organizational transfer climate and positive transfer of training. *Human Resource Development Quarterly, 4*(4), 377–390.

Russ-Eft, D., & Preskill, H. (2009). *Evaluation in organizations: A systematic approach to enhancing learning, performance, and change* (2nd ed.). New York: Basic Books.

Salas, E., Tannenbaum, S., Kraiger, K., & Smith-Jentsch, K. (2012). The science of training and development in organizations: What matters in practice. *Psychological Science in the Public Interest, 13*(2), 74–101.

Sharkey, L. (2003). Leveraging HR: How to develop leaders in "real time." In M. Effron, R. Gandossy, & M. Goldsmith (Eds.), *Human resources in the 21st century* (pp. 67–78). San Francisco, CA: Jossey-Bass.

Shrock, S., & Coscarelli, W. (2007). Measuring learning—Evaluating level II assessments within the eLearning Guild. In S. Wexler (Ed.), *Measuring success: Aligning learning success with business success* (pp. 155–164). Santa Rosa, CA: The eLearning Guild.

Smith, R. (2011). *Strategic learning alignment: Make training a powerful business partner.* Alexandria, VA: ASTD Press.

Sousa, D. (2011). *How the brain learns* (4th ed.). Thousand Oaks, CA: Corwin.

Sullivan, J. (2005). Measuring the impact of executive development. In J. F. Bolt (Ed.), *The future of executive development.* New York: Executive Development Associates, Inc.

Thalheimer, W. (2006). Spacing learning events over time: What the research says. Retrieved August 2013 from http://willthalheimer.typepad.com/files/spacing_learning_over_time_2006.pdf

Todd, S. (2009, October). Branding learning and development. Paper presented at the Fort Hill Company Best Practices Summit. Mendenhall, Pennsylvania.

Van Adelsberg, D., & Trolley, E. (1999). *Running training like a business: Delivering unmistakable value.* San Francisco, CA: Berrett-Koehler.

Vance, D. (2010). *The business of learning: How to manage corporate training to improve your bottom line.* Windsor, CO: Poudre River Press.

Visser, L. (2010). Motivational communication. In R. Watkins & D. Leigh (Eds.), *Handbook of improving performance in the workplace: Vol. 2. Selecting and implementing performance interventions.* San Francisco, CA: Pfeiffer.

Wehlage, G., Newmann, F., & Secada, W. (1996). Standards for authentic achievement and pedagogy. In F. M. Newmann & Associates (Eds.), *Authentic achievement: Restructuring schools for intellectual quality* (pp. 21–48). San Francisco, CA: Jossey-Bass.

Wick, C., & Papay, M. (2013). Feasting on achievement. *T & D, 67*(1), 57–60.

Wick, C., Pollock, R., & Jefferson, A. (2009). The new finish line for learning. *T & D, 63*(7), 64–69.

Wick, C., Pollock, R., & Jefferson, A. (2010). *The six disciplines of breakthrough learning: How to turn training and development into business results* (2nd ed.). San Francisco, CA: Pfeiffer.

Wick, C., Pollock, R., Jefferson, A., & Flanagan, R. (2006). *The six disciplines of breakthrough learning: How to turn learning and development into business results.* San Francisco, CA: Pfeiffer.

Wolf, K., & Stevens, W. (2007). The role of rubrics in advancing and assessing student learning. *The Journal of Effective Teaching, 7*(1), 3–14.

Index

Page references followed by *fig* indicate an illustrated figure; followed by *t* indicate a table; followed by *e* indicate an exhibit.

A

Aaron, B., 130, 633

Accountability: ensuring training transfer, 90–96; of managerial support of training, 90

Achievement stories: description and purpose of, 67; *Waggl* web-based system to collect, 67; use of in proficiency coaching, 477

ACTION conversation methodology: Lever Learning/ Moree Plain Shires Council case study on using, 462–464, 610; peer coaching use of, 610

Action planning: How-to Guide to engage learners in, 597–600; to increase accountability for learning, 95; Learning Andrago case study on using formal, 453–458; Lever Learning/Moree Plain Shires Council case study use of, 462e; Plastipak Packaging case study use of, 392e. *See also* 6Ds Personal Action Planner tool

Actions: Kaiser Permanente case study and summary of, 244*fig*; 6Ds Personal Action Planner tool for planning, 137, 223–229; Transfer Climate Improvement Planner tool, 84, 207–208; Turning Learning into Action approach focus on, 96; Underwriters Laboratories (UL) Green Belt training, 258–259

ADDIE model, xxiv*fig*, 80, 312, 506

AfferoLab case study: advice to colleagues from, 473; background information on, 469–470; disseminating corporate culture of Promon Engenharia during, 470–473; performance support deployed through mentoring at, 100, 470–473

AGES learning retention model, 568

Agile development process: DTCC case study on, 311–318

Agilent Technologies, Inc. case study (D2.3): advice to colleagues from, 332; background information on, 325–326; commitment form for managers and coaches during, 328e; creating learning

intentionality at, 34; Emerging Leaders Program Checklist, 329e; Emerging Leaders Program (ELP) for talent building, 326–332; example of a timeline for ELP business project, 330e; excerpt from ELP participant's personal board of directors illustration, 331e; on need for senior leader sponsorship during, 327e–328

Agilent Technologies, Inc. case study (D2.5): advice to colleagues, 343; agenda for complete learning experience, 339e; background information on, 337–338; enhancing first-level managers' learning experience, 338–343; redefining the finish line of leadership program at, 42; screen capture from SharePoint site for the program, 341e

Akram, S., 4, 135, 281, 519

Allianz SE Insurance Management Asia Pacific, 248

Amabile, T., 43

American Express study: on driving learning transfer, 88–89; on providing performance support for managers, 606

American International Assurance (AIA), 248, 249

Analyzing Performance Problems (Mager and Pipe), 17

Anderson, J., 567, 594

Apking, A., 33, 549, 630

Apple, 85, 593

ARCS model of communication, 546, 547–548

Ariely, D., 32, 43, 47, 88

Assessment: How-to Guide to improve predictive value of, 587–591; predictive value of, 587. *See also* Evaluation

"The Astounding Value of Learning Brand" (Dresner and Lehman), 135

Attention: AGES learning retention model on emotions and, 568; the challenge of paying, 57; how sensory overload impacts, 56*fig*; How-to Guides on gaining and holding learners,' 567–569; strategies to get the learner's, 546; using stories to gain and keep, 569; ten-minute segments best for keeping the, 57–58

Audience-response technology, 58

AXIS Minnesota, 346

B

Babbie, E., 619

Bajpai, A., 292

Baker, H., 86, 437

Banerjee, S., 4, 285

Banks, B. B., 67, 411

Barbazette, J., 17

Bardhan, I., 48, 353, 481

Bartlett, R., 86, 431

Bates, R., 84

Beech, P., 122, 503

Beginning with the end: Covey's principle on, 117, 118, 579–580; D6 (Document Results) on, 117*fig*–120; KnowledgeAdvisors case study on benefits of, 496–499

Behavior change: Emirates Group's SOAR program for, 122, 503–511; Lever Learning/Moree Plain Shires Council case study on workplace, 96, 459–468; Oneida Nation Enterprises (ONE) case study on, 67, 400–406; Underwriters Laboratories (UL) case study on Green Belt training for, 258–266; U.S. Military Academy (USMA) case study on, 67, 411–415

Bell, C., 66, 583, 584, 585

Bell-Wright, K., 122, 503

Bersin, J., 5, 129, 625

Block, P., 34

Bloom's taxonomy of learning objectives, 587–588*fig*

Brain Rules (Medina), 56

Branch, R., 590

Brand. *See* Learning brand

The Brilliant Report (Paul), 56

Brinkerhoff, R., 33, 89, 549, 579, 629, 630

Brinkerhoff's Success Case Method, 134*fig*–135, 629

Broad, M., 537

Brunet Relyea, M. B., 67, 399

BST case study: advice to colleagues from, 410; background information on, 407–408; "moments of truth" to shape safety culture at, 67; results of the, 409–410; turning front-line supervisors into safety leaders, 408*t*–409

Burke, L., 597

Business case: description of, 601; How-to Guide for making the learning transfer, 601–604

Business language, 626

Business objectives: clearly defining the, 117*fig*–120; differentiating between learning and, 20–21*fig*; examples of, 21*t*; used to explain benefits of training, 22–25; how to use the Outcomes Planning Wheel to clarify, 533–536; Quick Check: Business Objectives, 24–25; relevant measures for training, 125–127; traditional training failure to include, 81. *See also* Business outcomes; Learning objectives; Training outcomes

Business outcomes: of UL's Green Belt training, 266; creating results intentionality, 33–34, 549–553; differentiate business and learning objectives of training, 20*t*–21*t*; example of slide linking training to, 271*e*; Janssen Pharmaceuticals case study, 269; Kaiser Permanente case study on focus on results and, 86, 243–246; KLA-Tencor Corporation case study on defining, 376, 377*e*–379*e*, 380; performance-gap analysis to improve, 15–19; talk to your stakeholders to improve, 8–14; Tata Motors Academy's *iteach* and defined, 293–297; understanding the business you support, 5–7; Underwriters Laboratories (UL) Green Belt training, 25; Value Chain Planner tool to connect behaviors to, 66, 199–200. *See also* D1 (Define Business Outcomes)

C

"Can I?" question: Checklist for D3 tool to help answer, 201; D3 (Deliver for Application) issue of, 52–54; D4 (Drive Learning Transfer) and role of, 79*fig*; importance of, xxii, xxiii*fig*; performance support enhancing learning transfer by answering the, 98–99

Cape plc. *See* Primeast Ltd. case study

"Capstone call," 561

Car Talk (radio show), 106

Case studies: Agilent Technologies, Inc. (Case D2.3), 34, 325–332; Agilent Technologies, Inc. (Case D2.5), 42, 337–343; BST, 67, 407–410; Cox Media Group (CMG), 90, 449–452; Deloitte adoption of 6Ds, 275–279; Depository Trust & Clearing Corporation (DTCC), 29, 311–318; DirectWest, 86, 431–433; Emirates Group, 122, 503–511; Emory University, 33, 319–324; Fort Hill Company, 79, 417–422; General Electric, 513–518; Global Trainers, Inc., 247–250; Hypertherm, Inc., 81, 423–430; Institute for Learning Practitioners, 90, 106, 443–447; Janssen Pharmaceuticals, 269–273; Kaiser Permanente, 24; KLA-Tencor Corporation, 60, 375–386; KnowledgeAdvisors, 9, 117, 495–502; Learning Andrago, 94, 453–458; Learning Lever/Moree Plain Shires Council, 459–468; Learning Path Methodology, 48, 345–352; Mars University, 135, 523–526; Merck & Co., 9, 305–309; Methodist Le Bonheur Healthcare, 42, 333–336; Oneida Nation Enterprises (ONE), 67, 399–406; Oracle (Case D1.1), 4, 135, 281–284; Oracle (Case D6.4), 519–521; Plastipak Packaging, 67, 387–398; PowerUpSuccess/Visual Solutions, 48, 361–365; Primeast Ltd., 9, 299–303; Promon Engenharia-AfferoLab case study, 100, 469–473; Qstream, 86, 435–441, 561; ROHEI Corporation, 59, 367–374; by Royce Isacowitz on using 6Ds outline, 251–255; Tata Motors Academy imPACT, 481–486; Tata Motors

278; background information on, 275–276; photos related to using 6Ds, 277e, 278, 279

Deming Cycle (or PDCA), 80fig, 134

Deming, W. E., 80

Deploying performance support. *See* D5 (Deploy Performance Support) and Performance support

Depository Trust & Clearing Corporation (DTCC) case study: advice to colleagues from the, 318; background information on, 311–313; new Agile structure to create learning solutions, 314fig–318; treating learning as a process at, 29

Design for How People Learn (Dirksen), 22, 57

Designed complete experience. *See* D2 (Design the Complete Experience)

DeSmet, A., 78

Developing and Measuring Training the Six Sigma Way (Islam), 29

DirectWest case study: advice to colleagues from, 433; background information on, 431; example of reminder email to participants, 432e; on implementing low-cost, low-effort follow-up to training, 432e–433; reminder system used at, 86

Dirksen, J., 22, 57, 543

Documenting results: of UL's Green Belt training, 265; Brinkerhoff's Success Case Method for, 134fig–135; building a strong learning brand by, 135; Checklist for D6 for, 221–222; ensuring credibility when, 128–129, 131–132, 217–218; examples of goals for applying 6Ds to, 227–229; measurement issues of, 125–127t, 131. *See also* D6 (Document Results)

Donahue, T., 58, 110, 571

Donohoe, J., 122, 503

Drive: The Surprising Truth About What Motivates Us (Pink), 43

Driving learning transfer. *See* Learning transfer

Duarte, N., 197, 376, 381, 564

DuarteDesign, 383

Duggan, K., 424

E

Ebbinghaus, H., 436

Ebert, J., 257

eLearning Guild, 588

The elephant and rider analogy, 57, 58fig

Emirates Group case study: advice to colleagues from the, 511; application of Service Pillars by shift team leaders during, 510fig; background information on, 503–505; customer service training initiative by, 122; follow-up to the SOAR program, 507; Kirkpatrick Foundational Principles used during, 122, 504; leading indicators of change by Service Pillar, 508fig; number of customer complaints about Call Center Service following

training, 508fig–509; results of the SOAR program, 508fig–511; SOAR (Service Over and Above the Rest) program effectiveness, 122, 504–507

Emory University case study: advice to colleagues from, 324; background information on, 319–320; Learning and Organizational Development (LOD) department's Excellence Through Leadership program, 33, 320–324

Emphasizing training benefits, 34–37

"Error training" studies, 62

Essar Group case study: advice to colleagues from the, 290–291; background information on, 285–286; defining business outcomes at, 4; endorsement of the 6Ds approach by the Essar Hypermart CEO, 291–292; transforming a training program into a business transformation of Hypermart unit of, 286–290

Evaluation: Brinkerhoff's Success Case Method, 134fig–135, 629; Checklist for Evaluation Credibility tool for, 217–218, 624; clearly defining the business objectives prior to, 117fig–120; Covey's "Start with the end in mind" principle of, 117, 118, 579–580; credibility of, 128–129, 131–132, 217–218; decide what to measure, 125; efficient use of resources for, 130–133; Evaluation Planner tool for, 219–220; executive summary of, 626; How-to Guide to conducting a success case method, 629–632; How-to Guide to improve credibility of, 619–624; How-to Guide to make more compelling, 625–627; how to measure for, 118; make a compelling case for, 129–130; measuring the relevant outcomes for, 125–127; prove and improve training outcomes, 134fig–135. *See also* Assessment; Training outcomes

Evans, R., 9, 299

Evidence-Based Teaching (Petty), 56

Executive summary, 626

Exercises: description of effective training, 583; How-to Guide for introducing training, 583–585

Experiential learning: Agilent Technologies' enhancement of first-level manager, 42, 338–343; description and benefits of, 58–59; examples of goals for applying 6Ds to, 227–229; Plastipak Packaging case study on designing a, 67, 387–398; ROHEI Corporation's engagement of learners through, 59, 368–373; Underwriters Laboratories (UL) Green Belt training, 260–264.

F

Far Side cartoon (Larson), 59

"Feasting on Achievement" (Wick and Papay), 67

Feedback: imPACT program's Coaching Mirror as tool for, 482, 483e, 484; interaction of practice with, 61; providing performance support, 111;

Qstream case study on Qstream question and answer, 438*fig*; rubrics and scoring guidelines to improve, 590; Transfer Climate Improvement Planner tool to improve, 84, 207–208. *See also* Communication

Finish line. *See* Redefining the finish line

Friday5s model, 432

Flow Chart: Is Training Necessary? tool, 175–177

Flow Chart for Phase I Learning (Pre-Work) tool, 187–188

"Forgetting curve," 436*fig*

Fort Hill Company case study: advice to colleagues from, 422; Application Checklist to ensure learning transfer, 419–422; background information on, 417–418; Immediate Application Checklist, 420*e*–421*e*; "Immediate Transfer Checklist" used at, 79

Frese, M., 62

The Future of Executive Development (Sullivan), 625

G

Gagné, R., 65

Galford, R., 533

Gamification: Qstream case study on using, 437–439, 561; Qstream results from using, 439–440

Gawande, A., 98, 109, 577

General Electric (GE) case study: advice to colleagues, 518; background information on Crotonville Leadership Institute, 513–514; keys to success during, 517; Net Promoter Score (NPS) to improve customer satisfaction, 514, 515–516; results of the NPS, 516–517

Getting Your Money's Worth from Training and Development: A Guide for Managers (Jefferson, Pollock, and Wick), 606

Gettysburg Address parody (PowerPoint), 565

Gill, S., 579

Gilson, P., 94

Girone, M., 34, 325

Glance Test for Slides tool, 197

The Glance Test (KLA-Tencor case study), 380*e*, 381, 382*fig*, 384

Global Learning and Leadership Development (Agilent Technologies), 34, 42

Global Trainers case study: advice to colleagues based on the, 250; background of, 247–248; how they used 6Ds to differentiate their services, 248–249

Goh, C.S.K., 42, 337

Goldsmith, M., 610

Goldstein, I., 84

Green Belt training. *See* Underwriters Laboratories (UL) case study

Green, C., 533

Gregory, P., 4, 135, 281, 519

Grigorova, M., 135, 523

Grigsby, L., 387

Grossman, R., 81

H

Hackett, C., 81, 423

Haddon, E., 257

Haidt, J., 57

The Happiness Hypothesis (Haidt), 57

Harvard Business Review, 514

Hayes, W. J., 33, 319

Hinton, D., 67, 387

Hodell, C., 542, 588

Holton, E., III, 53, 66, 84, 579

How the Brain Learns (Sousa), 56

How-to Guides: build a value chain for learning, 579–582; build scaffolding, 575–577; communicate to motivate, 545–548; conduct a success case method evaluation, 629–632; create results intentionality, 549–553; decide whether training is necessary, 537–539; develop great performance support, 613–615; engage learners in action planning, 597–600; ensure your measures are relevant, 617–618; gain and hold learners' attention, 567–569; improve the credibility of evaluations, 619–624; improve the predictive value of assessments, 587–591; introduce exercises, 583–585; use learning objectives, 541–544*e*; make the business case for learning transfer, 601–604; make your evaluations more compelling, 625–627; move the finish line for learning, 559–562; use Outcomes Planning Wheel to clarify business purpose, 533–536; use PowerPoint, 563–566; provide performance support for managers and coaches, 605–607; re-engage learners after a break, 571–574; remind learners to apply their training, 593–596; start learning before class to improve efficiency, 555–557; utilize peer coaching, 609–611; write better surveys, 633–636. *See also* Training

How we: achieved lean improvements with learning transfer, 423; are incorporating the 6Ds methodologies into our culture, 527; are lighting up the fire of continuous improvement for our lean sigma green belts, 257; bring employees up to speed in record time using the Learning Path methodology, 345; build enterprise high-potential talent at Agilent, 325; created a high impact Mars University brand, 523; defined business outcomes and the learning continuum for iteach, 293; deployed performance support for a technical capability building initiative, 489; designed a complete experience for our signature induction program "Steerin," 353; designed a complete experience to deliver business results, 387; develop managers to leverage learning transfer, 443; engage key contributors to disseminate corporate culture, 469; engage managers to acknowledge the achievements of leadership program participants, 449; engage participants for optimal learning transfer, 481; enhanced and stretched our first-level managers' learning experience, 337; fostered a proactive approach to leader development, 411; guide our clients to design with the end in mind, 495; implemented a low-cost, low-effort follow-up, 431; implemented an immediate application checklist to ensure learning transfer, 417; improved the signal-to-noise ratio to transform the presentation culture at KLA-Tencor, 375; incorporated the 6Ds into our learning services tool box, 305; increased leadership effectiveness by delivering for application, 399; increased the volume and variety of learning solutions, 311; introduced the 6Ds to our team 275; made learning relevant to deliver business impact, 361; moved from order takers to business partners, 281; moved the finish line for leadership development, 333; prepare a proposal and design a process using the 6Ds outline, 251; sustain priority-management training, 453; transitioned our focus to results, 243; turn front-line supervisors into safety leaders, 407; turn learning into action, 459; turned a "feel good" training program into a successful business transformation, 285; use alumni to help set expectations for new program participants and their leaders, 319; use the 6Ds to differentiate our services, 247; use experiential learning to engage learners' hearts as well as minds, 367; use proficiency coaching to improve performance, 475; use success stories to communicate training's value, 519; used in-depth analysis to design the right intervention to achieve business objectives, 299; used measurement to drive "SOAR—service over and above the rest," 503; used NPS to track and improve leadership impact, 513; used spaced learning and gamification to increase the effectiveness of product launch training, 435; used the 6Ds framework to redevelop our sales leader curriculum, 269

Hughes, G., 60, 197, 375
Hurtado, J., 137
Hutchins, H., 597
Hypertherm, Inc. case study: advice to colleagues from, 429–430; background information on, 423–424; Lean P&S Program for Lean Principles and Six Sigma for learning transfer during, 81, 424–429; Lean P&S Program results during, 428–429

I

IKEA, 105
"If-then" relationships, 496
Implementation. *See* Deliver for application
The Improvement Guide (Langley, Nolan, Nolan, Norman, and Provost), 29
Initiating learning, 38, 39–41
Institute for Learning Practitioners case study: advice to colleagues from, 447; background information on, 443–444; Leveraging Results from Learning program to help managerial coaching, 90, 444–447; proficiency coaching used at, 106, 475–479; results from the Leveraging Results from Learning program, 446–447
Instructional-systems design (ISD) process, xxiii, 80, 311
Intrinsic motivation: moving the finish line for learning by harnessing, 560–561; sense of accomplishment as, 43–47
Isacowitz, R.: on preparing proposal and design using the 6Ds outline, 251–255; spreadsheet flow chart for the 6Ds, 252e–253e
Islam, K. A., 28, 29, 80, 311
Iteach program (Tata Motors Academy), 294–296*fig*

J

Jaccaci, A., 81, 423
Janssen, P., 269–270
Janssen Pharmaceuticals case study: using the 6Ds framework to redevelop sales leader curriculum, 270–273; advice to colleagues from the, 273; background information on, 269–270; example of slide linking training to business outcomes, 271e
Jefferson, A., 8, 38, 42, 94, 116, 121, 183, 186, 193, 206, 208, 229, 417, 584, 606, 611
Job aids: ensuring use of, 110, 112–113; have managers reinforce the use of, 111; introducing them before and during training, 110–111
Johnson & Johnson, 269
Johnson, C. W., III, xxv, 269
Joyce, T., xxvi, 275

K

Kahneman, D., 32
Kahudova, A., 277e
Kaiser Permanente case study: advice to colleagues based on the, 246; background information on, 243–244; Front Office Operations Improvement (FOOI) transitioning focus to results, 243–245; reminder messages system used by, 86
Kaizen, 81
Kazanas, H., 542
Keeton, J., 42, 333

Keith, N., 62
Keller, J., 546
Keller's ARCS model, 546, 547–548
Kelley, H., 32
Kerfoot, B., 86, 437
Khanna, S., xxv, 243
Kiefer, T., 568
Kinds of Performance Support and Their Application tool, 213–214
Kirkpatrick Foundational Principles, 122, 504
Kirkpatrick, J., 122, 503
Kirkpatrick, W., 122, 503
KLA-Tencor Corporation case study: advice to colleagues from, 386; background information on, 375–376; The Glance Test used during, 380e, 381, 382fig, 384; improving their signal-to-noise ratio (SNR), 380, 380e, 381e, 382e, 382fig, 383–386; results of the, 385–386; 6D steps used during the, 376–385; transforming the presentation culture in the, 60, 376–386
KnowledgeAdvisors case study: advice to colleagues from, 502; background information on, 495–496; cautions from the, 500; logic modeling used to talk to stakeholders at, 9, 496–501; mind map for a management development program, 498e; results of the, 500–501; on starting with the business objectives, 117; teaching clients to design with the end in mind during, 496–499; time line from training to results during, 499e
Knowles, M., 53, 66, 579
Kontra, S., 605
Kramer, S., 43
Krathwohl, D., 588fig

L

Lalande, M., 94, 453
Langley, G., 29
Lao-tzu, 137
Larson, G., 59
Le Nech, A., 278e
Lean Manufacturing: Hypertherm, Inc. application of, 81, 424–429; Underwriters Laboratories (UL) case study on Green Belt training, 257–267
Learners. See Participants.
Learning: connecting the dots for, 65–70; creating intentionality for, 33–34, 549–553; ensuring adequate practice for, 61–64; initiate before class, 38, 39–41; managing expectations about, 32–33; PowerUpSuccess delivering business impact through, 361–365; pre-work (Phase I), 187–190, 555–557; providing sense of accomplishment as fourth phase of, 43–46; scaffolding, 575–577; schematic key steps in storage,

retrieval, application, and, 59fig; "spaced learning" approach to, 61; teach how people process, 56–59; treat it as a process, 28–31. See also Experiential learning; Participants; Value Chain for learning
Learning Andrago case study: advice to colleagues from, 458; background information on, 453–454; cautions from the, 458; Commitment-to-Apply Contract (Bilingual Template) used during, 455e; engaging participant commitment to priority-management training, 94, 454–456; lessons of experience and keys to success, 457–458; results of sustaining priority-management training, 456–457
Learning brand: building a strong, 135; Mars University case study on creating high impact, 135, 524–526
Learning intentionality, 33–34, 549–553
Learning journals, 595
Learning objectives: Bloom's taxonomy of, 587–588fig; Checklist for Learning Objectives, 543e–544e; differentiating between business and, 20–21t; examples of, 21t; How-to Guides on using, 541–544e; as traditional training focus, 81. See also Business objectives; Training outcomes
Learning Path Methodology case study: advice to colleagues from, 351; background information on, 346–347; description of, 345–346fig; increasing employee proficiency, 347–351; putting it all together as core concept of, 48
Learning Paths International, 346
Learning transfer: applying process thinking for, 80–83; engage managers in process of, 88fig–90, 91–93; Essar Group case study on, 289; examples of goals for applying 6Ds to, 227–229; Fort Hill Company case study on using checklist to ensure, 79, 417–422; How-to Guide for making the business case for, 601–604; increasing accountability for, 90, 94–96; Institute for Learning Practitioners case study on leveraging, 90, 106, 443–447; as key to successful training, 77–80; KLA-Tencor Corporation case study on driving, 377e–379e, 384; Learning Andrago case study to sustain, 94, 453–458; maintain share of mind by reminding learners, 85–87, 593–596; ResultsEngine web-based tool to support, 95, 414; typical approach to (cartoon), xxfig; of UL's Green Belt training, 264e–265. See also D4 (Drive Learning Transfer); Training outcomes; Transfer climate
Learning Transfer Climate Scorecard tool, 203–206
Learning Transfer Systems Inventory, 84
Lennox, D., 86, 435
"Let's Roll" activity, 597–600
Lever Learning/Moree Plain Shires Council case study: ACTION methodology for action conversations, 462–464, 610; advice to colleagues

from, 468; background information on, 459–460; example of an impact dashboard used during, 465e–466; example of an individual case study used during, 467e; example of typical action plan used during, 462e; keys to success, 467–468; results and impact of the, 464–467fig; Turning Learning into Action (TLA) approach for work-place change, 95–96, 460–468

Lever-Learning: challenged to effect real workplace change, 459–460; Turning Learning into Action approach used by, 96, 460–468

Logic modeling: to answer questions about training, 9–10; KnowledgeAdvisors case study on using, 496–502

Long-term memory, 59fig

Louisiana State University, 84

Low, J., 48, 361

Low, R., 9, 305

M

Mager, R., 17, 538

Maister, D., 533

Managers: BST case study on making safety lead-ers out of front-line, 67, 407–410; use business objectives to explain training benefits to, 22–25; Corporate Executive Board survey on training perceptions of, 28; Cox Media Group (CMG) manager acknowledgment on training impact, 90, 449–452; creating learning intentionality with trainee, 33–34; engaging them in learning transfer process, 88fig–90, 91–93; How-to Guide on providing performance support to coaches and, 605–607; increasing accountability for support of training, 90; Institute for Learning Practitioners' approach to leveraging coaching, 90, 444–447; Manager's Guide to a Post-Training Discussion tool, 191–193; Manager's Guide to a Pre-Training Discussion tool, 181–183; providing performance support to, 104fig; reinforcing the use of job aids, 111; Sample Learning Contract tool for participants and, 185–186; self-fulfilling prophesies and training expectations by, 32–33; spectrum of actions related to training by, 88fig; training expectations for improved performance by, 29fig; Transfer Climate Improvement Planner tool for, 84, 207–208

Margolis, F., 66, 583, 584, 585

Markowitz, A., 34

Mars, F. C., 523

Mars, F. E., Sr., 523

Mars University case study: advice to colleagues from, 526; background information on, 523–524; on creating a high impact brand, 135, 524–526; Mars Five Principles foundation of the Mars culture, 524; Mars University Logo, 525e; results of creating the Mars University brand, 526

Massacesi, A., xxv, 257

Mayer, R. E., 565

McDermott, S., 257, 610, 611

McDonald's, 85, 593

McGurk, M., 78

McKensy & Company, 78

Measurements: comparing apples to apples, 622–623; Emirates Airline's SOAR program, 504–511; How-to Guide to ensure relevance of your, 617–618; obtaining actionable information for improvement through, 625; randomized control group, 622; return on expectations (ROE) indica-tor of value, 506, 602–603, 613

Medina, J., 56, 57, 567

Memory: challenges of remembering details, 98; "forgetting curve" and, 436fig; learning pro-cessed and stored in long-term, 59fig; using working memory to process information, 98

Menon, S., 110, 489

Mentoring: disseminating organizational culture through, 100, 469–473; requirement for success-ful, 470. See also Coaching

Merck & Co. case study: background information on, 305–306; benefits of using the Planning Wheel at, 9, 306–309

Merck Polytechnic Institute. See Merck & Co. case study

Methodist Le Bonheur Healthcare case study: advice to colleagues from, 336; background information on, 333–334; Coaching Clinic's redefinition of fin-ish line at, 42, 334–336

Minnesota Department of Economic Development, 346

Modra, D., 257

Moffett, R., 135, 523

Mok, P., 59, 367

Moment of truth, xxi–xxii

Monitoring: of perceived relevance and utility of training, 71–74; Quick Check: Monitoring Relevance, 73–74; by tracking participant-rated statements, 71–72t

Montesino, M., 33

Mooney, T., 630

Motivation: how experiencing early success increases, 99fig; How-to Guide on how to com-municate for, 545–548; moving the finish line for learning by harnessing intrinsic, 560–561; sense of accomplishment as intrinsic, 43–47; Transfer Climate Improvement Planner tool to improve, 84, 207–208

Motorola, 28

Multi-tasking myth, 57

mysask411 solution, 431

and where to use, 102–103; importance of post-training, 98; job aids used as, 110–113; Kinds of and Their Application tool for, 213–214; KLA-Tencor Corporation case study on deploying, 377e–379e, 385; mentoring as, 100, 470–473; as part of the training design, 100–101; Planner tool for, 211–212; proficiency coaching model used as, 106, 175–179; provided to managers, 104fig; ResultsEngine web-based tool for, 95, 414; Tata Motor's critical-to-quality (CTC) parameters as, 491–493; during UL's Green Belt training, 265; and working memory, 98. See also D5 (Deploy Performance Support)

Petty, G., 56

Pfizer study (2007), 605

Phase I learning (pre-work): Flow Chart tool for, 187–188; How-to Guide to, 555–557; Purposes and Examples tool for, 189–190

Phillips, J. J., 130, 633

Phillips, P. P., 130, 633

Phoon, R., 48, 361

Pike, R., 569

Pink, D., 43, 569, 626–627

Pipe, P., 17, 538

Plastipak Packaging case study: action plan to move from learning to results, 392e; advice to colleagues from, 398; background information on, 387–388; cautions when designing learning experience, 397; Impact Map developed during the, 389e; keys to success during the, 396; learning experience designed to deliver business results during, 67, 388–393; lessons of experience learned during the, 395–396; results of the learning experience impact during, 393–395; TOUGH Talks tools used during the, 388, 391e, 393, 396, 397; VitalSmarts Crucial Conversations program role in the, 388, 389e

Plotnikoff, R., 85

Poll Everywhere, 58

Pollock, R., 8, 15, 38, 42, 94, 116, 121, 183, 186, 193, 206, 208, 229, 417, 584, 606, 611

Post-training: importance of performance support during, 98; Manager's Guide to a Post-Training Discussion tool, 191–193; Qstream systems to engage learner, 86; reminding learners component of, 85–87, 432e, 593–596

"The Power of Peer Coaching" (McDermott), 611

PowerPoint: "Bullet Laws" for use with, 564; Gettysburg Address parody using, 565; Glance Test for Slides tool to use with, 197; How-to Guides for using, 563–566; Janssen Pharmaceuticals case study on using, 269–273; signal-to-noise ratio (SNR) used to prepare slides, 380e–382e, 564–565

PowerUpSuccess/Visual Solutions case study: advice to colleagues from, 364–365; approach

for delivering business impact during, 363e; background information on, 361–362; learning and development solution and impact during the, 362–364; putting it all together during the, 48

Practice: ensuring adequate, 61–64; interaction of feedback with, 61; tips on effective, 62

Pre-Work (Phase I learning): Flow Chart tool for, 187–188; How-to Guide to, 555–557; Purposes and Examples of tool for, 189–190

Predictive value: description of assessment, 587; How-to Guide to improve assessment, 587–591

Presentation Zen (Reynolds), 563

Preskill, H., 619, 633

Primeast Ltd. case study: advice to colleagues from, 303; background information on, 299–300; consultation with Cape plc, 299–303; PrimeFocus framework used at, 9, 300–302

Process thinking: PDCA or Deming Cycle for continuous improvement, 80fig; training that applies, 80–83

Procter and Gamble (P&G), 413

Productivity: don't confuse activity with, 121–124; Learning Path Methodology case study on increasing proficiency and, 48, 345–351; training for business ends, 121fig

Proficiency coaching model: Institute for Learning Practitioners approach to improved performance using, 475–479; as performance support, 106, 476–479

Promon Engenharia case study: advice to colleagues from, 473; AfferoLab's approach to disseminate corporate culture during, 470–472; background information on, 469–470; performance support deployed during, 100; "Praça de Aprendizagem" (Learning Plaza) meetings during, 472; results and lessons of experience during, 472–473

Provost, L., 29

Purposes and Examples of Phase I Learning (Pre-Work) tool, 189–190

Putting it all together, 48

Q

Qstream case study: advice to colleagues from, 440–441; background information on, 435–436; example of Qstream question and feedback on answer during, 438fig; forgetting curve issue of, 436fig; formal action plan used during, 437–439; results of the game-based sales reinforcement approach, 439–440; spaced learning and gamification for effective product launch training, 437–441, 561; success factors used during, 440; systems used to engage learner post-training, 86

About the Authors

Roy V.H. Pollock, D.V.M., Ph.D., is chief learning officer and co-founder of The 6Ds Company and co-author of *The Six Disciplines of Breakthrough Learning* and of *Getting Your Money's Worth from Training and Development*. Roy has a passion for helping individuals and teams succeed. He is a popular speaker and frequent consultant on improving the value created by training and development.

Roy has a unique blend of experience in both business and education. He has served as chief learning officer for the Fort Hill Company; vice president, global strategic product development for SmithKline Beecham Animal Health; vice president, Companion Animal Division for Pfizer; and assistant dean for curriculum at Cornell's Veterinary College.

Roy received his B.A. from Williams College *cum laude,* his D.V.M. degree with highest distinction, and his Ph.D. degrees from Cornell University. He studied medical education at the University of Illinois Center for Educational Development. Roy is a Fellow of the Kellogg Foundation National Leadership Program and, in 2013, was honored as a "Learning Luminary" by the Asian L&OD Roundtable. He lives and teaches at Swamp College in Trumansburg, New York.

Andrew McK. Jefferson, J.D., is co-founder and chief executive officer for The 6Ds Company. He is a co-author of *The Six Disciplines of Breakthrough Learning* and of *Getting Your Money's Worth from Training and Development.*

Andy is a frequent and popular presenter and consultant who excels in helping companies maximize the value they realize from their investments in learning and development. He is an accomplished executive with deep line-management expertise.

Andy views learning as a critical source of competitive advantage in an increasingly knowledge-based economy. He knows the challenges of running a company and making every investment count. Prior to joining The 6Ds Company, Andy served as the chief executive officer of The Fort Hill Company, CEO of Vital Home Services, and chief operating officer and general counsel of AmeriStar Technologies, Inc.

Andy is a graduate of the University of Delaware and graduated *Phi Kappa Phi* with honors from the Widener University School of Law, where he served on the school's board of overseers. He and his family make their home in Wilmington, Delaware.

Calhoun W. Wick, M.S. is the founder of the Fort Hill Company and co-author of *The Six Disciplines of Breakthrough Learning.* Cal is internationally recognized for his work on improving the performance of managers and organizations. In 2006, he was named "Thought Leader of the Year" by the Association of Learning Providers.

Cal recognized that the finish line for learning and development programs is no longer the last day of class; a trainee has completed a program only when improved performance has been achieved.

Cal earned his master's degree as an Alfred P. Sloan Fellow at MIT's Sloan School of Management.

About the 6Ds Company

The 6Ds Company was created to help organizations achieve even greater returns on their investment in training and development. We and our certified partners offer both open-enrollment and in-company workshops on the 6Ds and instructional design as well as consulting services. Since 2012, we have partnered with John Wiley & Sons to bring the 6Ds to a global audience.

Additional information is available on our website: www.the6Ds.com or by writing info@the6Ds.com.

Printed in Australia
10 Aug 2022
LP002872